The *CSI* Effect

Critical Studies in Television

Series Editor
Mark Andrejevic, University of Iowa

Advisory Board
Robin Andersen, Fordham University
Lynn Schofield Clark, University of Denver
James Hay, University of Illinois Urbana Champaign
Fred Turner, Stanford University

This series critically examines television, emphasizing in-depth monographic studies on a particular television series. By looking at television through a critical lens, the books in this series will bring insight into the cultural significance of television, and also explore how the lessons apply to larger critical and social issues. The texts in the series will appeal to communication, media, and cultural theory scholars.

Titles in Series:

Dawson's Creek: A Critical Understanding by Lori Bindig

Dear Angela: Remembering My So-Called Life edited by Michele Byers and David Lavery

Tribal Warfare: Survivor *and the Political Unconscious of Reality Television* by Christopher J. Wright

The CSI *Effect: Television, Crime, and Governance* edited by Michele Byers and Val Marie Johnson

The *CSI* Effect

Television, Crime, and Governance

Edited by
Michele Byers and
Val Marie Johnson

LEXINGTON BOOKS

A division of
ROWMAN & LITTLEFIELD PUBLISHERS, INC.
Lanham • Boulder • New York • Toronto • Plymouth, UK

LEXINGTON BOOKS

A division of Rowman & Littlefield Publishers, Inc.
A wholly owned subsidiary of The Rowman & Littlefield Publishing Group, Inc.
4501 Forbes Boulevard, Suite 200
Lanham, MD 20706

Estover Road
Plymouth PL6 7PY
United Kingdom

British Library Cataloguing in Publication Information Available

Library of Congress Cataloging-in-Publication Data

The CSI effect : television, crime, and governance / edited by Michele Byers and Val
Marie Johnson.
   p. cm. — (Critical studies in television)
   Includes bibliographical references and index.
   ISBN 978-0-7391-2470-3 (cloth : alk. paper) — ISBN 978-0-7391-2471-0 (cloth : alk.
paper) — ISBN 978-0-7391-3927-1 (electronic)
   1. CSI: crime scene investigation (Television program) 2. Forensic sciences on
television. 3. Criminal investigation on television. 4. Justice, Administration of, on
television. 5. Television—Social aspects—United States. I. Byers, Michele, 1971– II.
Johnson, Val Marie, 1967–
   PN1992.77.C75C75 2009
   791.45'72—dc22   2009011101

Printed in the United States of America

⊚™ The paper used in this publication meets the minimum requirements of American
National Standard for Information Sciences—Permanence of Paper for Printed Library
Materials, ANSI/NISO Z39.48-1992.

Contents

Figures and Tables

Acknowledgments

This book has been long in coming. It began, sometime in 2003 or 2004, out of heated discussions we were having about crime and TV, and *CSI* more particularly. Coming at the subject from different angles, we both saw a huge gap in the literature about criminality and TV. In fact, the whole production of this book has, in a sense, embodied the struggle to find or craft a language that attends to both the media and the crime in crime and media, as well as how crime and media are forged in broader governing dynamics. The book's essays make steps towards the creation of such a language. They are part of the inauguration of a long overdue dialogue between many different people talking about the same things, but rarely to each other. We hope this book will stimulate others, as it has stimulated us as colleagues, friends, and TV viewers. It has been quite a journey, but one well worth taking.

We would like to acknowledge the patience and hard work of Joseph Parry and Matthew McAdam, as well as many others at Lexington who have helped to make the publication of this book a reality.

Finally, and very importantly, this book would be nothing without the keen insights of the contributors. Thank you for your tenacity, openness to engage in dialogue, and ongoing enthusiasm for this project. We hope that, along with us, you will find it has been well worth the wait and the work.

—Michele Byers and Val Marie Johnson

CSI as Neoliberalism: An Introduction

Michele Byers and Val Marie Johnson

Sometime in 2003, we started talking about producing an edited collection on *CSI*, a TV series that seemed to be on the air every time we turned on our TVs. *CSI* was being heralded in many spheres of public discourse as a televisual revolution, its effects on the public unprecedented. Commentators tended to overlook *CSI*'s pedigree within the long-standing crime TV genre, perhaps because most of the people doing the talking were journalists and crime-related professionals. In an ongoing tradition, criminologists paid limited attention to the production of crime and criminality discourses in the popular public sphere.[1] Further, media scholars and cultural critics seemed unmoved to think about the series in a sustained way even if they were unable to avoid watching it.[2] This is made visible in the lack of critical scholarship available about the *CSI* franchise, and exemplified in things like the 2006 FLOW Critic's Poll. FLOW is an online forum of international but primarily U.S.-based TV scholars who were, in this case, invited to vote for their favorite TV series currently airing in first run. *CSI* received one vote. In fact, the only crime or policing series to get any votes were *The Shield* (4) and *24* (3). Other hit crime series like *Law & Order* (in any of its incarnations), *Cold Case*, and *Criminal Minds* did not merit any attention at all.

The top rated shows by these TV scholars were *Lost*, *Arrested Development*, *The Colbert Report*, *The Daily Show*, *Veronica Mars*, Stephen Colbert's White House Correspondents' Dinner Speech, *Deadwood*, *Project Runway*, *Battlestar Galactica*, and *The Office*.[3] These may seem rather eclectic, but they are tied together by the critical languages in which they have been produced vis-à-vis television as a particular medium of mass communication, with a particular history in the United States. These shows are, in large measure, exciting to scholars of mass communication because they offer something textually rich and innovative to the critical and TV-savvy viewer, like *Lost*'s five-season narrative arc, or the deeply satirical languages deployed by Colbert and the writers of *The Office*. Henry Jenkins muses on the poll: "I sometimes wonder if everyone who watches *Veronica Mars*, for example, has a PhD or more importantly, if every PhD in the world watches the series."[4] It is clearly important to acknowledge the split between the intellectual desires of some (even many) TV scholars and a more general televisual viewership, including scholars writing about TV from a variety of other academic disciplines.

We might speculate that TV scholars were not writing about *CSI* because, despite the claims made about its innovation as a cultural text, it was actually a pretty mundane example of mainstream TV production in the early 2000s. The first *CSI* series focuses on a team of CSIs (Crime Scene Investigators) led by Gil Grissom, a forensic entomologist who heads the night shift team in Las Vegas. Most episodes feature members of the team solving one or two crimes, focusing on their deployment of forensic technologies to expose the "truth" and to allow victims to "speak" from beyond the grave. The *CSI* franchise has been hailed a departure from standard crime dramas that focus on cops and/or lawyers—à la *Law & Order*—because of its subgenric categorization as a forensic crime drama. But this shift in focus to the more behind the scenes work of forensic scientists and coroners has important predecessors, and/or particularly the long-running *Quincy M.E.* (1976–83) starring Jack Klugman as the crime-solving Dr. Quincy. The *CSI* texts themselves, with the exception of a few examples of stunting[5]—most spectacularly the two-part fifth season finale of the original series directed by Quentin Tarantino—are rather ordinary crime scene episodics (series whose primary narratives are resolved within a single episode or two). We do not need to be avid or particularly devoted viewers to understand how *CSI* works.[6]

The *CSI* series do have serial elements, that is, elements that carry over and form arcs between episodes and across seasons, which is characteristic of much contemporary TV. This is particularly true of the franchise series *CSI: Miami* and *CSI: New York*. But by and large these series do not break radically from the parameters of the crime drama genre, as is explored in various ways—for instance in terms of genre, gender, class, and racialization—by the authors in this volume. What might be considered innovative about the *CSI* series is their shift in foci to literal "bodies of evidence," rather than the pursuit of the understanding, capture, and litigation of (criminal) subjects. The episodes of the three *CSI* series focus on the forensic aspects of crime, with particular appeals to audience fascination with the minute, the mundane, and the almost patently absurd details of crime and criminality. Small forays into human interest, including collegial and other relations, are allowable, but are barely even secondary to *CSI*'s focus through the forensic gaze.

   The appeal of this focus, and the catapult this appeal provided in terms of creating a seemingly limitless interest in *CSI* and series like it for nearly a decade, is at least two-fold. First, the series really capitalize on new technologies in their production and in the series narratives. The shows have extremely high production values and use special effects technologies extensively. Most significantly, these technologies allow viewers to ride bullets and blood spatter forwards and backwards in time; as a number of our authors explore they take us into bodies and in so doing suggest a venue through which the dead can speak. At the same time, the series are hyper-oriented toward a display of forensic technologies that is clearly fetishistic. These technologies are represented as necessary to solving crime (both particular crimes and "crime" as a whole) and mitigating risk. This brings us to the second fold: *CSI*'s appeal cannot be disentangled from the broader discourses and practices on risk that circulate within our neoliberal landscape. As we consider more closely below, *CSI* reinforces the notion that we have in some ways been abandoned by the state and its key players (including in some ways, the police, the law), and yet risk is constant even in the context of our most mundane acts.[7] In most episodes of *CSI* crimes are (re)solved less through litigation and sentencing then through the identification of an often elusive "truth"—about the criminal and how s/he "did it"—which is also often a moral lesson in the idiosyncratic nature of risk, and the impossibility of its mitigation. If crime and risk are impossible to mitigate; if lawyers and the police (and thus in some capacity the state) have failed, *CSI* tells us that we are left with the truth of the body, a truth that can only be discovered by objective forensic scientists under the guidance of the father figures of Gil Grissom, Horatio Caine, and Mac Taylor. Week after week that's what happens: these men show us that in a world in which risk cannot be mitigated, in which neither law nor order can necessarily be counted on, and in which the state is in many ways not accountable, only these individuals and their science can speak for and save us (and thus effect some redemption for law, order, the state).
   In exploring these and other questions, the strengths of this volume rest in the bridge that it builds over the deep and rocky gap between the study of media, including or particularly popular culture media, and the study of crime. We encouraged our contributors to consider the points of intersection between these very different realms of scholarship and in so doing have sought to foster the development of a new set of theoretical languages in which the mediated spectacle of crime and criminalization can be critically and carefully considered. We begin this effort at bridging the gap between the analysis of media and crime here by examining the political economy of both *CSI* as TV and how *CSI* has operated as, and in connection with, a set of cultural ideas and practices defined as neoliberal, particularly in the

post–September 11, 2001 era. The chapter concludes with an overview of the rest of the chapters in the volume.

CSI TV

In ways that are characteristic of the recent history of neoliberalism more generally, the period of—let us say—twenty years leading up to the turn of the millennium witnessed an unprecedented deregulation of the American broadcasting sector initiated under the administration of President Ronald Reagan and the U.S. Federal Communications Commissions. There followed a relaxation of the Financial Interest and Syndication rules (Fin Syn) for broadcast TV, as the three network system slowly gave way to a broadcast universe with what appeared to be more players: new networks, netlets, cable, satellite, digital cable, and so on. The Clinton administration completely disbanded Fin Syn and the Prime Time Access Rules, as well as bringing in the Telecommunications Act of 1996, which radically revised industry ownership rules. In this period when there seemed to be so many players at the bottom end, there was also a move to conglomeration, that is, a disappearance of players at the top end. By 2000 there were four major names in the U.S. television game: AOL Time Warner, Disney, Viacom, and News Corp., and they seemed to own *everything* even though many outside the industry could not actually see this.[8]

The implications of this move to conglomeration are more complex then they might seem on the surface, or at least more ambiguous. Fewer people were making decisions at the top end of the industry, and the money was running to the same few places, despite the fact that it was running from a wider variety of sources. At the production end of things, deregulation, coupled with the rationale of competitive global capitalism, suggested that we were getting more viewing possibilities because everyone was working harder to produce something (greater in number, as well as more diversified in nature) viewers were interested in seeing. And yet, maybe these productions did not really have to be so interesting: in a three network system you had to attract a lot more viewers to be considered popular than you do in the more fragmented televisual landscape we know today. *My So-Called Life*, for example, was considered by some to be a failure for ABC in garnering only about ten million—largely teen girl—viewers per episode in the mid-1990s, while only a few years later *Buffy the Vampire Slayer* became the lynchpin of the WB netlet's series roster with far fewer.[9] Conglomeration, fragmentation—what this will mean for us as viewers and cultural critics, and for television in the long run, is anyone's guess.[10]

In this context of the decline of the major networks and a boost in fragmented programming, one thing is certain: *CSI* has accomplished what many thought would never again be possible: the creation of a massive audience with a seemingly insatiable appetite for network television, culled from broad and diverse segments of the American viewing population, and all this for a *drama*.[11] There are many possible reasons for this. Let us trace two, which represent strands in a complexly woven tapestry of discourses through which U.S. conceptions of criminality and justice are (re)produced in the popular imagination and broadcast internationally: the social dominance of neoliberal and neoconservative discourses of the type that the *CSI* series deploy, and the synchronicity between the franchise's emergence and the events referred to as 9/11. In this way, we can locate *CSI* as a set of cultural texts in the context of contemporary developments in how we govern and think about ourselves and others more broadly.[12]

CSI AS NEOLIBERALISM,
CSI AS GOVERNING THROUGH CRIME

CSI was produced squarely and serendipitously in a moment when audiences were ripe for the particular sort of narratives it proffered in a compulsive fashion. *CSI: Crime Scene Investigation* first aired in late 2000 and got off to a somewhat slow start, ending up with a rank of ten overall for the season. By season two (2001-02) and through season five (2004-05) it held the number one or number two spot. Capitalizing on this popularity, *CSI: Miami* first aired in September 2002, and *CSI: NY* in September 2004. With U.S. audiences, the original series (generally the most popular of the franchise in North American markets) seems to have begun a slow decline, ending up number three in season six, number four in season seven, and slightly lower in the eighth season. However, the show still ranks in the top ten nearly every week according to Nielsen ratings, to say nothing of its near ubiquity in an unusually broad spectrum of channels in syndication, and its global appeal.[13] We begin here to consider how we might understand this arc and the franchise's international impact through an examination of *CSI*'s intersections with contemporary forms of governing.

A central way in which we see the *CSI* franchise as a reflection and re-enactment of neoliberal ideas and practices is that *CSI*'s primary narrative characteristics, and the dominant ways in which the franchise's social impact have been read, both reflect the workings of what Jonathan Simon terms "governing through crime."[14] We see governing through crime at work in the franchise's gestures via forensic heroism at both critiquing the state and legitimating policing powers as essential and moral-scientific; its refusal of the social as a realm informing human action, conflict, and solutions except through the local workings of forensic teams; its central focus on the individual responsibility of crime fighter and criminal. We also see governing through crime at play in the fact that commentators, particularly in the commercial media and the criminal justice system, have credited *CSI* with significantly impacting contemporary ideas and practices outside the televisual realm through what is ubiquitously known as the *"CSI* effect."[15] This is primarily understood to mean that watching *CSI* inspires an *anti-prosecution* tendency in North American and especially U.S. jurors,[16] by raising their expectation and perception of the need for forensic evidence of guilt in all criminal investigations and trials. In other words, the *"CSI* effect" is popularly understood as a dangerous *hindrance* to crime fighting on several fronts: it is framed as effectively delegitimizing the traditional policing and prosecutorial arms of the criminal justice system by showing that crime is best fought through the allegedly impersonal techniques of science and high technology, it is envisioned to over-empower juries with unrealistic expectations for forensic evidence in trials and to over-burden criminal forensic labs with endless testing of every molecule possibly relevant to crimes, and so on.[17] Both the further workings of governing through crime and the interplay between the televisual realm and "real" life are revealed in responses to this perceived set of dynamics, which center on *fortifying crime fighting* as a set of ideas and practices—from prosecutors attempting to educate juries on the limits of forensic evidence, to *CSI* actors and producers lobbying for increased state and private funding for forensic crime labs.[18]

This project began partly in response to a need we felt to broaden and problematize dominant readings of the so-called *CSI* effect, by locating these readings in a socio-historically grounded and critical analysis, something that we and other authors in this book argue *CSI*'s narratives do not often provide. By this we mean that understanding a TV franchise like *CSI* requires an analysis of the material social relations and political rationalities that provide the shows' context of production and circulation. This analysis is executed by bringing together the tools of critical media studies with those of criminology and socio-political theory—fields of study that are, strangely, often resistant to interdisciplinary collaboration.[19] Working in this manner, we situate *CSI* as a set of practices and ideas in the context of contemporary socio-economic and political dynamics. In the same way that *CSI* must be understood as *TV* in the context of the political economy of television, we argue that the fruits of the *CSI* franchise, including dominant understandings of and assumptions about the *CSI* effect, reflect and reinscribe contemporary forms of governing in advanced global capitalism, including governing through crime. As is reflected in the meteoric rise in popularity of the *CSI* franchise, and widespread speculation about how the series hinder or enhance the battle against crime that saturates contemporary governing tactics and rationales, in Simon's apt words, "We govern through crime when 'crime' becomes the problem through which we seek to know and act on the conduct of others. We govern through crime when 'crime' supplies the narratives and metaphors for people who seek to make claims on those who govern."[20]

We can particularly see *CSI* as a reflection and reinscription of contemporary governmentalities (ways of governing, and the mentalities that facilitate them)[21] if we consider how the franchise frames risk and responsibility, and by implication citizenship and governing more broadly. Specifically, the terrain of the *CSI* universe involves three key elements: risk as omnipresent, responsibility for risk (and agency more generally) as largely individualized, and the provision of security as one of the few collective enterprises (at times it seems the only) remaining to us. Risk is framed as a ubiquitous feature of contemporary experience, and as grounded primarily in individualized or arbitrary rather than socially conditioned responsibilities and relationships through the rationalities and tactics circulated around and within *CSI* and similar texts (it is argued in this book that *CSI* may be framed as something "new," but like all popular television it is intertextually linked to other crime and forensic texts from earlier and contemporaneous periods). By individualized or arbitrary we mean that human actions and relations are constructed first as occurring among autonomous, largely ahistorical individuals who make rational choices (whether they are forensic heroes or criminal villains), and second as involving the workings of chance. In other words through neoliberal rationality—here in a fictional universe of criminal offenders and victims—human subjects, actions, and relations operate just as "free" markets do. Thus, within *CSI*'s televisual *diegesis*—the world of the text with its particular rules—human subjects and relations are imagined to require and be shaped by minimal social intervention. The key exception to the functioning of individualism and play of chance in this imagined televisual realm is the state and private provision of policing, security, and criminal justice perceived to be necessitated precisely by the ubiquitous, atomized, and arbitrary character of risk, which is defined almost exclusively as individual acts of violent crime. In terms of citizenship and governance more broadly, in this *CSI* universe the rationalities and practices that construct crime, crime fighting, and victimization, are central to defining the contemporary parameters of individual and collective action, identity, and belonging.[22]

The terrain of the *CSI* universe is also the terrain of contemporary neoliberalism. These products of the *CSI* franchise—the imagining of ubiquitous and/or arbitrary risk, of responsible criminals and crime fighters, of criminal justice as an essential collective enterprise—are also deployed extra-diegetically outside of these texts in locally, regionally, and nationally specific frameworks, and within the globally mobile crime-fighting contexts that are used in advanced capitalist societies such as North America, the UK, and Australia to address not just crime,[23] but a range of social issues that were once largely addressed through the welfare state. Under this rubric, welfare provision, affordable housing, and immigration and refugee policy, are reconfigured as the policing of welfare fraud, the street-engaged poor, and potentially terrorist foreigners.[24] However, we argue that these narratives of risk management that carry traces of the welfare state in their criminal justice reimaginings are largely *absent* from the narratives of *CSI*, which focus instead on the carefully calculated and/or arbitrary violent crimes of white, middle-class rational actors. In fact, chapters in this volume illustrate from multiple angles that a key way in which *CSI* has sold good television is by *tidying up the damage* of contemporary neoliberalism and neoconservatism: rendering criminality and crime fighting as rational calculation purged of social messiness, error, and power relations, deploying representations of scientific and technological wizardry to purify policing, law, and justice, all of course in the time of an episode with commercial breaks.

Thus we argue that the dominant popular criminology narratives[25] offered by the *CSI* franchise, their huge (and interestingly now waning) commercial success, and the primary definition of the *CSI* effect as inspiring an anti-prosecution tendency in jurors, reflect a wider shift in the end-goals of popular culture and criminal justice, but also an illustration of how fiction and fantasy can bring pleasure and catharsis through engagement with risk in a relatively formulaic manner, and a repeated resolution that is impossible in "real" life. Unsurprisingly, commercial network television productions seeking mass audiences come to reflect dominant cultural discourses (here around crime) at the time of production, that in turn resonate strongly with viewers as familiar and comfortable.[26] By way of illustration, scholars have analyzed how, in tandem with the rise of what David Garland calls "crime control culture," television drama representations of law and policing over the 1980s and 1990s shifted away from defense attorneys' and private detectives' exoneration of the innocent accused and toward a vision of justice presented, in Mariana Valverde's terms, "wholly from the point of view of victims, cops and prosecutors."[27] Similarly, criminal defense lawyer and crime novelist Scott Turow highlights that *defense* lawyers predominantly used high-technology identification techniques (such as the DNA analysis routinely portrayed on *CSI*) during their initial widespread deployment in the late 1980s and early 1990s, leading to the reversal of many wrongful convictions. Initially skeptical that the science could be easily manipulated, prosecutors started using such forensic evidence to solve "cold" murder cases in the 1990s. Turow argues that the popularizing of forensics as a way to catch and punish bad guys via shows like *CSI* has helped to bolster public pressure for the wider *prosecutorial* application of such techniques, including the removal of prosecutorial restraints surrounding their use (such as statutes of limitations in non-murder cold cases).[28] Here again we see the contemporary characteristics of discourses and tactics in the battle against criminals (rather than, say, the defense of the innocent) forged as they move back and forth between televisual and "real" life.

These complex operations of televisual and "real" life governing through crime are crucially inflected by commerce (would they be neoliberal if they were not?). On the one hand, those who write and produce *CSI* sell their show by tapping into dominant contemporary ways in which we think and talk about crime, criminality, and citizenship already in circulation and by creating dramatic narratives in which these discourses circulate (which in turn reinscribes and disseminates them as a cultural language). On the other hand, Harvey and Derksen in this volume indicate that media commerce in crime and celebrity has helped produce and widely circulate a specifically anti-prosecution narrative—referred to as the *CSI* effect—in popular and legal discourse, despite the narrative's lack of empirical substantiation. Although there is evidence to suggest that regular *CSI* viewers may actually develop a *pro-conviction* bias as jurors, on the judicial side of things the perceived anti-prosecution *CSI* effect has begun producing legal and criminal justice tactics intended to facilitate more certain prosecution, such as questioning jurors about their TV-viewing habits, wider use of forensic evidence testing, and vastly increased U.S. federal funding for state and local crime labs.[29] In a related way, VanLaerhoven and Anderson's chapter examines how the *CSI* effect's perceived promotion of science has manifested markedly in the educational and professional realms through the fortification of forensic science as a field of knowledge and expert practice. Widening the lens to consider how these developments fit in contemporary political economy leads us to consider how knowledge production around science and technology (as well as through social sciences such as criminology) is harnessed to modes of governing through crime.[30] Examining this web of popular cultural, corporate commercial, educational, and professional practices and ideas linking and valorizing science, technology, and crime fighting adds new dimensions to our understanding of the contemporary operations of governing through crime.

As Bonnycastle's piece in this book illustrates nicely, this web reflects and allows for the performance of new forms of knowledge production characteristic of a shift from the human sciences associated with the modern welfare state—such as social work and psychology, which measured and aided in the management of things such as normalcy and the potential for rehabilitation—to the actuarial sciences linked with neoliberal governing—such as those in the insurance and finance (and increasingly prison) industries, which assess risk through statistical and mathematical measures and set practices accordingly.[31] Importantly, knowledge production via the actuarial sciences is also better suited to circulation through capitalist markets. In a sense what Bonnycastle's arguments show us is that, in the same way that actuarial assessments reduce risk calculation to a set of easily manipulated numbers, *CSI*'s televisual construction of risk as embodied and responded to through discrete and rational individuals both avoids the social messiness of how harm and violence are actually produced, and makes for an extremely reproducible and saleable pop cultural product.

We thus argue that commodification and commercial exchange are key dynamics in the circulation of neoliberal rationalities and practices through all dimensions highlighted in a critical reading: of *CSI* as must see TV, of a perceived *CSI* effect producing a prosecutorial burden or inspiration for forensic science awareness and funding, of *CSI* as a reflection and reinscription of ideas and practices around governing through crime. Of crucial importance in this commodification and exchange is the fact that the *CSI* franchise's hegemony in the network television grid, and elsewhere in syndication and within international televisual and post-televisual flows (particularly through the world wide web), has facilitated the wide circulation of ideas and practices characteristic of governing through crime through arguably the most influential cultural medium in North America and other advanced capitalist societies. This hegemony peaked in *CSI*'s direct rating supremacy between 2002–2005, and through the 2005–2007 blooming of similar shows across a variety of networks and specialty stations. And what does the slow decline in the franchise's popularity beginning in 2005 tell us about these dynamics? Are we tired of a televisual and "real" world where fear is everywhere, risk and responsibility are individualized, and governing through crime is the best that we can imagine for a collective enterprise?

CSI TV IN THE ERA OF SEPTEMBER 11, 2001

Given that the series tripped lightly onto the televisual scene virtually on the eve of what is now called "9/11," we can understand the arc of the series' prominence as following the trajectory of public preoccupation with those events, particularly in the United States but also internationally. In her essay on television culture after the events of September 11, 2001, Lynn Spigel argues that after these events "traditional forms of entertainment had to reinvent their place in U.S. life and culture."[32] Part of this reinvention involved a push for a "return to normal" through the "repositioning of audiences back into television's fictive times and places."[33] *CSI* might be read as a particularly useful creature in this regard; it allowed us to return to normal, but a different normal, one that was so important after 9/11, that is, a normal where fear was lurking behind every corner, but certainty and justice, rendered through fantasies of scientific criminal justice, also held sway.

This is not to suggest that *CSI* bore explicit traces of 9/11 (with the exception of the second series spin-off, *CSI: NY*, this has not generally been the case). Other shows, like *The West Wing*, *24*, and Showtime's *Sleeper Cell* have dealt with those particular fears more directly. Rather, the series, like all television, is "haunted" by the specter of 9/11 through discourses and practices—around fear, risk, crime, evidence, truth, science, the state, and so on—that predated and were reinforced by the events of that fateful day and U.S. and international responses to them.[34] Media and communications scholar Murray Forman makes the argument that in the first post-Columbine season, we saw several TV series about teens that, although they developed complex narratives about adolescent social relations, all skirted a direct engagement with the 1999 events that occurred at Columbine High. Forman suggests that, despite the direct avoidance of the school shootings, these events felt like the invisible and yet inevitable end point of a trajectory that the social relations depicted in these teen dramas set in motion—social exclusion, hierarchy, humiliation, collusion of adults and community. The author writes: "the explicit violence and rage displayed at Columbine High School have been excised . . . displaced in favor of the exhibition of social and psychological forces that engender contemporary eruptions among disenfranchised teens."[35] In a similar fashion, Mikita Brottman argues that the horror of 9/11 is less in what we saw on that September day than in what we did not, could not, have not been allowed to see.[36] That is, in both cases narrative coherence around these events—whether these stories are told as fiction or news—is achieved by alluding to terror, risk, disaster, without ever actually forcing the viewer to confront their fears or the social realities that produce them.

CSI plays successfully into this dynamic in particular ways. We argue that its rise in popularity after the 2000–2001 season is linked to the *fantasy* of full disclosure it gives us every week. Unlike the dominant news footage produced in the wake of 9/11, in which there was a marked absence of the type of explicit imagery that we have come to associate with graphic representations of violence—blood, broken bodies, the dead—*CSI*'s graphic manipulations take us up close and (im)personal with blood and dismembered, violated bodies week in and week out. As Glynn and Kim demonstrate in this volume, we the audience do not expect—nor are we offered—these images as "real," in fact, their status as digital recreations of impossible to see/experience events is part of the accepted production conventions of the show (the tracing of a bullet as it leaves the wound and travels backwards into the gun, the moment leading up to a crime told several times from slightly different angles).[37] The focus on what Joel Black calls the "graphic imperative" obscures what is more likely to suture the viewer to this cultural text: its activation of discourses that validate the *conceptual* framework of the risk society and put forward a mythology that crime fighting and justice through science—in the old-fashioned understanding of science as objective and thus the bearer of impartial anterior truths—hold the key to our collective safety and salvation. We suggest that this is central to the catapulting of *CSI* into the televisual stratosphere, especially in the wake of 9/11 and the global and domestic uncertainty and structural brutality exacerbated through the U.S.-led response to it.

As suggested by our analysis above, not only did the timing of *CSI*'s emergence seem to almost guarantee its popularity: this timing linked in with the franchise's consistent deployment of neoliberal and neoconservative discourses, that on the one hand posit a citizenry that is self-reliant and self-responsible within the current, hyper-disaster-capitalist system, and that at the same time construct that citizenry within very tightly circumscribed moral and historically amnesiac discourses.[38] Contemporary television series cannot easily, if at all, disentangle themselves from these types of dominant social discourses; indeed, they are constitutive of these TV series, the institutions that produce them, and the institutions that such series represent in their narratives. TV series such as *CSI* do not critique the state in order to offer a vision that will better serve the public (any public), but instead offer a vision of a state that better serves particular ideological ends: the accumulation of capital/the shoring up of allegedly Christian morality/the legitimization of police and militarist power.

Yet *CSI* engages in a typically neoliberal balancing act. It offers up a critique of the state even as it relegitimizes state power, in that each franchise centers on a neoliberal hero (white, male, middle-class, educated, straight, technologically advanced) who has to do the work of truth and justice that the state and its representatives have failed to do. Although they work on its behalf, as men (and secondarily women) of science, the CSIs are presented as beyond the state. As Bonnycastle and Rajiva illustrate in this volume, these neoliberal heroes live by a moral code that, while not explicitly bigoted, is informed by neoconservative values through which historical matrices of power and oppression are naturalized to the point of almost complete erasure, and a "scientific" code through which policing, criminal justice, and state force are largely cleansed of references to these matrices. As discussed by several authors in what follows, when Grissom tells us again and again to look/listen to the evidence, we are also being told not to look at the context through and in which the evidence, the harm defined as crime, and the accused and victimized come into being.

TV scholar David Lavery, in his afterword to *Reading 24*, the recent edited collection on the series *24*, ruminates on whether he has missed something in considering the essays in the volume. Lavery touches on the potential dangers of the deep investment that we as viewers (and as critical, scholarly viewers in particular) make as fans. Lavery suggests that as fans we often like series because they offer us the familiar. Quoting Echo, he describes how "[t]wo clichés make us laugh but a hundred clichés move us because we sense dimly that the clichés are talking among themselves, celebrating a reunion."[39] This is a useful way to consider the popularity of *CSI*: as a reunion of innumerable neoliberal and neoconservative clichés about citizenship, criminality, the state, truth, justice, and power; that is, neoliberalism and neoconservatism are so omnipresent in social discourses today that they have become clichés.[40] We see this familiarity evoked by the ubiquitous presence of these discourses on *CSI* as one of the things that has made the series so popular. Having been somewhat sidelined in the period preceding the series' rise to dominance, they offer mainstream viewers a reunion of discourses with which they are well versed—even new or younger viewers have had the opportunity to become intertextually acquainted with both neoliberal and neoconservative narratives in a range of media and a variety of crime and forensic genre texts, as they occupy so much televisual and filmic space in both first run and syndication, in mainstream and alternative venues of distribution. And clearly this reunion is a pleasurable one for many.

Further, maybe the relative downward slope of the *CSI* arc in recent years, particularly among U.S. audiences, suggests that the pleasure produced by this particular constellation of clichés is beginning to lose its appeal. To borrow from another critique of cultural and political economy in the wake of Columbine, maybe we are finally growing tired of the "limited choices found within the ideological framework of this [neoliberal and neoconservative] alliance."[41] Do all reunions or clichés, if they don't eventually end, turn into something else? Jerry Seinfeld made the point that it was better to leave on a high note then to hang around for another season even if it meant relinquishing more than a proposed million dollars per episode. Is *CSI*, like all TV series do eventually, burning itself out? With current financial crises and attendant questioning of the capitalist market as the model for wise governance, the election of Barack Obama, and so on, dare we hope (yes, hope) that neoliberalism and neoconservatism are also on the wane?

CHAPTER OVERVIEW

The chapters in this volume are produced at the intersection of media and communications studies, and the history and theory of crime, governance, and regulation. Working from diverse disciplines—film, television, and cultural studies, sociology, criminology, forensic science, history, musicology—and interdisciplinary frameworks, our authors also read *CSI* as a compelling and sometimes disturbing phenomenon from multiple sites: in the United States and Canada, the UK, and Australia. This book also provides an introduction to a range of media (and more broadly cultural) studies methods, including discourse analysis, content analysis, and various forms of textual analysis.[42] As an anonymous reviewer noted, there are some gaps here, including studies of the global political economy of *CSI* as a franchise that has achieved transnational popularity, of audience and/or fan analyses, of *CSI*'s place within television's new convergence culture, of *CSI* and/in the Internet landscape. These are all important areas for further research, and this is, we hope, a point of departure from which others will carry on.

The volume is divided into three parts. Part I opens the book with four chapters that deconstruct the "effect" of *CSI* as a cultural text, with particular attention paid to the ways in which *CSI* produces dramatic television narratives of justice and science. The three chapters that make up part II consider the various ways in which evidence as a concept is configured and how bodies are produced as evidence within the mediated landscape of *CSI*. The volume concludes with three chapters that investigate how *CSI* imagines a range of late modern subjects, including crime experts, villains and victims, dramatic heroes and heroines, human and urban bodies. Both the second and third parts consider how this imagination is shaped by a neoliberal political economy, relations of race, class, gender, and sexuality, and postmodern configurations of identity and space, and ask what *CSI* tells and shows us about memory, forgetting, and what is knowable in the world.

Part I's four chapters examine the *CSI* effect from multiple angles. In chapter 1, Liz Harvey and Linda Derksen set the tone of the book by tackling head on the question of whether the "*CSI* effect" is science fiction or social fact. The massive bibliography of sources on *CSI* and its perceived effects compiled by the authors is notable in itself (see Appendix C), but also grounds their content analysis of popular press reports. As the authors illustrate, the *CSI* effect—"usually defined as a belief in the near-infallibility of forensic science and its ability to solve all crimes"—is sometimes now perceived as a matter of serious concern for forensic and legal professionals. Harvey and Derksen underscore, however, that there has been little "systematic inquiry into what comprises the CSI effect, or what its immediate and long-term consequences may be." Harvey and Derksen conclude from their analysis "that the jury is still out on what the *CSI* effect is, and whether it has any systematic ramifications," and, crucially, "that all reports of the *CSI* effect have been based on very few sources . . . cited time and time again."

In chapter 2, Sherah VanLaerhoven and Gail Anderson bring their expertise in forensic entomology and professional forensic consulting to bear on the ways that the *CSI* franchise has helped to make science "exciting, glamorous, and sexy." They acknowledge that the franchise's "intent is to entertain," but ask what it means when *CSI* does not provide "an accurate or full portrayal of science." First VanLaerhoven and Anderson scrutinize the science and science careers represented on the franchise. Second, they "clarify the practical career options in the field of forensic science" and consider how *CSI* has contributed to "the proliferation of forensic graduate and undergraduate programs" across Canada.[43] The authors express both their gratification with increased public and academic interest in the sciences, as well as their concern about the unrealistic expectations viewers and students may come to have with regard to forensic science programs and practices.

In chapter 3, U.S. historian and former criminal lawyer Kurt Hohenstein argues that the dramatic crime series *CSI* and *Law & Order* "demonstrate a dueling set of public values about criminal justice institutions and processes." While *Law & Order* centers on the conflict, uncertainty, and unfairness inherent in legal systems in formal liberal democracies, all three *CSI* series center on claims of truth offered by forensic science and scientists. Hohenstein concludes that, "both dramas encourage the nagging suspicion among Americans" that their criminal justice system cannot be trusted; *CSI*'s forensic model, however, minimizes the role of police, lawyers, judges, juries, and conflict and complexity in the legal system, and in so doing raises important questions about neoliberal fantasies of truth and justice. While Hohenstein's investigation suggests that at least some viewers derive pleasure from and crave the fantasy of certainty on offer by the *CSI* franchise, it also suggests that the longevity of *Law & Order* reflects a significant population of viewers' persistent desire to engage with the (dramatized) complexities of law and justice.

In chapter 4, TV and media studies scholar Nichola Dobson examines how the series in the *CSI* franchise both conform to, and have produced innovation in, the TV crime drama genre. Deploying film and television genre theory, consideration of other "genre-innovative shows," and analysis of all three *CSI* series, Dobson argues that while the series adhere to many generic conventions, *CSI* has also significantly impacted the genre through the series' use of "narrative structure, narrative space, and visual effects." The franchise's generic innovation in TV crime drama is reflected in the forensic-centered dramas that have proliferated in the wake of *CSI*. Moreover, Dobson demonstrates how the visual effects developed through the *CSI* franchise have particularly influenced TV drama beyond the crime genre.

The chapters in part II investigate what we see and hear in *CSI* about the production of bodies and/or evidence on *CSI*. In chapter 5, film, television, and cultural studies scholars Basil Glynn and Jeongmee Kim examine how "the graphic destruction" and scrutiny of the human body are "presented as an unproblematic and essential aspect of crime solving" on *CSI*. The authors argue that *CSI*'s "stylistic and aesthetic strategies" make "a body horror extravaganza" acceptable to a mass audience, and particularly that the series' "up-front fakery" undercuts the violence toward bodies that it represents. Glynn and Kim conclude that *CSI* has been so successful because it does not cross the "line between fantasy and reality" or remind viewers too much of "their human vulnerability" and mortality. The authors also raise key questions about citizenship, identity, and governing in contemporary societies, asking what it means when bodies serve more as objects than subjects, as marketable fantasy products, that is, that allow us to dabble in but not confront our embodiment and mortality.

Cultural studies scholar Patrick West engages related issues of embodiment in chapter 6. By reading the insights of urban and social theory in tandem with a close examination of *CSI: Miami*'s story arcs and visual languages, West demonstrates how the series reflects contemporary characteristics of the city of Miami, but also suggests that the series "offers television viewers a sneak preview of tomorrow's Miami," and thus of other twenty-first century cities and citizens. Perhaps the most fascinating dimension of West's analysis is his exploration of "how bodies on the show . . . contain the transgressive potential to bring alive" the spaces around them, particularly interior and "intimate" urban spaces. West posits that the spaces represented on *CSI: Miami* offer "bolt holes down which the urban body might escape from the identity dissipations of globalization and virtualization." Reading West on *CSI: Miami* leads us to ask what the broader consequences are for identity, community, citizenship and material social change in these virtualized, globalized, and interiorized realms, as well as who has access to these new urban experiences.

In chapter 7 environmental historian William Turkel provides a reading of the first five seasons of the original series that contrasts "the televisual world of orderly verisimilitude portrayed on *CSI*" with the complications of actual forensic practice and "the historian's crime scene"—with their "infinite number of clues with almost as many possible interpretations," and their "tangled skein of science and politics, where knowledge is power and vice versa." Turkel shows us how *CSI* abstracts complex social relations into decontextualized and individualized physical relations, primarily through the fantasy of scientific certainty achieved through the "objective" measurement of neat, isolatable forms of physical evidence. Turkel shows us how science and physical evidence are fetishized on *CSI* in much the same way that Marx described commodity fetishism: as social relations that assume "the fantastic form of a relation between things."[44]

Like Bonnycastle's analysis of *CSI*'s production of "Cartesian" crime experts and "free-will" villains (see below), and Glynn and Kim's consideration of the franchise's "upfront fakery" around bodily destruction, Turkel's examination reveals how *CSI* absents human relations from its definitions of justice and truth. Turkel's examination also suggests that *CSI*'s evidentiary fetish helps to facilitate the series' reproduction as a commodity—via franchising, serialization, global TV and internet flow, and the marketing of forensic science and high technology as sexy. *CSI* creator Anthony Zuiker underscores this by framing *CSI* as "a fantasy love affair between the viewer and science." Zuiker suggests that *CSI* makes for a particularly marketable product through a rendering of forensic science as fun high technology that compels audiences more than social relations do: "We feed the machine in terms of doing more and more shows that are on the cutting edge of technology. People cannot get enough of that. If you go to all of our testing dials, emotion of the show and character stuff (don't test as well). But when we ask about the rock music and the eye candy. . . . They love it."[45]

Part III aptly concludes this volume with three explorations of how *CSI* produces particular types of late modern subjects. In chapter 8, criminologist Kevin Bonnycastle examines how the first four seasons of *CSI: Crime Scene Investigation* provide what she terms "a neoliberalizing public education" to its viewers. Bonnycastle argues that not only does *CSI* "dramatize sensational and rare forms of violence," it neoliberalizes that violence and its policing by, first, glamorizing the crime scene investigator as a new type of crime expert whose forensic technologies decenter traditional police and the human sciences as subjects of crime expertise. Second, *CSI* presents violent death as ungrounded in social context or conventional causal explanations of crime, and especially obscures how political economy and institutionalized racism shape actual violent deaths. Bonnycastle argues that *CSI* instead produces the accused as "rational choice free-will subjects" and both victims and accused as white, bourgeois citizens. In this way, *CSI* produces a version of governing through crime that renders invisible the social realities produced through neoliberalism and masks the *neoconservative* dimensions of recent U.S. governance.

While Bonnycastle is interested in how *CSI*'s narratives work through the marked invisibility of a racialized U.S. "underclass" and the brutal tactics that are used to contain it outside the realm of TV drama, in chapter 9 sociologist

Mythili Rajiva examines how race, gender, class, and sexuality are absent, present, projected, and displaced in *CSI: Crime Scene Investigation*. Using a feminist psychoanalytic framework to analyze the first season, Rajiva provides a reading of how "phallic mastery and anxiety" are expressed in the series storylines and character arcs through tropes of white male mastery, lost white female innocence, black masculinity as either dangerous or failed, and diffuse and complex anxieties over various forms of Otherness. She also argues that the infrequent presence of black femininity in the first season constructs it "as a dummy presence, a form of tokenism that re-asserts the series' dominant racialized, gendered, aged, and classed norms." Rajiva's chapter concludes with a "counter-reading of the show that recognizes the 'multiple, shifting and highly subjective' nature of viewer interpretations."[46]

In chapter 10 musicologist Lawrence Kramer provides an apt final chapter to our volume by demonstrating how *CSI: Crime Scene Investigation*, *CSI: Miami*, and *Cold Case* "epitomize the recent trend toward forensic romance in crime narratives," in significant part because they help to channel the trauma surrounding the events of September 11, 2001, through normative stories about the way things should be. Through his examination of what he terms "forensic music"—particularly these series' titles sequences—Kramer argues that, "led by *CSI*, television's forensic melodramas have tried to recover the value of traumatic shock by constructing narratives that reanimate trauma on a small scale and demand that it be . . . discharged by narrative." Like the parallel that Turkel draws for us between evidentiary and commodity fetishism, Kramer's analysis of the packaging of trauma helps explain the commercial success of *CSI* and other "forensic romances." In keeping with the arguments of several of our authors, in Kramer's telling the reproduction of trauma is as much about forgetting as it is about remembering. Kramer argues that the music of *CSI*, joined to hi-tech forensic visuals, helps to associate "the search for justice" with a co-joined "devotion to technocratic rationality" and "a deep, irrational rage" for revenge. Further, Kramer shows us how commercial pop cultural fantasies help to reconcile us to these contradictions inherent in contemporary events and practices. Like *CSI*'s narratives of omnipresent risk meeting certain justice that they preface, the phrases of these series' musical title sequences "unite across gaps to form a whole. . . . The music gives the fantasy-patchwork a consistency resonant with the practices of post-9/11 memory while absolving the audience of the need to name the connection. . . . The fantasy can remember for them."

Many issues are considered in the pages of this book. We hope that this introduction has helped to illustrate why we must not lose sight of the fact that *CSI*, whatever else it might be, *is* TV. Insofar as it is first and foremost a TV franchise *CSI* cannot be fully considered outside of the matrices through which TV itself is constituted. In the same way, in our view, one cannot fully consider *CSI* without examining the broader, extra-textually circulating social discourses through which it is constituted. As our reviewer underscored, it is this "spell[ing] out the socio-political context that makes cultural analysis worth doing." To ignore either of these broad analytical frameworks is to give a problematically partial reading of *CSI*, one that imagines that the text exists outside of televisuality or outside of the social sphere. In what follows we create a space in which *CSI* is interrogated across these various, overlapping, and ultimately partial terrains of inquiry. We enter into this knowing that we cannot possibly meet all expectations, but it is our sincere hope to begin to challenge the disciplinary and theoretical boundaries that have obstructed the study of mediated criminalities. If any text produced in recent memory begs for this type of analysis, it is clearly *CSI*.

NOTES

1. The dearth of critical criminological work in the areas of media and popular culture is astounding. Some shift in this has been evident, particularly in the UK context. A new SAGE journal, *Crime, Media, Culture*, launched recently' offers promise in this regard. The work that has been produced by critical criminologists has tended to ignore the long history and vast scholarly materials related to media and other popular culture texts. That is, they tend to forget that these are texts and mediums with their own specific histories and bodies of scholarship. At the same time, cultural and media theorists haven't engaged with critical criminological literatures that might offer insight into the popular representations of crime and criminality that circulate today. See, for example, J. Ferrell. and C. R. Sanders "Toward a Cultural Criminology." In J. Ferrell and C. Sanders, eds., *Cultural Criminology* (Boston: Northeastern University Press, 1995), 297–326; Robert Reiner, "Media Made Criminality," in *The Oxford Handbook of Criminology*, ed. M. Maguire, R. Morgan & R. Reiner (Oxford: Oxford University Press, 2002) 376–416; Bill Chambliss, Aaron Doyle and Jimmie Reeves, "Panel Discussion on 'Deviance,'" *Velvet Light Trap* 53 (Spring 2004): 4–9; Nicole Rafter, "Crime, film and criminology: Recent sex-crime movies," *Theoretical Criminology* 11, n.3 (2007): 403–20.

2. One book of essays (M. Allen, ed., *Reading CSI: Crime TV Under the Microscope* [London: IB Tauris, 2007]), as well as the following articles about *CSI* have been published since we began this work: G. Barak, "Mediatizing law and order: Applying Cottle's architecture of communicative frames to the social construction of crime and justice," *Crime, Media, Culture* 4, no.3 (2007): 101–9; G. Cavender and S. Deutsch "*CSI* and moral authority: The police and science," *Crime, Media, Culture* 3, no.1 (2007): 67–81; E. Burton Harrington, "Nation, identity and the fascination with forensic science in Sherlock Holmes and *CSI*," *International Journal of Cultural Studies* 10, no.3 (Sept. 2007): 365–82; R. Diehl Lacks, "The 'Real' CSI: Designing

and Teaching a Violent Crime Scene Class in an Undergraduate Setting," *Journal of Criminal Justice Education* 18, no.2 (July 2007): 311–21; M. Mopas, "Examining the 'CSI effect' through an ANT lens," *Crime, Media, Culture* 3, no.4 (2007): 110–17; T. Tyler, "Viewing CSI and the Threshold of Guilt: Managing Truth and Justice in Reality and Fiction," *Yale Law Journal* 115, no.5 (March 2006): 1050–85; M. Gever, "The spectacle of crime, digitized," *European Journal of Cultural Studies* 8, no.4 (Nov.2005): 445–63.

3. "The Best of Television: The Inaugural Flow Critics' Poll" (Posted by Jason Mittell, September 22nd, 2006) <http://flowTV.org/?p=8> (30 Jan. 2009).

4. "Flow Critics' Poll."

5. On stunting see John Caldwell, "Covergence Television," in *Television After TV*, ed. Lynn Spigel and Jan Olsson (Durham & London: Duke University Press, 2005), 46–47, 61–65.

6. On such viewers see Jimmie Reeves, Marc Rodgers, and Michael Epstein, "Rewriting Popularity: The Cult *Files*," in *"Deny All Knowledge," Reading the X-Files*, ed. David Lavery, Angela Hague, and Marla Cartwright (New York: Syracuse University Press, 1996), 25–26.

7. One excellent example of this is found in the episode "Coming of Rage" (4010). A woman dies of a gunshot wound although no one around her has a gun. The big reveal comes in the form of a neighbor who has fired his gun into the air from his backyard; the bullet has migrated back to earth and right into this woman's chest, killing her. Even stepping outside of your house is risky.

8. Jennifer Holt, "Vertical Vision: Deregulation, Industrial Economy and Prime-Time Design" in *Quality Popular Television*, ed. Mark Jancovich and James Lyons (London: Bfi Publishing, 2003), 11–31. For a great one-page representation of ownership structures from about 2001, see "Ultra Concentrated Media" <http://www.mediachannel.org/ownership/chart.shtml> (30 Jan. 2009). This chart, produced by the Media Channel, includes the four players identified by Holt, as well as Bertlesmann and Vivendi Universal.

9. Michele Byers and David Lavery, eds. *"Dear Angela:" Remembering My So-Called Life* (Lexington, 2007).

10. Henry Jenkins, "Why Fiske Still Matters," FLOW. June 10, 2005. http://flowTV.org/?p=585

11. The period in which *CSI* vaulted into the public spotlight is the same time frame in which we see a resurgence in the reality-TV genre, again a recycling of old forms that was heralded as both a major innovation and an imminent indicator of the end of culture and TV itself.

12. Wendy Brown's "American Nightmare: Neoliberalism, Neoconservatism, and De-Democratization," offers an insightful discussion of the intersection of these two rationalities (*Political Theory* 34, n.6 [2006]: 690–714). She asks how we are to understand the intertwining of "American neoconservativism—a fierce moral-political rationality—and neoliberalism—a market-political rationality . . . that does not align with any particular persuasion." That is, she reminds us that neoconservatism and neoliberalism are two different rationalities that "converge at crucial points to extend a cannibalism of liberal democracy already underway" (691). It is the separateness but

also the opportunistic interpenetration of these two rationalities that Brown describes so eloquently, asking: "how does a rationality that is expressly amoral at the level of both ends and means (neoliberalism) intersect with one that is expressly moral and regulatory (neoconservatism)? How does a project that empties the world of meaning, that cheapens and deracinates life and openly exploits desire, intersect one centered on fixing and enforcing meanings, conserving certain ways of life, and repressing and regulating desire? How does support for governance modeled on the form and a normative social fabric of self-interest marry or jostle against support for self-governance modeled on church authority and a normative social fabric of self-sacrifice and long-term filial loyalty, the very fabric shredded by unbridled capitalism?" (692). She draws our attention to the way that neoliberalism effects the "saturation of the state, political culture, and the social with market rationality [which] effectively strips commitments to political democracy from governance concerns and political culture" (695). Neoconservatism is more elusively described as "[T]he open affirmation of moralized state power in the democratic and international sphere" (697). These two rationalities act as bolsters: "the moralism, statism, and authoritarianism of neoconservativism are profoundly enabled by neoliberal rationality" (702). Bonnycastle in this volume also addresses the convergence and distinctions between neoliberalism and neoconservatism. For research on television and governmentality see Mick Dillon and Jeremy Valentine. "Introduction: Culture and Governance," *Cultural Values: The Journal for Cultural Research* 6 (2002): 5–9; Gareth Palmer, *Discipline And Liberty: Television and Governance* (Manchester: Manchester University Press, 2003); Laurie Ouellette and James Hay, *Better Living through TV: Television and the Government of Everyday Life* (Oxford: Blackwell, 2008).

13. TV Ratings are notoriously difficult to measure and read. Differing annual ratings for *CSI: Crime Scene Investigation* can be found at TV By the Numbers and Wikepedia: "Final 2007–8 Season To Date Broadcast Shows By Viewers" (Posted 25 September 2008 by Bill Gorman) <http://tvbythe numbers.com/category/nielsen-network-tv-ratings-season-to-date/nielsen-tv-ratings-top-broadcast-shows-season-to-date> (30 Jan. 2009); "CSI: Crime Scene Investigation"<http://en.wikipedia.org/wiki/CSI:_Crime_Scene_Investigation#U. S._television_ratings; www.nielsen.com> (30 Jan. 2009). On the franchise's popularity internationally, and especially that of *CSI:Miami*, see Elizabeth Guider, "'CSI' on Euro most-wanted list," *Variety* (Oct. 12, 2005);" "CSI show 'most popular in world,'" (31 July 2006) <http://news.bbc.co.uk/1/hi/entertainment/5231334.stm> (30 January 2009).

14. Simon, *Governing through Crime*. See also David Garland, "The Limits Of The Sovereign State: Strategies of Crime Control in Contemporary Society," *British Journal of Criminology* 36 (1996): 445–71.

15. See Kimberlianne Podlas, "'The CSI Effect:' Exposing the Media Myth," *Fordham Intellectual Property, Media and Entertainment Law Journal* 16 (2006): 429–65 and Harvey and Derkson's contribution to this volume, as well as the sources listed in appendix C.

16. Even in the United States, the country where the highest percentage of legal cases are decided by jury, the vast majority of cases are not decided by juries. In

countries such as Canada and in the UK juries decide even fewer trials. In Canada, for example, only a very small percentage of serious charges (for indictable offences) offer the accused the right to trial by a judge or a judge and jury.

17. A secondary (and related) dominant understanding of the CSI effect suggests that the extreme popularity of the franchise has inspired a markedly increased public interest in science, and particularly forensic science, as reflected, for example, in rising enrolments for or the initiation of educational programs in this field. See VanLaerhoven and Anderson in this volume. The much less common conception of the CSI effect is that watching the shows *lower* jurors' standards for reasonable doubt making it *easier* to convict. We discuss this below. For detailed exploration of all three of these understandings of the *CSI* effect see Podlas, "'The *CSI* Effect.'" For an illustration of the ubiquitous character of the dominant definition of "the *CSI* effect" see the Wikepedia definition at <http://en.wikipedia.org/wiki/CSI_Effect> (30 April 2008).

18. See, for example, Janine Robben, "The 'CSI' Effect: Popular culture and the justice system," *Oregon State Bar Bulletin* (October 2005), online at <http://www.osbar.org/publications/bulletin/05oct/csi.html or Henderson> (30 Jan. 2009), Nevada's Forensic Science Center's "Crime Lab Fundraising Project" at <http://www.henderson crimelab.com/media_coverage.html> (30 Jan. 2009).

19. See, for example, J. Ferrell and C. R. Sanders, "Toward a Cultural Criminology" in *Cultural Criminology*, ed. J. Ferrell and C. Sanders (Boston: Northeastern University Press, 1995): 297–326; Robert Reiner, "Media Made Criminality" in *The Oxford Handbook of Criminology*, ed. M. Maguire, R. Morgan, & R. Reiner (Oxford: Oxford University Press, 2002), 376–416; Sheila Brown, *Crime and Law in Media Culture* (Buckingham and Philadelphia: Open University Press, 2003); Mariana Valverde, *Law & Order: Images, Meanings, Myths* (New Brunswick, NJ: Rutgers University Press, 2006).

20. *Governing through Crime*. The quote is on page 5 of the pre-publication Draft (August 2005) in the possession of V. Johnson.

21. Graham Burchell, Colin Gordon, Peter Miller, eds., *The Foucault Effect: Studies in Governmentality* (Chicago: University of Chicago Press, 1991).

22. As Jonathan Simon aptly sums it up, "Crime governs when the experience of being a victim of crime becomes one of the dominant models of the citizen much as the yeomen farmer, the industrial worker, and the biologically vulnerable consumer have been at different moments in our history." *Governing through Crime* (August 2005 Pre-Press Draft from the author), 9. See also David Garland, *The Culture of Control* (Chicago: University of Chicago Press, 2001), 144.

23. See, for example, the following: Ulrich Beck, *Risk Society: Toward a New Modernity* Translated by M. Ritter (London: Sage, 1992); Burchell et al., *The Foucault Effect*; Richard Ericson and Kevin Haggerty, *Policing the Risk Society* (Toronto: University of Toronto Press, 1997); Garland, *The Culture of Control*, Pat O'Malley, ed., *Crime and the Risk Society* (Brookfield: Ashgate, 1998); Simon, *Governing through Crime*; Zygmunt Bauman, "Living (Occasionally Dying) Together in an Urban World" in *Cities, War and Terrorism*, ed. S. Graham (Malden, MA: Blackwell, 2004), 110–19.

24. See, for example, the following: Dorothy Chunn and Shelley Gavigan, "From Welfare Fraud to Welfare as Fraud: The Criminalization of Poverty" in *Criminalizing*

Women, ed. Comack and Balfour (Halifax, NS: Fernwood Publishing, 2006), 217–35; Joe Hermer and Janet Mosher, eds., *Disorderly People: Law and the Politics of Exclusion in Ontario* (Halifax: Fernwood Publishing, 2002), Anna Pratt and Mariana Valverde, "From Deserving Victims to 'Masters of Confusion': Redefining Refugees in the 1990s," *Canadian Journal of Sociology* 27, no.2 (2002): 135–62.

25. For dramatic narratives (in this case in film) as popular criminology, see Rafter, "Crime, film and criminology."

26. Cavender and Deutsch "*CSI* and moral authority," 69. See also G. Cavender, "Media and Crime Policy: A Reconsideration of David Garland's The Culture of Control," *Punishment & Society* 6, no.3 (2004): 335–48, Elayne Rapping, *Law and Justice as Seen on TV* (New York: New York University Press, 2004), N. Rafter. *Shots in the Mirror: Crime Films and Society*, 2nd ed. (New York: Oxford University Press, 2006).

27. Valverde, *Law & Order*, 99 (quote). Valverde is drawing on the work of Rapping, *Law and Justice as Seen on TV*. See also Cavender and Deutsch, 69, Cavender, "Media and Crime Policy."

28. Scott Turow, "Still Guilty After All These Years," *New York Times* April 8 2007.

29. Again, prominent *CSI* personnel have lobbied for this. For detailed critique of the evidence and reasoning behind the dominant construction of the *CSI* effect as decreasing jury likelihood of conviction, see Podlas, "'The *CSI* Effect.'" She also conducted a correlated survey of television viewing and respondent verdict responses to a criminal trial rape case scenario among 291 U.S. students that disproved any significant "anti-prosecution CSI Effect" among frequent viewers of CSI, but did provide some evidence of a pro-prosecution bias among these same viewers. For the impact on prosecutorial tactics of the perceived anti-prosecution *CSI* effect, see, for example, Karin H. Cather "The *CSI* Effect: Fake TV and its Impact on Jurors In Criminal Cases," *The Prosecutor* 38, no.2 (March–April 2004); Robben, "The '*CSI*' Effect"; "CSI: Maricopa County. The *CSI* Effect and its Real-Life Impact on Justice. A Study by the Maricopa County Attorney's Office" (June 30, 2005), <www.maricopacountyattorney.org/Press/PDF/CSIReport.pdf> (21 Sept. 2007).

30. For an exemplary examination of how these trends manifest in the Canadian discipline of criminology see Dorothy Chunn and Robert Menzies, "'So what does all of this have to do with Criminology?': Surviving the Restructuring of the Discipline in the Twenty-First Century" *Canadian Journal of Criminology and Criminal Justice* (September 2006): 663–76. The home institution of Byers and Johnson is currently marketing itself (and our department's criminology program) through the promotional slogan "I want to get into crime. *Understanding, not committing.*"

31. On the actuarial sciences and neoliberal governmentalities, see Richard Ericson and Aaron Doyle, *Uncertain Business: Risk, Insurance and the Limits of Knowledge* (Toronto: University of Toronto Press, 2004), Bernard Harcourt, "The Shaping of Chance: Actuarial Models and Criminal Profiling at the Turn of the Twenty-First Century," *University of Chicago Law Review* 70, no.105 (2003): 105–28.

32. Lynn Spigel, "Entertainment Wars: Television Culture after 9/11," *American Quarterly* 56, n.2 (June 2004): 235.

33. Spigel, "Entertainment Wars," 238.

34. Spigel, "Entertainment Wars," 262. Useful here is Derrida's notion of "hauntology" (*Spectres of Marx* [New York: Routledge, 1994]). Also see Lawrence Kramer's essay in this volume, and a related discussion in that by Basil Glynn and Jeongmee Kim. On discourses and practices around fear, risk, and crime that predated 9/11 see, for example, Jonathan Simon, *Governing through Crime: How the War on Crime Transformed American Democracy and Created a Culture of Fear* (New York: Oxford University Press, 2007).

35. Murray Forman. "Freaks, Aliens, and the Social Other: Representations of Student Stratification in U.S. Television's First Post-Columbine Season," *Velvet Light Trap* 53 (Spring 2004): 80.

36. Mikita Brottman. "The Fascination of the Abomination" in *Film and Television after 9/11*, ed. W.W. Dixon (Carbondale IL: Southern Illinois University Press, 2004), 163–77.

37. As Joel Black argues, the "increasingly graphic depiction of reality does not necessarily entail greater realism" *The Reality Effect* (New York and London: Routledge, 2002), 29.

38. On the shift from welfare liberalism to advanced or neoliberalism see Andrew Barry, Thomas Osborne and Nikolas Rose, eds., *Foucault and Political Reason: Liberalism, Neo-Liberalism and Rationalities of Government* (Chicago: University of Chicago Press, 1996), Nikolas Rose and Peter Miller, "Political Power beyond the State: Problematics of Government," *British Journal of Sociology* 43, no.2 (June 1992): 173–205, Nikolas Rose, "The death of the social? Refiguring the territory of government," *Economy and Society* 25, no.3 (1996): 327–56, Thomas Lemke, "'The birth of bio-politics': Michel Foucault's lecture at the Colle`ge de France on neo-liberal governmentality," *Economy and Society* 30, no.2 (2001): 190–207. On neoliberalism and neoconservatism see Wendy Brown, "Neo-liberalism and the End of Liberal Democracy," *Theory & Event* 7, no.1 (2003): 1–19. See also Bonnycastle in this volume.

39. Lavery, "Afterward," 211–12.

40. Drawing on Antonio Gramsci's theory of hegemony, David Harvey makes a related argument about how neoliberal understandings of the world have become "common sense." See Harvey, *A Brief History of Neoliberalism* (New York: Oxford University Press, 2005), 3, 5, 39 ff.

41. Tyson Lewis, "The Surveillance Economy of Post-Columbine School," *The Review of Education, Pedagogy, and Cultural Studies* 25 (2003): 349.

42. We would like to that our anonymous reviewer for highlighting this.

43. For the U.S. dimensions of this phenomenon see also Podlas, "'The CSI Effect,'" 442–43.

44. Karl Marx, *Capital*, vol. 1 (London: Penguin Classics, 1990), quote from 165, cited in Turkel.

45. Zuiker quoted in Saira Peesker, "New '*CSI*' game lets viewers in on the mystery," CTV News. ca (Dec. 11 2006), <http://www.ctv.ca/servlet/ArticleNews/story/CTVNews/20061205/CSI_interview_061205/20061211/> (17 Aug. 2007).

46. Herman Gray, *Watching Race: Television and the Struggle for Blackness* (Minneapolis: University of Minnesota Press, 1994), 4–10, cited in Rajiva.

Part I

PRODUCING JUSTICE, SCIENCE, AND TELEVISION DRAMA

Chapter One

Science Fiction or Social Fact?: An Exploratory Content Analysis of Popular Press Reports on the *CSI* Effect

Elizabeth Harvey and Linda Derksen

Beginning in 2002, a spate of newspaper and television news pieces point to what is alleged to be a new phenomenon called the "*CSI* effect." This is usually defined as a belief in the near-infallibility of forensic science and its ability to solve all crimes. At the 2005 conference of the American Association for the Advancement of Science (AAAS) forensic anthropologist Max Houck described the *CSI* effect as an "infallible juggernaut" which leads people to believe that science, as portrayed on television, can determine guilt or innocence beyond the shadow of a doubt.[1] The effect's name comes from the extremely popular television series *CSI: Crime Scene Investigation* (*CSI*),[2] its spin-offs *CSI: Miami* and *CSI: New York*, and similar shows such as *Crossing Jordan, Law and Order, Bones, ReGenesis, NUMB3RS, F2:Forensic Factor* and *Cold Squad*.[3] Law professor Robert Weisberg noted in the *Stanford Law and Policy Review* that "[t]he public, in part because of the unfortunately misleading influence of television shows like CSI, has come to believe that DNA is, or soon will be, the magic solution" to problems with evidence in the criminal justice system.[4]

To date, there have been few academic publications based on systematic inquiry into what comprises the *CSI* effect, or what its immediate and long-term consequences may be.[5] That a television show may influence the criminal justice system bears critical and systematic investigation.[6] In this paper we begin the process of determining whether the *CSI* effect is a media-inspired tempest in a teacup, or a real, growing, and potentially problematic phenomenon. We do so through an analysis of the only currently available literature on this subject: media reports about the *CSI* effect. We are interested in whether this purported effect is an empirically testable phenomenon or is something created by media hype that has subsequently become a self-fulfilling prophecy because people believe what they read in the press and may act on it.[7] To this

3

end, we performed a content analysis of seventy press reports on the *CSI* effect to see if we could determine just who it may be affecting and in what ways.

The *CSI* franchise plays to a western cultural predisposition to believe that science offers the kind of certainty that *CSI* delivers compellingly each week[8] and many times a day in syndication. Some prosecutors have claimed that the *CSI* effect has caused them to lose cases, and that juries are demanding that *all* evidence should be backed by infallible scientific proof.[9] The prosecutors' argument is that jurors expect proof to be presented with the same visual flair and speedy scientific certainty dished up to them on television, rather than through the dull reports of statistical probabilities that often characterize the courtroom presentation of forensic evidence. Anecdotal reports abound that jurors are giving short shrift to eyewitness testimony and older forms of evidence in favor of what they perceive to be "hard science."[10] In practice, most cases that come to trial in the United States do not have DNA or other scientific evidence available.[11] Prosecutors have complained to the media that juries sometimes acquit cases where no suitably scientific evidence is presented. [12]

Other reported ramifications of the *CSI* effect include the following: increased enrollment in university forensics courses, the increased social belief that forensic science is infallible, the perception that these shows educate people, the belief of prosecutors that jurors will acquit because they generally have inflated expectations of forensic science, the perception of defense attorneys that juries will convict their clients because these shows portray forensic evidence as providing a definitive truth and proving guilt beyond a reasonable doubt, and the contention that *CSI* is cleaning up forensic science's image as error-and-fraud prone.[13] If true, some of the effects attributed to *CSI* may pose a problem for a justice system that is already strapped for resources.[14] Since jurors are drawn from the television viewing public, it is a disturbing possibility that *CSI* and other similar television shows may spawn a new generation of jurors who believe that real life science can—and *should*—deliver the kind of certitude possible only on the small screen.

The *CSI* storylines present evidence, as revealed through forensic science techniques, as an infallible source of truth. An exchange between two of *CSI's* main characters in "Bloodlines" (4023) illustrates this absolute faith in "the evidence:"

Catherine Willows: The evidence is *wrong*.

Gil Grissom: No, it isn't. You can be wrong, I can be wrong. The evidence is just the evidence.

This interchange presents a compelling image of science free from human intervention (and error), in which evidence simply speaks for itself. This image is misleading and may have consequences for the criminal justice system if it is believed by people who participate in the system. Physical evidence, where it is available and suitable for forensic analysis, must undergo extensive, expensive, and time consuming mediation before it can "speak" to anything[15] (see also Anderson and Van Laerhoven in this volume). Even when evidence has been subjected to forensic analysis, there is no guarantee that the process will yield incontrovertible results. As much as we wish that science could answer our questions unequivocally, subjective judgment and individual expertise are an irreducible part of the production and interpretation of forensic evidence.[16] The *CSI* shows present forensic science in a way that denies the potential fallibility of scientific processes and hides the skill, expertise, and subjective judgments involved from the time evidence is collected until it is delivered in a courtroom. Instead, small-screen forensic scientists are presented as allowing the evidence itself to reveal the identity of the perpetrator, as they manipulate that evidence with a myriad of high-tech procedures indicated by flashy visual effects and machines.

This image of truth in the service of justice presented by the *CSI* franchise is so compelling that it has commanded the attention of one of the most prestigious scientific bodies in North America. At the 2005 annual meeting of the American Association for the Advancement of Science (AAAS), prominent forensic scientists held a symposium titled: "The CSI Effect: Forensic Science in the Public Imagination," where forensic scientists enlisted the support of *CSI* producers to test the authenticity of professional practitioners' science against that portrayed on television.[17] Forensic experts and criminal justice authorities have been quoted in the press as being bemused by the scientific license exercised in the shows, concerned by the growing expectations of jurors for high-tech equipment and scientific evidence in the courtroom, or pleased that jurors are becoming increasingly sophisticated as a result of watching the shows.

BACKGROUND

Can Television Affect Viewers' Constructions Of Reality?

As reported in the media, the *CSI* effect is premised on the belief that watching television shows such as *CSI* can actually *cause* a viewer to have heightened expectations of what science can do. There is some evidence, especially in the case of criminal justice shows, that television may act as an arbiter of viewers' perceptions of reality.[18] Some viewers may construct their perceptions of reality based on information gleaned from fictional crime shows, movies, or reality-television series such as *COPS*, rather than on their own life experiences.[19] Television's ability to collapse reality into reframed manageable segments, carefully delineated in time and space, may create a hyper-reality in which television portrayals appear to be more immediate and real than the correspondingly slower-moving pace of daily life. This immediacy draws viewers in and inspires them to create new realities that are actually media-inspired events.[20] Research also shows that viewers often simply forget where they learned specific pieces of information with which they construct their world-views.[21]

Media scholar Ray Surette points out that people create the worldview through which they experience lived reality from four sources: personal experience, interactions with significant others, knowledge disseminated by agencies, institutions, or organizations that collect and distribute data, and the mass media.[22] Personal experience, or "experienced reality" is the result of your interactions with others and provides direct information about the world.[23] "Symbolic reality" consists of all knowledge one has not personally witnessed, gathered, or experienced, but nevertheless believes to be factual.[24] The synthesis of reality from these four sources creates one's worldview, which although subjectively individual, is often similar to that of others with whom one frequently associates and shares ideas. This fusion of realities provides the platform for individual consciousness and is the springboard from which we act.[25]

Surette argues that the mass media make knowledge claims about social phenomena gleaned from popular culture, which help to create the "symbolic reality" we participate in as a culture. When disseminated through electronic and print media, these knowledge claims come to be accepted by the public as reliable facts.[26] Television's cultural symbols and signs present viewers with a worldview that most people consciously or unconsciously internalize and use to mediate their perceptions.[27] Legal theorist Richard Sherwin goes so far as to argue that post-modern societies replace reality with symbolism to the extent that many people have lost the ability to recognize where the barrier between reality and representation exists.[28] The only contact most people will ever have with the criminal justice system is through images in the mass media,[29] and even the American Civil Liberties Union claims that crime and justice programming are an "excellent legal education for the public."[30]

Communications scholar Heintz-Knowles[31] argues that television is a "cultural storyteller," which simultaneously shapes its viewers and reflects their norms and values. Fictional characters that represent success, or ideals valued by the viewer are more likely to stimulate imitative behavior.[32] This claim has been used in numerous press reports to explain the recent upsurge in female admissions to forensics programs at many universities. The argument is that the positive and sexy portrayal of females on *CSI* appeals to young women and may stimulate interest in a forensics career because they have been led to believe that this will allow them to look good, solve mysteries, and participate in exciting investigations.[33]

The *CSI* Effect: Part of a Fifty-Year Old Tradition, or Something New?

There is anecdotal evidence that previous criminal justice television shows have influenced courtroom practices, which would mean that the *CSI* effect may be just a new wrinkle in an old story. In the 1960s quintessential television defense attorney *Perry Mason* reassured television audiences and menaced witnesses by leaning on the witness stand, a device television producers used to get Mason and the witness in the same frame for filming.[34] At that time, real-life attorneys were not allowed to approach the witness stand lest they intimidate witnesses. Soon, however, jurors in trials all over North America began to expect Mason-like courtroom tactics in actual cases.[35] In the 1970s, pathologist-cum-sleuth *Quincy* managed to find fingerprint evidence in case after case. Subsequently, there was an upsurge in the demands of jurors for fingerprint evidence at their trials.[36] In the 1980s, *Judge Judy* and *Court TV* prompted jurors to complain if professional judges did not behave as television's syndi-court judges did.[37] Through repetition in each episode, *NYPD Blue* taught jurors and viewers their Miranda Rights.[38] Each new television show has prompted media scholars and criminal justice professionals to decry every new phenomenon as it appears in relation to new TV shows, as indicated in the examples above, and subsequently speculate about its possible effects on the criminal justice system.[39] Now, *CSI: Crime Scene Investigation* and its spin-offs, *CSI: Miami* and *CSI: New York* are being touted as a threat to the criminal justice system.

Since the average viewer has limited exposure to significant criminal activity in their own life it may seem reasonable for people to construct a view of the criminal justice system based on what they see on television.[40] Some claim that television "educates and amuses people" and "makes them informed citizens," but that it also "creates illusions" and "destroys literacy."[41] In reference to a video-reenactment of a crime that was presented as part of a court case and viewed by the jury on an in-court TV monitor, two years *before CSI* hit the airwaves, attorneys Lee and Page claimed that "[w]hen people see something on television, they think it is real even when it is not."[42] That two noted attorneys reported a *CSI*-like effect on a jury before *CSI* was produced points to the possibility of a more generalized effect of television shows in the crime genre.

There is evidence that people do learn from what they watch on television. Rogers, Singhal, and Thombre[43] found that subtle messages about fashion, clothes, hairstyles, and other image-based ideas were easily integrated into personal lifestyles and meaning schemes by a sample of television viewers from India. The Media Literacy Resource Guide of the Ontario Ministry of Education goes so far as to state:

> The media are responsible for the majority of the observations and experiences from which we build up our personal understandings of the world and how it works. Much of our view of reality is based on media messages that have been pre-constructed and have attitudes, interpretations and conclusions already built in. The media, to a great extent, give us our view of reality.[44]

The presence of television cameras and the media in courtrooms, through both *Court TV* and celebrity trials, has effectively recast legal proceedings as entertainment that people may draw on to help them understand social issues.[45] However, Sheila Jasanoff—a science and technology studies professor with a specialization in law—has argued that because many people subscribe to the belief that the camera does not lie, televising legal proceedings may serve to legitimate them as the source of truth claims in the minds of viewers.[46]

Because television is a source of learning about the social environment, if a viewer knows that even part of what is being portrayed there is true they may be more likely to accept all of what is portrayed in a given show as within the bounds of possibility.[47] When actual criminal justice experts lend their expertise to the creation of shows such as the *CSI* trilogy, it is not unreasonable for viewers to believe that some of what is depicted on these shows must be true, and that the involvement of credible experts lends authority to what is presented through them for public consumption.[48]

The *CSI* Effect: A Generational Effect?

Television shows are created for and targeted to specific audiences who are determined to be most receptive to a given advertising ethos.[49] Some evidence points to the conclusion that the *CSI* effect is partly a generational effect, due to the coming-of-age of jurors from Generation X (who were the first generation to live their entire lives in the television age). Litigation communication consultants Foley and LeFevre indicate that this generation's familiarity with television and computer technology has influenced them as jurors to accept and expect cutting-edge courtroom presentations incorporating formats with which they are intimately familiar.[50] Similarly, Generation Y have lived their entire lives in the computer age.[51] This is meaningful because together, Generation X and Generation Y comprise more than forty percent of the possible jury pool in the United States.[52] It is thus not unreasonable to conclude that the characteristics and perspectives of these two generations may influence the criminal justice system.[53]

Some Generation X jurors may walk into courtrooms expecting to be part of the fast-paced, infallible legal machine they see on television. They tend to expect multi-media courtroom presentations[54] rather than "dated and boring" oral summaries, and they respond well to cases presented as stories with recurring themes of morality and ethics.[55] Some argue that Generation X'ers have been socialized to reject the knowledge claims of traditional sources of evidence such as eyewitness testimony or authority figures.[56]

CSI creates a sense of urgency and hyper-reality through fast-paced, clear, and uncomplicated depictions of events, a portrayal that Sherwin asserts is preferable to Generation X viewers who are habituated to this form of information.[57] While they may not be influenced by one particular show, there is evidence that Generation X'ers are influenced by the familiarity of this format: rapid visual learning and sound bite information that provides a bottom-line analysis based on purportedly scientific facts, and which leaves viewers feeling as if they have solved a complex mystery or puzzle.[58] The *CSI* shows use mood lighting and stirring music, and present fast-paced close-ups of bodily cells, fibers, and other evidence in microscopic detail to signal to the viewer "something scientifically awesome has taken place."[59] Viewers are conditioned to see scientific evidence as the result of exhaustive and rigorous investigation. Law professor Peter Bensinger Jr. argues that criminal justice professionals who emulate this style of story-telling in the courtroom[60] are more likely to reach and influence Generation X jurors[61] because they will respond positively to a format with which they are already familiar.[62] Foley and LeFevre also argue this, observing:

> Whether it is *voir dire*, opening statement, or cross-examination, they do not want to wait an hour for you to get to the point. . . . Show Generation X jurors early that you have the facts and the data to back up your words. The key is to package information in the way they are accustomed to receiving it. . . . Observe how information is presented in newspapers, on television, and on websites: there is always a headline (the point) followed by supporting data.[63]

METHODS AND RESEARCH

What Do Professionals in the Criminal Justice System Say about the *CSI* Effect?

In the absence of systematic research on the *CSI* effect, in the summer of 2005 the authors conducted an informal e-mail survey of 205 (mostly American) criminal justice experts and real-life crime scene investigators who had been identified in media reports. Among other questions, we asked if they had observed any effects of television criminal justice programming in their practices, if they had heard of the *CSI* effect and, if so, whether they felt the *CSI* effect was impacting their work. Due to the non-random nature of the sample and a low response rate, the results cannot be generalized to a wider group.[64] However, the survey provided some evidence that members of the criminal justice system feel that something exists that they identify as the *CSI* effect. Seventeen respondents reported that they believed television crime shows had impacted their duties significantly and three of these respondents sent us links to specific news pieces about the *CSI* effect.[65]

In general, lawyers who responded felt that what they were experiencing as a *CSI* effect in the courtroom was due to the public's response to press reports *about* the *CSI* effect, and not anything specifically about the program *CSI* itself. One defense attorney wrote, "As I understand it the *CSI* effect is the impact on juries of watching television shows in which brilliant science and careful investigation of scientific facts yields the truth." Some lawyers said that they believed the television shows influence what jurors expect from them in relation to the types of evidence presented, and the technology used to present it. They also felt that the *CSI* effect influenced the ways in which lawyers conducted their jury selections. A district attorney told us that the *CSI* shows create confusion in the mind of the public, particularly jurors, between what television creates and what happens in real-life cases. In sum, both defense and prosecuting lawyers tended to express a belief that the *CSI* shows have an impact on juries.

Respondents who were crime scene professionals, and those working in forensic laboratories, expressed different concerns. The director of a forensic science laboratory defined the *CSI* effect as "an unwarranted level of expectation regarding the abilities of forensic science engendered through science fiction detective shows, especially *CSI*." The chief of another crime laboratory said the *CSI* effect was "heighten[ing], even exaggerate[ing], expectations for crime laboratory work from investigators and jurors." Finally, a police chief wrote "*CSI* leaves viewers with the impression that cases will be solved immediately, with little 'leg work' and that the evidence will stick like glue."

Clearly, to identify more definitively whether there is a *CSI* effect as described above would require systematic research with real life jurors and those who work in the criminal justice system. However, until just previous to our submission date, virtually all reports on the *CSI* effect came from the popular press.[66] We decided that a logical first step would be to interrogate just what the press was saying about the *CSI* effect.

Going to the Source: an Exploratory Content Analysis of Popular Press Reports on the *CSI* Effect

To find out what the press is saying about *CSI* and its effects on the public, we conducted a content analysis of publications that mentioned the *CSI* effect.

We wanted to determine what has been reported as the *CSI* effect and what evidence has been brought to bear to support its alleged effects. We wondered whether and in what ways the *CSI* effect is an actual phenomenon, or if it may have been created primarily by the media. We wondered who has been reported as being impacted by the *CSI* effect, and how? Has *CSI* been alleged to affect any real life cases since the show first aired?

DATA SELECTION

Between May 1 and August 10, 2005, we conducted an internet search for newspaper articles and other media content, using Google© for our search engine, and a consistent search strategy with terms involving *CSI* and the *CSI* effect.[67] There were many duplicate hits in the retrieved data, so we reduced the data to seventy unique newspaper articles, and audio and video sources. We kept only sources that were widely available to the general public, either in print media such as newspapers and magazines, or on the radio, television, and the internet. Sources that were relatively obscure or generally only accessed by professional communities were discarded (see Appendix C for a full list of the sources that constitute our dataset).

We first scanned the data to identify broad themes, such as "unrealistic juror expectations," and "effects of *CSI* effect on real-life justice professionals." Axial coding allowed us to focus the themes more narrowly and to refine our search for concepts or categories within our codes. [68]

DESCRIPTIVE FINDINGS

When and Why Are Articles about the *CSI* Effect Published?

One of our first and most obvious findings was that there was an increase in the number of unique articles published in each year since *CSI* first aired in 2002 (Figure 1.1). Mapping the publications over time shows that two of the articles we found were from 2002, nine were from 2003, while twelve articles and one internet audio source were from 2004. The other forty-six articles were all from 2005.

Second, we noticed that a large number of publications about the *CSI* effect cite just a tiny handful of original sources. The content of the articles from 2002 and 2003 were primarily based on the content of just one article (included in the dataset): a *Time* magazine piece on *CSI* published in October 2002.[69] The *Time* article was one of only two unique articles mentioning the *CSI* effect published in 2002.[70] Only five sources in our dataset explicitly

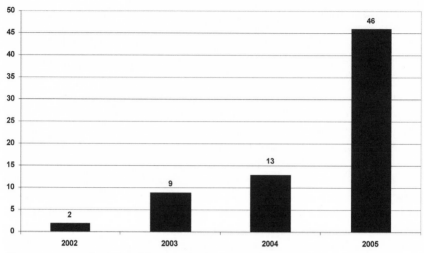

Figure 1.1. Number of Articles Mentioning "*CSI* Effect" by Year

cited news services such as Associated Press or Reuters as the source of their information.[71] However, it is our impression that many more news items than this five actually used news services for the content in their items on *CSI*, without mentioning the services as their primary source of information, because the same few prosecutors, CSI technicians and defense attorneys are mentioned repeatedly in the range of news items. Names that appear repeatedly include forensic anthropologist Max Houck, who spoke at a session on the *CSI* effect at the 2005 general meeting of the American Academy for the Advancement of Science (cited in ten articles).[72] Clatsop County D.A. and Oregon director for the National Defense Attorneys Association (NDAA) Josh Marquis was quoted in eleven articles.[73] Elizabeth Devine, former L.A. Sheriff's department CSI tech and current consultant on *CSI: Miami* was quoted in six sources,[74] and *CSI* franchise Executive Producer Anthony Zuiker was also mentioned in six sources.[75]

Of the seventy articles in our content analysis, thirty-two articles contained references to the positive or negative impacts of the *CSI* effect on both defense attorneys and prosecutors. D.A. Josh Marquis was quoted ten times as stating that there was a negative effect for prosecutors and once as opining that the *CSI* effect was a positive benefit for defense attorneys (in article number 14). Defense attorney Betty Layne des Portes was quoted in two articles (14 and 61), as saying that the *CSI* effect had negative consequences for defense attorneys, and once (in article 14) as stating that she felt it was a positive thing for prosecutors. District attorney Christine Mascal was quoted in two articles (numbers 1 and 61), and she presented the *CSI* effect as being both positive and negative for prosecutors. Fifteen articles mentioned effects on attorneys, but listed no names to which the results in the article could be attributed.[76]

Real cases, some local to the place of publication,[77] some featuring high-profile and shocking crimes such as the Laci Peterson case,[78] and others featuring celebrity accused such as Robert Durst,[79] Ted Binion,[80] Robert Blake,[81] and Jayson Williams,[82] were mentioned in thirty-three of the seventy sources (see Figure 1.2). Twenty-nine sources intimated that juror awareness of forensic techniques, or the lack of DNA evidence such as that presented on *CSI*, had impacted the verdict in particular cases.[83] Figure 1.2 shows the number of unique articles that mention these cases.

Major cases such as the Laci Peterson case in 2003, and the trials of Robert Durst and Ted Binion in 2004, drew a lot of media attention. As jury selection proceeded, there was almost daily speculation on television and in the dailies as to whether the jurors on these cases were watching *CSI* or not. By mapping the publication dates across time, Table 1.1 shows how articles that mention the *CSI* effect tend to cluster around the dates of major cases. This may indicate that the *CSI* effect is not an independent phenomenon, but is more of a catchphrase that the media uses to draw readers into their stories when real-life cases are being tried.

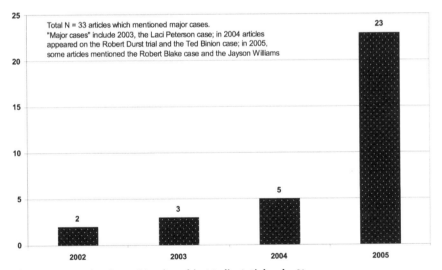

Figure 1.2. Major Cases Mentioned in Media Articles, by Year

Table 1.1.   Frequency of Cases by Date and Case Name

Cases	2002	D	J	2003	D	J	2004	D	J	2005	A
Williams										1	
Peterson			1								
Durst							1	1		1	
Binion								1		1	
Blake										2 4 1 1	
Local		1	1				1	1	1	4 3 4	2
O.C.N.	1		1					1		1	
No Case			1 2	1 1 1 1			1	3 1	1	2 5 2 6 3 3	2

LEGEND

Williams	Jayson Williams manslaughter trial, starts Jan. 2004 in New Jersey; jury deadlocked in May 2004. Could face retrial in 2006.
Peterson	Laci Peterson Case, start June 2004, Scott Peterson convicted November 2004 in San Francisco.
Durst	Robert Durst Case, Galveston County Texas, November 2003, found not guilty because head of victim was not found.
Binion	Ted Binion Trial, November 2004, Las Vegas, both accused killers of Ted Binion were acquitted
Blake	Robert Blake Case, March, 2005 in Los Angeles, jury acquits Robert Blake of murdering his wife.
Local	Local cases
O.C.N.	Other Cases of Note
No Case	No Cases Mentioned in the article

(In November of 2004 the Binion case ended. In March of 2005, Robert Blake was found 'not guilty' of the murder of his wife. In May of 2005, the Binion case was back in court and the news, as people started filing claims on the buried silver he left behind in the Nevada desert outside Las Vegas.) Stories about the *CSI* effect in 2005 cluster around the Blake and Binion media circus.

The *CSI* effect was cited in the Blake murder case because of an alleged dearth of evidence proving that the gun used to shoot his wife was in Blake's hand, and because of footage of Blake on the show *20/20*, where, in an interview with Barbara Walters, Blake declared his innocence. His defense team used this footage as a video deposition at Blake's trial, although he did not take the stand in his own defense (Bringardner 2005).

The *CSI* effect was cited in the Durst murder trial because the head of the victim was never found, thus allowing jurors to cite an incomplete evidence chain and acquit Durst (Willing 2004). In the Binion case, the jury could not be convinced that every last piece of evidence led conclusively to the two accused, and acquitted because of reasonable doubt (Puit 2005).

THEMATIC FINDINGS

Major Themes

The major themes that we found in the media sources were as follows:

1. unrealistic juror expectations allegedly created by *CSI*;
2. the alleged impacts of the *CSI* effect on practicing justice professionals;
3. positive and/or negative results of the *CSI* effect in the lives of, or on the work or duties expected from, prosecutors, jurors, defense attorneys and CSI technicians;

4. the possible consequences of the *CSI* effect on forensic school enrolment;
5. effects similar to those associated with *CSI*, but from earlier television shows;
6. how the *CSI* effect has allegedly impacted real-life cases;
7. the difference between real life forensics and television representations of those practices.

Juror Expectations

Figure 1.3 illustrates how many times each of these themes was found in our seventy sources. The words "juror expectation" or "unrealistic expectations" appeared fifty-six times. Jurors were alleged to have been impacted positively in thirteen articles,[84] and negatively impacted in twenty-eight sources.[85] Reports of positive impacts included educating jurors, increased juror awareness of scientific techniques, and more people looking forward to jury duty. Reports of negative impacts included biased jury pools, punishing defendants for forcing jurors to sit through boring trials that did not include sexy technology such as that portrayed on television, jurors dismissing eyewitness testimony (as opposed to scientific evidence) as irrelevant, jurors expecting more bombastic performances and technical proficiency from criminalists, lawyers and expert witnesses expecting increased use of Power Point, Smart Boards and visual cues such as docudramas, juror perceptions that they are now experts because of their television viewing, and unrealistic expectations

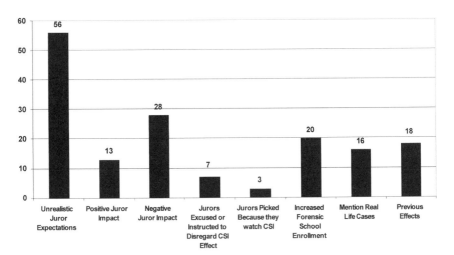

Figure 1.3.   Major Themes in which "*CSI* Effect" Is Mentioned in Media Articles

about what real-life science can provide in terms of technology used, items suitable for testing, and time-frames for results.

Seven articles or sources mentioned that, as a result of the perceived impact of *CSI*, in some jurisdictions jurors are now either issued instructions to disregard what television may have led them to expect in regards to the types and quantity of evidence that may be presented in court or they are excused from jury duty if they admit to watching *CSI*.[86] Two sources mentioned the Robert Durst trial, where defense jury consultant Robert Hirschorn specifically picked jurors who watched *CSI* because he anticipated that they would be proficient at spotting faulty evidence.[87] Blake trial juror Cecilia Maldonado appeared in newspapers, radio shows, and on television in 2005 to discuss why she voted for Robert Blake's acquittal.[88] Maldonado and other jurors in this case said that they thought the state's crime scene procedures were "sloppy" because they did not match those portrayed on *CSI*.[89] On CBC's radio show *The Current,* Prosecutor and District Attorney of Clatsop County, Oregon, Josh Marquis expressed worry that jurors such as Maldonado were not sufficiently instructed about the possible influence of fictional shows such as *CSI* during jury selection, and that most jurisdictions do not have the financial and technical resources that television presents as being readily available. He argued that this does not mean that actual evidence collection techniques are lacking, but that crime scene technicians are doing the best they can with limited resources.[90]

By early 2005, media reports suggested that jurors were increasingly being drawn from a public watching *CSI* and other crime shows on television, with one source, *USA Today,* citing that over seventy percent of the jurors in the Robert Durst jury pool of five hundred watched *CSI*.[91]

Who Is Reported as Being Impacted by the *CSI* Effect?

Next we determined who, besides jurors, the *CSI* effect is alleged to have impacted, and in what ways (see Figure 1.2). Prosecutors were listed as being negatively impacted by the *CSI* effect in twenty-nine articles,[92] while only eight articles listed a positive impact for them.[93] Negative impacts posited for prosecutors included the following: increased costs to try a case because press reports indicate that jurors expect all pieces of evidence collected to be tested whether germane to a case or not, increased expectations that a prosecutor will provide supporting forensic evidence or "negative evidence" explaining why this is not possible, jurors who feel that a lack of evidence means that someone did not do their job correctly, and disruptive jurors who act as armchair criminalists and second-guess the prosecutor. Positive effects posited for prosecutors were listed in eight articles and included the suggestion that jurors (especially those who watch *CSI*) are more educated and are thus less likely to miss crucial evidence because they can't follow the proceedings. Two articles mentioned that some judges feel prosecutors are trying cases differently and are working harder to make sure that all of their facts are supported.[94]

Defense attorneys were reported as experiencing negative impacts of the *CSI* effect in nine articles, primarily due to juror over-reliance, in deliberations, on the scientific evidence presented in the case.[95] In these nine articles, defense lawyers were generally represented as believing that jurors do not sufficiently take into account the possible errors made at forensic labs and at crime scenes. A positive impact of the *CSI* effect for defense attorneys was mentioned in twelve articles.[96] These articles suggested that jurors routinely demand DNA tests for virtually every case tried, so many defense attorneys simply have to ask where the supporting physical evidence is to win over jurors in cases where there is a lack of such supporting evidence.[97]

The *CSI* effect is also alleged to affect the practicing crime scene investigators who collect evidence at crime scenes, and technicians working in forensic labs. Twenty sources asserted negative impacts from the *CSI* effect such as increased workloads, insufficient staffing, unrealistic expectations (from prosecutors, detectives, crime victims, and their families), and lack of scientific equipment.[98] Ten sources mentioned positive effects such as increased recognition of forensic techs as heroic figures, a better educated and growing pool of applicants for lab jobs, increased public awareness and demand for funding for forensic labs and programs, and increased awareness of forensic work as a satisfying and positive career choice.[99]

Are most prosecutors and defense attorneys being stressed by the crime shows on television? We do not know. However, as justice professionals cited in our survey pointed out, if criminal justice personnel try their cases in a more vigorous and rigorous manner, it may have positive long-term effects. We do not know how most real-life forensic practitioners are affected by these shows. There are reports that they are being asked to collect evidence as it is done on television. However, further research is required to determine how widespread this demand actually is. In the long term it is possible that increased public interest in forensic science may highlight the need for increased funding, more and better lab facilities, and more trained and fully accredited personnel.

Impacts on Enrolments in Forensic Programs

Another reported impact of *CSI* and related television series is that applications to forensic programs are reported to have "skyrocketed" at many

North American universities, with twenty sources[100] listing vastly increased enrolment by females in particular in forensics programs as a result of the *CSI* effect.[101] Of these, nine either directly mentioned the University of West Virginia where aforementioned forensic anthropologist Max Houck teaches, or used some form of direct quote or paraphrase of Dr. Houck's words about increased enrolment and its consequences. Only one of these nine articles (Unknown News, Sept 7, 2003: AP), listed a primary journalistic source such as Associated Press as its information source.[102] Five of these nine articles paraphrased Dr. Houck or mentioned the program of which he is the director, but did not attribute the information about increased enrolment to him or to another source such as AP or Knight-Ridder. To us this indicated that the articles citing Max Houck are recycling one or two primary sources, thus amplifying the *CSI* effect through media circulation. Very few of the nine articles mention Max Houck's full quote about increased enrolment in forensics courses, which goes on to say that most of the new recruits drop out when they realize that there is a significant mathematics, biology, and chemistry requirement to complete the degree, and that the work is often tedious and unromantic. Further investigation is required to understand whether enrolments have gone up and stayed up, and whether this is attributable in any way to the *CSI* franchise.

Reported Impacts of Previous Crime Shows

Seventeen sources[103] mentioned effects from previous television shows, books, or phenomena to which the *CSI* trilogy of shows has purportedly added its influence (see figure 1.5). Earlier effects include reports that the O.J. Simpson trial awakened public interest in forensic science and the use of technology in the courtroom. The *Perry Mason* show is said to have affected lawyers being allowed to physically approach the witness stand.[104] *Dragnet* is reported to have affected public knowledge of the Miranda ruling because it was read to suspects in every show.[105] *Quincy* is reported to have caused an upsurge in the demand for fingerprint evidence by jurors,[106] and *Hill Street Blues* is credited with introducing social politics and police psychology to viewers.[107] *The Untouchables* is reported to have familiarized viewers with crime scene procedures,[108] and *L.A. Law* is credited with introducing potential jurors to the use of trial transcripts by juries to assist them during court proceedings and later deliberation stages.[109] Fictional heroes and heroines Sherlock Holmes, Miss Marple,[110] and Kay Scarpetta[111] are reported to have informed readers of scientific procedures and taught them to expect detectives' use of intellectual abilities to deduce facts from the evidence presented.

These reports indicate that phenomena that resemble what is perceived as the *CSI* effect predate *CSI*. At this point, we believe that what is called the

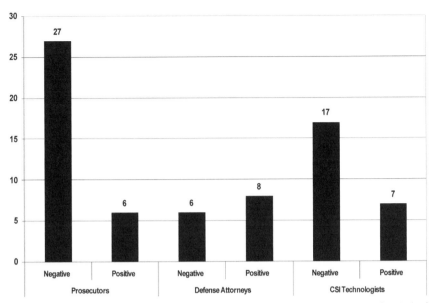

Figure 1.4. Perceived Impact of the *"CSI* Effect" on Three Categories of Criminal Justice Professionals

CSI effect is predicated on a long line of literary characters and television shows that have cumulatively helped to shape the public's perception of how the criminal justice system operates for well over sixty years.

Perhaps because major media sources such as *Time* and *USA Today* have claimed in print that jurors are again asking for what their latest favorite television shows are presenting as reality, many media outlets are dramatizing the *CSI* effect as a new phenomenon. Is this a new effect? We don't believe so. There is, as yet, no systemic evidence of any tangible effect of the *CSI* programs on the criminal justice system. Instead, media reports inflate the comments of a tiny number of people, repeating them over and over again, until it seems that the *CSI* effect is everywhere. At this point, the *CSI* effect appears to be merely a new wrinkle in the continuing interplay between audiences and television, media and popular culture.

CONCLUDING THOUGHTS

What, precisely, the *CSI* effect is remains to be determined. Some of *CSI*'s principal actors and producers have appeared before the U.S. Congress, and may have positively influenced a funding increase to some forensic labs.[112] However, the legislation for increased long-term funding for forensic labs in the United States, specifically DNA laboratories, was first enacted in the 1990s, long before *CSI* aired.[113]

Forensic science as portrayed on *CSI* appears to offer viewers certainty in the face of doubt about forensic evidence and the guilt of an accused. Some scientists believe that *CSI*'s biggest flaw is that it represents science as always infallible and impeccable.[114] Journalist and juror Sophia Smardz reported that contemporary jurors do not want to grapple with reasonable doubt: they want no doubt.[115] It is unlikely that the desire for scientific certainty in the court-room will vanish. However, the relationship between popular television, and courtroom and criminal justice practices needs to be interrogated more deeply and systematically before any conclusions can be drawn about whether the *CSI* effect is primarily a media creation, or a new set of social practices. This would require research with jurors and those who work in the criminal justice system. To date, we are not aware of any such research.

We believe that the jury is still out on what the *CSI* effect is, and whether it has any systematic ramifications or not. This exploratory content analysis shows that all reports of the *CSI* effect have been based on very few sources: the 2002 *Time* article,[116] repetitions of a single quote from forensic anthro-pologist Max Houck,[117] and a few defence attorneys and prosecutors who are cited time and time again. We have demonstrated that media reports on the *CSI* effect tend to cluster around major cases and celebrity trials that draw

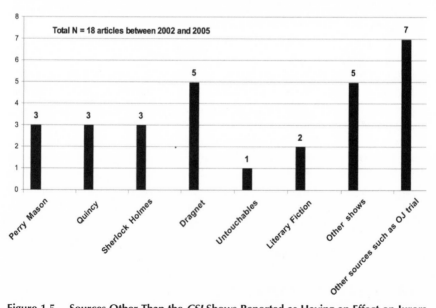

Figure 1.5.   Sources Other Than the *CSI* Shows Reported as Having an Effect on Jurors

a lot of media attention. There is currently no systematic research indicating that the *CSI* effect exists, or what its impacts may be.

Bearing in mind that eighteen sources cite earlier crime books and shows as similarly affecting public attitudes and juror demands, at this point it seems unlikely that the *CSI* franchise has spawned anything new. It is more likely that the media have turned the persistent effects of television on popular culture into a catchy phrase that encapsulates the latest instalment of the public's long-term fascination with crime and mystery genres. It is not surprising that given the overall popularity of the *CSI* trilogy, some of its viewers are demanding that the criminal justice system live up to the certainty of justice that they see on television. Earlier viewers of similar shows did the same. Artistic depictions of realism may have morphed to equate with reality in the minds of some viewers. The *CSI* effect is conceived of, and may exist, at the juncture where viewers' faith in science and dramatic license merge.

NOTES

1. Several online dictionaries have posted definitions for the "CSI effect" which are essentially the same as Dr. Houck's definition. For example, "CSI Effect," *Do You Speak American: Track That Word at PBS.org.* (2003) <http://www.pbs.org/speak/words/trackthatword/ttw/?i=513> (15 Nov. 2005); and Double-Tongued.org, "CSI Effect," *Double-Tongued Dictionary* 2005 <http://www.doubletongued.org/index.php/citations/csi_effect_1/ > (15 Nov. 2005).

2. Franzen cites viewership of *CSI: Crime Scene Investigation* at near fifty million weekly. Robin Franzen, "'CSI Effect' on Potential Jurors Has Some Prosecutors Worried," *Almenconi News*, December 19 2002 <http://www.almenconi.com/news/dec02/121902.html> (10 May 2005).

3. The Nielsen ratings for the week from July 25–31, 2005, near the end of our study, demonstrated that out of the sixteen most watched shows, ten were crime genre shows. CBS, with its *CSI* triptych led the pack with an average of 7 million viewers in prime-time for the week (4.8 rating, 9 percent share). CBS-*CSI: Crime Scene Investigation* had 13.4 million viewers; CBS-*Without a Trace* had 11.3 million viewers; CBS-*CSI: Miami* had 10.3 million viewers NBC-*Law and Order: Criminal Intent* got 9 million viewers; CBS-*NCIS* had 9 million; CBS-*Cold Case* had 8.4 million; and NBC-*Law and Order* (original) got 8.3 million people tuning in. "Crime Shows Dominate Ratings" <http://www.cnn.com/2005/SHOWBIZ/television/08/03/nielsens.ap/> (3 Aug. 2005).

4. Robert Weisberg, "Introduction," *Stanford Law and Policy Review* 15 (2004): 323–28.

5. However, CSI is currently "hot" on the academic conference circuit, if the AAAS session in February 2005, and the August 2005 American Bar Association

conference titled: "*CSI Meets the Courts: The Brave New World of Forensic Science*" are any indication.

6. Kimberlianne Podlas, "'The CSI Effect:' Exposing the Media Myth," *Fordham Intellectual Property, Media and Entertainment Law Journal* 16 (2006): 429–65.

7. Simon Cole and Rachel Dioso, "The Law and The Lab: Do Television Shows Really Affect How Juries Vote? Let's Look At the Evidence," *The Wall Street Journal* (2005), <http://www.truthinjustice.org/law-lab.htm> (23 May 2005).

8. Elizabeth Foley and Adrienne LeFevre, "Understanding Generation X" *Trial* (June 2000): 58–62.

9. Marsha Kazarosian, "Hollywood: Fact or Fiction in Court?" *Power of Attorney* Radio Show. <http://www.legaltalknetwork.com/modules.php?name=News&file=article&sid=20> (2005).

10. Leo Adler, "Commentary: Convicted by Juries, Exonerated by Science," *The Voice of the Criminal Defence Bar* (1996), (13 June 2005); Michael Lynch, "God's Signature: DNA Profiling, the New Gold Standard in Forensic Science," *Endeavour* 27, no. 2 (June 2003): 93–97; Mark Hansen, "The Uncertain Science of Evidence," *ABAJournal.Com* (2005) <http://www.abanet.org/journal/redesign/07fcle.html> (17 July, 2005).

11. Kazarosian, "Hollywood."

12. Brian Hayes, "Wisconsin's Lethargic Response to the 'CSI Effect,'" *Wisconsin Interest* (Fall 2005): 7–13.

13. Cole and Dioso, "The Law and The Lab."

14. Some *CSI* cast members participated in a special awareness day at the Kern County Regional Crime Lab in Bakersfield, California, to highlight the lack of funding for forensic labs, and to allow the public and the media to see the conditions under which a real lab operates. Gregory E. Laskowski, "The CSI Effect: Good or Bad For Forensic Science" 2005, <http://www.clpex.com/Articles/TheDetail/100-199/TheDetail187.htm.> (20 June 2005).

15. Linda Derksen, "Towards a Sociology of Measurement: The Meaning of Measurement Error in the Case of DNA Profiling," *Social Studies of Science* 30 (2000): 803–45.

16. Derksen, "Towards a Sociology."

17. Attendees included journalists, AAAS members, and featured speakers including ballistics expert Richard Ernst, West Virginia University forensic anthropologist and trace evidence expert Max Houck, forensic pathologist Patricia McFeeley, and AUS Armed Forces DNA expert Demris Lee. Cast members invited from the *CSI* shows were unable to attend although they had accepted the invitation. To compensate, *CSI* producers provided video clips from the show for use by presenters at the conference to highlight key points in their presentations. American Academy for the Advancement of Science, "The CSI Effect: Forensic Science in the Public Imagination," Symposium, in *Worldwide Public Understanding of Science*, American Academy for the Advancement of Science 2005 Annual Meeting (Audio-Visual Education Network, 2005), AS5187.

18. Michael Hallett, '*COPS*' and '*CSI*': *Reality Television?* 2005, <www.unf.edu/coas/ccj/Faculty/Hallett/COPS%20and%20CSI%20Reality%20Television.doc>

(15 Oct. 2005); David S. Meyer and William Hoynes, "Shannon's Deal: Competing Images of the Legal System in Primetime Television," *Journal of Popular Culture* 27 (Spring 1994): 31–41; Monica L. P. Robbers, "The Media and Public Perceptions of Criminal Justice Policy Issues: An Analysis of Bowling For Columbine and Gun Control," *Journal of Criminal Justice and Popular Culture* 12, no. 2 (2005): 77–95.

19. S. H. Chaffee and A. R. Tims, "Interpersonal Factors in Adolescent Television Use," *Journal of Social Issues* 32, no. 4 (1976): 98–115; Marie-Louise Mares, "The Role of Source Confusion in Television's Cultivation of Social Reality Judgments," *Human Communication Research* 2 (23 December 1996): 278–97; J. Meyrowitz, "Television and Interpersonal Behavior: Codes of Perception and Response," in *Inter/Media*, ed. G. Gumpert and R. Cathcart (New York: Oxford University Press, 1979), 253–72; Jan Van den Bulck and Heidi Vandebosch, "When the Viewer Goes to Prison: Learning Fact From Fiction. A Qualitative Cultivation Study," *Poetics* 31 (2003): 103–16.

20. Peter K. Manning, "Media Loops," in *Popular Culture, Crime and Justice*, ed. Frankie Bailey, Y. and Donna C. Hale (Belmont, CA: West/Wadsworth, 1998), 25–39.

21. Mares, "Source Confusion," 278–97; Van deb Bulck and Vandebosch, "When the Viewer."

22. Ray Surette, "Some Unpopular Thoughts About Popular Culture," in *Popular Culture, Crime and Justice*, ed. Frankie Y. Bailey and Donna C. Hale (Belmont, CA: West/Wadsworth, 1998), xiv–xxiv; Surette, *Media, Crime, and Criminal Justice: Images and Realities* (Pacific Grove, CA: Brooks/Cole Publishing, 1992).

23. Surette, "Some Unpopular" and *Media, Crime*, vx.

24. Surette, "Some Unpopular" and *Media, Crime*, vxi.

25. Surette, "Some Unpopular" and *Media, Crime*, 1998.

26. Surette, "Some Unpopular" and *Media, Crime*, 1998.

27. George Gerbner, Larry Gross, Michael Morgan, and Nancy Signorelli, "A Curious Journey Into the Scary World of Paul Hirsch," *Communication Research* 8 (1981): 39–72.

28. Richard K. Sherwin, *When the Law Goes Pop: The Vanishing Line Between Law and Popular Culture* (Chicago: University of Chicago Press, 2000).

29. Connie L. McNeely, "Perceptions of the Criminal Justice System: Television," *Journal of Criminal Justice and Popular Culture* 3, no. 1 (1995): 1–20.

30. M. Gunther, "You Have the Right to Remain Silent," *TV Guide*, 18 December 1971, 8.

31. Katharine E. Heintz-Knowles, "Images of Youth: A Content Analysis of Adolescents in Prime Time Entertainment Programming" 2000, 13 <http://www.frameworksinstitute.org/products/youth.pdf> (13 Oct., 2005).

32. Albert Bandura, "Social Cognitive Theory of Mass Communication," in *Media Effects: Advances in Theory and Research*, ed. J. Bryant and D. Zillman (New Jersey: Earlbaum, 1994), 121–53.

33. Susan LaTempa, "The Women of CSI," *Written By* (2002) <http://www.wga.org/WrittenBy/1002/csi.html> (20 June 2005).

34. Franzen, "CSI Effect."

35. Amy Lennard Goehner, Lina Lofaro, and Kate Novack, "Where CSI Meets Real Law and Order," _Time_ 164, no. 19 (8 November 2004).

36. Franzen, "CSI Effect"; Goehner et al, "Where CSI Meets."

37. Podlas cites editorials in the _New Jersey Lawyer_ which detail public complaints about the judges and attorneys in actual cases who do not measure up to what viewers have come to expect from Judge Judy and her ilk. Kimberlianne Podlas, "Should We Blame Judge Judy? The Messages Television Courtrooms Send Viewers," _Judicature_ 86, no. 1 (July–August 2002): 38–43.

38. Susan Bandes and Jack Beermann, "Lawyering Up," _Green Bag_ 2 (Autumn 1998).

39. Goehner et al, "Where CSI Meets."

40. Connie L. McNeely, "Perceptions."

41. Susie O'Brien and Imre Szeman, _Popular Culture: A User's Guide_ (Scarborough, Ontario: Nelson, 2004), 156.

42. Joseph Lee and A. G. Page, "Use and Admissibility of 'High Tech' Evidence," _California Litigation_ 11, no. 3 (Spring/Summer 1998): 1.

43. Everett M. Rogers, Arvind Singhal, and Avinash Thombre, "Indian Audience Interpretations of Health Related Content in The Bold and the Beautiful," _Gazette: The International Journal for Communication Studies_ 66, no. 5 (2004): 437–58.

44. Barry Duncan, et al. _Media Literacy Resource Guide_ (Toronto: Ontario Ministry of Education, 1989).

45. Elayne Rapping, _Law and Justice As Seen On Television_ (New York: New York University Press, 2003).

46. Sheila Jasanoff, "The Eye of Everyman: Witnessing DNA in the Simpson Trial," _Social Studies of Science_ 28, nos. 5–6 (October–December 1998): 713–40.

47. Joseph Lee and A. G. Page, "Use and Admissibility of 'High Tech' Evidence," _California Litigation_ 11, no. 3 (Spring/Summer 1998).

48. Dave Scheiber, "Crossing the Line: Reality Becomes Fiction When a Real-Life Detective, Who Makes His Home in St. Petersburg, Embarks on a New Career Advising The CBS Drama, CSI: Miami," _St. Petersburg Times Online_ (1 January 2004), <http://www.sptimes.com/2004/01/01/news_pf/Floridian/Crossing_the_line.shtml> (17 July 2005).

49. O'Brien and Szeman, _Popular Culture_, 149.

50. Gen X'ers are defined as those born from 1966 to 1981. They are represented by the letter "X" because, like the symbol which represents them, they are perceived as an unknown quantity. Lisa Brennan, "Pitching the Gen X Jury," _The National Law Journal_ (June 6 2004), <http://www.judicialaccountability.org/trialsusingtechnology.htm> (July 19 2005); Foley and LeFevre, "Understanding Generation X." For an explanation of what litigation communication consulting entails see the website for Zagnoli McEvoy Foley LLC <http://www.zmf.com/> (28 Aug. 2007).

51. Gen Y are those born after 1982. Brennan, "Pitching."

52. Brennan, "Pitching."

53. Brennan, "Pitching"; Foley and LeFevre, "Understanding Generation X."

54. Decision Quest, "How Jurors Really Think"; Sherwin, _When the Law Goes Pop._

55. Foley and LeFevre, "Understanding Generation X."

56. Foley and LeFevre, "Understanding Generation X"; Hansen, "Uncertain Science." Defense attorneys often aggressively dispute the use of more traditional forensic practices such as fingerprint analysis or ballistics reports, or try to negate the value of them to jurors. Hansen, "Uncertain Science."

57. Richard Sherwin makes the claim that continued exposure to the 'reality' of television, and its high-speed, sound-bite format has left many people incapable of processing information which is not presented in this manner. Sherwin, *When the Law Goes Pop.*

58. Brennan, "Pitching"; Sherwin, *When the Law Goes Pop.*

59. Raymond A. Schroth, "The Case of the Beautiful Corpse: A Comparison of Today's Television Crime Dramas With Crime Novels of the Past Shows How Our Culture Has Changed," *National Catholic Reporter* 40, no. 19 (12 March 2004): 16.

60. As cited in Brennan, "Pitching."

61. Decision Quest, "How Jurors Really Think"; Foley and LeFevre, "Understanding Generation X"; Sherwin, *When the Law Goes Pop.*

62. Brennan, "Pitching."

63. Foley and LeFevre, "Understanding Generation X," 6.

64. We conducted a small e-mail survey during the summer of 2005 of justice professionals such as attorneys, judges, CSI technicians and law professors whose names and e-mail addresses we pulled from news articles about the CSI effect. The response rate was small (thirty-five out of 205): many e-mail addresses were no longer valid, and many professionals were out of the office for the summer.

65. Points that respondents made included: crime scene staff collected all possible traces of evidence even in minor cases where such evidence is not generally needed to make a case; that citizens are demanding immediate answers from CSI techs at the site of crimes; an increased request for information about the CSI effect from the administration of organizations they worked for. One respondent noted that he follows the trends on television so that he can predict how jurors may react to evidence. A respondent from an armed forces lab noted that her superiors were seduced by the instant results shown on television and have stepped up their demands for faster results from her lab. Lab techs told us that agents in the field such as detectives are requesting that unrealistic tests be performed on evidence.

66. Dr. Kimberlianne Podlas, Assistant Professor of Media Law, Dept. of Broadcasting & Cinema, University of North Carolina, Greensboro, and Former Associate Appellate Counsel of The Legal Aid Society (Criminal Appeals Bureau), after ascertaining that no empirical evidence existed to substantiate claims of a CSI effect, conducted a study using 254 adults who were eligible to serve as jurors. She found no evidence of a CSI effect that either interferes with prosecutors and or how they try their cases. Podlas, "'The CSI Effect.'"

67. To retrieve sources we used the following search terms: CSI; CSI effect; juror effect; effects of CSI; effects of CSI on jurors; effects of CSI on potential jurors; CSI and jurors; jurors and CSI effect; CSI effect and the public. We conducted weekly searches from May 1 to August 10, 2005.

68. Lawrence W. Neuman, *Basics of Social Research: Qualitative and Quantitative Approaches* (New York: Pearson Education Inc., 2004); Michael Patton,

Qualitative Research and Evaluation Methods (Thousand Oaks, California: Sage Publications, 2002).

69. For all dataset sources we will be providing the dataset number and the year it was published as listed in Appendix C.

70. Dataset numbers 1 and 2.

71. Dataset articles 2, 11, 13, 16 and 30.

72. Immediately after this February 2005 conference quotes by session partici-pants began to appear in media sources directly and indirectly (dataset numbers 28, 29, 39, 42, 49, 50, 70). Max Houck's "science as juggernaut" is the most popular and oft repeated quote. Since the 2005 AAAS Conference tape that we ordered hinted that conference numbers were not very large and that space was limited, it can be inferred that most reporters either got their stories from wire services or ordered taped copies of the conference sessions as we did.

73. Articles 2, 11, 14, 19, 27, 30, 31, 50, 53, 65, and 69.

74. Articles 3, 5, 7, 13, 14 and 61.

75. Article numbers 18, 27, 31, 50, 65 and 69.

76. 11, 22, 24, 26, 28, 29, 32, 39, 40, 41, 42, 47, 48, 49, and 50.

77. Articles 1, 2, 7, 11, 14, 22, 23, 27, 31, 36, 38, 39,41, 42, 51, 52, 53, 55, 56, 59, 60, 61, 62, and 64 mention local real-life cases.

78. Article 4 mentions the Peterson case.

79. Durst was mentioned in articles 14, 19, and 47.

80. Binion was mentioned in articles 22 and 47.

81. Actor Robert Blake was mentioned in articles 28, 30, 31, 39, 41, 50, 60 and 65.

82. Williams appeared in article 38.

83. Articles 1, 4, 7, 8, 9, 10, 11, 14, 16, 17, 19, 22, 28, 30, 38, 40, 41, 44, 47, 48, 49, 51, 53, 56, 57, 58, 62, 65, and 68.

84. Articles 7, 9, 11, 14, 19, 29, 48, 50, 53, 57, 58, 68, and 69.

85. Articles 1, 4, 7, 11, 14, 19, 21, 27, 31, 30, 31, 32, 38, 39, 41, 42, 47, 48, 49, 50, 53, 56, 57, 58, 59, 60, 65, and 68.

86. Articles 2, 11, 38, 47, 51, 53, and 57.

87. Articles 14 and 18.

88. Susan Ormiston, "The Current Part 2: The CSI Effect," *The Current* <http://www.cbc.ca/thecurrent/2005/200504/20050405.html> (5 April 2005).

89. Ormiston, "The Current."

90. Ormiston, "The Current."

91. Richard Willing, "'CSI Effect' Has Juries Wanting More Evidence," *USA Today* (8 May 2004) <http://www.usatoday.com/news/nation/2004-08-05-csi-effect_x.htm> (10 May 2005). Only one source in our dataset (number 65), CBC Radio's "The Current," actually interviewed a juror, Cecilia Maldonado, from a famous case, Robert Blake's trial. However, subsequent searches in Google, using terms such as "Blake case" or "Binion case," found numerous such interviews. Interviews or studies with actual jurors in the above cases need to be conducted to determine whether the jurors felt that they were impacted by *CSI* or something else. By way of illustration,

Los Angeles County criminal defense attorney Michael Cavalluzzi, a consultant to NBC's drama *The Law Firm*, notes that generally, in his experience, jurors require much more stringent evidence than usual to convict someone they know or admire such as friends or celebrities. Kazarosian, "Hollywood."

92. Articles 1, 11, 14, 19, 22, 23, 24, 26, 27, 28, 29, 30, 31, 32, 34, 42, 46, 47, 48, 49, 50, 53, 56, 57, 60, 61, 62, 65, and 69.

93. Articles 1, 11, 14, 31, 34, 39, 61 and 69.

94. Articles 27 and 34.

95. Articles 14, 23, 28, 29, 32, 34, 46, 50, and 61.

96. Articles 14, 19, 22, 30, 34, 41, 47, 48, 49, 53, 57, and 60.

97. Barry Scheck of the Innocence Project indicates that it is a good thing that jurors are demanding more of the criminal justice system, and that increased public demand may lead to increased funding for better equipment at forensic labs. Goehner et al, "Where CSI Meets."

98. Articles 1, 7, 10, 16, 17, 19, 27, 28, 33, 35, 38, 41, 42, 49, 51, 55, 57, 61, 67, and 69.

99. Articles 7, 9, 11, 14, 19, 27, 35, 37, 47, and 48.

100. Articles 1, 4, 7, 11, 13, 14, 18, 28, 29, 33, 34, 42, 49, 50, 52, 53, 61, 64, 67 and 70.

101. The original *Time* article (Dataset Number 1, 2002) states that females still suffer from bias in the sciences and that may be why they are turning to forensics careers. A poll mentioned in the same article suggests that more women are concerned about crime as a problem than are men. Lieberman writes that popular culture may be influencing women towards forensic careers, paraphrasing Max Houck. Bruce Lieberman, "Forensics: Fact or Fiction. TV Shows Make Crime Solving Look Easy But In Real Life It's Not So Simple," *The San Diego Tribune* <http://www.signon-sandiego.com/uniontrib/20050221/news_1n21forensic.html> (28 May 2005).

102. Unknown News, Sept. 7, 2003; MSNBC, Feb.20, 2005; *San Diego Union-Tribune*, Feb. 21, 2005; *The Scotsman.com*, April 24, 2005; *US News and World Report*, April 25, 2005; BBC News, May 10, 2005; *Wall Street Journal*, May 13, 2005; *Popular Mechanics*, July 2005; and Nancy Beardsley Report on News VOA, October 20, 2004.

103. Articles 2, 3, 4, 5, 7, 13, 16, 18, 19, 23, 27, 32, 34, 58, 60, 62 and 67.

104. Franzen, "CSI Effect"; Goehner et al., "Where CSI Meets."

105. Bill Brioux, "Chalk It Up to Experience: How the Experts Make Television's Hottest Show Seem So Realistic," *Canoe-Jam!* (2003) 8 May, 2005; Philip J. Lane, "The Existential Condition of Television Crime Drama," *Journal of Popular Culture* 34, no. 4 (2001): 137–51.

106. Franzen, "CSI Effect"; Goehner et al., "Where CSI Meets."

107. Lane, "The Existential Condition."

108. Brioux, "Chalk It Up."

109. James Poniewozik, Jeanne McDowell, Desa Philadelphia, and Kate Novack, "Crimetime Lineup: How the Slick Show Changed Television-in Part By Dragging It Back Into the Past," *Time* 164, no. 19 (11 August 2004).

110. Mark Sappenfield, "From Lindbergh to Laci, a Growing Forensics Fallacy," *The Christian Science Monitor* (24 April 2003) <http://www.csmonitor.com/2003/0424/p01s01-ussc.htm> (5 Aug. 2005).

111. Carlene Hempel, "Television's Whodunit Effect," *The Boston Globe Magazine* (2003) <http://www.bafo.org.uk/television1.htm> (28 May 2005); Sappenfield, "From Lindbergh."

112. Sappenfield, "From Lindbergh."

113. Linda Derksen, "Agency and Structure in the History of DNA Profiling: The Stabilization and Standardization of a New Technology" (Ph.D. Dissertation, University of California San Diego, 2003).

114. Clarence Walker, "CSI (Television Crime Dramas) Affects the American Criminal Justice System," *American Mafia.Com* (2005), <http://www.americanmafia.com/Feature_Articles_301.html> (21 June 2005).

115. Sophia Smardz, "The Jury's Out." *WashingtonPost.Com* 25 June 2004, <http://www.washingtonpost.com/wpdyn/content/article/2005/06/25/AR2005062500078_p.htm> (17 July 2005).

116. Jeffrey Kluger, "How Science Solves Crimes," *Time*, 12 October 2002.

117. American Academy for the Advancement of Science, "The CSI Effect" *Public Understanding of Science*, 2005.

Chapter Two

The Science and Careers of *CSI*

Sherah VanLaerhoven and Gail Anderson

The *CSI* television franchise has captured the interest of the viewing public. Science, once considered boring or difficult by many, is suddenly exciting, glamorous, and sexy. The old image of the scientist as a quiet bespectacled white-coated elderly man has morphed into that of the forensic scientist: an attractive, well dressed, suave, sophisticated, witty, and highly intelligent individual that everyone wants to be. Science has finally made it!

In some respects this is a good thing. Everyone should have a better grasp of science, not just students struggling with basic physics, biology, and chemistry, but also the average person, as scientific knowledge helps in their day-to-day understanding of such global issues as pollution, climate change, and the spread of disease. In these ways, bringing science into everyone's living room is a good thing. However, this chapter demonstrates that forensic science as portrayed on *CSI: Crime Scene Investigation* is, of necessity, not an accurate or full portrayal of science. In order to make the science more interesting and easy to understand, and in order to present crimes that can be solved in sixty minutes (including commercials), the scientific aspects of *CSI* are often incorrectly represented. In some cases, the correct tests are done, but results are achieved in hours or minutes, rather than the more realistic period of days or weeks. In other cases, incorrect tests or scientific methods are used, or ones that do not (yet) exist. In defense of the series, one can argue that *CSI* is not on the Knowledge Network; its intent is to entertain. However, we acquire a great deal of our common knowledge from TV. This is true not just of the science itself, but also of the career expectations of the viewer who decides that they want to be a "CSI."

The information portrayed on the show not only appears to influence the general public, but perhaps also juries and judges. Today's viewer is tomorrow's jury member. There is anecdotal evidence from police officers who testify in court and from lawyers that some jurors now expect to see forensic evidence in the cases they participate in, just as they see it provided on *CSI*.[1] After the recent prosecution of Robert Blake for the murder of his wife, the Los Angeles District Attorney, Steve Cooley, argued that the raised evidentiary expectations of the jury due to *CSI* were partially responsible for the *Baretta* star's acquittal.[2] Newspaper reports provide examples of juries that have refused to convict defendants because a test they saw on television was not performed in the case under their scrutiny.[3] In one U.S. case, the prosecutor alleged that the jury would not convict a man of murdering his girlfriend with a knife because a half-eaten burger at the scene was not tested for his DNA, despite the availability of other evidence that indicated his guilt.[4] In a recent Illinois rape case, the prosecutor told the jury "You've all seen *CSI*? Well this is your CSI moment. We have DNA." However, according to the jury, they acquitted the suspect as they felt the prosecution should have produced more physical evidence, in particular, they should have tested virtually every item and available surface at the scene.[5]

According to a police specialist from the Forensic Identification Services of the Toronto Police Department, experts are being called to the stand simply to explain "the *CSI* Effect" in more and more court cases.[6] According to journalist Jamie Stockwell, in some cases, lawyers have based their closing arguments on the assumption that jurors have a certain knowledge base obtained from watching *CSI*.[7] Max Houck, director of the Forensic Science Initiative at West Virginia University, argues that juries have developed a very unrealistic expectation of what the forensic laboratory can actually do; they now wonder why every blood spot and item at the scene were not tested when, in most cases, not every item needs to be tested in order for a particular case to be made.[8] To test every single glass and surface at a crime scene would be prohibitively expensive and time consuming, and unlikely to be relevant in every case. Houck states that prosecutors have put "negative witnesses" on the stand to explain that real-life detectives do not always find physical evidence. Another result of this increase in awareness of the existence, if not the understanding, of forensic science, is the tremendous burden it has placed on the crime labs, which struggle to handle the immense backlogs of evidence that must be analyzed. According to Houck, as jurors and the public expect more and more of science, the police are obliged to collect increasing amounts of evidence.[9]

On the other hand, it could be argued that it is now easier to present complex scientific principles to jurors as the terms and tests involved are now more familiar to them because of their exposure to fictional and documentary television shows about forensic science.

This chapter examines how *CSI* has also had a massive impact on both young and old television viewers, especially students in terms of their career choices. Suddenly everyone wants to be a CSI, but their understanding of this career path comes primarily from television. As with so many television programs, the jobs on *CSI* are portrayed as glamorous and exciting, never boring. Perhaps of more concern is the portrayal of the actual career path. In most cases on *CSI*, individual characters play roles that would, in real life, be occupied by a number of different scientists and police officers, all with very different types of training, experience and career paths.

Part one of the chapter looks at the science and the scientific careers represented on *CSI*, with an emphasis on entomology (the specialty of both the authors), but also biology (DNA), chemistry, toxicology, questioned documents, firearms and toolmark examinations in crime scene investigation. We discuss the parts of the science that are accurately depicted and where the exaggerations lie. Part two of the chapter briefly clarifies the practical career options in the field of forensic science, and considers how the show has contributed to people's increased interest in entering the field of forensic science. We also discuss the proliferation of forensic graduate and undergraduate programs that are appearing across Canada in response to this new interest. Although, to those of us in the field of science, it is gratifying to see such increased academic interest, we are concerned that students have unrealistic expectations of career paths and job availability. Many students are unaware of the real job opportunities, or lack thereof, in the field, and of the necessary educational path required to enter any of the myriad different careers in forensic science. We hope this chapter may help to clarify some of these misunderstandings.

PART ONE: SCIENCE AND CAREERS IN CRIME SCENE INVESTIGATION—REAL LIFE VS. *CSI*

Many people wish to be a so-called crime scene investigator after watching *CSI: Crime Scene Investigation*. Viewers may love the idea of this type of work but usually have little understanding of what real careers are available in the field. *CSI* lead characters such as Gil Grissom, Sara Sidle, Nick Stokes, Warrick Brown and Catherine Willows are characters whose knowledge spans several fields of forensic science and police work at once. In the pilot episode (1001), Willows and Warrick interview suspects at the crime scene, process the scene for fiber and pattern evidence (shoe prints), analyze the fibers in the lab, carry a gun, and are present for the arrest of the suspect. What we see these television CSIs doing is a myth. In reality, homicide detectives or major crime officers interview suspects and make arrests; forensic identification officers collect evidence at the scene; and lab scientists perform the trace analysis of fiber evidence.

Forensic Identification

In Canada, and in many other countries, crime scene investigators are usually police officers. Very rarely do civilians collect evidence at crime scenes. These Identification Officers are highly specialized officers with many years of advanced training in areas such as fingerprints, photography, and evidence collection. In most cases, forensic evidence is not analyzed by the identification officer, but by civilian scientists who never or rarely leave the lab (and do not carry guns). The only exceptions to this involve pattern evidence analysis, such as fingerprints, bootprints, and blood stains, which is analyzed by Identification Officers.

In Canada, practicing CSI (Identification Officers) are police officers who have a minimum of three years experience as general duty officers before they can apply for the Identification section of the police force. Most have completed many more years of service before entering this specialized field. Each applicant must undergo basic testing, including a Physical Comparison Abilities test, which looks for an ability to recognize shapes and patterns. The potential candidate then undergoes a three-week assessment period to determine their suitability as a future Identification Officer. During this assessment, experienced Forensic Identification Specialists monitor and test each candidate's ability and potential ability for analyzing crime scenes and working in all areas of Ident including photography and fingerprint analysis. If accepted they undergo the eight or nine week training program in Identification. This is a very intense program focusing on all aspects of basic Ident, including photography and fingerprint analysis. It is so intense that, despite the fact that the course lasts only 8–9 weeks and covers a range of methods; a leading camera manufacturer considers its graduates' training to be equivalent to that of the normal two year course of professional photographers.[10]

After the basic training program, successful graduates enter a four-year apprenticeship, which includes courses, research, casework, exams and mock trials under the guidance of a senior Identification Officer. At any point during training, or during the entire length of their career, if an Identification Officer in Canada ever misidentifies a fingerprint as being a match when it is not, they immediately lose their position in Ident.[11] They are allowed no mistakes.

In Canada, Identification Officers collect evidence at crime scenes. They do not interrogate suspects, or in fact, analyze most of the evidence themselves. In addition to the fingerprint, bootprint and blood stain pattern evidence that Identification Officers' analyze, they are responsible for the collection of evidence for other specialists who do not attend the crime scene, such as forensic biologists, chemists and toxicologists. Identification Officers specialize in recognizing evidence and collecting it in an appropriate manner and minimizing destruction and contamination of evidence, in order to deliver it to the relevant scientists at the crime lab for analysis.

Why would Identification Officers in a real crime scene not use the methods used on *CSI*? Every contact between the scene and individuals entering/leaving the scene leaves a trace, so no crime scene that involves interpersonal violence should ever be entered or processed by anyone who is not covered head to toe in an officer protection suit, which protects the crime scene from the officer and the officer from the scene. Locard's Exchange Principle dictates that when two objects contact each other, materials are transferred from one object to another.[12] This is one of the most basic tenets of forensic science: every time a person or an object touches something or someone else, some trace is left behind, and something is taken away. This could be a fiber, a fingerprint, a footprint, blood or semen or hair or any other type of trace evidence. This happens in all walks of life at all times. In a crime scene, this means that every time someone enters the scene, they leave something of themselves behind, such as hairs, fibers, or skin cells. At the same time, they also pick up something from the crime scene, such as blood and fibers. Hence, a rapist's semen and sweat may be found on the victim, and pubic hair from the victim and fiber from her sweater may be found on the suspect. During a crime scene investigation, all Identification Officers should wear an officer protection suit to prevent transferring evidence themselves. They should even have their mouths covered with a protective mask to prevent them from contaminating the scene with saliva as they speak. A scene can be contaminated in this manner within 15 minutes of entry into the scene.[13]

Officer protection suits, commonly called "bunny suits," should include hoods, booties, masks and gloves. However, such "bunny suits" are not flattering and, were they used on the television series, they would prevent the viewer from seeing the characters, so they are rarely used on *CSI*. While *CSI* often acknowledges the need to prevent contamination of the evidence by having the characters wear gloves, there are notable examples where even this basic principle is forgotten. In the episode "Friends and Lovers" (1005), Gil Grissom searches a car without putting on gloves. In "Blood Drops" (1007), Gil Grissom and Sergeant O'Reilly put on protective booties to enter the scene, but only after they have already walked through it once. The most striking example, however, is in the episode "I-15 Murders" (1011), where Gil Grissom doesn't put on gloves before handling a missing woman's purse. This is followed by Grissom putting his unprotected finger in a yellow substance spilled at the base of a shopping cart and then tasting the substance. It turns out to be mustard but could easily have been something more dangerous. In "Crate 'n' Burial" (1003), we can contrast this behavior with Sara Sidle's comment to another investigator to "Get a picture of the security pad. Someone touches it before it's dusted, I break their fingers," which demonstrates an awareness of the potential contamination of fingerprint evidence.

Pattern evidence is often analyzed by Identification Officers, rather than civilian forensic scientists. On *CSI*, the characters routinely dust for latent fingerprints that are otherwise invisible to the naked eye, using powders, brushes and lifting tape. However, other techniques are also used to visualize latent prints. In "Anonymous" (1008), Sidle uses a fluorescent powder and alternate light source to search for prints, and Nick Stokes fumes a car with cyanoacrylate (or super glue) to make prints visible. In the field, the police use both of these techniques, but *CSI* takes current techniques and pushes them into the realm of science fiction. In "Burked" (2001), Detective Brass asks Warrick Brown, "Can you get a print off those balloons?" Warrick replies, "I can get a print off of air." Statements such as these may make the viewing public, including potential jurors, believe that fingerprint evidence is always recoverable. In actual fact, fingerprints may not be available for any number of reasons, including the fact that many materials are not conducive to retaining prints, such as the rough surface of the butt of a gun; weathering of surfaces may have also removed any prints. As well, although prints taken from a suspect in police custody are beautifully clear, people rarely leave the type of crisp, clean and complete latent prints in crime scenes that we commonly see on television. When most people touch something in real life, they only contact the surface with part of the fingerpad, and often move their fingers in such a way that they smudge the print. Therefore, although fingerprints may be recovered from a scene, they may not be identifiable. Further, as noted above, Canadian police regulations indicate that every time a fingerprint is analyzed an Identification Officer puts his or her career on the line; thus, if the print is not definitely and clearly identifiable, it will not be individualized.

Every scene is also covered in fingerprints from normal daily activity and identifying the most important ones may be impossible. There may literally be hundreds of unknown prints at a scene that have no relevance to the crime. Jurors who watch *CSI* may become very concerned when unidentified prints are found at a scene, forgetting that their own home may have hundreds of prints belonging to any number of people that visit and pass through. Even when a clear fingerprint is found on a suspicious object such as a knife, it has no value until the fingerprint can be linked to a specific person. Only a very limited number of people have their prints on record, such as those with criminal records. Once a suspect has been identified, then the print has great value, but if no suspect is found, even a pristine fingerprint may have no value.

It is not just the way that fingerprint evidence is collected on *CSI* that may be misleading. On the show, fingerprint evidence is analyzed by either an AFIS (Automated Fingerprint Identification System) technician, who compares the print to those found in a computer database compiled by law enforcement agencies, or by one of the show's main characters, such as Stokes or Brown. On *CSI*, the computer completes the matches. In reality, a fingerprint is always matched to an individual by a human being, not a computer. An AFIS technician will determine a number of possible matches from the database based on the class characteristics of the fingerprint. However, two Identification Officers conduct the final match of a fingerprint, with one making the initial match, and a second officer confirming the match.

Other types of pattern evidence routinely collected and analyzed by Identification Officers are tire tracks and shoe prints. Depending on the medium in which the prints are found, different techniques are used. In the pilot episode (1001) of *CSI*, Willows and Brown use ink to get shoe print impressions. In "Blood Drops" (1007), Grissom uses an alternate light source and electrostatic dust lifter to find and lift bootprints while Brown uses plaster to make a mold of tire tracks.

When it comes to matching evidence such as bootprints, in forensic practice in the field it is important to distinguish between both class and individual characteristics. Class characteristics link an object to a group of similar objects, but not to a specific example of that group. In pattern evidence analysis, class evidence would be the original pattern of the footwear sole when the footwear was produced. Class evidence might indicate that a Nike runner, size 11, in a style produced from 2002–2004, made the footwear imprint. Individual evidence is evidence that links an item to one source; it indicates that this print was made by a particular shoe and only by that shoe. This type of evidence includes all the tiny nicks, scratches and marks imposed on an object during manufacture and use, such as wear patterns, cuts, nail marks, *etc.* In professional practice, computer databases are used to assist in identifying footwear and tire tread patterns, but only indicate the class or group that the evidence comes from. In order to match a specific impression to a shoe, both the impression and the shoe or tire that made it must demonstrate individual patterns specific to that shoe or tire, such as a wear pattern.

In "Anonymous" (1008), Brown matches a shoe print to a class of shoe and Stokes matches tire tracks to a class of tire and vehicle, but without the more individual characteristics in the patterns, they would not be able to make a conclusive match to a single shoe or tire.

The final type of pattern evidence that is collected and analyzed by Identification Officers is bloodstain patterns. In "Friends and Lovers" (1005), Nick Stokes recreates the blows received by a victim who was beaten to death by calculating the trajectory and velocity of each blood droplet using strings to find their points of convergence. This is quite accurate, although in reality, modern policing most often utilizes computerized methods. In "Blood Drops" (1007), Willows uses the shape and size of blood droplets to recreate the sequence in which victims were killed, as well as the movement of both the attacker and victims. Because blood is not always visible at crime scenes or on other evidence, presumptive tests are used to identify or locate blood and bloodstain patterns. A presumptive test is one that is quick, cheap and easy to use and will indicate if a substance is possibly blood. These are very useful to eliminate stains that may look like dried blood, such as juice or oil, but such tests can have false positives. Therefore, presumptive tests are used to determine whether a spot or stain may be worth testing further, but do not prove that the substance actually is blood. Confirmatory tests will show conclusively that the substance is or is not blood. Some presumptive tests can be used to make blood or other body substances visible under certain conditions. In "Scuba Doobie-Doo" (2005), Grissom sprays luminol on the carpet at a crime scene to reveal the pattern of bloodstain and finds voids in the stain that indicate something was in that space during the bloodletting. In "Sex, Lies and Larvae" (1010), Nick uses phenolphthalein to test if blood is present. All of these are realistic techniques used by Identification Officers in the field.

In professional practice in most countries, some types of evidence are collected by Identification Officers, but not analyzed by them. These Ident Officers collect hairs and fibers through hand picking or tape lifts. They gather DNA from the scene, although a medical professional usually does sampling from suspects, most often through mouth swabs. Samples of body fluids such as blood and semen are collected for DNA evidence from items at the scene. Other items such as chewing gum or sealed envelopes or stamps may also be seized in order to obtain DNA evidence. If these types of evidence are not readily visible, alternate light sources (ALS) are used to find body fluids, hairs and fibers. In "Chaos Theory" (2002), Sidle uses ALS to search dorm room beds for body fluids, she then circles the spots using a black marker to enable them to be identified later under regular light. These are realistic techniques used by Identification Officers to collect these types of evidence.

All evidence that is collected must be correctly documented. This allows the triers of fact (judges and juries) to see that the evidence has never been left unattended or unsecured and that every moment of time from collection to presentation in court can be accounted for in a legitimate manner. Without such documentation, defense could and should argue that the evidence may have been tampered with. *CSI* often fails to demonstrate this meticulous procedure and there are many examples of one of the main characters picking up evidence before it has been photographed *in situ*. One of the few correct dramatizations of this process is found in "Crate and Burial" (1003), where evidence markers, including rulers to depict the scale of the photographs, are used to photograph a scooter before it is moved from its original position in the crime scene. A second example is found in "Blood Drops" (1007), where Nick photographs a cigarette butt before collecting it. In an actual crime scene, all evidence would be photographed *in situ* and notes, sketches and measurements would be made before the item was seized. The act of the seizure would also be photographed, as would the scene after the item had been seized, so that all of the original aspects of the scene are recorded, and the collection of evidence and condition of the scene after collection are documented. This is required to reconstruct the specific conditions of the scene for the court.

Without such rigorous documentation, all continuity of evidence would be lost. Continuity refers to the extensive note taking, photography and other documentation that make up a central mandatory aspect of the investigation. The original position, collection and analysis of evidence within the crime scene—be it something as substantial as a gun or as ephemeral as a fingerprint—must be documented from the moment it is first observed until it is finally presented as evidence in court. In this manner, the court has lengthy documentation concerning the movements of each item of evidence, from its collection at the scene, to its analysis at the lab, to its storage and eventual presentation in court. Continuity includes a list of every person who has been in contact with a piece of evidence, every test and examination that has been performed on it, any changes that may have taken place (such as the extraction of 0.01 mg of the sample for toxicological analysis), and the timing of each of these events. Continuity of evidence is demonstrated in the plot line for "Pledging Mr. Johnson" (1004):

Judge: You're going to do something for me.

Brown: Judge, I thought we were even. How much longer am I under your thumb?

Judge: You do what I ask, slate's clean. Henderson rape case, state's evidence.

Brown: Damn, I knew you were in tight.

Judge: Judges aren't appointed on a whim. I owed the family. I need you to compromise the chain of custody.

Brown: Just like that. We've got a slam dunk on a three time rapist and he's just going to walk.

This is followed by Brown returning to the crime lab and talking to Grissom about the conversation Brown had with the judge. Brown arranges to meet the judge at a park and gets the judge to incriminate himself on tape, asking Brown to violate the chain of custody, allowing the hidden Detective Brass to come out and arrest the judge.

The Crime Laboratory

Most forensic scientists work in a crime lab, but only attend crime scenes in extremely rare situations. They are civilians with at least an honors baccalaureate degree in their specific field of science, and frequently a graduate degree or two. They are bench scientists who play an impartial role in analyzing the evidence. Their name reflects the fact that such scientists rarely leave the lab bench, except to testify in courts of law. Unlike on *CSI*, these scientists are specialists in one particular area of science, acquiring training and post-secondary education in only that one particular area. According to criminologist John Houde: "*CSI* has as much to do with criminalistics as Baywatch has to do with being a lifeguard."[14] He refers to the way in which *CSI* frequently portrays its characters doing several jobs, suggesting that a single person could cover all of these scientific areas simultaneously. In practice, each specialty is a separate career, requiring extensive education. On *CSI*, the same character may collect evidence such as paint chips at the crime scene and proceed to the lab where this individual conducts a chemical analysis of the chips. In practice, Identification Officers do not perform laboratory science. Although this misrepresentation may make the *CSI* characters appear more intelligent and exciting, it is misleading for young people who are interested in pursuing a career in forensic science. The following section discusses some of the real sciences and scientists in a crime lab and how these relate to *CSI*.

Forensic Chemistry

Forensic chemistry is the analysis of compounds found at crime scenes, such as powders, soils, explosives, or other non-biological samples (i.e. not hairs, body fluids or DNA evidence). It is frequently referred to as the science of the everyday as it involves analyzing the trace evidence produced in connection with crime scenes by the everyday activities of the offender and victim. In our daily lives, we are continually collecting, transferring and exchanging traces from ourselves to our surroundings and vice versa. Offenders and victims in crimes do the same. Further, crimes frequently occur in everyday places such as the home, workplace, bar or street where there may be trace evidence from many people. It is this trace evidence: glass particles, paint chips, fibers, glue, explosives etc. that is the provenance of the forensic chemist. Forensic chemists are civilian scientists who enter the crime lab with, at a minimum, an Honors B.Sc. in chemistry, although many have more advanced degrees. Once hired, the scientists undergo an understudy period of 12–18 months. This includes extensive education in the forensic application of their science, and the study of the science itself, casework and court presentation of evidence. All scientists in the lab undergo ongoing training throughout their career.

On *CSI*, forensic chemistry analyses are conducted using a variety of lab equipment, such as a gas chromatograph-mass spectrometer or infrared spectrophotometer that are current tools of the trade in most forensic labs. Many different techniques are used depending on the evidence. On *CSI*, a variety of characters, including the main investigators, conduct forensic chemistry analyses. In "Chaos Theory" (2002), Nick Stokes and Gil Grissom analyze paint chips:

> Grissom: The car that impacted the dumpster was originally white, then red and now it's black.
>
> Nick: With two coats of primer between each paint job. Quality work, probably a dealership.
>
> Grissom: Every paint has a unique light absorption rate. We ID the paint, we get to the car.
>
> Nick: Really. Cherokee '89 or '93 paint jobs all factory stock: Stone White, Flame Red and there's your Midnight Black there.

As we described before in relation to class and individual evidence, the above sequence would pinpoint a type of car, but would not individualize one specific car. If the car has been repainted several times (keeping in mind that each paint job requires three to four paint layers) that fact would suggest circumstantially that this is the car that they are searching for. However, further evidence would be required to specifically identify the vehicle. In professional practice, the usual clincher would again be transfer evidence: if the paint from the dumpster were to be found on the vehicle, this would be highly probative. In "I-15 Murders" (1011), Sara Sidle and Warrick Brown question a suspect:

Suspect: You found what on my pants?

Sidle: Glass. Any idea how it got there?

Suspect: Well, it's just a guess. Someone broke into my car last weekend and smashed my window and made off with my CD player. I must have been wearing those pants.

Sidle: Did you file a police report?

Suspect: No, but you can check with my insurance company.

Sidle: I already checked with my lab. They do this test and guess what? The glass? It floated.

This is followed by Sidle and Warrick testing the density of the glass found on the suspect's pants, comparing it with that at the crime scene, and with a piece of glass found in the butt of a gun discovered at the scene. In practice, analysis of paint chips or glass would be conducted by scientists in the chemistry section of a forensic laboratory, not by an Identification Officer. Even though *CSI* portrays these jobs as the domain of a single character, they are separate careers with very different educational requirements.

Frequently, prior to the more specialized confirmatory tests that are run in the lab during forensic chemistry analyses, presumptive tests will be used during the collection of evidence. These tests are an extremely useful tool in the field for determining the presence of potential evidence. In "Bully for You" (2004), Grissom questions a suspect:

Grissom: I'd like to do a test on your shirt, if I may.

Suspect: What kind of test? [Grissom sprays the shirt and a blue stain appears.] What is that?

Grissom: GSR. When someone fires a weapon, gun shot residue plumes back onto their hands and clothes. This means that you fired a gun within the last three to six hours.

What they do not mention in this episode is that, in actual forensic practice, although such evidence could indicate that the suspect fired a gun, it could also indicate that they were simply near someone who fired it. As well, as presumptive tests, such as those for gunshot residue (GSR), do not confirm the structure of the chemical compound under scrutiny, they are subject to error through false positives. Here, the material suggested by the GSR test could also be any substance that contains nitrates, including urine, faeces, tobacco and cosmetics. Therefore, further confirmatory tests would be required to determine that the material found by the presumptive test is, in fact, GSR. For instance, a confirmatory test for primer residue might be used that identifies very specific trace elements (including lead styphnate, barium nitrate and antimony sulfide) that are not found in the same combination outside of GSR.

Forensic Biology

Forensic biology is the analysis of biological compounds such as saliva, blood, semen, and hair. DNA analysis has become the major component of forensic biology sections in crime laboratories. In the past, blood groups were used as class evidence, but with the advent of DNA, most biological evidence can be individualized to just one person. In Canada, forensic biologists have a minimum of an Honors B.Sc. in Biology, primarily molecular biology, and many also have graduate degrees. Once accepted into the lab, these scientists undergo an understudy period under the supervision of an experienced forensic biologist, during which they analyze cases, receive on-going training and present evidence in mock trials.

During the first few seasons of *CSI*, the character Greg Saunders portrayed a forensic biologist. On *CSI*, the time taken to process and analyze evidence is compressed far beyond what is possible in reality, in order to make the story work in the approximately forty-five minutes of air time allotted to each episode. Occasionally, the writers recognize this flaw and bring it to the attention of the viewer. In "Overload" (2003), when asked why some test results are not done yet, Greg Saunders states: "FYI–thrity swabs in six hours. Not realistic, even for me." In reality, the processing time for DNA evidence is not hours, but in the order of days, for the required tests to be run. This may extend to months, depending on the degree of backlog a particular lab is experiencing.

Furthermore, although modern science can now retrieve DNA from many items that it was not possible to retrieve it from before, there are still limits. *CSI* often ignores this, but in "Alter Boys" (2006), Saunders is unable to amplify (recover and increase the amount of) any DNA from a blood sample taken from jeans because they were dry-cleaned, denaturing or destroying the DNA molecules. This meant that no identifiable DNA could be recovered.

A few years ago, the average person had never heard of DNA; with the O.J. Simpson case, DNA became part of most North Americans' vocabulary. However, it is only since *CSI* has gained such enormous popularity and visibility that the public, including jurors, have come to expect that DNA will be present at and collected from every crime scene. In reality, DNA is not retrieved from many crime scenes, because offenders may clean up after themselves, or use protective measures such as gloves or a condom while committing a crime (criminals watch *CSI* too). In other cases, collecting DNA would be pointless. For instance, in a domestic violence case at a couple's home, the DNA of both victim and assailant will be present everywhere and collection and analysis would have little value. As well, DNA analyses are time consuming and expensive and so cannot be performed on every single drop of blood that might be present at a crime scene. On television, the seemingly random blood drops chosen for analysis inevitably lead to the perpetrator, but in professional practice, only a sample of drops present at a scene can realistically be analyzed, and it is entirely possible that those analyzed are not probative. For instance, in a battering case, there may be millions of blood spatters on the walls, but most will, naturally, belong to the victim. One or two out of the many spatters may belong to the perpetrator if he or she was injured, but the chance of finding those spatters will be minimal.

Access to resources and time limits impact what can actually be done in DNA analyses. However, we have anecdotal evidence to suggest that some juries and judges now expect that such analyses will be performed on every unknown substance found at a crime scene and are reluctant to convict if such analyses are not done, even when other, more relevant evidence is presented at trial. In Los Angeles, jurors complained that a bloody coat at the crime scene was not tested for DNA that would have proved that the defendant was present at the scene. However, this was entirely unnecessary as the defendant had already admitted in court that he was at the scene.[15] In this case, the judge stated that "TV had taught jurors about DNA tests but not about when they should be used."[16]

Forensic Toxicology

As toxicology is a specific part of the bigger science of chemistry, the general public frequently confuses forensic toxicologists with forensic chemists, but, in practice, the two are quite different. Forensic toxicologists deal with toxins and alcohol found in the body and body fluids, as well as with drug paraphernalia, whereas chemists handle all other non-biological materials. Forensic toxicologists are civilian lab scientists with a minimum of an honors B.Sc. in pharmacy, biochemistry or chemistry, followed by an in-house understudy program in the forensic laboratory. They analyze fluids from suspects and victims for the presence of drugs or alcohol and also determine what pharmaceutical affects such toxins would have, such as whether a certain drug is likely to cause amnesia or paranoia. They are among the rare lab scientists that might actually attend a crime scene if it involves a clandestine drug laboratory, as such labs are extremely volatile and dangerous. The toxicologist can assist by showing the Identification Officers potential booby-traps, including explosive chemicals or other items left behind that could be hazardous to the unwary.

Forensic Toxicology plays a major role in the episode "Friends and Lovers" (2005):

Grissom: You want to know what killed this kid? Benny Hanna the maggots.

Brown: What the maggots?

Grissom: Tox the maggots we found on the victim. Whatever he ingested probably evaporated from the sun but the maggots are like little refrigerators. They preserve what we digest for longer periods of time. . . .

Brown: I did the whole tox maggot thing, found Gypsom weed in their blood.

Grissom: Which means?

Brown: Gypsom weed in Eric's blood.

The procedure in actual practice is to conduct presumptive tests, followed by confirmatory tests, to identify an unknown substance found in body fluids or stomach contents. Presumptive tests would be conducted to eliminate large numbers of substances that could be at play, and to attempt to narrow the possible relevant substance down to a smaller group. Only at that point could a particular substance be more specifically identified using confirmatory tests. Normally toxicological analyses are performed on body fluids such as blood and urine, or body organs such as the liver or vitreous humor of the eye. As "Friends and Lovers" accurately demonstrates, you are what you eat and insects are no exception. If a person ingests a drug and then dies, it is often possible to identify the type of drug from the maggots present in their body at a crime scene. This is usually relevant when the body is extremely decomposed and it is often impossible to perform analyses on body fluids. Insects that feed on a dead body bioaccumulate the body's toxins and can often be tested to determine a victim's drug use prior to death.[17]

Back in the *CSI* lab in the same episode, Brown and Saunders test and compare a sample taken from a drug dealer's vehicle to a sample from the victim's intestine:

Brown: The chemical compositions break down the same.

Saunders: Yeah, but that doesn't necessarily prove that the seeds from the dead kid's gut came from the same place as the seeds from the dealer's car.

Grissom: We need the pods to do a DNA match and we don't have them.

Saunders: Truth is, it wouldn't matter. I ran the seeds Eric ingested. Toxic levels are low, too low to have killed him.

Toxicologists not only determine what toxin is present, but also interpret how the drug, at the levels found in the person, might affect a person's behavior. This is particularly valuable when an accused person or victim will not or cannot say what happened. For instance, a person accused of assault may claim that they have no recollection of the incident, or that the drug made them do it. The toxicologist, with his or her knowledge of pharmacology, will be able to state whether the drug type and the levels of the drug and its metabolites found in the relevant party, could result in a person forgetting an incident, or becoming violent. This process is demonstrated later in "Friends and Lovers," when Grissom and Brown talk with the suspect:

> Grissom: It's not about memory now, Bobby. It's about the evidence and the evidence sucks. You and Eric bought Gypsom tea from Ethan that night.
>
> Brown: But you guys have never taken J weed before, so you weren't aware of the side effects of photophobia.
>
> Bobby: Photo what?
>
> Brown: Photophobia, it's just a big word for lights freaking you out. You guys were hallucinating and whatever Eric was seeing was scaring him, big time. The coroner states that Eric's dose shot his temperature through the roof. He was boiling in his own skin so he stripped, which is why we found him naked.
>
> Brass: We just don't know if it was an act of aggression or self-defense.
>
> Bobby: I love that guy.
>
> Grissom: That's why I tend to believe it was an act of self-protection. The lights were scaring him. At the same time, we conjecture you were suffering auditory hallucinations. Both of these symptoms are routine with this drug.

Questioned Documents

Another common form of forensic analysis is that of questioned documents. This is an area that combines both science and art. Questioned documents (QD) examiners are civilian lab scientists with a minimum of an honors B.Sc. in a natural science, followed by the longest understudy period in the crime lab of two and a half years. A common mistake made by the public and the *CSI* series concerning QD examiners entails confusing QD examination with graphology. QD examination involves the scientific analysis of all aspects of documents and writing, including how the documents are made, chemical analyzes of inks, writing styles etc. Graphology, on the other hand, analyzes a person's handwriting, with the intention of determining a person's personality and has no scientific basis.

A questioned document is anything that contains visible, partially visible or invisible signs, symbols or marks, which could possibly convey a meaning relevant to the criminal investigation. Questioned documents are usually thought of as pertaining to writing on paper, but can also include things such as graffiti. The main areas of interest for a QD examiner are handwriting and handprinting comparisons. These are used to determine whether a person wrote a certain questioned document, and to examine the means, media and materials used to make it (such as paper, ink, pens, pencils, computer printers, faxes and photocopiers), or how a document may have been altered in some manner. The largest part of the job of a QD examiner involves comparing two documents, the suspect document and one written by a known person, in order to determine whether they were written by the same person. QD examination thus entails a scientific examination, comparison and analysis of a questioned document. QD examiners do not determine anything about the person themselves, any more than a fingerprint specialist would look at a fingerprint and claim to be able to tell the age, race, personality and religion of a person from their fingerprint. Both sciences involve comparisons.

In "I-15 Murders" (1011), Gil Grissom and Catherine Willows take writing found on a bathroom door to be analyzed by a questioned document examiner. In this episode, the examiner combines both actual QD examination techniques and graphology into his analysis:

QD examiner: The person who wrote this is left-handed.

Grissom: And we know that because?

QD examiner: The t bar in "catch." It's left tending. And uneducated. The contraction in "I've" is misplaced. Then we have the large arched hook in the letter "Y" and the arches in the letter "L's." This indicates criminal tendency, which is supported by the heavy pasteiosity, which suggests low impulse control.

Catherine: Heavy pasteiosity?

QD examiner: The pressure, how firmly you put pen to paper.

Grissom: Or marker to metal. Do we know anything else?

QD examiner: Yes. Overall, the handwriting is cursive and round. This tells me it was written by a woman.

Although right or left handedness is something that can be determined by a QD examiner, as well as pressure levels and other class characteristics, criminal tendencies cannot be determined from a person's handwriting any more than they can be determined by simply looking at a person (as was once believed). Such speculation is only found in the world of the graphologist.

Fire Arms, Ballistics, and Tool Marks

A major part of any television show involving forensic science is that of firearm identification, and *CSI* is no exception. Long before the word DNA was general knowledge, bullet and gun matching was found in virtually all police shows. Firearms and toolmark examiners determine whether a particular tool was used at a crime scene. The term tool is used fairly broadly. It does not necessarily refer to the usual sort of tools found in one's shed (such as hammer and chisel), but is used in the more scientific sense of any object that leaves a mark in a softer object. So this may indeed be a chisel marking a wooden window frame when the burglar breaks in, but could also involve the impression left from a tire in snow, blood or even skin. A gun is also a tool, as the barrel is a hard object that leaves minute marks from the rifling and barrel surface onto a softer object, the bullet, when the gun is fired. Firearms examination is therefore a specialized form of toolmark examination. Firearms examiners must have at least an honors B.Sc. in science, usually engineering, and then must undergo an understudy training period in the lab. Such examiners also work closely with forensic chemists and pathologists in examining gunshot residue and determining the distance a shot may have been fired from.

The term ballistics is often used on television to refer to bullet matching, when in actuality it means something quite different. Ballistics refers to the practice of determining the trajectory of a bullet. In the episode "Bully for you" (2004), ballistics is used in its correct sense, that is, to determine the angle that a gun was pointed at when the victim was shot and how tall the perpetrator was. Grissom puts a straw in the bullet hole in the wall, holding a string to the straw, while giving Brown the other end of the string. Brown moves away from the wall, keeping the string at the same angle as the straw until he has walked past where the victim was shot. From here, they are able to determine the precise spot the shooter stood in when the shot was fired, as well as to ascertain, with some certainty, that the shooter was short, possibly only 5'3" or 5'4".

In "Overload" (2003), toolmark examination is used to match a tool to a suspect, which enables the CSIs to place the suspect at the scene of the crime. In the lab, Brown cuts an electric plug with the suspect's pliers and puts it under a comparison microscope with the plug found at the crime scene. When the two plug sections are overlapped, we see that the striations made by the pliers match. This is a classic example, although abbreviated, of the job of a toolmark examiner. In the lab, the suspect tool is used to mark a substance soft enough not to damage the tool in any way, but hard enough to take an impression on the soft substance, most often wax or soft lead. The examiner will then compare the impression recovered from the crime scene with the controlled impression made in the lab by the suspect tool. This comparison is done under a comparison microscope: two compound microscopes joined together and viewed through one set of eyepieces, allowing the examiner to see the two impressions in one field. The impressions are then minutely compared to determine whether the same tool created them both.

As with most forensic evidence, toolmarks show both class and individual characteristics. Class characteristics link the mark to a group of tools, such as a type, brand and size of chisel, or a model of gun. Minute striations that come from manufacture and use cover every object that acts as a potential tool. When an object, such as a chisel or gun barrel, is made, dust and grime create tiny imperfections in the machinery used to make the tool. As each tool is made, the dust and filings in the machinery move, or are changed. Thus every tool or gun barrel is unique from the moment of manufacture. Once the tool is used, these individualizing striations change and more are added. It is these minute characteristics that allow a toolmark examiner to determine that a particular tool made a specific mark or that a bullet was shot from a specific gun. Again, lab scientists perform these examinations, not Identification Officers or CSI.

In "Slaves of Las Vegas" (2008), Sara Sidle and the firearms expert, Bob, discuss bullet evidence from her case. Bob explains: "Look at the bullet from your victim's thigh. Five lands and grooves on it. That would be a Colt, .38 caliber." This exchange illustrates the class characteristics associated with a gun. When a gun is manufactured, the barrel is produced by drilling a centre hole in a solid bar of steel with a roach. This produces a tube of steel. The inside diameter of the tube is referred to as the caliber, which is a class characteristic of a gun. Caliber can be described in metric terms, such as "a 9mm," or in imperial terms, such as a "357," which refers to a caliber of 0.357 inches. Once the roach has drilled a hole the length of the barrel, a second drilling is performed to cut a long spiral pattern inside the barrel. This is referred to as rifling and is intended to put a spin on the bullet as it passes down the barrel, so that it flies straight. The spiral cuts are referred to as the grooves, and the remaining surface is referred to as the lands. The caliber, the number and direction (clockwise or anti-clockwise) of the grooves are all class characteristics that can identify a type and make of gun. When the original roach drills the barrel, and again when the rifling is added, minute striations are created in the barrel. These are unique to each individual gun, even two guns produced one after the other on an assembly line are individualized, as tiny iron filings and dust move in and out of the barrel with every drill. As the gun is fired and cleaned, more striations are added and previous ones are changed or obliterated.

It is these many tiny marks that are meticulously examined in both a suspect bullet found at a crime scene or in a victim, and a bullet test-fired from a suspect weapon, to determine whether a particular gun is the one that fired the bullet found at the crime scene. This is a time consuming endeavor as every tiny striation must be examined and compared. The bullets (the suspect bullet and, for comparison, one fired from the suspect weapon into water so as not to damage it) are rotated on their platforms under the comparison microscope until two points of convergence between the two bullets are seen. Then the bullets are slowly rotated 360° to ensure that every striation matches. In order to be sure that a bullet was fired from a particular gun, or that a particular gun was used to fire a particular bullet, the class characteristics such as caliber and rifling must match, and all the striations must match. In order for the examiner to state that the same weapon fired each bullet there must be no unexplained differences. However, an example of an explained difference might be something as common as the fact that half of the bullet retrieved from the victim is damaged due to impact with bone.

Forensic Pathology

Forensic pathologists are medical doctors with advanced training in pathology and forensic pathology. They perform autopsies and determine cause, manner and mode of death. At a minimum, pathologists have an undergraduate degree, usually in science, followed by a second degree in medicine with a specialty in pathology. In *CSI*, the roles of coroner and pathologist are combined into that of coroner, portrayed by the characters Dr. Albert Robbins (as coroner) and Dr. David Phillips (as assistant coroner). The differences between coroners and medical examiners on television have always been confusing, perhaps because they are actually somewhat confusing in real life. In North America, some jurisdictions have medical examiner (ME) systems and others have coroner systems. In both cases, the ME or Coroner usually works for the province or state. However, many coroners and MEs are not actually forensic pathologists.

Both Coroners and MEs investigate unexplained deaths, but the background and role of each profession may be quite different. Both act as ombudspersons for the dead and investigate the who, what, where, when and how of the death. Their primary role is to investigate all the details of a death and then attempt to prevent further such deaths from occurring. Medical examiners are always medical doctors but they are not necessarily forensic pathologists. In fact, In Canada, in provinces which use an ME system, usually only the Chief ME and Deputy MEs are forensic pathologists. It is the forensic pathologist who will perform autopsies and their place of work is in a hospital, primarily in a morgue. Most other MEs are usually general practitioners who investigate death cases on a fee for service basic. If an autopsy is required, they refer it to a forensic pathologist.

Coroners do not usually have to be medical doctors, although in Ontario and some U.S. states the coroner does have an MD; in such cases the coroner might also be a forensic pathologist. Coroners come from a variety of backgrounds including those in the judicial, legal, law enforcement, and medical professions, and their primary workplace is based out of an office, although much of their time may be spent at death scenes. One of the main differences between a coroner and an ME is that coroners also hold a quasi-judicial role and conduct inquiries and inquests into the death of a person in order to determine what happened and how such a death may be prevented. In most deaths, an investigation into the death is all that is required, for instance, in the case of a drug overdose. In other cases, such as that of a death in custody, a more formal inquest may be required that includes a jury and is presided over by a coroner. MEs do not hold such a judicial role and a separate board of individuals, independent of the Medical Examiner's Office decides whether a case should go to a Public Inquiry held before a judicially appointed judge.

In the pilot episode of *CSI* (1001), the forensic pathologist glances at the wound and states: "this person was shot from 6–7 feet away." Normally, a joint team involving both the firearms specialist and the pathologist determine the distance from the weapon to the victim. Ammunition today is propelled toward its target by the expanding gases created by the ignition of smokeless powder or nitrocellulose in a cartridge. In the ideal situation, it is expected that all the gunpowder (which actually consists of fine granules) would be consumed during this process. What actually happens is that the powder is not totally burned, and so there are burned and unburned gunpowder particles, as well as partially burned particles, together with soot from smoke, which are propelled out of the barrel and, if close enough, are deposited on the target. You can, therefore, get an idea of the distance the gun was fired from the target by analyzing the discharged residue on the target. However, it is impossible to determine this distance without knowing the weapon used and the ammunition employed; both of these will have a dramatic impact on gunshot residue projection, as will the presence or absence of a silencer.

Some pathologists have training in interpreting skeletal remains, but many do not. For expertise in determining the sex, age, stature and bone wounds of a particular set of remains, forensic anthropologists are usually called upon. Training in forensic anthropology requires a PhD in forensic anthropology. Board certification requires further experience and education. Most forensic anthropologists are university professors who consult with the police when needed. Although a pathologist will conduct the autopsy in all cases, a forensic anthropologist may assist them when the remains are skeletonized.

In usual *CSI* fashion, in the following scene from "Who Are You?" (1006) Nick Stokes and especially Gil Grissom are credited with knowledge that would normally be the province of the pathologist and forensic anthropologist:

> Grissom: Based on the auricular surface, I'd say she died when she was about twenty.
>
> Stokes: She?
>
> Grissom: It's in the hips. Pelvic bones definitely female. You know, for a ladies man, you don't know much about bone structure.
>
> Stokes: Well, I know all I need to know. I figure she was killed before her cement bath.
>
> Grissom: Yeah? How?
>
> Stokes: She was stabbed, at least a dozen times . . . screwdriver, maybe like a spike.
>
> Grissom: No. The gouges on her ribs are unusual. The instrument had to be slightly curved . . . with some kind of serrated edge . . . like crocodile teeth. Whatever killed this girl was not a traditional weapon.

Grissom continues in this multiple-roled fashion—as pathologist, anthropologist, and forensic identification officer—when he gives the following description of two bodies at a crime scene in "Blood Drops" (1007):

> Male Caucasian, approximately forty years old, laying in a pool of blood. No drag marks. Body does not appear to have been moved. Multiple stab wounds to the back and neck. Looks like a single edged blade. Force to such a degree that the left and right internal jugular veins have been transected. Female Caucasian. Appears to be one stab wound to the throat, transection of the left and right carotid arteries with exsanguinating haemorrhage. No defense marks. Cursatory opinion: she was killed in her sleep.

In practice, all of the above would be determined by the forensic pathologist and not by a police officer or lab scientist.

Forensic Entomology

Forensic entomologists,[18] odontologists,[19] and botanists[20] are civilian specialists in their field, usually employed as university professors. They have graduate degrees in their field and are specialized in one very particular area. Each of these areas requires approximately ten to twelve years of post-secondary education, so people do not have expert knowledge in several fields. On *CSI*, the character Dr. Gil Grissom acts as a forensic identification officer collecting evidence, a pathologist interpreting wounds, an anthropologist determining the sex and age of victims from bones, and a homicide detective interviewing suspects, but his Ph.D. is in entomology and he often interprets insect evidence. In the unlikely event that someone did undergo training in all these fields, they would have to have at least 46 years of university education and training to be minimally qualified, so they would retire before they were able to commence their career.

In all of his multiple roles, Grissom frequently interprets insect evidence. One example of this is found in "Sex, Lies and Larvae" (1010). At the scene, Grissom uses hot coffee to kill beetles and keeps some beetles alive with beef jerky. He states: "These are the first witnesses to the crime." In forensic practice, hot water is used to kill larval flies as it destroys their internal enzymes and so allows a better preservation, although insects must not be left in the hot liquid for long or they will degrade. When dealing with larval fly evidence, half are kept alive to rear to adulthood, the rest are preserved for court purposes. However, although dry meat is eaten by some beetle species, beef jerky (with its myriad preservatives) would not be an appropriate substance to use in this context.

In the same episode, a body that was found in the mountains is removed to the morgue and during the autopsy Grissom identifies a fly on the body. Later, Sara Sidle and Detective Brass question him about using insect evidence:

Sidle: Insects arrive at a corpse in a specific order, right?

Grissom: Like summer follows the spring.

Sidle: And you can pinpoint time of death based on the type and age of insects present on the body.

Grissom: I watch the insects mature from eggs to larvae to adults and then count backwards.

Sidle: Linear regression . . . .

Grissom: *Synthesiomyia nudiseta* is the Latin name.

Sidle: It's a muscid fly that only breeds in urban areas but Grissom found one on our girl which means she was probably killed downtown and then carried into the mountains.

It is possible to use insects to determine whether a body has been moved from one location to another if the insects being examined have specific habitat preferences. However, Grissom's interpretation of the insect evidence in this case is riddled with inaccuracies. His insect evidence log states "*Phaenicia cuprina*" and "*Piophilia casai*" both of which are flies used to estimate time of death. Grissom measures a beetle from the body, which appears to the authors to be an adult June beetle (Scarabidae), but he looks up size growth charts for immature Round fungus beetles (Leiodidae) that supposedly give estimates of the growth rate of the immatures over time as measured by length. To the best of our knowledge as professional entomologists, this information does not exist for these beetles. As well, an adult beetle does not grow larger once it matures. However, on the series precisely this sort of growth allows Grissom to estimate that the victim has been dead for three days. *Piophilia casai* is a carrion insect, but is not attracted to such fresh bodies. The presence of beetles, again normally later invaders to a decomposing body, could not indicate such a precise elapsed time since death, particularly for such a fresh corpse.

In this "Sex, Lies and Larvae" case, the hypothesized time of death is five days based on circumstantial evidence, so Grissom uses a pig carcass in an attempt to recreate the scene conditions as closely as possible:

> Brass: Well, let me ask you this. You killed a pig just for this?
>
> Grissom: This poor ham was already on his way to someone's Christmas dinner table.
>
> Brass: I mean, wouldn't a rabbit be easier?
>
> Grissom: Gotta be a pig. Interestingly, they are the most like humans.

Pigs are indeed used as the main model for human decomposition in forensic entomology research. Grissom watches the pig decompose and records insects arriving on the carcass. This method was actually used by forensic entomologist Dr. Lee Goff to recreate the crime scene for one of his own cases.[21] After performing the experiment, Grissom tells the Sheriff based on this new evidence that the victim died five rather than three days earlier.

Insect evidence plays another major role in the episode "Scuba Doobie-Doo" (2005), when Sidle and Grissom are looking for evidence:

> Warrick: We already know this beetle feeds only on human blood so why are we extracting its stomach contents?
>
> Sidle: Ah, not so. According to Grissom, Mr. bug guy, the silphid beetle will actually feed on any decomposing mammal, so we need to show human DNA or we are not going to get a warrant to break down any walls.

In scientific practice, although it should be possible to recover human DNA from insect stomach contents and this has been done experimentally, it has never been tested in an actual case.[22]

Many episodes of *CSI* feature forensic entomology because Grissom is presented as an entomologist. A number of the scenarios presented are taken from real cases, but in some situations Grissom makes major conclusions without conducting any analysis. In the pilot episode (1001), Grissom and Brass walk into a bathroom, where they find a man in a tub. Grissom leans over the tub, collects a maggot and states: "Pupae stage 3. The third stage of larval metamorphosis. This guy's been dead 7 days." Insects are commonly used to determine time since death but the results are not instantaneous. An entomologist can no more look at an insect and give an exact time of death than a biologist can look at a bloodstain and name the bleeder. In order to use insects to determine time since death the species must be identified and the temperature of the crime scene for the forgoing time must be known. Larvae or maggots must be identified by rearing them to adulthood, followed by dissection under a microscope or DNA analysis. Simply looking is not good enough. As well, without knowing the temperature of the scene for the preceding days, time of death cannot be determined.

CSI often draws from classic cases involving forensic entomology. Sun Tzu's account of events in a Chinese village is often cited as the first time insect evidence was used to solve a crime.[23] At the end of the episode "Sex, Lies and Larvae" (1010), Grissom has the following conversation with Sara:

> Grissom: You know, there was a murder recently, in a village on the other side of the world. Every man in the village denied having any part in it. The victim's throat had been slashed with a shovel. This one guy, I guess you could call him a science nerd, asked all the men in the village to bring their shovels to the center of town and hold them spade side up and he waited. Eventually, flies stared showing up on one specific shovel looking for microscopic bits of blood and flesh.

> Sidle: First witness to a crime.

> Grissom: The investigator got his murderer and—

> Sidle: —and forensic science was born. Sun Tsu, 1285 AD. You call 800 years ago recent?

> Grissom: To an astronomer it is.

Another classic case is used as the basis for using insect evidence in "Burked" (2001). Gil Grissom compares chigger bites on Nick Stokes to those found on a suspect:

> Grissom: Nick, I need your leg. Show me your bite.

> Stokes: Ah, it's no worries. I got some cream.

> Grissom: Hey.

> Stokes: Alright, it's no big deal, really.

> Grissom: What time did you log in at the Braun house?

Stokes: 9:15 that morning.

Grissom: How long after that did you start processing the backyard?

Stokes: About a half an hour.

Grissom: You're not the only one with chigger bites.

Stokes: Who is this?

Grissom: Walt Braun. It's now 9:30 at night, approximately thirty-six hours ago you were bitten. Three hours earlier than that, Tony Braun was murdered. Chiggers run a predictable course. A chigger attaches itself to a hair follicle, injects a digestive enzyme into the skin which ruptures the surrounding cells allowing the chigger to suck them up, leaving behind a red itchy bump.

Stokes: So?

Grissom: Walt Braun lied. We now have an entomological timeline that places him at the house on the day his brother was murdered.

This scenario too, is borrowed from a real life case in which chiggers were used to link a suspect with the crime scene and the time of death of a victim.[24] Chiggers are not only blood feeders, but are also extremely patchy in their distribution so this has been used to help link a suspect not only to a time frame but also to a particular location.

This episode, like many others, has borrowed from real life. It glamorizes and extends the reality of forensic science and does have some foundations within science, and actual cases. As we have shown, some of the cases and examples used on the show are quite accurate, whereas others make rather large fictional leaps. This is true of the majority of television and is not intended as a criticism. Our criticism, as forensic scientists, is perhaps less with the TV show itself and more with the TV viewing audience who, from our myriad encounters with them through public talks, lectures and emails, seem more and more inclined to believe what they see, despite the fact that they know the series is fiction. Of more concern perhaps than the stretching of the scientific truth on *CSI*, is the exaggeration and misinformation related to the education and careers of the characters on the show.

PART TWO: EDUCATION AND
CAREERS IN THE CSI FIELDS

Although *CSI* makes some scientific leaps that are not entirely grounded in actual practice, the show has never claimed to be anything more than fiction. However, perhaps the most significant gap between fiction and practice that is represented through *CSI* is in the education and careers of the characters themselves. In some respects, this causes the most concern to those of us in science education. Many young people base their career aspirations on people who inspire them. These people may be teachers, parents, or mentors. However, the dramatic increase in related program enrolments since *CSI* first aired suggest that people also make career choices based on TV characters rather than people in their lives. This is especially true when these careers are portrayed as glamorous and exciting as well as socially responsible. In other TV shows that highlight lawyers or doctors, the viewer is at least fairly cognizant of the usual career paths required or can access information as to how to achieve them, for instance, through an appropriate university bachelors degree, followed by a law or medical degree, further training or specialization, then a job in the field. This is not so simple when we look at *CSI*, as the main characters are shown to work across so many varied careers, each, in reality, involving years of very different training.

　CSI capitalizes on human beings' interest in mysteries and puzzles, combined with their fascination with death. The same morbid yet compelling interest that causes drivers to slow down to look at an accident on the other side of the highway has been used in movies, television and books in the mystery, horror, and drama genres to capture our interest. In the past, criminal justice was considered to be something dealt with by judges and their word was final. However, in the past ten or twenty years, we have seen many real life cases where lawyers, journalists, scientists, and police officers re-examine previous judicial decisions and right terrible wrongs involving unjust convictions. Perhaps it is this that has brought criminal justice to the heart of the average person and the desire to become a part of this whole picture, to right wrongs and serve justice. *CSI* has shown many people that they, too, can work in this field. As portrayed on television it is glamorous, exciting, and fulfilling.

　The influence of television on career choice is certainly not new. Professionals in specific fields have probably witnessed popular television shows about their specialty increase interest in the choice of professions such as law, policing, and medicine. As a child, the second author (Gail Anderson) watched this very phenomenon sweep the UK and later North America when the TV show *All Creatures Great and Small* portrayed the adventures of a North Yorkshire veterinarian. Veterinary schools were swamped with applications from people who had never previously considered such a career. We are, potentially, what we watch.

　Thus it is not surprising that incoming first-year undergraduate students often appear to choose their area of study based on what they have seen on television. *CSI* has opened the eyes of students to the wide variety of careers in forensic science. However, in the case of law, medicine, and policing, undergraduate and professional programs already exist for students who desire to pursue these areas of interest. As well, faculty and advisors in such programs can mentor potential students on the realities of their chosen career and disabuse them of any preconceptions gained from television. Therefore, these students can easily learn the realities of the job involved. Further, law and medicine are specific career choices with specific directions. The show *CSI*, on the other hand, suggests that being a CSI—as this is presented on the series—is a single career choice, when in actual fact the show covers a myriad different careers with very different educational backgrounds, often all enacted by the same character. As there is no such thing as a CSI, as portrayed on the show, it is very difficult for potential students and even for advisors and counsellors, to understand that the job as shown on television is fiction and that it actually represents many very different career possibilities.

Prior to *CSI*, forensic courses were available at some Canadian universities, primarily in traditional areas such as forensic anthropology, entomology, odontology, pathology, and psychiatry, when practicing experts were members of the university faculty. However, very few formalized forensic programs existed. In this educational vacuum, the interest in *CSI* and forensic science has resulted in the rapid development of Canadian programs specializing in forensic science that did not exist ten years ago (table 2.1). The majority of these programs were created after *CSI* debuted in 2000.

Students in these programs are attracted by the idea of becoming a CSI, but soon learn that the reality is very different from the glitz and glamour of Hollywood. Those students who persevere gain degrees in various areas of science. Some may enter the world of forensic science, either as police officers or civilians, but the demand for jobs by these new graduates will dramatically outweigh the supply in any one particular field of forensic science, as these positions are extremely limited. For instance, there are fewer than one hundred forensic chemists employed across all of Canada, yet many students are pursuing this field. That said, there are many outlets for students graduating from forensic programs that do not entail a specific career in forensic science, such as careers in non-forensic applications of science, social science, as well as law (which would require further education and certification), investigating human rights violations (such as working for the United Nations), policing, and corrections.

Students pursuing forensic science degrees may have to settle for more traditional scientific careers. Instead of the traditional undergraduate science degrees leading to professional schools, many students now choose forensic programs prior to applying to medicine, pharmacy, or dental school. Because of forensics' immediately apparent application of science, it is an ideal tool to interest students in science, especially those who might not have considered

Table 2.1.   Higher Education Programs in Forensic Science in Canada

Province	Institution	Program	Specialty
AB	Mount Royal College	Certificate	Forensic Studies
BC	British Columbia Institute of Technology	B. Technology	Computer Crime; Economic Crime Forensic Investigation;
BC	University of British Columbia	MSc.	Forensic Odontology
NS	Dalhousie University	Certificate	Forensic Psychology
NS	Saint Mary's University	Diploma	Forensic Science
ON	Lakehead University	H.B.Sc.	Applied Bio-Molecular Science
ON	Laurentian University	B.Sc.	Forensic Science; Anthropology; Analytical Chemistry; Psychology
ON	Seneca College of Applied Arts & Technology	Certificate	Applied Forensic Investigative Sciences
ON	Trent University & Fleming College	B.Sc.	Forensic Science (Molecular Biology)
ON	University of Ontario Institute of Technology	H.B.Sc.	Forensic Science
ON	University of Toronto	Diploma; H.B.Sc.	Forensic Science (Anthropology; Biology; Chemistry; Computer Science; Psychology); Forensics and Criminology
ON	University of Windsor	H.B.A.; H.B. Forensic Science	Biology; Chemistry; Molecular Biology; Anthropology

H.B.Sc. Honors Bachelor of science
HBA, Honors Bachelor of Arts
H.B. Forensic Science Honors Bachelor of Forensic Science.

a career in science otherwise. As long as the degree program provides good core scientific training in at least one particular science, these students will be as likely to find employment as any other science major. Therefore, the careers that are portrayed in *CSI* may be mythic, but the show's popularity may result in increased scientific training in the next generation. This interest has even reached high school textbooks, which now frequently use forensic science to teach basic science,[25] and general interest science books for elementary students that incorporate forensic science mysteries to pique their interest.[26] Science is no longer boring, nor only for the nerds!

Thus in specific ways, *CSI* does educate people about science, if only by opening their eyes a little wider to the world around them and the possibilities that science holds. The trick is to remember that it is just an interesting and fun TV show and is not designed to instruct people in science or career path.

NOTES

1. J. Stockwell, "Defense, Prosecution Play to New "CSI" Savvy: Juries expecting TV-style Forensics," *Washington Post*, May 11 2005, A01. For a different reading of the press coverage of the *"CSI* effect" see Harvey and Derksen in this volume.
2. Max M. Houck, "CSI: Reality," *Scientific American* 295 (2006): 85–89; A. Massie, "'CSI effect' evident in U.S. courtrooms," *Scotsman*, April 24 2005.
3. Houck, "CSI: Reality."
4. J. Stockwell, "Defense, Prosecution Play to New 'CSI' Savvy; Juries expecting TV-style Forensics," *Washington Post*, May 11 2005, A01.
5. Massie, "'CSI effect' evident."
6. Personal Communication W. Knapp, Forensic Identification Services, Toronto Police Department. 2005.
7. Stockwell, "Defense, Prosecution Play."
8. Houck, "CSI: Reality."
9. Houck, "CSI: Reality."
10. Personal Communication, Sgt. Luc Maltais, Instructor, Senior Identification Course, Canadian Police College, 2004.
11. Personal Communication, Insp. Brian Andrews, OIC Integrated Forensic Identification Service E Division, RCMP.
12. Richard Saferstein, *Criminalistics. An Introduction to Forensic Science.* 9th ed. (Upper Saddle River, N.J.: Prentice Hall. 2007), 638.
13. N. Port et al. "How long does it take to contaminate a scene by talking?" paper presented at The International Association of Forensic Sciences. Hong Kong, August 21–26 2005).
14. A. Massie, "CSI effect' evident in U.S. courtrooms" *Scotsman.* 2005.
15. Max M. Houck, "CSI: Reality." *Scientific American*, 295 (2006): 85–89.
16. Max M. Houck, "CSI: Reality." *Scientific American*, 295 (2006): 85–89, p86.
17. Francesco Introna, Carlo Pietro Campobassa and Madison Lee, Goff, "Entomotoxicology" *Forensic Science International* 120 (2001): 42–47, D. W. Sadler et al. "Drug accumulation and elimination in *Calliphora vicina* larvae" *Forensic Science International* 71(3) (1995): 191-7, Madison Lee Goff and Wayne D. Lord, "Entomotoxicology. A new area for forensic investigation." *American Journal of Forensic Medicine and Pathology* 15(1) (1994): 51–57, J. C. Beyer, Y.F. Enos and M. Stajic, "Drug identification through analysis of maggots." *Journal of Forensic Science* 25(1980): 411–12, Z. Wilson, S. Hubbard, S., and D.J. Pounder, "Drug analysis

in fly larvae"*American Journal of Forensic Medicine and Pathology* 14(2) (1993): 118–20.

18. Forensic entomologists study the insects associated with a dead body in order to estimate elapsed time since death as well as other factors at a crime scene, such as whether the body has been disturbed or moved. Both authors are forensic entomologists.

19. Forensic odontologists are dentists who use dental evidence to identify a person, as well as analyze bite mark evidence to implicate the biter.

20. Forensic botanists study any botanical evidence associated with the victim, suspect and scene and can use this to establish whether a person was present in a particular area, link a person to a scene or area, and determine the age of remains by considering plant growth rates over or through the body.

21. Madison Lee Goff, "Problems in estimation of postmortem interval resulting from wrapping of the corpse: A case study from Hawaii." *Journal of Agricultural Entomology* 9(4) (1992): 237–43.

22. Kosta Y. Mumcuoglu et al. "Use of human lice in forensic entomology." *Journal of Medical Entomology* 41(4) (2004): 803–6, Jeffrey D. Wells and Felix A. Sperling, "DNA-based identification of forensically important Chrysomyinae (Diptera: Calliphoridae)." *Forensic Science International* 120 (2001): 110–115, Wayne D. Lord et al. "Isolation, amplification, and sequencing of human mitochondrial DNA obtained from human crab louse, *Pthirus pubis* (L.), blood meals." *Journal of Forensic Science* 43(5) (1998): 1097–1100.

23. Brian E. McKnight, *The Washing Away of Wrongs: Forensic Medicine in Thirteenth Century China by Sung T'zu.* (Ann Arbor: Center for Chinese Studies, Univ. Mich.,1981), 181.

24. James P. Webb, Jr. et al. "The chigger species *Eutrombicula belkini* Gould (Acari: Trombiculidae) as a forensic tool in a homicide investigation in Ventura County, California." *Bulletin of the Society of Vector Ecology* 8 (1983): 141–46.

25. Richard Saferstein, *Forensic Science, An Introduction* (Pearson/Prentice Hall, 2007), 732.

26. Vivien Bowers, *Crime Science: How Investigators Use Science to Track Down the Bad Guys* (Toronto: Owl, 1997), 64.

Chapter Three

CSI and *Law & Order* : Dueling Representations of Science and Law in the Criminal Justice System

Kurt Hohenstein

The longevity of *Law & Order* and meteoric rise of *CSI* reaffirms the American public's infatuation with anything criminal.[1] Long a staple of popular programming, depictions of the resolution of policing and criminal justice processes on television crime dramas are linked in complicated ways with public attitudes about the criminal justice system evidenced by public opinion polling. However, the original *Law & Order* series and the evolution and immense popularity of *CSI: Crime Scene Investigation* evoke something different from what viewers watched on television crime dramas of the 1980s. This paper argues that, to a remarkable degree, these two shows present competing representations of public views about the efficacy, fairness, and values of the American criminal justice system. Rather than simply opening a window into public attitudes about that system, they demonstrate a dueling set of public values about criminal justice institutions and processes that many Americans view with skepticism.[2]

Each original series represents a particular thematic vision of the role of traditional policing and legal institutions and processes in achieving justice. *Law & Order* thrives on the legal conflict inherent in the American, and perhaps in any formally democratic, legal system. In nearly every episode, defense lawyers seek to suppress various kinds of evidence discovered by the shows' detectives and occasionally the forensic professionals, to the mutual frustration of the police and prosecution team seeking to convict what appears to be the so-obviously-guilty defendant. On *Law & Order*, the conclusive action takes place in the courtroom, and generally not the forensic laboratory. *Law & Order* depicts a legal system that, while interesting because it explores a variety of contemporaneous legal conundrums, often appears conflicted, uncertain, and even unfair. For example, in an episode entitled "Everyman's Favorite Bagman" (1006), Detectives Logan and Greevey investigate a murder that involves suspected police corruption. A local mob boss has important evidence but he demands immunity for his help. The prosecutors and the viewer are confronted with the moral dilemma of granting immunity to a character framed as criminal in order to solve the murder, with altogether unsatisfying results.[3] *Law & Order* is replete with these kinds of legal, moral, and social dilemmas that accentuate the criminal justice system's often conflicted goals and methods.

The *CSI* franchise, on the other hand, promotes the forensic scientist as a virtually infallible legal fact-finder. Here, only very rarely do crimes get resolved in a courtroom. In *CSI: Crime Scene Investigation* the only significant police figure, Captain Brass, more often than not appears simply as an afterthought, confirming with the ubiquitous confession wrought from a hapless criminal because of the irrefutable forensic evidence discovered by the CSIs. Even in cases where a courtroom comes into play or there are questions surrounding the accuracy of forensic evidence the science wins the day. In "The Closer" (1022), *CSI: NY* Detective Mac Taylor testifies in a trial that a bloody, DNA-covered hammer ties the defendant to the murder. The defendant maintains his innocence at trial and, after he is convicted, calls Taylor from jail to confront him about his conclusions. "The evidence never lies," Taylor advises him. Viewers later find out that the forensic scientists in Mac's team misinterpreted the physical evidence because an *eyewitness*, a traditionally influential form of legal evidence, lied. The viewer is led to question, as Detective Taylor does, the value of eyewitness testimony when faced with the newly discovered forensic evidence. The truth wins out only because Taylor, despite the resistance of a prosecutor who has a conviction he wants to keep, testifies on behalf of the defendant at a new trial as to why the experts misinterpreted the evidence in the earlier conviction.[4] Here we also see that in *CSI*, when prosecution or defense lawyers are involved, they act as impediments to the truth-seeking goals of the more reliable actors in the system by using the rules of procedural evidence to obstruct the discoveries uncovered by the *CSI* team. The *CSI* model, which centers on forensic science, generally minimizes the role of police investigators, lawyers, judges, juries, and courtrooms, as procedurally instrumental parts of the criminal justice system. For *CSI*, justice is best served by avoiding the procedural complexities of the criminal justice system and cutting to the forensic chase with hard scientific evidence that appears both clear and conclusive.

These dueling representations of how the criminal justice system operates, represented by *CSI*'s fictionalized and often inaccurate portrayal of the role of forensic science,[5] and by the procedural conflicts of *Law & Order*, point out a central dilemma of modern criminal jurisprudence. These shows' fictional portrayals of the conflict between swift and sure justice and the values of procedural and constitutional fairness illuminate the frustration of some Americans with a criminal justice system that they see as overly solicitous of the civil liberties of criminal trial defendants.[6] It is my contention that the popularity of *CSI* developed in the wake of high profile criminal cases that challenged the beliefs of some Americans about the capability of the legal system to act as a competent arbiter of justice. The trials of four white Los Angeles police officers accused of beating African-American Rodney King (1992) and of O.J. Simpson (1994–1995), where defendants perceived as guilty were acquitted, called into question for some the competency of juries to impartially assess the evidence.[7] Between 1992 and June 2007, the Innocence Project, an organization that uses new forensic techniques of evidence discovery and analysis to overturn wrongful convictions, also successfully fought to reverse the convictions of 202 defendants. Their work has raised serious questions about the competency of the truth-finding function of the criminal justice system and challenged in the court of public opinion the fairness of traditional procedural determinations of reasonable doubt.[8] In addition, the highly publicized Scott Peterson trial (2005)—in which Peterson was convicted of the murder of his wife and unborn son based on forensic evidence in an otherwise largely circumstantial case—enhanced the public credibility of forensic evidence. Major legal-cultural events, along with the banal ubiquity of shows like *Court TV* (1991–2007), with its moderator Nancy Grace rolling her incredulous eyes at witness testimony, have reinforced a belief among some Americans that the criminal justice system cannot adequately determine the guilt or innocence of defendants because, in the new *CSI* world of forensic science, traditional evidence and legal procedure through which most cases are made is unreliable and biased.[9]

Recent media reports have suggested that the cultural phenomenon that is the *CSI* franchise reflects and perpetuates these growing doubts, and is perceived to have created unrealistic perceptions that forensic science can replace the work of lawyers, judges and juries.[10] With Americans expressing concern about the effectiveness of the criminal justice system in fairly determining and convicting guilty defendants, the popularity of *CSI* exposes a lack of public respect for a system that some Americans find out of touch with, or even opposed to, their values. This essay examines the dueling representations of the law and science as finders of fact on the original *Law & Order* and *CSI* series, and asks how the immense popularity of the fictionalized science-based justice of *CSI* may be linked with public understanding of and support for the criminal justice system as it currently exists.

PUBLIC PERCEPTIONS OF THE
CRIMINAL JUSTICE SYSTEM

The idea that many Americans are contemptuous of the condition of their justice system is nothing new. When polled in May 2005 "How much confidence you had in a list of institutions in American society," only nine percent of Americans expressed a "great deal of confidence" in the criminal justice system. While forty-five percent of 1,004 respondents expressed "some confidence," twenty-six percent had "very little" confidence in the system." As a total of respondents expressing "some, very little, or none," only organized labor, the U.S. Congress, big business and HMOs ranked lower.[11] In a February 2005 Harris Poll, when 1,102 adult respondents were asked which institutions they had a great deal of confidence in, the criminal justice system received the affirmation of only twenty-two percent of Americans, ranking barely ahead of major corporations, organized labor, Congress, television news, Wall Street financial institutions, the press and law firms.[12] This approximate level of public confidence in the criminal justice system has remained consistent since 1980. While these polls are reflective of a wider lack of confidence in a variety of public institutions, I argue that the low confidence expressed by American adults in the criminal justice system demonstrates a problem with public perceptions of the workings of U.S. criminal justice. A recent study that analyzed public attitudes about governmental institutions found that more than eighty percent of those questioned preferred the idea of "totally revamping the way the criminal justice system works for violent crime"; seventy-five percent said the same with regard to how the system works for all crime. Respondents cited the perception that victims lack rights and offenders are not made to pay restitution or accept responsibility for their crimes as key reasons that major changes were needed in the operation of the system.[13]

Racial minorities, who often experience disproportionate contact with the criminal justice system personally or through family members, express a more intense distrust of the system.[14] But these citizens cite as their chief complaint a lack of procedural fairness rather than a perceived violation of victims' rights. Harsh treatment by police officers, unfair sentences for drug crimes and lack of equal access to quality legal representation are some of the particular concerns of racial minority Americans who express distrust of the system.[15]

Yet, most Americans have little or no direct contact with the criminal justice system. Their impressions come not from family, friends or acquaintances that have faced the system and related their own experiences, but from ubiquitous media representations on the news or in entertainment programs. Lawrence W. Sherman, Director of the Jerry Lee Center of Criminology at the University of Pennsylvania, has convincingly argued that for the majority of Americans that have no actual contact with the system, the level of civic trust in criminal justice "may depend on what they hear about criminal justice encounters with other citizens."[16] For that majority, Sherman suggests that the three major domains affecting their confidence in criminal justice are the practices of the criminal justice system, the changing values and expectations of the culture the system serves, and the images of the system presented in the electronic media. Sherman asserts that public trust is likely to grow only where changes in the three domains work to create values in the system "perceived to be fair, inclusive, and trustworthy."[17]

My analysis of the immense popularity of *CSI*, which dwarfed the longstanding but drastically smaller audiences for *Law and Order*, leads me to argue that Americans desire the values of certainty and efficacy in the operation of the criminal justice system. Post-conviction exposés of criminal procedural inequity have contributed to Americans' diminished faith in the criminal justice system. The Innocence Project, and other private efforts working to uncover forensic proof of the innocence of previously convicted defendants, have suggested to the public that the miscarriage of justice may be more commonplace than anecdotal. These post-conviction exposés, along with high profile trials that serve as a lightening rod for public debate and popular perceptions of potential jury members' exposure to new forensic technologies through the media, create the perception that the concept of reasonable doubt is changing as a principle fairly assessed by ordinary courts and juries.[18] Politicians such as former Illinois Governor George Ryan recently called for capital punishment moratoriums because they believed that their systems have executed and/or were likely to execute innocent defendants. Although scientific evidence was not the only reason for Governor Ryan's actions, in an address to the Bar of the City of New York, he made clear his concern about executing defendants who might later be found innocent as a result of DNA testing. Governor Ryan stated that "As you all know, DNA is a very powerful tool for everybody that is involved in the criminal justice system. It can either convict the guilty or exonerate the innocent."[19] Recent news reports suggest that some defense lawyers, aware of public uncertainty about the criminal justice system produced by wrongful conviction projects and popular impressions from shows like *CSI*, have used the perception that forensic evidence is absolutely trustworthy and universally available at crime scenes to lead juries to believe that a lack of forensic evidence in itself creates reasonable doubt.[20]

There is also evidence to suggest that Americans have come to believe that justice must be swift in order for it to be just. This type of fast-food mentality demands solutions to criminal justice problems in a way that can be compartmentalized and expressed in simple, immediate results. Long delays caused by legal maneuvering before trial and long tedious trials themselves are often cited by segments of the public as a major concern.[21] The recent emphasis on victims' rights creates in the public an unreasonable expectation that justice must be efficiently meted out in order to achieve "closure," that illusive psychological concept that has become as important a goal of the system as state-exacted punishment.[22]

FORENSIC SCIENCE AND LEGAL PROCEDURE ON *CSI* AND *LAW & ORDER*

While both *CSI* and *Law & Order* compress the machinations of the justice system into hour-long slots, the procedural emphasis of *Law & Order* makes it clear that the trial process is often long and winding in practice. *CSI* instead emphasizes the speed through which dramatized forensic science can obtain results, spitting the facts about a suspect's DNA and fingerprint or voice analysis out of machines as the characters sip their morning coffee. In *CSI,* certainty is a virtue not merely because it avoids the ambiguity of human error, but because it unrealistically promises results in minutes for those viewers grown weary of legal delay.

Despite its depiction of legal complexity and conflict, the *Law & Order* franchise has remained popular for over a decade. The original series has morphed to include the prosecution of crimes against "special victims" in what may be the unhappiest show on television (*Law & Order: Special Victim's Unit*), and *Law & Order: Criminal Intent*, which focuses in part on the workings of the criminal mind. That *Law & Order* has been able to sustain an audience for so long suggests a measure of audience awareness and engagement with the complexity and conflict of the legal process. However, I argue that *CSI*'s intense popularity, on the other hand, stems from its portrayal of quick and certain justice. Audiences of *Law & Order* have engaged with the procedural and legal complexities depicted in that series, but the values of certainty and efficiency that *CSI* emphasizes appear to have helped it win the ratings race among viewers. *CSI* and *Law & Order's* two very different dramatizations of the system demonstrate that their dueling conceptions of criminal justice represent a contemporary showdown over the values Americans expect from their criminal justice system.

While both shows seek the conviction of often-reviled suspects, *Law and Order* depends on the traditional legal model of rule-bound interpretation. In the episode "Dissonance" (11232),[23] physical evidence is excluded from trial because a judge who is presented as biased rules that the police mistakenly, and therefore illegally, seized it from the wrong source. The ruling protects the civil rights of the defendant, but the judge's decision leaves Executive Assistant District Attorney Jack McCoy, and one suspects some viewers, frustrated, questioning the fairness and rationality of a system that promotes procedural perfection while possibly allowing a presumably guilty defendant to go free.

CSI liberates viewers from that frustration by playing to it, making all legal rules and procedures irrelevant through an end run around them. On *CSI*, the scientific examination of facts leads to clear and concise conclusions. *Law and Order* relies on human intuition and interpretation, and legal-procedural rigor, to arrive at justice; *CSI* finds order in a forensic science that appears to make human interpretation avoidable by easily matching bullet fragments under a microscope or DNA samples to a known offender in a database. In U.S. society, where the sad state of science and math education is a common lament, *CSI*'s popularity suggests that viewers desire the unrealistic forensic science displayed in the Las Vegas laboratory of Gil Grissom and his associates without necessarily understanding it. Americans have embraced the scientific model for criminal justice widely popularized by *CSI* because it appears to offer easy answers to complicated conflicts among legal ideas and institutions, the law, and the perceived dichotomy between the rights of the accused and victims.[24]

CONSTITUTIONAL PROTECTIONS VERSUS A MODEL OF INDIVIDUALIZED JUSTICE

The Office of Victims of Crime, a federal office within the U.S. Department of Justice established in 1983, announces on its official website: "justice isn't served until crime victims are." It promotes the concept that individual victims should have a role in the criminal justice process and that their interests are as important as societal goals of apprehension and punishment.[25] The explosion of victim's rights movements over the last decade or so has provided an important voice for a minority that some argue was formerly silent, but it has also individualized criminal justice to the point where communal values which promote civil rights as essential to a proper working of the system are seen as counterproductive if they interfere with the conviction and incarceration of presumably guilty parties. The individualization of justice in order to support victims adds to public confusion about the form and function of our criminal justice system. Procedural protections of civil rights like the exclusionary rule, which excludes evidence seized in violation of the *U.S. Constitution*, are designed to promote broader goals such as promoting the communal values of equal justice and constitutional fairness. Victims' rights movements, however, have come to define procedural protections like the exclusionary rule as antithetical to the increasingly individualistically defined rights of and justice for crime victims.[26]

Law & Order and *CSI* play heavily on these themes, but in distinctly different ways. In *Law & Order,* a narrator intones over the opening credits: "In the criminal justice system, the people are represented by two separate yet equally important groups: the police who investigate crime and the district attorneys who prosecute the offenders. These are their stories." By compartmentalizing their stories into two halves of each episode, *Law & Order* focuses on the interrelationship of the institutions of policing and prosecution as equally necessary elements of criminal justice system as a whole. The values espoused in *Law & Order* are traditional and communal values like equal justice, procedural fairness and impartiality. Even the obligatory wisecrack the police deliver each episode over the body of the victim minimizes the victim's part in the investigation in favor of the larger purpose of satisfying the values of communal and societal justice.[27]

Law & Order emphasizes the conflict between procedural justice and victim's rights. In nearly every episode, Executive Assistant DA McCoy faces a motion to exclude police-gathered evidence because of some inventive loophole craftily exploited by scheming defense lawyers. The judges often agree with the defense, leaving McCoy and undoubtedly some viewers exasperated by the perceived nonsense of the system as the prosecution scrambles to overcome the effect of the ruling.[28] Even within the DA's Office the Assistant DA, who is often depicted as less conservative than McCoy, questions the ruthless and dogged methods McCoy uses to gain a conviction. Yet McCoy's sustaining appeal is that despite the procedural setbacks and the disapproval of some of his colleagues, he remains affirmed in his faith in the system, his belief that the jury will right technical wrongs. His jury summations usually cut to the chase, appealing to the commonsense that he believes every juror possesses. However, the dilemmas explored in *Law & Order* leave us wondering, asking large and small ethical questions about the legal system, not one hundred percent certain about its effectiveness and ability to dispense justice fairly.

CSI, on the other hand, appeals directly to Americans' apparent need for judicial certainty. In a society where some people have come to believe that common law rules and civil procedure impede more often than impel justice, the arcane procedures implicit in the rule of law become anathema to the pragmatic resolution of criminal conduct. *CSI* often excludes the jury, the courtroom, and its actors completely from the visible drama, with an unspoken yet clear implication that we, the viewers, ought not to trust to juries the important function of interpreting legal facts. Facts are stubborn things that can often be misunderstood, so *CSI* finds its footing by depicting forensic science as the solution to that problem. It is the evidence, we are constantly reminded by Grissom and his associates, that never lies and that leads to the truth; in this fictionalized account, we can be confident that there is but one version of the truth that the certainty of science will disclose. These dramatized principles make juries and judges appear to be not only unnecessary but even impediments to discovering the truth. Viewers may find themselves wishing, in a *CSI* cornucopia of scientific revelation, that we could have discarded the verdicts of juries and judges in well-known cases where they seemed to have gotten things so very wrong.

Unlike *Law & Order* (with some exception in *Law & Order: SVU*), *CSI* revels in the victim, opening up their lives and especially every intimate detail of their traumatic deaths to the forensic scientists who use them as the source for a very individual kind of forensic redemption. The dead bodies of the victims often provide the evidence that is central to identifying and apprehending the suspect—the decomposing bugs time-stamping their demise, the skin samples under their nails from the struggles that led to their deaths, their stomach contents as a sort of messianic last supper message. It is as though victims exert, from the autopsy table, the kind of personal agency critics believe the criminal justice system has stripped from them. In this personal (and particularly circumscribed) focus on victims, *CSI* echoes cries for the recognition of victim rights as a paramount value of criminal justice. Jack McCoy speaks for the legal system in *Law and Order*, but in *CSI* the victims, through the CSIs as their forensic translators, quite aptly speak for themselves.

However, this appeal to victims' rights subverts the communal interests served through the broad protection of civil rights and constitutional principles in our criminal justice system. Personalizing the interest of the victim as a fundamental criminal justice value appeals to popular audiences because many Americans have come to believe that every worthy value is individualistic. The criminal justice goals of promoting collective judgment on guilt and punishment or reinforcing the idea that criminal acts, while directed against individuals, are an affront to the state or society as a whole, become less important as we accord victim's rights an exalted place in our criminal justice pantheon of values.[29] Through its fictionalized forensic approach *CSI* emphasizes that, even as viewers rapaciously witness the most grotesque iteration of the victims' wounds and violent deaths, it is science that vindicates them. This sensationalizing and effective privatization of criminal justice values makes it more difficult to advocate that the collective wisdom of juries and the constitutional protection of civil rights are worthy of preservation.

THE DUELING TELEVISUAL STYLES
OF JUSTICE OF *LAW & ORDER* AND *CSI*

The darkly stylish approach of *CSI: Crime Scene Investigation* also contrasts with the clean, clear shots prevalent on *Law & Order*. Shot in Las Vegas, the home of long odds, the urban *CSI*'s cinematography is enveloped in dark back-lit tones, slowly unveiled in the pornographic depictions of crime scenes, autopsy examinations, or evidence retrieval. The camera shots at the crime scenes are intentionally dimmed, and the focus redirected to the green luminescence of the flashlight seeking the telltale evidence from the luminal sprayed on blood-spattered walls. It is as if the entire world goes dark in the presence of forensic science because it alone holds out hope and thus light, in the search for the truth. *Law & Order,* on the other hand, uses bright, high contrast scenes where everything becomes crystal clear as the legal principles and rulings remain conflicted and contentious. *Law & Order* maintains a presumption of cinematic innocence, even as viewers might grow angry at the legal opacity that clouds some of the most unambiguously guilty defendants.

The characters from each of the shows also reinforce the dichotomy between *CSI* and *Law & Order*. *CSI* is replete with nerdy scientists, no nonsense geek chic characters like Gil Grissom and Catherine Willows who steadfastly focus on the science and their work, sublimating all the comfortable angles of their own humanity. Greg Sanders, the boy wonder DNA expert, represents the high forensic competence of the show, but also the burning desire to leave the laboratory. In season four, his exceptionally diverse forensic talents are subordinated, to the consternation of his colleagues, by his boyish sense of humor and his drive to get out of the laboratory and into the field where the real action takes place. However, it is his laboratory work that in many episodes directly leads to the discovery of the most important evidence. Greg does his work in the lab surrounded by marvelously advanced yet at times unrealistically portrayed scientific technology. His high competence represents the epitome of forensic science as fictionalized by *CSI*, even as he strives to escape from the lab to the more interesting fieldwork his colleagues engage in. In "Who Shot Sherlock" (5011), he desires and ultimately achieves the luminescence of fieldwork and his final proficiency, surrounded by blood and bones and mystery, separated from his familiar forensic machinery and techniques.

At various points in the show's seasons, every character on *CSI* has portrayed some human frailty. Catherine, a divorcée, attracts a series of abusive relationships. Nick Stokes is a survivor of sexual abuse and cries a lot, betraying his machismo. Sarah Sidle drinks too much. Warrick Brown has a gambling addiction that repeatedly puts him on the criminal edge. Captain

Brass, a hardnosed cop with a seriously troubled daughter, finds his solace in police work instead of human relationships. Grissom is an emotionally detached workaholic, often incapable of expressing his love for anything but the evidence from his forensic unit. Only Dr. Albert Robbins, who performs the autopsies, seems stereotypically normal, but he has physical frailties, and walks with a cane. Each character's distinctive frailties appear intended to humanize them for the viewer, even as they drive the televisual focus of the viewer to their work, where like many of us facing similar problems, they can find peace and happiness and emotional satisfaction, a respite from their personal distress or foibles.

Americans who demand exacting and swift justice from their legal system are frustrated by complicated legal-cultural events, such as the LAPD-Rodney King and O. J. Simpson cases or the more recent Andrea Yates trial and appeal, which suggest that justice, like the cases on *Law & Order*, lies in the hands of a jury that could go either way.[30] While *Law & Order* plays to this uncertainty and complexity, *CSI* represents a fictional way out of the moral wilderness, through which science can reliably and rapidly resolve doubt about the facts in every case. *CSI* emulates a public desire for sure justice, for a criminal justice system than can rest on sure facts by avoiding lawyers, courts, and juries. *CSI* relies on science to answer criminal justice questions because the show presents science as providing certainty in an uncertain world. The legal system depicted in *Law & Order*, with its lawyers, rules of evidence and civil liberties is rife with ambiguity. The representation of forensic science on *CSI* promotes the goal of certainty, not by working with the legal system, but by making its procedural operation irrelevant.

CSI and *Law & Order* are more than mere entertainment; they are cultural phenomena that depict and reinforce public attitudes about the values Americans desire in the criminal justice system. The coarsening of American legal-political rhetoric—in partisan debates on issues such as judicial activism, the argument about the original intent of the *Constitution*'s framers, the role of juries, the rights of criminal defendants and the value of civil liberties versus the rights of victims—hastens public distrust of the judicial system. This dynamic is fortified when our major contentions about criminal justice values are played out, not in deliberative democratic forums, but in the dueling televisual representations of *CSI* and *Law & Order*. This chapter has demonstrated that both dramas encourage the nagging suspicion among Americans that we have a criminal justice system we cannot trust. The desire to elevate science as the arbiter of criminal justice fact-finding is a quixotic attempt to achieve absolute certainty in criminal justice, enacting a smoking-gun syndrome through which nuance can be managed by science because complexity is made irrelevant. The truth behind *CSI*'s scientific solution is epithelial-deep: by presenting a fictionalized and unrealistic representation of forensic science as certain avenger of the victim it masks more fundamental problems in the system, such as the social roles of race, gender and economics in shaping criminal justice inequity. In a democratic society the legal role of interpreter of fact in a criminal trial can only justly belong to judges and juries because facts remain predominately human expressions demanding careful examination and *communal* interpretation. Ironically, in seeking to eliminate mistakes, *CSI*'s fictionalized forensic model eliminates the human role in criminal justice procedure by relying exclusively on science, which in actual practice itself remains a human enterprise. There is a place for the criminal justice tools presented on *CSI*, but especially given the rarity of conclusive forensic evidence in determination of guilt or innocence in most criminal cases, science alone cannot provide justice.

NOTES

1. Philip Lane, "The Existential Condition of Television Crime Drama" *Journal of Popular Culture* 34 (Fall 2001): 137–51. This article focuses primarily on the two original series, *Law & Order* and *CSI: Crime Scene Investigation* rather than their several spin-off series.

2. *The Gallup Poll. Public Opinion 2005* (Lanham, MD: Rowman & Littlefield, 2007), 201 ff (hereafter Gallup May 2005). As discussed in more detail below, in several U.S. public opinion polls measuring the public approval of major institutions, the criminal justice system has ranked consistently low.

3. 1006 was first broadcast 30 October 1990, Writer Dick Wolf, Director John Patterson. See also "Nullification" (8162), first broadcast 5 November 1997, Writer David Black, Director Constantine Makris.

4. Summaries of the storylines of *Law & Order* and *CSI: Crime Scene Investigation* can be found on www.tv.com.

5. S. L. VanLaerhoven and G.S. Anderson, "The Science and Careers of CSI," in this volume.

6. Gallup May 2005.

7. Jewelle Taylor Gibbs, *Race and Justice: Rodney King and O. J. Simpson in a House Divided* (New York: Josey Bass, 1996). In a Poll of 635 adults nationwide conducted on October 3, 1995 in the aftermath of the Simpson verdict, fifty-six percent of those surveyed disagreed with the verdict. Seventy-two percent of the respondents said that racial issues were either "considered by the jury" or "determined the verdict." CNN/USA Today-Gallup, "Simpson verdict opinion poll" (October 3, 1995), <http://www.cnn.com/US/OJ/daily/9510/10-04/poll/index.html> (2 Feb. 2009).

8. James Brovard, *Attention Deficit Democracy* (New York: Palgrave Macmillan, 2005), 171–188. On the Innocence Project see <http://www.innocenceproject.org/> (2 Feb. 2009).

9. Jeffrey Toobin, "The CSI Effect," *The New Yorker*, May 7, 2007.

10. Richard Willing, "'CSI Effect Has Juries Wanting More Evidence," *USA Today* (August 5, 2004). See also Harvey and Derksen in this volume.

11. Gallup May 2005.

12. For results from the annual Harris Poll on Major Institutions (2004–2008) see <http://www.pollingreport.com/institut.htm> (2 Feb. 2009). The Harris Poll queried 1,102 adults nationwide with the following question: "As far as people in charge of running [insert the institution] are concerned, would you say you have a great deal of confidence, only some confidence, or hardly any confidence at all in them?" The responses for the criminal justice system ranked them with twenty-two percent of people surveyed expressing a great deal of confidence, just ahead of major companies, organized labor, congress, television news, Wall Street, the press, and law firms.

13. Lawrence W. Sherman, "Trust and Confidence in Criminal Justice," *National Institute for Justice Journal* 248 (2002): 22–31.

14. David Cole, *No Equal Justice* (New York: New Press, 2000); Yesilernis L. Peña, Christopher Federico, and Jim Sidanius, *Race and Support for the Criminal Justice System: A Matter of Asymmetry.* Working Paper 181 (New York: Russell Sage Foundation, 2006): 1–32

15. Eschholz, Sarah, Brenda S. Blackwell, Marc Gertz, and Ted Chiricos. "Race and Attitudes Toward the Police: Assessing the Effects of Watching 'Reality' Police Programs," 30 *Journal of Criminal Justice (2002)*: 327–41.

16. Sherman, "Trust and Confidence," 29.

17. Sherman, "Trust and Confidence," 30.

18. Willing, "CSI Effect."

19. "Governor Ryan's Capital Punishment Moratorium and the Executioner's Confession: Views from the Governor's Mansion to Death Row," 75 *St. John's Law Review* (Summer 2001): 401–18.

20. "Defense Lawyers Hinge Cases on 'CSI' Savvy," *The Washington Post*, May 22, 2005, A1.

21. Brian J. Ostrom and Roger A. Hanson, *Efficiency, Timeliness, and Quality: A New Perspective From Nine State Criminal Trial Courts* (Rockville, MD: National Institute of Justice, 2000).

22. Mark Dubber, *Victims in the War on Crime: The Use and Abuse of Victims' Rights* (New York: New York University Press: NY, 2002); Paul H. Robinson, "Should the Victims' Rights Movement Have Influence Over Criminal Law Formulation and Adjudication?" *McGeorge Law Review* 33 (2003): 749–88

23. "Dissonance" (11232), first aired 1 November 2000, Writer Wendy Battles, Director Lewis H. Gould.

24. 18 United States Code §3771. The passage of the Crime Victims' Rights Act in 2004 was specifically intended to provide rights to victims that its sponsors stated the *Constitution* had "ignored."

25. National Center for Victims of Crime, *America Speaks Out: Citizens' Attitudes About Victims' Rights and Violence, Executive Summary* (Arlington, VA: National Center for Victims, 1991).

26. Robinson, "Victims' Rights Movement."

27. The spin-off of *Law & Order: SVU* tends to focus much more on the interests of the victim as essential to the police work dramatized in that series than does the original *Law & Order* series.

28. For examples of this dilemma, see "Kiss the Girls and Make Them Die," which depicts the legal inability of the prosecution team to use evidence of prior bad acts to try a violent defendant" (1004, first broadcast 11 October 1990, Writers Robert Stuart Nathan and Dick Wolf, Director Charlie Correll); "Black Tie" where forensic medical evidence contradicts the prosecution theory and prevents them from presenting their case as they desired (4071, first broadcast 20 October 1993, Writers Michael S. Chernuchin and Walon Green, Director Arthur W. Forney); and "Past Imperfect" (7156, first broadcast 14 May 1997, Writer Janis Diamond, Director Christopher Misiano) where the prosecution's main witness also happens to have created attorney-client privilege communication problems.

29. U. S Department of Justice, *New Directions from the Field: Victims' Rights and Services for the 21st Century* (Washington, DC: Office for Victims of Crime, 1998) <http://www.ojp.usdoj.gov/ovc/new/directions/> (2 Feb. 2009). The Crime Victims' Rights Act of 2004 specifically mandates a wide range of protections for victims of crime that were previously only voluntary in the federal system.

30. For a quick popular summary of the Yates conviction, appeal, and over-turned conviction, and its spotlighting of the legal dynamics around insanity pleas see "Andrea Yates" <http://en.wikipedia.org/wiki/Andrea_Yates> (2 Feb. 2009).

Chapter Four

Generic Difference and Innovation in *CSI: Crime Scene Investigation*

Nichola Dobson

This chapter assesses the extent to which the shows in the *CSI* franchise conform to the generic verisimilitude of television crime drama. This examination will highlight the generic variation and innovation produced through the *CSI* shows, as well as the construction of a generic verisimilitude through the franchise. By generic verisimilitude I mean not the realism of the text but rather the text's conformity to the rules of the genre that I explore throughout the chapter. The success of *CSI: Crime Scene Investigation* is evident in its consistently high ratings, and that of its franchise spin offs *CSI: Miami* and *CSI: NY*. This chapter considers the effect that the *CSI* franchise has had on the development of the television crime drama genre. While the original *CSI*, *CSI: Miami* and *CSI: NY* conform to many of the generic conventions of contemporary television crime drama, there are unique features in these shows that have had a significant impact on the genre itself, including how the shows use narrative structure, narrative space and visual effects. Drawing on film and television genre theory I consider these features and the effects that the *CSI* shows have had on the development of television crime drama.

Film genre theorist Steve Neale suggests that "Genres are inherently temporal: hence, their inherent mutability on one hand, and their inherent historicity on the other."[1] Genre is not static and therefore modification and diversity within genres are natural occurrences; genres are "marked fundamentally by difference, variation and change."[2] Georgina Born suggests that while television genres are inherently repetitive they also manage "to innovate within the existing rules."[3] It is this variation, innovation and difference within television crime drama that is key to *CSI*'s continuing success and the focus of this essay.

The style and narrative of crime drama, like other genres on television, has developed over the years with new filming and editing techniques. The content of crime shows has also changed to reflect cultural changes and audience tastes with, for example, the addition of female detectives and glamorous drug squads. Feuer, Kerr, and Vahimagi's[4] examination of MTM studios' *Hill Street Blues* (1981–87) demonstrated that television could produce crime drama at a level of quality and sophistication previously only seen in feature length cinema. The quality of writing, acting and camera work in the show led to a generic shift in television crime drama. Feuer et al's analysis of *Hill Street Blues* demonstrates the impact one show can have on generic development, and I refer to their work throughout this essay.

CSI: Crime Scene Investigation, like other crime dramas such as *Law & Order* (1990–) and *Homicide: Life on the Streets* (1993–99), is influenced by *Hill Street Blues* and integrates many of the earlier series' narrative techniques. One of the most notable differences in the *CSI* franchise, however, is the heavy use of special effects, through both models and Computer Generated Imagery (CGI). *CSI* also repositions the traditional law enforcement narrative space of the police station by concentrating most of the episode in the science lab. This shifts the focus away from what would be found in the conventional cop show—the police—to highlight instead the forensic science element of police work, traditionally kept behind the scenes. This has proved extremely popular and thus has effectively hybridized the crime drama television genre, resulting not only in two additional shows in the *CSI* franchise, but also in new season line ups since *CSI* debuted in 2000 that include variations on the science/cop show theme, such as *Cold Case* (2003–), *Bones* (2005–) and *Waking the Dead* (2000–) (UK). The chapter will first outline genre theory, which I apply to the franchise, and then look at some key television crime dramas which have shaped the development of the genre. By considering the conventions and history of the genre I will then examine the franchise in some detail and offer conclusions as to the extent to which the *CSI* franchise has developed both as a brand and as an influence on television crime drama.

GENERIC CONVENTION

In order to examine the generic innovations in *CSI*, it is necessary to consider how the crime drama genre has been produced within television. While there is not space here to consider the long history of crime drama in detail, it is important to reflect upon the crime television shows, especially *Hill Street Blues*, which have significantly impacted the genre and thus the *CSI* franchise.

Television genre theory is informed by film theory. In this regard, this essay draws from Steve Neale's examination of the origins of film genre theory. Neale suggests that generic verisimilitude (defined as the rules of the genre) is "central to an understanding of genre, as is the question of the social and cultural functions that genres perform."[5] He explains that "Genres do not consist only of films [texts]: they consist also, and equally, of specific systems of expectation and hypothesis which spectators bring with them . . . and which interact with films during the course of the viewing process."[6] Verisimilitude thus refers both to generic verisimilitude, and to social or cultural verisimilitude: the audience's acceptance of a genre text is dependent on their interaction with the social or cultural conventions displayed in that text. For producers in a genre to develop new characteristics in that genre, their audiences must accept change within the genre's texts. If the producers want to attract a mass audience, it is therefore important that they consider audiences' generic expectations when they create new shows, and that they ensure that their shows conform to at least a few recognized and accepted generic characteristics.[7]

All popular narrative forms, including cinema and television, have key generic elements that inform the narrative and allow the viewer to identify the form by its generic dominant. Neale suggests that because there are so many possible components of each genre, the most obvious ones (hence dominant) tend to be those by which texts in a particular genre are identified.[8] The generic dominant is often identifiable in the iconography of the text, such as the setting or costumes in a Western. However, Neale also suggests that television as a medium complicates genre categorization; particular programs can be classified by mode of production, style, consumption and institutional marketing as opposed to the more simplistic institutional categorization of film genres, more akin to literary genres.[9] The crime television series can be categorized as a dramatic form. However, the particular characteristics and conventions of crime television, which can be further categorized as "police, detective and crime drama," set it apart from other drama series.[10]

As Neale suggests, no list of generic characteristics can be exhaustive, therefore I would suggest that the dominant features of crime television include the following: i) the commission of a crime and action surrounding it, often of a violent or dangerous nature; ii) a crime solving process entailing arrests, the questioning of witnesses and suspects, examining, chasing, prosecuting; iii) a narrative space—police station, detective's office, court, city; iv) the characterization of heroic cop/detective, clever sidekick, officious superior; and v) a resolution/outcome of the justice system.

While these characteristics are generally present in all television crime series, the genre has developed over the last five decades, with new shows reflecting the changing culture in which the series have been produced.[11] There is space here to consider a few of the shows that have contributed significantly to the genre's development and served as predecessors for the *CSI* franchise.

Quincy, M.E. (1976–83) moved crime solving away from the police station and into a scientific (medical) space. The series' lead character was a medical examiner who solved police cases using forensic medicine as a detection tool; he was always more accurate in his detection than the police force. This hybrid of medical drama and cop show was a forerunner of *CSI. Quincy M.E.* contributed to the development of the genre in its use of narrative space, or location, and structure. The narrative structure used the prologue to tease the audience about the circumstances of the crime. The body of the victim would then arrive at Quincy's lab for autopsy. It is at this point that his medical and scientific expertise are utilized as he questions the police findings. The use of the lab as the key narrative space reinforced the importance of the medical examiner's work in aiding crime solving with most of the crucial aspects of solving the cases occurring there. Quincy usually worked alone though his main assistant Sam was a fixture in the lab. The two other main characters, Quincy's boss and the police Sergeant, each helped and hindered Quincy's methods equally; however Quincy always found the truth by his own perseverance. This differentiates *Quincy M.E.* from the ensemble crime shows that would follow through the development of what Feuer calls "quality" television, and which provide a further precedent for the ensemble teams of *CSI*.

"QUALITY" TELEVISION

In the 1980s there were two television shows that were significant in the generic development of television crime drama. *Hill Street Blues* (1981–87), portrayed the events of an entire police precinct, and *Miami Vice* (1984–89) featured two main (male) detectives working undercover in the glamorous, but dangerous, vice world of Miami.[12]

Jane Feuer suggests that with *Hill Street Blues* MTM studios produced a new standard for television at that time: "NBC's ad campaign of fall 1983 was based on a notion of 'quality' for which MTM programmes provided the model."[13] (The line up also included hospital drama *St Elsewhere* (1982–88) and intellectual comedy *Newhart* (1982–90). The term "quality demographics" was used to refer to both the economic value of a show's audience for advertisers and the quality of a show's content. MTM shows had high production values, intelligent content and writers/producers with cinematic credentials. MTM quality shows like *Hill Street Blues* became a studio trademark, just as

Jerry Bruckheimer's[14] *CSI* franchise has similarly created a signature style. The cinematic influences evidenced in the *CSI* aesthetics have, like MTM with *Hill Street Blues*, helped to elevate the television show to a form comparable to feature length cinema at a time when television was marginalized in favor of film. *CSI* may not be quality television according to the standards set by Feuer et al, however as this chapter will demonstrate it has affected the generic development of crime television, and indeed other genres, in a similar manner.

Neale's notion of the possibility of innovation within genre is reinforced by Caughie who suggests that despite the complications of a mass medium, possibilities of difference can exist in television, and it is in the difference that we find value.[15] *Hill Street Blues'* difference from previous cop shows was highlighted in the network's promotion of the series when it was released[16]: "*Hill Street Blues* is not a run of the mill prime time hit, it is one of those landmark shows that announce the trend for a decade."[17]

The show did maintain the characteristics of the television crime genre outlined above. However, the show's use of film techniques not commonly used in television drama, its "more complex narrative strategies"[18] and its realism, marked out *HSB*'s difference from other crime series. Steve Jenkins notes, "This is police life complete with the warts! The idea of 'believable realism' was constantly picked up and confirmed by newspaper reviews" of the show.[19] This "believable realism" also led to the development of some controversial, violent and/or political storylines that gave the show a darker and more graphic feel overall than what had been found on previous crime television series.

HSB featured an inner city police precinct with thirteen main characters, an unusually large number in a television drama series, particularly in the early 1980s. The storylines featured nearly all of the characters in each episode by using multi-layered narratives, often focusing on more than one plot or case within the episode. Shot in documentary style, using hand held cameras and long shots that were often blocked with other action outside the central plot thread of the episode the audience was presented with a chaotic, realistic vision of the busy police station. This shooting style clearly echoed the "semi documentary authenticity"[20] of the long running police procedural *Dragnet* (1949–70) which Mittel suggests, while largely overlooked, was influential on the style of later police shows. While it is undoubtedly the case that *Dragnet* was a stylistic innovator in the genre, the content, narrative style and characterizations were not considerations in *HSB*.[21] The character driven plots displaced the crime solving conventions of earlier crime dramas and the plots were often left unresolved giving the show a soap opera quality.

Hill Street Blues' hybridization of cop show and soap opera did lead to some generic classification confusion among mainstream audiences and critics.

Initially the subject of criticism, the show's multiple plot threads became the element that highlighted its difference from contemporaries and reinforced its "progressive status."[22] Despite initial resistance from audiences as evidenced in poor ratings,[23] *HSB*'s new narrative forms, filming style and multi character plots became familiar to and accepted by television viewers, allowing genre development that influenced the crime dramas which followed *HSB*.

Like *HSB, Miami Vice* presented audiences with high production values and a cinematic approach. However, rather than the gritty documentary feel of *HSB, Miami Vice* had the appearance of a slickly produced music video, capitalizing on the success of newly launched MTV. The police work of the undercover vice squad was glamorized through the inclusion of trendy fashion and cars, and the use of popular music in the soundtrack. The show conformed to most traditional crime drama generic conventions, and focused largely on the crime solving process, particularly the arrests and questioning of suspects. *Miami Vice's* stylistic differences from other crime dramas did not affect the genre as significantly as *Hill Street Blues* did. However it is a clear predecessor to the *CSI* franchise. Like *MV, CSI* also relies heavily on music to set scenes and advance the plot. In *MV* scenes featuring the lead characters driving, or in a chase sequence, would be set to music with no dialogue; similarly, in *CSI* there are scenes with experiments being carried out set to music with no dialogue.[24]

Television crime series of the 1990s attempted to emulate the success of *Hill Street Blues* by portraying a gritty, realistic version of police life. Both *NYPD: Blue* (1993–2005) and *Homicide: Life on the Street* (1993–99) were long running examples of such series, and were more graphic in terms of sexual and violent content than previous crime dramas, including *Hill Street Blues* and *Miami Vice*. These newer shows reinforced the conventions that their predecessors had introduced. After 2000, television crime series such as *The Wire* (2002–08) and *The Shield* (2002–2008) (and to a lesser extent *The Sopranos* [1999–2007]) took the realism of *HSB* and the graphic nature of *NYPD* and *Homicide* to new levels. A key difference however, is that these shows were broadcast on cable networks which are not bound by the same regulations as their network counterparts and as such could show more graphic scenes. While these shows and others like them forged new boundaries in the genre with explicit content, the procedural elements and familiar generic characteristics remain. Like its contemporaries, *Law & Order* (1990–) largely maintained the generic verisimilitude of earlier crime dramas. However, its focus shifted away from *HSB's, NYPD: Blue* and *Homicide*'s pseudo-documentary style to a more procedural style in a nod to one of the original television police procedurals: *Dragnet*. This was reflected in a narrative structure that divided each episode into two halves, presenting the criminal justice system from policing and crime solving to the courtroom. This structure has not been particularly influential in the genre as a whole. However, the creation of three *L&O* series was significant because it created a brand model for the series and set a precedent for the possibility of spin offs for the Networks which didn't necessarily require the move of one character into a different show as had occurred in the past.[25] This franchising trend was quickly emulated by *CSI: Crime Scene Investigation. CSI* saw its second franchise established only two years after the original series aired, and the third show in the franchise premiered two years after that.

GENERIC DIFFERENCE AND INNOVATION: THE *CSI* FRANCHISE

The preceding discussion has suggested that the generic innovation of *Hill Street Blues, Quincy M.E* and *Miami Vice* were influential in the television crime drama genre. Shows after *HSB* generally reinforced and conformed to the generic conventions set out by their predecessors. The foremost developments in the genre have been in narrative structure, the franchise model of *L&O* and style, especially regarding the importation of a cinematic aesthetic into television. The shows discussed above challenged audiences' expectations with each new approach to the genre, which over the course of twenty years became accepted generic conventions[26] and were then reinforced by new shows that adopted these characteristics.

In 2000 *CSI: Crime Scene Investigation* premiered, presenting viewers with a new crime series, which was both influenced by and distinct from the aforementioned shows.[27] The show's high production values announced its difference from its contemporaries; its style had a high gloss and glamour similar to that of *Miami Vice.*

CSI takes each of the generic conventions outlined here and engages with them through a strict narrative sequence used throughout the three series. The crime is either shown as it is occurring (with the identity of the perpetrator obscured) or through discovery of the aftermath, often by an innocent who has happened upon the scene. The CSI team then arrives to assess the crime. This entire section happens as a prologue, a pre-credit teaser sequence. Likewise the outcome of the crime or resolution of the CSIs' contribution to the criminal justice system is often dealt with in the epilogue. The rest of the episode is focused almost entirely on crime solving, following the processes of the CSIs rather than the police detectives. This was unusual in contemporary crime drama in 2000, with other shows considering several aspects of the justice system. Here we see the influence of *Quincy M.E,* which also concentrated heavily on the crime solving element of the criminal justice system, rather than the style of policing and detective work that audiences had previously been familiar with. However, while Quincy discussed the evidence and its importance to police work, and was shown performing autopsies, the body was never shown in any graphic detail. Likewise any detail of evidence was discussed as Sam or Quincy sat at the microscope but the audience did not see this visualized as they do in *CSI*.

The gathering of clues and examination of evidence provides the basis of most of the *CSI* narrative. The lead characters are shown processing the gathered evidence inside the lab in scenes graphically representing in visual terms each step in the crime solving process: from finding fingerprints at the scene to reconstructing the journey of a bullet as it traveled inside the body of the victim. Integral scenes in each episode consist of lab based experiments accompanied by background music or characters discussing in detail the factors in the crime scene, and explaining their reasoning about the crime to each other and, more importantly, to the audience. These scenes are often accompanied by flashbacks that visually represent how the crime took place or how the evidence supports the CSIs' theories.

In these scenes, the level of detail and graphic realism achieved using special effects is comparable to that commonly featured in big budget Hollywood blockbusters. The use of such effects was unusual in television crime drama when *CSI: Crime Scene Investigation* debuted and, as such, provides another mark of *CSI's* difference from its contemporaries. In the *CSI: Crime Scene Investigation* episode "Spark of Life" (5018), one scene features a burn victim in hospital; the audience is shown a close up of the burns. In a later evidence-gathering scene in the same episode there is a flashback to the victim actually being burned while the lead *CSI* character describes what happened. This is not the type of realism that was seen in *Hill Street Blues*, which depicted the socio-cultural issues of the time and the challenging nature of police work through realistic storylines and documentary style camera work. Realism in *CSI* is portrayed through the graphicness with which the violence in crimes and the injuries sustained are rendered for the audience. In this way the show pushes the boundaries of realism on North American prime time television, just as *Hill Street Blues* did twenty years ago.[28]

CSI: Crime Scene Investigation's success led to the formation of two new shows creating a franchise after only two years: in 2002 *CSI: Miami* debuted, and *CSI: NY* debuted in 2004. These new shows feature new characters and cities, but the content is essentially the same as that found in the original Las Vegas based show. All three shows follow the basic narrative structure outlined above, but with slight differences.

The credits for each show use a different theme song, though the rock group The Who sings them all.[29] As with most television crime dramas, the credit sequence imagery is indicative of the genre's iconography. In all of the series of the *CSI* franchise the credit sequence presents a montage of evidence gathering depictions, close-ups of forensic experiments, and shots that introduce the characters at work. The cast is presented in the order of importance of the characters they play in the show, which introduces their hierarchical positions within the show to the audience. The evidence gathering in the opening credits makes the audience aware of what to expect within the content of the show. The similarity of the title sequences for all three shows and the use of songs by the same band establish the brand and rules of the *CSI* franchise. In all three shows there are also shots of each show's respective city within the opening sequences, to differentiate the shows from each other. There are numerous city shots within each show, as well as in the credit sequences; these are often used between scenes or to frame a particular scene. This reminds the audience of the show's location and often reinforces aspects of the storylines that may concern issues of life in these particular cities.

The narrative space or setting of each show consists of a combination of city and crime lab spaces. In the original *CSI: Crime Scene Investigation*, the lab and the police interview rooms are the locations for the majority of the action, with crime scene locations also featured. The interview rooms are quite dark but the labs have a hi-tech feel with a lot of computer equipment and stainless steel fixtures. There is a similar spatial organization in *CSI: Miami*. However, the police building on this show is often shot from the exterior. This exterior space is often used at significant scene breaks (or during the epilogue), as if by coming outside into the sunshine the work in the crime lab is marked as concluded, giving the relevant character(s), and the audience, a moment to reflect on what has taken place in the episode. This specific use of the outdoor space is unique within the franchise; the other shows do not spend as much time outside and indeed do not use a specific place within the lab or station to anchor the narrative in the same way as *CSI: Miami*. The space featured in season one of *CSI: NY* is quite different again. The police offices are small and busy, with a suggestion of claustrophobia; the crime lab is contained within a large, old building with vaulted ceilings. The morgue in *CSI: NY* has a decidedly gothic atmosphere with dark lighting and the sense of an enclosed basement space, whereas in the other two shows the morgue areas are sterile and modern. This gave the *NY* series a darker feel and tone that some initial viewers did not like. In response, creator Anthony E. Zuiker decided to overhaul the show for the second season and the atmosphere was lightened, this will be discussed later in the chapter.[30]

From its first episode, *CSI: Crime Scene Investigation* has centered on evidence as the most important factor in crime work. This emphasis varies within the franchise and can be seen in the character groupings outlined in table 4.1 below.

While each series features a similar number and set of character types, *CSI: Miami* and *CSI: NY* feature more characters working in a policing and criminalist role rather than in scientist roles. This is particularly noticeable in *CSI: NY* where the main criminalists, Mac and Stella, are ranked as detectives.[31] In *CSI: Crime Scene Investigation* the main character, Dr Gil Grissom, is a scientist working with the police, but his primary concern is always the physical evidence. He will help the police question suspects but is more interested in science than in the morality of the crime. This is a generic distinction characterizing the original *CSI*, as most television crime drama is concerned with the morality of crime and the notion of justice. *CSI* is in many ways a "How Dunnit" rather than a "Who Dunnit." However, in *CSI: Miami* there is more emphasis, especially via the lead CSI, Lieutenant Horatio Caine, on obtaining justice. Horatio is a cop working in forensics and possesses a strong sense of moral justice; he is keen to protect the innocent and often promises victims positive results as though cases are his personal quests. *CSI: NY* finds a middle ground between the two earlier series. Detective Mac Taylor is a cop working in forensics; like Gil he considers the evidence vital in solving each case, while exhibiting less of a sense of personalized justice than Horatio.

These characterizations are typical of the television crime genre, historically featuring a maverick "lone" protector working outside the system such

Table 4.1. *CSI: Crime Scene Investigation* Character Groupings

	CSI	CSI: Miami	CSI: NY

CRIME SCENE INVESTIGATOR	Dr. Gil Grissom
	Catherine Willows
	Warrick Brown
	Nick Stokes
	Sara Sidle
		Lt. Horatio Caine
		Calleigh Duquesne
		Eric Delko
		Tim Speedle/
		  Ryan Wolfe
		Det. Yelena Salas
		(left in Season 4)
			Det. Mac Taylor
			Det. Stella Bonasera
			Danny Messer
			Aiden Burn/
			  Lindsay Monroe

POLICE
LAB TECHNICIANS
	Captain Jim Brass
	Greg Sanders (CSI
	  in season 5)/
	  various
		Det. Frank Trip
		Various/ Natalia
		  Boa Vista (CSI in
		  season 5)
			Det. Don Flack
			various

MEDICAL EXAMINER	Dr. Albert Robbins	Dr. Alexx Woods	Dr. Sheldon Hawks

as "Kojak" or the lead characters in *Starsky and Hutch* (1975–79), as the moral center of the show such as *Dragnet's* Joe Friday or *Hill Street Blues'* Captain Frank Furillo, or more recently as the anti-hero exemplified by *The Sopranos'* Tony Soprano, *The Shield's* Vic Mackey and the titular lead of *Dexter* (2006–). Both Horatio and Mac are also representative of the socio-political climate of the U.S. with Horatio the avenger and protector, and Mac the patriot and ex-marine. Like most film and television genres, the crime series reflect the anxieties of the viewing public and, in the case of the two *CSI* franchise shows, post 9/11 society is writ large on these lead characters. Each show has a distinct style and approach to the relationship between forensic science and more traditional police work, providing the audience with a different experience within the familiarity of the franchise rules.

The narrative sequence in the original *CSI* outlined earlier is present in the other two series and reinforces the rules of the franchise brand. Comparing two examples from *CSI: Miami* and *CSI: NY* demonstrates the conformity. In the *CSI: Miami* episode "Freaks and Tweaks" (1023). Lieutenant Horatio Caine, and his two younger colleagues, Tim "Speed" Speedle and Eric Delko, stand in the lab discussing the evidence spread out on the table before them, trying to find out what triggered a warehouse explosion. As Horatio describes the evidence the audience is shown a flashback of the explosion as well as short visual representations of what he is describing, in this case, an electrical charge passing through a wire. Once the team develops a theory as to what was used as a detonation device they have to prove it by testing the theory. In the next scene we see Horatio testing the charge through a piece of wire. These lab scenes are accompanied by hip music and advance the narrative. When the music stops Horatio has solved this element of the case and has essentially caught the guilty party. In the *CSI: NY* episode "The Fall" (1017), the same type of scene occurs. CSIs Aiden and Danny are analyzing evidence separately but are shown through simultaneous inter-cuts. Just as in the *CSI: Miami* example, this scene features a musical accompaniment and numerous close shots of experiments being carried out. These examples are typical throughout both series and demonstrate their conformity to the narrative structure established in *CSI: Crime Scene Investigation*.

The *CSI* shows conform to some of the generic characteristics outlined earlier, and thus are recognizable to the audience as television crime dramas. The generic difference seen throughout the franchise can be summarized thus: (i) The use of special effects, including extreme detail and realism; (ii) the narrative space, the focus on the crime lab; (iii) Narrative structure, focus on forensic processes—'How Dunnit'; and (iv) the use of music and descriptive visuals. These generic differences, and the resulting brand experience for the series' audiences, have created a generic verisimilitude for the franchise separate from that of the television crime drama genre.

Within the verisimilitude of the franchise brand there are also distinct characteristics that distinguish the shows from each other. These are seen in the opening sequences, the opening music and the differences among each show's set of character types, particularly with regard to the lead characters' relationships to science and justice. The thematic differences displayed through the attitudes of the lead characters seem to reinforce the difference in tone set by the colors and narrative space as described above. The case of *CSI: NY* is unusual as the show changed significantly between the first and second seasons. The second and subsequent seasons were visually lighter than the first year. The character of Mac was introduced as a grieving widower who had lost his wife in 9/11 and while he fought to uphold the law he knew that the evidence was crucial and accepted the occasional lack of resolution. He and his team were shown to struggle with moral issues, perhaps to reflect the grey areas of New York City living, as opposed to the bright sunshine of Miami. In the episode "Grand Murder at Central Station" (2002), CSI Aiden was depicted as having tampered with evidence in order to secure a conviction; however, we later found out that after she did not tamper with the evidence and resolved the issue by quitting her position. The character left the show and was replaced by a younger, more optimistic character. The season continued with bright outdoor daytime scenes and plots featuring models and other glamorous aspects of New York life as opposed to the darker street life exemplified in season one. Mac Taylor's character was also softened; he was seen playing in a band during his time off and even dating. The changes in *CSI: NY* have left the show less dark than it had been previously but still different from the other two shows in the franchise.

The limits to the *CSI* franchise's generic innovation are evident in the producers' response to viewer criticism of *CSI: NY* by lightening up the atmosphere and character relationships on the show. These limits support Neale's notion that audience acceptance is important to generic development. Perhaps innovation and genre progression has to be a gradual process in commercial television seeking a broad audience (and advertisers). The brand's success and longevity seems to rely on the audience engaging with, and accepting, the rules of the franchise.

Due to the sophistication of *CSI*'s special effects, innovative narrative space and the feature film credentials of many of the franchise's creative teams, the notion of "quality" that was applied to *Hill Street Blues* can also be applied to the *CSI* franchise. The huge success of the *CSI* franchise has also allowed Jerry Bruckheimer to create a quality brand that, like the productions of MTM, sets a standard in the industry and the genre.

CONCLUSION: THE *CSI* FRANCHISE
AND GENERIC INNOVATION

This essay began with an outline of the generic characteristics found in television crime drama. The brief examination of genre-innovative shows—*Quincy M.E.*, *Hill Street Blues*, *Miami Vice*, and to a lesser extent *Law & Order*—as well as shows such as *NYPD Blue*, *Homicide*, *The Wire* and *The Shield*, that reinforced their generic innovations, illustrates the genre's development. These shows' innovation in theme, style and narrative within the repetitiveness of television altered the generic verisimilitude of crime drama, and with it audiences' systems of expectation (Born 1993). By analyzing the *CSI* franchise and the differences that mark it out from other contemporary crime series I have tried to establish that *CSI*'s innovation has both contributed to the generic development of crime drama and created a brand with its own generic verisimilitude.

My earlier discussion suggested that prior to *CSI: Crime Scene Investigation's* debut in 2000, television crime drama essentially reinforced the generic conventions set by *Hill Street Blues* and its predecessors. With the exception of *Law & Order's* brand creation there was little to suggest any development within the genre, other than more explicit scenes enabled by the cable channels, which have become home to many new crime series. Cable television has provided a home for the return of the hero outside of the system, or in post *CSI* series, the anti-hero. These shows, such as *The Shield* and *Dexter*, have been heralded as "ground-breaking" due to their graphic visual styles and grittiness (and protagonist as anti-hero); however in generic terms they reinforce the contribution to graphic style of *CSI* and the aforementioned realism of *Hill Street Blues* as well as the characterizations of a long history of crime series.

CSI's contribution to the generic development of television crime drama is already evident in new hybrid crime series that have been introduced since the original show's debut in 2000. A number of these have featured forensics as the key components of the series' narrative and structure, such as the Bruckheimer-produced *Cold Case* (2003–) and *Bones* (2005–). These post-*CSI* forensic-centered shows demonstrate the success of *CSI*, but also the progression of the generic conventions demonstrated by audiences' acceptance of a degree of generic innovation. The level of detail and sophistication of the effects used in the *CSI* franchise have also had a wider influence outside the genre and are now seen in other drama series, such as the medical drama *House* (2004–) and the filmic effects of drama series *Lost* (2004–). All three shows in the *CSI* franchise remain successful with audiences and advertisers at the time of writing. Despite the initial audience resistance that was reflected in the production changes to *CSI: NY*, the franchise's innovations continue to impact on the generic development of television crime drama.

NOTES

1. Steve Neale, *Genre and Hollywood* (London: Routledge, 2000), 56.
2. Neale, *Genre and Hollywood,* 56.
3. Georgina Born, "Against Negation, for a politics of cultural production: Adorno, aesthetics, the social." *Screen* 34 no. 3 (1993): 223–42.
4. Jane Feuer, Paul Kerr, and Tish Vahimagi, eds., *MTM 'Quality Television.'* (London: BFI Books, 1984)
5. Steve Neale, 'Questions of Genre.' *Screen*, Volume 31 no. 1 (1990): 45–66.
6. Neale, "Questions," 46.
7. Neale, *Genre and Hollywood.*
8. Neale, "Questions," 57.
9. Steve Neale, "Studying Genre, Genre and Television" in *The Television Genre Book*, ed. Glen Creeber (London: BFI Books 2001), 2–4.
10. Lez Cooke, "The Police Series" in *Television Genre*, 19.
11. Jeremy G Butler, "Police Programs" *The Encyclopedia of Television,* <http://www.museum.tv/archives/etv/P/htmlP/policeprogra/policeprogra.htm> (Jan. 2004).
12. Another series that was significant in the development of the genre was *Cagney & Lacey* (1982–87). The show featured two female detectives as the lead protagonists in a male dominated police world. The show had a great impact leading to more shows with strong female characters, if not leads. There is not enough space in this essay to consider the show further, and it does not directly relate to *CSI*.
13. Jane Feuer, "The MTM Style" in *MTM 'Quality Television'* eds. Jane Feuer, Paul Kerr, and Tish Vahimagi (London: BFI Books 1984), 32.
14. Jerry Bruckheimer is well known for producing blockbuster feature films and has created a successful television production company, which at January 2006 had 6 shows on the air.
15. John Caughie, "Adorno's reproach: repetition, difference and television genre," *Screen* 32 no. 2 (1991): 133.
16. Paul Kerr, "Drama at MTM: Lou Grant and Hill Street Blues," in *MTM 'Quality Television,'* 133.
17. Michael Pollan in Jane Feuer "The MTM Style" in *MTM 'Quality Television,'* 26
18. Steve Jenkins, "Hill Street Blues" in *MTM 'Quality Television,'* 183.
19. Jenkins, "Hill Street Blues," 185.
20. Jason Mittel, *Genre and Television* (London: Routledge, 2004), 145.
21. Mittel describes the peculiar narrative style of the first person narrator and the lack of character development or personal interaction in his chapter on "Policing Genres—Dragnet's Texts and Generic Contexts. The show has clearly been influ-

ential in the genre in later years but was not explicitly, or quickly, emulated in the creation of a new generic cycle to the extent that *HSB* was.

22. Jenkins, "Hill Street," 186.

23. Jenkins, "Hill Street," 186.

24. See Chapter 10 by Lawrence Kramer, "Forensic Music: Channeling the Dead on Post-9/11 TV."

25. The spin off shows were as follows: *Law & Order: Special Victims Unit* (1999–present), *Law & Order: Criminal Intent* (2000–present) and a third *Law & Order: Trial by Jury*, that was cancelled during its first season. The shows have a similar narrative and often feature cross-over episodes, though the themes and content are very different across the franchise.

26. Neale, *Genre and Hollywood*, 212.

27. I refer to the original series by its full title to differentiate from the other two series in the franchise. *CSI* is used to refer to the whole franchise.

28. The gore shown in the *CSI* franchise has perhaps also become more acceptable to mainstream audiences through an influx in surgery based reality shows, as well as the continuing success of hospital dramas such as *ER* (1994–).

29. See Kramer, "Forensic Music."

30. Creator Anthony E. Zuiker was interviewed between the first and second season in 'Jam Showbiz' and said viewers were turned off by the 'dark, underground feel' <http://jam.canoe.ca/Television/TV_Shows/C/CSI_NY/2005/06/14/1087223.html> (26 July 2007).

31. The official CBS website lists characters of each show, in the original and Miami the CSI's are listed by name only but in NY the leads are listed as 'Detective Mac Taylor and Detective Stella Bonasera' <http://www.cbs.com/primetime/csi_ny/> (26 July 2007).

Part II

BODIES OF EVIDENCE

Chapter Five

Corpses, Spectacle, Illusion: The Body as *Abject* and *Object* in *CSI*

Basil Glynn and Jeongmee Kim

In the *CSI: Crime Scene Investigation* (*CSI*) episode "Sex, Lies and Larvae" (1010), a muscid fly is plucked from the leg of a murdered woman during an autopsy. The fly is found in urban areas yet the body has been discovered in the mountains. How can this be?

In *CSI* the close examination of bodies raises many difficult and puzzling questions such as this, the answers to which usually bring a killer to justice. The questions the program poses explicitly are ones of logic: how did a fly get there, in what particular way did a woman die up in the mountains? Yet certain more ethical questions are seldom dwelt upon in the program, such as whether *CSI* agents have the right to strip, handle, prod, probe and disfigure bodies in order to find their clues. In the world of the fictional series, experimentation, dissection and scrutiny of bodies is presented as an unproblematic and essential aspect of crime solving. Few characters in the show question the ethics of such practices—not the *CSI* team, the police or the relatives of the victims. Perhaps most notably, the audience does not seem to take offense at the graphic destruction of the human body week after week.

As Mike Clarke points out, different crime fictions make "very different 'contracts' with their audiences." Each one "has to work hard to establish its particular character for audiences; once this is achieved, the expectations created have to be fulfilled."[1] In the case of *CSI* we have come to expect a body horror extravaganza and in most episodes we get one. Yet through a series of stylistic and aesthetic strategies such grisly images are not as disturbing as perhaps they should be. *CSI* has managed to make extreme imagery palatable to a mainstream audience rather than just a niche horror fan audience. This chapter will suggest that the program has achieved this by undercutting the violent imagery it displays by advertising its artificiality so that audiences recognize and are constantly reminded of the fictional nature of what they are watching.

What we are watching in *CSI* are medical procedures conducted on the dead in order to ensure the well being of the state (in this case, Nevada), without the prior consent of the deceased or the permission of next of kin. The requirements of the state take precedence over the sanctity of the body. Sophocles' *Antigone* debated whether such a social contract was acceptable over 2000 years ago, when the eponymous heroine objected to the dead body of her brother, Polyneices, remaining unburied in order to serve as a warning to those who refused to comply with the laws of the state. The gods cursed the state (in this case, Thebes) as a result of this sacrilege.

A mere 175 years ago the state again stepped in to decide that the needs of society outweighed the rights of the deceased individual with the introduction of The Anatomy Act in Britain (1832), which resulted in significant social panic. For years before this act, medical experimentation for research purposes had been conducted only on a specially selected sector of society. As medical historian Ruth Richardson explains in *Death, Dissection and the Destitute*, only the dead bodies of hanged murderers were subjects for medical dissection. This practice was viewed as "a *post-mortem* punishment," an additional deterrent to murder.[2] Due to the demand for bodies for medical research, however, a change in the law in 1832 "recommended that instead of giving hanged murderers, the government should confiscate the bodies of paupers dying in workhouses and hospitals, too poor to pay for their own funerals. What had for generations been a feared and hated punishment for murder became one for poverty."[3]

The Anatomy Act created a situation whereby a large proportion of the population could picture themselves unwillingly sliced open upon the anatomist's table. Ordinary working class people suddenly faced the prospect of being experimental cadavers should they face any financial misfortune before death. As Joyce Tyldesley explains, in Britain "saving for a decent funeral—and thereby avoiding dissection—became a working class obsession, one which has continued almost to the present day."[4] The Anatomy Act provides an interesting historical example of the anxiety that the prospect of involuntary post-mortem investigation can create. In many respects *CSI* might present a chilling modern parallel to historical post-mortem and one could imagine it arousing many of the same emotions with its depictions of human dissection. Bypassing the class boundaries that once regulated dissection, the members of any socio-economic group, irrespective of their wishes, are depicted in the show as potential fodder for the examiner's knife. Rather than murderers, they are now the victims of post-mortem, who can be cut up or dismembered in the name of the greater good. In *CSI* we are, one might argue, looking at bodies on a weekly basis that could belong to any one of us. Yet rather than wishing for the wrath of the gods to descend on the CSIs for desecrating the body as Sophocles may have deemed fit, or turning away in fear that we could be the next potential victims of the contemporary version of the Anatomy Act, we tune in week after week to watch the body butchered. So many of us in fact appear to enjoy this spectacle that the *CSI* franchise has achieved remarkable popularity around the world.

Dystopian fiction author J.G. Ballard, in a feature on *CSI* in *The Guardian*, identifies the program's dead bodies as the answer to its popular appeal. Not unlike those who dreaded the Anatomy Act, he suggests that the program's impact lies in the cold fact that it forces us to face what will one day become of us, that we are deeply affected by the corpses we witness on *CSI*. Ballard asserts that we face our own mortality and see ourselves on the mortician's table through the show's images: "I suspect that the cadavers waiting their turn on the tables are surrogates for ourselves, the viewers. The real crime the C.S.I. team is investigating, weighing every tear, every drop of blood, every smear of semen, is the crime of being alive. I fear that we watch, entranced, because we feel an almost holy pity for ourselves and the oblivion patiently waiting for us."[5]

Ballard's bleak viewpoint of the body that has fallen beyond the limit of life as we know it is a familiar one. Numerous writers have informed us that the corpse is a reminder of the final condition awaiting all of us and Ballard's hypothesis is particularly in tune with cultural theories on the corpse and our reaction to it. Julia Kristeva, in *Powers of Horror: An Essay on Abjection*, describes how her physical processes remind her that her body is both keeping death away and at the same time moving towards it. Her body reminds her of her mortality by continually leaking the fluids that Ballard referred to above: "Such wastes drop so that I might live, until, from loss to loss, nothing remains in me and my entire body falls beyond the limit—*cadere* [to fall], cadaver."[6]

Kristeva contends that "the corpse represents fundamental pollution. A body without a soul," and is therefore *abject*.[7] For Kristeva, our identity has boundaries. In order for there to be an "I," there is that which is defined in opposition to "I": the abject. She asserts; "Refuse and corpses show me what I permanently thrust aside in order to live."[8] What repulses us sets our boundaries, making us shrink into ourselves, and helping to create the "I." When the body that was alive becomes a corpse, non-life, this "most sickening of wastes" encroaches upon everything so that ultimately "It is no longer I who expel, 'I' is expelled."[9] Anthropologist Mary Douglas, in *Purity and Danger: An Analysis of the Concepts of Pollution and Taboo*, adopts a similar stance by relating the corpse to the notion of abomination because it reminds us that we are inextricably stranded in a material world in which death is certain.[10] Like bodily wastes such as excrement, vomit and menstrual blood, the corpse reveals the body to be organic and therefore passing away. The dead body is the moment when the body ceases to be human. Film theorist Jonathan Lake Crane, in his history of the horror genre, correspondingly asserts that "the most menacing piece of waste, far more threatening than any mere bodily excretion, is the corpse. A dead body has nothing to do with what is really human."[11]

Given such examples of western cultural thinking on the corpse and its effects upon the living, it is not difficult to see where Ballard is coming from with regard to *CSI*. *CSI* deliberately flaunts its corpses in various stages of decomposition or mutilation in virtually every episode. It repeatedly foregrounds human bodies lying dismembered, sliced and experimented upon by dispassionate scientists. Yet the question is, do the spectacularly gruesome corpses displayed in *CSI* really have the profound effect upon us proposed by Ballard, or the repulsion suggested by Kristeva, Douglas or Crane? Or is literary theorist and novelist Patricia Duncker's reply to Ballard's *Guardian* comments more useful in understanding the effects that *CSI* has upon us:

> Are we really all sitting there shivering with pity at the corpses in the autopsy room and contemplating the void that awaits us? I don't think so. I for one have laid my brains to rest for the day by the time it comes on. I'm there to enjoy the slick dialogue, the non-naturalistic methods of narration, to marvel at the new technology, ogle the very sexy cast, and then fall asleep reassured that reason and science are in charge, the crime scene yields its secrets and the truth will out.[12]

In contrast to Ballard, Duncker here suggests a far less metaphysical appeal to the show. The viewer is fully aware that s/he is watching a fiction. Although she claims to lay her brains to rest for the day before approaching *CSI*, Duncker's comments on her viewing suggest her appreciation of the skill with which the program is manufactured for her. Perhaps most interestingly, the corpses and the gore do not even feature in her evaluation. They do not get in the way of (or apparently feature in) her enjoyment of the program at all.

It is actually unsurprising. Duncker emphasizes the program's clever construction because *CSI* consistently illustrates its own inauthenticity. We marvel "at the new technology" of the program, in part, because of the skill with which it illustrates the workings of the human body through CGI effects and high-tech lab equipment. *CSI* invites us to look at the mapping of the human body in the same dispassionate way that we would read an anatomical text or model. Further, by adopting an almost metafictional approach, the program makes its destroyed bodies more bearable to the viewer. In literature metafictional stories, such as John Barth's *Lost in the Funhouse* and William H. Gass's *Willie Master's Lonesome Wife*, self-consciously draw attention to the mechanics of narrative construction through which their fictions are conveyed. They constantly remind the reader that they are reading works of fiction. Similarly, it is not just the *CSI* companion books and DVD special features that reveal the show's secrets but also the TV series itself, which consistently draws attention to its own fakery and reminds us all not to worry—the gore and violence are all only fabrications. The corpses are actors, models or body casts, the severed limbs are prosthetics, the wounds are latex and make-up, and the blood is fake.

The counterfeit character of the gore on display is made clear as early as the opening credits where a head is split open with a golf club: but wait a minute, it is only a dummy head. The credits set the tone for how we are invited to watch the spectacle of bodies on *CSI*. In many episodes we watch members of the *CSI* team create moulds and casts of victims' body parts, thereby mimicking what the show's special effects team does to create model corpses of the show's victims in the first place. In "Compulsion" (5017), for example, a model of the victim is doused in fake blood from a squeeze bottle and beaten repeatedly on the head by various members of the team to check a blood spatter pattern. In "Grave Danger" (5024) Grissom shoots two dummies tied together through their heads to determine that one bullet killed two victims. In "Who Are You?" (1006) a face is constructed from a skull through model-work and sculpturing. The program itself, by foregrounding how bodies and their parts and fluids are artificially recreated, reassures the audience that what it is watching is a series of effects. The body is represented as an object, rather than an *abject* thing.

CSI also encourages us to distrust or dismiss what it shows us through narrative. In numerous episodes the same brutal murder is shown to us again and again in a variety of ways as the team contemplate how a particular victim was killed. In "Anonymous" (1008), for example, Nick and Warwick both have their distinct opinion (and actually make a bet) on how a car crash occurred. Both scenarios are shown and neither turns out to be what actually happened. If we watch the show regularly, we know from the show's format that the first portrayal of a murder will generally be inaccurate. We are allowed to enjoy the initial version of the killing as sheer spectacle because we are sure it will later be revealed that this is not exactly how the victim died at all. Divorced from narrative factuality, the special effects and double-fictionalized creation of an event that never was serves as a distancing device that moderates our reaction to the bloodshed on display.

Indeed, *CSI* constantly distances us from the events we are witnessing as viewers. It does not pretend to offer depictions of realistic forms of brutal murder and its consequences. Instead it presents overtly implausible, often mildly comic crime scenarios: a dead scuba diver on top of a tree ("Scuba

Doobie Do" 2005), a victim found drowned in the middle of the desert ("Anatomy of a Lye" 2021), a corpse disguised as an alien ("Viva Las Vegas" 5001) or as a raccoon ("Fur and Loathing" 4006). The killers themselves are often equally bizarre, as in the cases of a murderous stage magician ("Abra Cadaver" 3005), special effects artist ("Pilot" 1001 and "Identity Crisis" 2013), Sherlock Holmes recreationist ("Who Shot Sherlock?" 5011), and cannibal nutritionist ("Justice Is Served" 1021).

As weird and wonderful as any of the killers or victims are in the series, they are surpassed by the *CSI* team itself, whose characters are rendered through personal idiosyncrasies, horror movie clichés about mad scientists like Dr Frankenstein, and cultural stereotypes about people who work closely with the dead. *CSI* offers us far more than professionals simply going about their jobs. The glee with which "Gruesome Grissom" performs his experiments and the casual manner in which medical examiner Robbins carves open bodies and pulls apart ribcages reach comic proportions, recalling images of Frankenstein up to his elbows in gore in films like Hammer Studios' *The Curse of Frankenstein* (1957) or Andy Warhol's *Flesh for Frankenstein* (1973). The dispassionate perspective the *CSI* team members have towards the dead body give him or her a peculiar and outsider status, further emphasized by the series adhering to conventional preconceptions that those who make their living from the dead are not like the rest of us. They are instead somehow strange and separate from the world that we inhabit. Rather than being prey to the broader cultural anxieties surrounding mortality that Ballard proposes we as viewers have, the *CSI* team members most often appear immune to them and invite us to share their attitude.

The CSIs' almost un-human attitude towards and treatment of the human body should, one could argue, be extremely difficult for the viewer to identify with. However, such familiarity with the dead is what we have become accustomed to from the death worker as represented in popular culture and such portrayals, to varying degrees, have long been par for the course on television. In a wide range of network, cable, and public television series we have watched forensic pathologists, medical examiners, coroners and morticians go about their lives.[13] They all suffer trials and tribulations in the pursuit of their careers, but are generally undisturbed by the nature of their work and the proximity to the dead that it entails. Bodies launch investigations and personal journeys and problems arise in the course of these ventures, but examining the bodies themselves in all their varying states of injury and mutilation are taken in each character's professional stride. Indeed, this strangely ambivalent attitude towards the dead is one of the main reasons that such characters interest us so much and make such regular subjects for television drama.

Horror novelist Stephen King suggests that we are fascinated with death workers and view them with wonderment and curiosity because of their occupational presence in a taboo world that most of us will never see while we are alive: "Morticians are modern priests, working their arcane magic of cosmetics and preservation in rooms that are clearly marked 'off limits.' Who washes the corpse's hair? Are the fingernails and toenails of the dear departed clipped one final time? Is it true that the dead are encoffined *sans* shoes? Who dresses them for their final star turn in the mortuary viewing room? How is a bullet hole plugged and concealed? How are strangulation bruises hidden?"[14] Since as long ago as ancient Egypt, people have been fascinated by those who take charge of dealing with the dead in that veiled interval between death and burial. Just like today, in ancient Egypt the deceased were removed from the presence of friends and relatives: embalmers practiced their art in ritual secrecy, resulting in a mystique surrounding them. Bodies were made to look lifelike through highly guarded techniques passed on through generations, such as the application of special make-up, use of artificial eyes and stuffing the cheeks with linen pads. As a result of proximity to death, the mortician was seen as a mysterious, almost sinister figure. The ancient Papyrus Sallier III (in the British Museum) informs us that "the embalmer's fingers are evil-smelling, for their odor is that of corpses."[15] It was even suggested that embalmers/morticians were unnaturally drawn to the bodies they treated. The ancient Greek historian Herodotus reported that such was the fear of necrophilia that "the wives of important men, when they die, are not handed over to be embalmed at once, nor women who are especially beautiful or famous. . . . They do this to prevent the embalmers violating the corpse."[16]

Perhaps we have come full circle. Today we can once again only imagine, as Stephen King notes, what occurs behind closed doors. Films such as *Kissed* (dir. Lynne Stopkewich, 1996) and *Nightwatch* (dir. Ole Bornedal, 1997) suggest a contemporary unease that the dead are still not entirely safe from sexual assault by those charged with caring for them. As in ancient Egypt, the dead are commonly dealt with in a segregated manner, this time in the West, making quarters and procedures for the dead once again ripe for speculation and morbid curiosity. Television theorist Mandy Merck, in her survey of Gothic motifs in *Six Feet Under*, asserts that death has become "America's best-kept secret" since the commodified management of death by the modern funeral business has taken the treatment of the deceased out of the hands of family members.[17]

CSI takes us through the doors, showing us the hidden rooms where the dead are stored and studied in a modern high-tech world full of amazing and strange devices. Yet in many ways the characters that populate these rooms still embody the age-old preconception that if they spend their lives in the company of the dead they must be different from the rest of us. Just like the Egyptian embalmer, in "Bully for You" (2004) Sara Sidle is told she has a "smell like the dead" after the odor of a decomposed corpse has clung to her (a fact that brings a premature end to a romantic rendezvous with a minor character in the scene). Grissom identifies human bones by tasting them ("To Halve and to Hold" 1014) and keeps blood for experiments in the communal work fridge ("Burden of Proof" 2015). Robbins eats his lunch and has a coffee machine in his autopsy room ("Table Stakes" 1015). Such depictions of being so at home with the dead not so subtly suggest that the program's main characters enjoy an unnatural closeness or even intimacy with the dead. In *CSI: Miami* as well, the medical examiner Alexx Woods regularly talks to the dead. Her *CSI: NY* counterpart Sheldon Hawkes emerges in one episode from a morgue drawer where the dead are stored: he even has a bed to sleep among them ("Recycling" 1012).

The CSIs have grown accustomed to the dead as a commonplace presence in the workplace. To remain objective, they have learnt to objectify the body and to view it scientifically as a receptacle of information. The evidence that the body contains points the way to "the truth" and the quest for this truth and the dehumanization of the body required to find it results in the CSIs often being cut off from ordinary living people not involved in their line of work. They have become so comfortable with the dead at a cost to their personal relationships, to the point that their lives among the dead often take precedence over their lives among the living. Grissom, for example, is most comfortable in aspects of his professional (and personal) life that do not involve live people. In "Chaos Theory" (2002) he states "I'll take prints over people any day." In "Butterflied" (4012) he explains that the only time people like him "ever touch other people is when we're wearing our latex gloves." This alienation of the CSIs is compounded by the fact that we see very little of their home lives, relatives or relationships outside of work. We see them almost exclusively where they are most at home, with the dead and, perhaps secondarily, with each other.

As television theorist Geoff Hurd states, in crime dramas it is the law enforcers that we usually come to know intimately: "It is only policemen who have 'characters.'" Criminals, he points out, are normally "represented by a cycle of cameo actors in opposition to the stability of recurrent police stars."[18] Mike Clarke additionally notes that it is the heroes that we see "'off-duty,'" while villains only ever appear in order to advance the narrative."[19] In *CSI* members of the team such as Sara and Nick are rarely seen off duty and we certainly do not know characters like Grissom intimately. Only the briefest glimpses are given into the private lives of the CSIs and even when we are given limited access, such as when we are introduced to Nick's parents and Catherine's father, it is usually in the context of work. Nick's parents appear when he is buried alive (the trauma of which prompts Warrick to marry, a fact he admits in "Bodies in Motion" 6001) whilst Catherine's relationship with her father is so defined by her job that she only discovers she is his daughter through her work as a CSI ("Inside the Box" 3023). Her ex-husband also eventually becomes a case to be investigated ("Lady Heather's Box" 3015).

Familiar cultural stereotypes of law enforcement officials and death workers are crucial to but complicated in the presentation of the central characters in *CSI*. Clarke suggests that crime series usually "conform to some social or cultural notions of what the police are like and how they behave."[20] This can only be extended to a limited degree to include the central characters of *CSI* because the program deliberately blurs the lines between police, CSIs, medical examiners and scientific specialists. This indistinctiveness enables Grissom and his team to display the required medical clinical detachment or police-like dogged determination to find the killer required by the demands of a particular episode or scene. Making their roles ill defined makes slightly less implausible the team's often remarkable understanding of subjects as diverse as architecture (Catherine in "$35K O.B.O" 1018), birds (Nick in "The Finger" 2014) and the occult (Greg in "Spellbound" 6019). This variety of encyclopaedic knowledge is further enhanced by useful nuggets of information provided from the seemingly endless array of jobs that the main characters undertook before becoming CSIs. Warrick, for example, knows about the intricacies of the numbers racket because he worked as a runner in college ("Fahrenheit 932" 1012). The characters display a variety of expertise that prevent their work-bound personas from becoming stale, whilst allowing diversity in the format and adhering to the expectations we might have of the characters as (interchangeably) police workers, medical examiners, crime scene investigators or lab-bound forensic scientists. Thus we are prepared to accept Grissom as obsessed with solving an infanticide in "Gentle, Gentle" (1019), as a cop warning Catherine against any emotional involvement with a victim in "Pledging Mr Johnson" (1004), as a scientist who interviews suspects like an interrogator in "Who Are You?" (1006), as a negotiator with a suitcase full of money to exchange for a hostage in "Grave Danger" (5024), and as a helicopter pilot in "Crate 'N Burial" (1003). He displays diverse jobs skills whether in the lab, the morgue, the crime scene, court, shooting range, etcetera. The knowledge and skills of the CSIs are so assorted and extraordinary that they frequently appear tailor made to the demands of each particular crime scene. The CSIs just happen to have the specialist knowledge required to crack a particular case, revealing the constructed-ness of the show and further enhancing its fantasy aspect.

The personal information we are given about the CSIs does not bring us closer to knowing them as people, just to understanding how they relate and are suited to their jobs. In Season 3 Grissom struggles with a hearing problem. Rather than seeing how this impacts upon his everyday life we see how it impacts upon his job, interfering with his ability to interrogate suspects and communicate with colleagues. His affliction additionally signifies his isolation and insularity as a man, as audibly disconnected from the world as his career has made him personally. He is also inaccessible to us, the program self-consciously playing with its practice of rationing personal information about him by having him relate a personal story about his relationship with his deaf mother in sign language to Dr Gilbert ("Sounds of Silence" 1020).

Like Grissom, each of the main characters in *CSI* is cut off from the world in which they live as a result of their job. On the one hand, they are all in many ways quintessentially Vegas people: Grissom paid his way through college as a poker player ("Revenge Is Best Served Cold" 3001), Warrick has a gambling addiction, Catherine is a former exotic dancer, Sara has an alcohol problem and Nick is a womanizer whose longest on-screen relationship is with the sex worker Kristy Hopkins ("Pilot," "1-15 Murders" 1011, "Boom" 1013). Yet on the other hand their job excludes them from truly fitting in with life in the city. Grissom, consumed by work, acknowledges that he is not good with people ("Face Lift" 1017) and that he is not used to having visitors to his house ("Strip Strangler" 1023). Sara, lonely to the point of alcoholism and an insomniac ("Blood Drops" 1007), spends much of her free time reading forensic books and listening to the police scanner ("Too Tough to Die" 1016). Little wonder perhaps that—as the two most isolated, work-obsessed characters—Grissom and Sara have had the longest running romantic frisson in the series. The job has made all of the CSIs outsiders, different, as we imagine anybody who does what they do must be. In order to be clinically detached enough to do their jobs, their ability to interact with people outside of their professional sphere has been compromised.

Richardson argues that historically clinical detachment represented "a defensive barrier" that enabled those who had to surgically cut or dissect human flesh to execute tasks, "which would, in normal circumstances, be taboo or emotionally repugnant. The term 'clinical detachment' carries with it both the positive connotation of objectivity, and the negative one of emotionlessness."[21] In the televisual world of *CSI* emotional detachment is taken beyond ordinary professionalism. It not only induces social alienation in the private lives of the CSIs but also at times a scientific inhumanity in their professional ones. On the whole they are not haunted but stimulated by the strange and puzzling injuries that have been done to the corpses they examine. In "Jackpot" (4007), for example, an off-duty Grissom rushes excitedly back to work when he hears somebody has found a head. On the whole, the CSIs display few feelings of curiosity about the lives of the dead under investigation unless the circumstances are deeply personally connected to them or truly exceptional (such as when a corpse reminds Grissom of Sara in "Butterflied," 4012). Just as the personal lives of the CSIs are kept to a minimum, so too are the lives of the victims of murder: their story begins at their end and is pieced together retrospectively and only forensically by the CSIs. Their bodies are presented in close detail, but not so their personal stories unless this pertains to the physical evidence of the case. Without any biographical exegesis the dead bodies are little more than props that carry clues, a view the presentational style of the series actively encourages us to take.

In his discussion of realism in televisual crime fictions, Richard Sparks argues that "the realist text both conceals its own work of representation and, in so doing, conceals from the 'viewing subject' the way in which s/he is thereby situated and addressed."[22] *CSI* does not attempt to present a realist text in this manner. It does not try, as Noël Carroll suggests realist film typically does, to give "the illusion of reality narrating itself."[23] *CSI* does not seek to "conceal" its fictional world. Its gory model work, intrusive computer graphics and special effects instead reveal its textual boundaries and the constructed-ness of its representations. We get impossible or spectacular views of bullets traveling through the body, knives penetrating organs, a spinal chord snapping and a heart exploding in "Bully for You" (2004), of the CSIs themselves from inside an ice-storage tank in "Assume Nothing" (4001) and of Nick buried alive from beneath his coffin in "Grave Danger" (5024). Such representations do not conform to what we have come to associate with realism in the TV crime drama.

Particularly with the development and popularity of reality crime programs such as *Crime Watch UK* (BBC, 1984–present) and *America's Most Wanted* (Fox, 1988–present), the realism of crime dramas has come to be associated with a certain style. Anita Biressi and Heather Nunn explain how in such reality crime television "the aesthetics of realism (badly framed images, poorly lit shots, images caught against bright light) underpin and authenticate the immediate realism and documentary posture of the footage."[24] We can find these strategies deployed in the construction of realism in crime dramas such as *NYPD Blue* (ABC, 1993–2005) and *The Shield* (Fox, 2002–). In contrast, *CSI* is a slick, beautifully photographed and lit series that shies away from gritty realism. Rather than simply offering style over substance, its style, heavily shaped by post-production manipulation, informs its substance: it regularly reminds us that it is fiction.

In the opening lines to her *Frommer's* guidebook on Las Vegas, Mary Herczog introduces her subject by stating that "Las Vegas is the city of sin and illusion, the town that Bugsy built, and it's like nothing you've seen before — a façade of a façade with some neon on it."[25] Where better than this "city of sin and illusion" to set *CSI*, with its neon-noir post-production gloss and finish? As film theorist Joel Black argues, the more digitalized effects are used and the more the key work in filmmaking shifts from production (recording the film) to post-production (manipulating the images), the less lifelike become the results: "As little as possible is left to chance, to the contingencies of real life, and to the vagaries *and* verities of the recorded image."[26]

CSI's foregrounding of its own artifice is crucial to making it consistently among the most viewed TV franchises since 2002. Just as Horatio in *CSI: Miami* usually observes autopsies from behind a video screen, so too do we have the glass of the television separating us from the proceedings of murder and violence. Were we not aware of this screen, and that we are watching a graphically manipulated fiction of detailed gore through it, the corpses would be more likely to have the shocking impact that Ballard outlines as noted above. Such an impact was evident in a 2000 *Sunday Mirror* newspaper report on the response to one filmmaker's attempt to use real corpses, thus removing the comforting knowledge that the filmic presentation of the dead is all pretend:

> BBC chiefs came under fire last night over plans to use real dead bodies in a new movie. Controversial British director Michael Winterbottom intends to feature corpses in the opening scenes of his latest film, *Kingdom Come*. The film's producers claim the move is in the name of realism but Shadow Home Secretary Ann Widdecombe and outraged pressure groups are demanding to know why the BBC and the Arts Council of England are among the project's backers. . . . Dr. Adrian Rogers, of the pro-family group Family Focus, said: "It is macabre, unnecessary, in bad taste and disrespectful of the dead." . . . Dr Rogers, a GP, said: "Once the person has died a body has the right to rest in peace, I would be very upset if it was a relative of mine who appeared in a film." He demanded: "Did the person who died give permission for his body to be used in a film? Did he receive payment for it or did his family?"[27]

When the filmed body is perceived as real all of the questions that *CSI* leaves unasked are raised: the indignity of manhandling the body, the duty to abide by the wishes of the deceased, whether deceased human bodies are subjects for popular entertainment at all. By keeping its tongue in its cheek and drawing attention to its state-of-the-art artifice *CSI* manages to sidestep such controversy. It does this so well that it has managed to get away with arguably the goriest content yet seen in a network television dramatic series, offering images such as a rat emerging from a dead model's mouth ("The Hunger Artist" 2023) and the skin being peeled from the face of a dead gambler ("Revenge Is Best Served Cold" 3001).

By highlighting its own dramatic construction, *CSI* constantly reminds us that the show's extreme images are a crucial part of the fictional narrative. The visually sensational corpses provide clue after clue to propel the story forward. With respect to this relationship between blood, guts and narrative, the series has much in common with the medical dramas that (along with *CSI*) have helped to up the gore stakes on TV. In the case of contemporary medical dramas like *ER* (NBC, 1994–), the bloodshed motivates the narrative as we watch the doctors struggle, the patients suffer and the relatives worry along the journey from sickness or injury to health. Importantly, however, as Jason Jacobs states in *Body Trauma TV: The New Hospital Dramas*, in the medical drama we do not see the "invasion and exploration of the body cavity offered to us as horror spectacle . . . the meaning of such butchery that we see is firmly closed, directed to positive healing rather than violent destruction."[28] Although there is clearly a visceral effect in medical drama, it is the containment of horrific images within a particular fictional narrative that makes the spectacle bearable. Just as graphic images are a constituent part of the narrative journey of the medical drama, so *CSI* also justifies their use as a necessary element in the solving of violent crime.

In the medical drama, mutilated and wounded flesh is generally healed to reveal the skills of the doctors. Whilst the gore in *CSI* similarly serves to illustrate the skills of the main characters, as opposed to the medical drama it is the corpse, not the living body, that is the focus. Rather than something to be repaired, quasi-surgical procedures further mutilate the corpse because the body is clue more than flesh, evidence more than human tissue. The skills of the CSIs—as played out in relation to their explorations of the corpse—are very specifically in service to the police and the judicial system, and thus the body in *CSI* recedes from view once it has yielded its secrets, often very early in an episode. When bodies are repeatedly returned to over the course of an episode it tends to be for information rather than pathos. When they are ultimately closed, morgue drawers signify the end of a body's usefulness in a case more than the end of a life, and we are infrequently shown more than fleeting scenes of the human cost of death to family and friends.

CSI is rooted in the worldview of Grissom, as the *paterfamilias* of the show, who instructs both the viewer and his CSI subordinates how to respond to the corpse: to see it as representing part of a puzzle rather than the end of a life. As writer Katherine Ramsland describes him in the unauthorized *CSI* tie-in book *Investigating CSI*, he "adopts a mental stance, eschewing emotion to analyze crime scenes with logic, esoteric knowledge, and the scientific method."[29] In "Too Tough to Die" (1016), for example, Grissom explains to Sara, who feels compassion for a victim in a coma, that "She's evidence." He constantly reminds everybody, including the viewers, to understand bodies as clues, to dehumanize and objectify them, not, as Ballard suggests, to see them as dead versions of our future selves.

Like numerous programs on the air today—such as *Silent Witness* (1996–), *Waking the Dead* (2000–, both BBC) and *Bones* (Fox, 2005–)—*CSI* uses bodies to forensically piece together puzzles. In the late 1990s, TV theorist Charlotte Brunsdon quite correctly perceived that in British television crime drama the focus was "moving away from the police as the solvers of riddles to pathologists and criminal psychologists [accompanied by] . . . a detectable tendency towards a spectacularization of the body and site of crime."[30] It is not the professionalism of the police but of the pathologists, coroners and DNA experts that we have increasingly come to admire.

Although the CSIs sometimes behave like the police when they try to get inside the heads of suspects through interrogation or to find clues by interviewing distraught relatives, it is the victims' bodies and where they died that are generally the focuses of their investigations. As a result of this relative disinterest in who a victim was (other than how they died and where), violence in *CSI* is more removed from its social context than is the case in police dramas such as *NYPD Blue* or *The Shield* in which the societal causes (poverty, gangsterism, drug addiction, etc) and consequences of crime are regularly depicted. When CSIs do occasionally struggle against their emotional responses to and moral outrage at violent crime as viewers might do, Grissom reminds them and us of the right way to approach investigation, to follow the evidence and take the victim's humanity out of the equation. The price for forgetting Grissom's advice is usually high, as Catherine learns when she becomes emotionally involved by identifying with a victim's relative, and as a result inadvertently instigates a murder in "Pledging Mr. Johnson" (1004).

Rather than being disturbed by their jobs, the CSIs are taught, through Grissom's guidance, to actually enjoy working with the dead so that they (along with the viewers) can enjoy the solving of riddles. As Catherine states to a rookie in "Pilot" (1001) when she is explaining the attraction of being a CSI: "I really love my job. We're just a bunch of kids that are getting paid to work on puzzles." The causes and consequences of crime become less important than the puzzle of how particular crimes are executed. As Grissom says in "Chaos Theory" (2002), the *CSI* team "stick with the how and deal with the why later." With each case framed as a forensic puzzle, motivation and emotion are less important than how the death occurred. As a result, both the killer and the victim are depersonalized: who they *are* does not matter as much as what they do or what is done to them. This has led to some criticism of the program. For example, in a discussion on *CSI* that took place on *BBC Radio 4,* British writer and critic Adam Mars-Jones complained that *CSI* "seems to dishonor the human body by using it only as a way of solving the problem of how somebody died."[31]

Mars-Jones is accurate in his assessment to a certain extent: *CSI*, through Grissom's insistence upon clinical detachment, does encourage the body to be viewed as little more than evidence for the CSIs, as opposed to human remains worthy of respect and emotional engagement. Importantly, it is through this very distancing effect that the series enables us as viewers to gaze upon the gore as spectacle: it rarely offers us the body of a person whose *life* we have meaningfully come to know. A corpse is essentially a prop that acts as the catalyst for the *CSI* narrative, framed as a mystery about how a particular corpse became a corpse.

Despite the graphic presentation of gore and brutality in contemporary genres such as the horror film, some argue that audiences are still unaccustomed to particular graphic images, especially those that are presented in a realistic fashion or that offend particular social taboos. Ballard posits, concerning *CSI*, that "Faecal matter and toilet paper are never shown, perhaps reflecting Americans squeamishness, though evidence of anal intercourse and vaginal bruising are snapped out like the tennis scores."[32] If the program did present the corpse or crime scene covered in the human refuse of excrement or vomit, it would bring the body closer to the abject image Kristeva proposes and perhaps have the sobering effect of reminding audiences of themselves as Ballard suggests. Yet in a sense he has countered his own reading of the show, because *CSI* does not do this. Rather than the abject, *CSI* presents its bodies as constructed objects. They may be gory and covered in goo sometimes, but it is gore and goo that we can cope with on a weekly basis. What we cannot cope with is not offered. There is a line that is not crossed. British writer John Taylor, for example, makes the point that in newspapers the most alarming pictures of murders and disasters are not printed:

> The press is not an unrestricted or unregulated horror show of bodies in distress, dying or dead. Pictures of bodily harm in the press are not as bad as they might be: commercial success is not clearly served by the relentless publication of photographs that provoke visceral reactions and disgust among readers and viewers. No newspaper offers an unrelieved diet of such pictures. On the contrary, reporting curtails or constrains hideous sights. The industry works within largely self-imposed limits that exclude the most detailed, close-up and disgusting photographs.[33]

The gore on display in *CSI* illustrates that audiences are not yet fully comfortable with "unrestricted" horror, but are happy to enjoy the fantasy of horror when it is clearly presented as such. Audiences do not want to see real body parts, but if they are skillfully recreated, and the fact that they are recreated is understood, then a gory spectacle can be enjoyed. Were *CSI* not to remind us that its graphically gruesome images are all illusion, and part of an entertaining puzzle, then the series would no longer be popular entertainment.

In fact, the line between real horror and the fantasy of horror did become blurred in the UK in the case of "Grave Danger" (5024), giving the impact of the televisual blood and guts on display in the *CSI* episode a very different resonance. In this episode a man with bombs strapped to his body blows himself up before Grissom's eyes. The team then has to investigate the remains of his blasted apart body in order to find clues as to where he has buried the kidnapped CSI team member Nick. This episode was scheduled to air on July 12 2005 on England's Channel 5. It had been promoted all week long as a special *CSI* double bill from celebrity guest director Quentin Tarantino. Yet ultimately the screening was postponed as a result of real-life events: on July 7 2005 four suicide bombers blew themselves up in London killing fifty two and injuring hundreds of bystanders.[34] The media responded by showing survivors emerging from the wreckage as bleeding and injured victims, but did not show the fragments of bodies on the trains or bus where the explosions occurred. What *CSI* unwittingly achieved through its timing was a verisimilitude that made viewing the program unbearable for Britons, at least while images of the London explosions were fresh in the minds of viewers. For a brief time, *CSI* crossed that line between fantasy and reality with its bomb-created body parts, reminding Britons too much of themselves, their human vulnerability and the flesh and bone scattered around London.

What *CSI* more commonly offers is an alternative to viewing the corpse as potentially ourselves. It does not confront us with real horrors that we might have to face one day or ask us to struggle with our own mortality on a weekly basis. It presents to us, instead, with a stream of mysteries framed through self-conscious fantasy horror that the viewer can enjoy with the dead body and all its fluids and organs as elaborate effects and props. Yet this particular "*CSI* effect" depends upon a contract that can be broken when overlap with real-life events occurs. As happened with episodes of *Buffy the Vampire Slayer* following the Columbine shootings, the intended effect of *CSI* became altered following July 7 2005 (or 7/7 as it is commonly referred to in Britain). Lisa Parks' "Brave New Buffy: Rethinking TV Violence" makes the argument that the *Buffy* episodes should have been shown even though they depicted student on student violence within an American school, because the overlap between fiction and real life was a missed opportunity for discussion of a violent reality. It would have enabled parents to talk with their children and allowed television to "confront the issue of violence rather than encourage it."[35]

As Mark Lawson wrote in *The Guardian* nine days after the London bombings, following such real-life horror the question arises of whether showing such programs as scheduled "cheapens or deepens the experience of the terrible event." He concluded that *CSI* should have been shown because "all art is changed by the context in which it is seen, and each of these is strengthened not weakened by the recent reality their audience has seen."[36] For Lawson, "such collisions of fiction and reality"[37] throw additional light upon both the programme we are watching and the world we are living in through them being lashed together, forcing us to take account of fact and fiction in relation to each other. For a program like *CSI*, however, which depends so much on upfront fakery and illusion, the question arises as to whether it would still be art if shown in the immediate aftermath of such an event. Or would the image of the human body in pieces following a bomb blast, when stripped of its metafictional quality, unintentionally become instead an unbearable snapshot of real abject horror ambushing viewers unaware that their contract with the program is about to be broken. As with the crime scene tape that surrounds each incident of actual murder, maybe some lines we just do not knowingly want to cross.

NOTES

1. Mike Clarke, *Teaching Popular Television* (London: Heinemann Educational in association with BFI, 1987), 40.

2. Ruth Richardson, *Death, Dissection and the Destitute,* 2nd ed. (London: Phoenix, 2001), xv.

3. Richardson, *Death,* xv.

4. Joyce Tyldesley, *The Mummy: Unwrap the Ancient Secrets of the Mummies' Tombs* (London: Carlton, 1999), 87.

5. J. G. Ballard, "In Cold Blood," *Guardian,* June 25 2005, Review sec., 19.

6. Julia Kristeva, *Powers of Horror: An Essay on Abjection,* trans. Leon S. Roudiez. 1980 (New York: Columbia University Press, 1982), 3.

7. Kristeva, *Powers,* 109.

8. Kristeva, *Powers,* 3.

9. Kristeva, *Powers,* 3.

10. Mary Douglas, *Purity and Danger: An Analysis of the Concepts of Pollution and Taboo* (London: Routledge & Kegan Paul, 1969).

11. Jonathan Lake Crane, *Terror and Everyday Life: Singular Moments in the History of the Horror Film* (Thousand Oaks, CA: Sage, 1994), 31.

12. Patricia Duncker, Letter, *Guardian,* July 2 2005, Review sec., 8.

13. For example: *Diagnosis: Unknown* (CBS, 1960), *The Hidden Truth* (A-R, 1964), *The Expert* (BBC, 1970–75), *Quincy, M.E.* (NBC, 1976–83), *Diagnosis Murder* (CBS, 1993–2001), *One West Waikiki* (CBS/SYN, 1994–96), *Silent Witness* (BBC, 1996–present), *Da Vinci's Inquest* (SYN, 1998–2005), *Waking the Dead* (BBC, 2000–present), *Six Feet Under* (HBO, 2001–2005) and *Crossing Jordon* (NBC, 2001–present).

14. Stephen King, *Danse Macabre* (London: Warner, 1993), 158.

15. Ange-Pierre Leca, *The Cult of the Immortal: Mummies and the Ancient Egyptian Way of Death*, trans. Louise Asmal (London: Souvenir, 1980), 157.

16. Carol Andrews, *Egyptian Mummies*, 2nd ed. (London: British Museum, 1998), 13.

17. Mandy Merck, "American Gothic: Undermining the Uncanny," in *Reading "Six Feet Under": TV to Die for*, ed. Kim Akass and Janet McCabe (London: I.B. Tauris, 2005), 64.

18. Geoff Hurd, "The Television Presentation of the Police," in *Popular Television and Film: A Reader*, ed. Tony Bennett et al. (London: BFI/Open University, 1981), 58.

19. Clarke, *Teaching*, 42.

20. Clarke, *Teaching*, 44.

21. Richardson, *Death*, 31.

22. Richard Sparks, *Television and the Drama of Crime: Moral Tales and the Place of Crime in Public Life* (Buckingham: Open University Press, 1992), 102.

23. Noël Carroll, *Theorizing the Moving Image* (Cambridge: Cambridge University Press, 1996), 78.

24. Anita Biressi and Heather Nunn, *Reality TV: Realism and Revelation* (London: Wallflower, 2005), 120–21.

25. Mary Herczog, *Frommer's Portable Las Vegas for Non-Gamblers*, 2nd ed. (New York: Wiley, 2005), 1.

26. Joel Black, *The Reality Effect: Film Culture and the Graphic Imperative* (New York and London: Routledge, 2002), 11.

27. *Sunday Mirror*, May 12 2000, 11.

28. Jason Jacobs, *Body Trauma TV: The New Hospital Dramas* (London: BFI, 2003), 69.

29. Katherine Ramsland, "IQ, EQ, and SQ: Grissom Thinks and Caine Feels, but Taylor Enlightens," in *Investigating CSI: An Unauthorized Look Inside the Crime Labs of Las Vegas, Miami and New York*, ed. Donn Cortez (Dallas: BenBella Books, 2006), 146.

30. Charlotte Brunsdon, "Structure of Anxiety: Recent British Television Crime Fiction," *Screen* 39, no.3 (1998): 242.

31. *Front Row*, BBC Radio 4, July 13, 2005.

32. Ballard, 18 (Review).

33. John Taylor, *Body Horror: Photojournalism, Catastrophe and War* (Manchester: Manchester University Press, 1998), 6.

34. *Daily Telegraph*, August 4, 2005, 11.

35. Lisa Parks, "Brave New Buffy: Rethinking TV Violence," in *Quality Popular Television: Cult TV, the Industry and Fans*, ed. Mark Jancovich and James Lyons (London: BFI, 2003), 129.

36. Mark Lawson, "Art in the Aftermath," *Guardian*, July 16, 2005, 22.

37. Lawson, "Art," 22.

Chapter Six

The City of Our Times: Space, Identity, and the Body in *CSI: Miami*

Patrick West

This chapter foregrounds televisual representations of the city of Miami in *CSI: Miami* to develop a broader argument about the combined impact of globalization and virtualization on twenty-first century cities and their inhabitants. I argue that some of the contemporary characteristics of Miami as a city are reflected in *CSI: Miami* and that, more than this, the show offers television viewers a sneak preview of tomorrow's Miami. While my argument is not equally valid for all cities, I claim that Miami is at the forefront of an international urban development trend that will influence the futures of many cities. *CSI: Miami* reflects a break from past experiences of urbanism through its focus on the virtuality of Miami. It suggests new modes of virtual identity in its diegesis and effects, while the show's dissemination along the television trade routes of global flow emphasizes the postmodern nexus between virtualization and globalization.

The convergence of globalization and virtualization concerns the inhabitants of cities like Miami because it further destabilizes postmodern urban environments in which identity already tends towards the schizophrenic or "psychasthenic" state described, by Celeste Olalquiaga, as a "feeling of being in all places while not really being anywhere."[1] Globalization dislodges identity from an allegiance to any one city, while virtualization compromises the connections people enjoy to the physical world; each concerns transports of identity. Quoting the work of Paul Virilio, Ackbar Abbas merges an analysis of globalization with attention to virtualization through his discussion of "a more and more insistently globalizing space" in which the "boundaries of the city itself have come into question, largely because of new informational and communicational technologies that introduce a novel idea of space: space, in an important sense, as non-physical and dematerialized."[2]

This is not to say that the city is no longer identifiable. According to Zygmunt Bauman, "the globalizing process goes on decomposing one by one all the familiar settings of human life, together with the conceptual frameworks in which we have grown used to grasp[ing] them."[3] Even so, there is a continuity of meaning in notions of urbanism that allows us to (re)experience and (re)conceptualize it; television show titles centered on actual cities—and the narratives that these shows convey—are in fact a cultural instrument in sustaining this sense of urbanism.

As a postmodernist site, the city of Miami reveals the processes of globalization and virtualization. Indeed, drawing upon the work of the Miami-based scholar Jan Nijman, I present evidence that Miami (*pace* Olalquiaga) trumps Los Angeles as the city of our times in demonstrating the global and virtual forces of postmodern urbanism in action. Miami's postmodern urbanism differs from modern urbanism in that decentralization has replaced centralization in urban forms, and the distinctions between public and private spaces therein have been problematized.

Nijman's sociological thesis is supported by the televisual representations of *CSI: Miami*. As Karen Lury observes, "the use of color, digital effects and lighting often mean that *CSI* creates an excessively expressionistic and even fantastic impression."[4] In terms of form, this sets off all three of the *CSI* shows from otherwise similar forensic dramas such as *Numb3rs* (CBS, 2005–) and *24* (Fox, 2001–). But within the franchise, *CSI: Miami* stands out from *CSI: Crime Scene Investigation* and *CSI: New York* for a style of cinematography that exaggerates the global and virtual characteristics of the city of Miami and, by extension, gestures towards the consequent disorientation visited upon Miami's inhabitants. Merging a formalistic inquiry into the show's cinematography with traditional plot and character analysis demonstrates that the show's lead character, Lieutenant Horatio Caine, represents a reaction against the globalized multi-nationalism, multi-racialism and multi-ethnicities of Miami.[5] Caine's hegemonic assertion of white community stands in opposition to Miami's pluralized reality as a postmodern city shaped by globalization and virtualization.

The portfolio method of formalism and content analysis used in this chapter reveals a rift in *CSI: Miami* suggestive of sociological tensions, as manifested especially in Caine, over the constitution of community in Miami, now and in the future. I also argue that *CSI: Miami* anticipates the further disintegration of urban spatiality due to the conjunction of globalization and virtualization pressures, but also counteracts this with a new postmodern version of space. In particular, I show how human bodies in the show reformat lived space within a problematized opposition of inside and outside—rather than within the modernist opposition of private and public space—and thus suggest a new way of locating (bodily) identity in the city.

Accordingly, I argue that *CSI: Miami* performs three linked functions: it illustrates how urban spatiality is mutating as an effect of the intersection of globalization and virtualization; it underscores the crisis of identity that this intersection provokes; and, it explores the potential of the body to address this crisis through a reconfiguration of space. A separate section in this chapter will be dedicated to each of these functions. But first, I consider Jan Nijman's views on the hierarchy of postmodern development in Miami and Los Angeles.[6]

MIAMI VERSUS LOS ANGELES

Arbitrating between the competing claims advanced for Miami and Los Angeles as *the* exemplar of postmodern urbanism underscores the relevance of *CSI: Miami* to my investigation into the future of the city because the show engages with the various criteria by which this competition between cities is judged in academic circles. Furthermore, while the show is produced and partly shot in Hollywood, the *diegesis* of *CSI: Miami* firmly sutures the show to the actual city of Miami; hence my analysis of *CSI: Miami* in relationship to Miami and other postmodern cities like it.

In his article "The Paradigmatic City," Jan Nijman interrogates the Los Angeles School's claim that this city "displays more clearly than other cities the fundamental features and trends of the wider urban system."[7] Using the same criteria through which Los Angeles has been assigned this paradigmatic status, Nijman shows that Miami represents a later stage of urban evolution than Los Angeles: he "renders Los Angeles as the quintessential twentieth-century city and points to Miami as the paradigmatic city of our time."[8]

In order to see how Nijman performs this Los Angeles-to-Miami shift, and to detail its importance to my chapter, the Los Angeles school position will be rehearsed here. Key members of the school (including Celeste Olalquiaga, Michael Sorkin and Edward Soja) all draw upon Fredric Jameson's "schizophrenic" diagnosis of Los Angeles in "Postmodernism, or The Cultural Logic of Late Capitalism."[9] Here, Soja describes Los Angeles as an "exopolitan" rather than conventionally metropolitan site:

> Perched beyond the vortex of the old agglomerative nodes, the exopolis spins new whorls of its own, turning the city inside-out and outside-in at the same time. The metropolitan forms that have become so familiar to us–with dominating

downtowns, concentric rings of land uses spreading out from the tightly packed inner city to sprawling dormitory suburbs, density gradients declining neatly from core to periphery—are now undergoing radical deconstruction and reconstruction, exploding and coalescing today in multitudes of experimental communities of tomorrow, in improbable cities where centrality is virtually ubiquitous and the solid familiarity of the urban melts into the air.[10]

Soja's gloss on his hometown is misplaced only to the extent that he characterizes Los Angeles as *the paradigmatic city* exhibiting exopolitan traits. In this respect, his words better describe another place, and that place is Miami.

Nijman sets forth Miami as a hyperbolic version of Los Angeles. Compared to Los Angeles, "Miami finds itself *one step further* in this evolutionary scheme: as the first global city;"[11] even more saliently, "Miami is unique in the sense that no other major US city has an absolute majority of recent immigrants."[12] Included in the list of what distinguishes Miami from Los Angeles, is the way that Miami functions as an international, multi-lingual communications and media node. John Sinclair underscores "the role of Miami as the locus of production, distribution, and exchange for both the Spanish-speaking television industry in the United States and the major television companies of Latin America."[13]

CSI: Miami is not a clone of the city of Miami. The Hispanic and Latin American television industries have a large presence in Miami, but *CSI: Miami* does not even figure in the Nielsen ratings for Hispanics. And as previously noted parts of the show are shot in Hollywood. It is, however, precisely this gap between the city of Miami and its televisual representations that creates room for an interpretation of *CSI: Miami* as a commentary on postmodern Miami and, by extension, on international urban development trends. If Miami, as Nijman suggests, is a portal onto the cities of tomorrow, then *CSI: Miami* helps us to better understand the nature of these future urbanisms today.

URBAN SPATIAL MUTATIONS

CSI: Miami represents Miami's usurpation of Los Angeles as the city of our times by exploiting the *CSI* franchise's visual repertoire. The aerial cinematography of the show maximizes the postmodern characteristics of Miami. Specifically, two features of the cinematography match with the double aspects of globalization and virtualization that makeup Miami's postmodernism.

Firstly, the camera often scrutinizes the margins of land and water that form much of Miami's physical geography, and these visual glissandos along the coastal strip and canals reinforce Miami's centre-less exopolitanism. Rather than homing in on the city, the camera brushes over it, as if Miami lacks solid purchase on the landscape. Furthermore, when the viewer's perspective trails away over the water, or ascends skywards, it is as if the process of Miami's separation from national place (under the dislocating pressures of globalization) has reached a televisual apogee.

A second, related aspect of the cinematography introduces another mode of detachment into the viewing experience: a detachment between the viewer and the city of Miami. Acting with a kind of omniscience, attuned to everything yet connected to nothing, not only does the camera record Miami's physical dislocation—tarrying over the margins such that any residual sense of a centre is lost—it also cuts the viewer off from the referent city. This second detachment (on this occasion, through the virtualization of the television image itself) suggests another way in which Miami involves a loss of the sense of relative permanence associated with the traditional city.

This cinematographic decentering of the city and suggestion of its virtualization is evident throughout *CSI: Miami*. Early on in "Spring Break" (1021), as if under the influence of the title sequence's pyrotechnics, the pitching camera makes drunken sorties up and down the shoreline. The disorientation this produces for the viewer carries over into a sense that the city itself has lost its bearings in localized (or national) space. Simultaneously, we are separated from the city to the extent that the medium of television drama interposes itself between Miami and us. The camera skims over the content of the images, and the images evince a preoccupation with their own status as images. In this sequence of shots, the beachgoers and umbrellas more resemble pixilations (that is, virtualizations) than actual people or things. In this way, *CSI: Miami* demonstrates the salience of Karen Lury's insight that "it is also sometimes the very restrictions of television—related to budget, technology, and even the conventions of television itself—which produce engaging and evocative images."[14] The pixilating qualities of the television image employed here underscore the virtualization of the city of Miami.

A similar example of the dual globalization and virtualization of the cinematography in *CSI: Miami* is provided by "Cop Killer" (3013). At one point in the episode, the ascending camera scans the apex of an office block, as if the building itself were about to change by alchemical means into air in order to tower still higher over the city. Meanwhile, it is the camera that floats even higher, abandoning the city as a site firmly located in place, in favor of an organization of globalized space that also involves the virtualization of the image itself, rather than its putative content. The camera draws attention to its own movement as an agent of virtualization, at the same time as the sense of Miami's urbanism is dissipated into exopolitan space.

Episodes of *CSI: Miami* also typically conclude with close-ups of Horatio Caine (played by David Caruso)—sometimes in company but more often alone—in scenes that disrupt the viewer's sense of his position in space because, at such close range, one is unable to locate him within a decipherable location. The editing procedure of cutting straight to these close-ups (excising the expected intermediate mid-range establishing shot) is one trigger of this effect. But the *tangential* framing of the human figure(s) in the concluding close-ups is particularly what sustains the uneasy relationship between person(s) and urban architecture in these scenes. Caine might be shown tucked into a side aspect of the entrance to the crime lab, or shot at an odd angle within the confines of a stairwell. Wherever he is, the impression persists of his being embedded uncomfortably within the architecture, rather than being in control of his spatial surroundings. Film scholar Cher Coad has observed that Caruso's hunched posture in his portrayal of Caine similarly suggests his being weighed down by the architecture.[15] It is not that the cinematography and acting styles of *CSI: Miami* necessarily reinforce narratives or storylines of spatial dislocation, but that the text taken broadly presents a parallel series of effects through mainly non-narrative visual means.

Michael Sorkin, another member of the Los Angeles School, describes "the dissipation of all stable relations to local physical and cultural geography, the loosening of ties to any specific space" as key features of exopolitan spatiality.[16] The aerial cinematography of *CSI: Miami* maximizes the viewer's sense of Miami's exopolitanism along the lines Sorkin suggests, but these televisual techniques can also be interpreted as a visualization of the city that alerts us to *new configurations* of urban spatiality. Besides tracing the architectural and geographic features of postmodern Miami, the cinematography of *CSI: Miami* can be understood as engaged in a mapping process akin to Fredric Jameson's notion of "global cognitive mapping," which he sees as a necessary response to postmodern disorientation.[17]

Those moments when the camera seems most detached from Miami—as it trails away over the water, or kisses the sky—are also moments when space itself becomes elastic and utopian. For a few seconds approximately three quarters of the way through "Whacked" (3023), for example, a vertiginous view down into the ocean ends with the camera hurtling upwards into an abstract explosion of brilliant white light. Such encounters of movement and image are external to the *diegesis* proper; they operate in counterpoint to the plot, often punctuating sequences of high drama. But they also function as cinematographic experimentations with space, which incite new possibilities for experiencing the spatiality of post-exopolitan sites by suggesting to the viewer (perhaps subliminally) new affective and intellectual relationships to urban space. In turn, this feeds into the project of addressing the problems of schizophrenic identity that postmodern urbanism produces. The computer-screen urban schematic that punctuates the titles sequence of *CSI: Miami* Seasons One and Two, for example, can be seen as a fleeting expression of the potential architectural blueprints for a future form of urban spatiality. Such forms are created from the elasticity of space that the show's cinematography opens up by presenting movements and non-representational images that destabilize the usual ways in which we engage with space. *CSI: Miami* thus prompts its image-literate audience to newly manipulate everyday spaces.

Form, thus, has content in *CSI: Miami*. However, in a gesture validated by Lury's recognition that the *CSI* franchise "explicitly reflects the increasing confidence of television producers to imitate cinema," it is in recent scholarship on cinema that the best rationale for focusing on the aesthetics of *CSI: Miami* emerges.[18] Adrian Martin champions a re-evaluation in "modern pop culture"[19] of "a particular and specific power of cinema, what I will call descriptive power: it shows, it traces, it unfolds a certain space and time."[20] Such a notion of form facilitates sensitivity to the spatial permutations characteristic of the post-exopolitan city. Pointing towards those texts "where form in some way overtakes content, swallows it up, and bares its architectonic soul with complete explicitness," Martin suggests that "maybe it is not the human substance of a story that sometimes matters, but the kinds of connections or free associations it allows us for playful formal possibilities."[21] I suggest that these "connections or free associations" emerge from *CSI: Miami*'s cinematographic flourishes in the context of the show's televisual representations of that city.[22]

At the same time as the cinematography of *CSI: Miami* re-maps urban spatiality under the pressures of globalization, the show also engages the virtualization of Miami; a re-mapping is in evidence on this level too. According to Raymond A. Schroth, the shows in the *CSI* franchise are "written for the cell-phone generation, for those whose overwhelming absorption in e-mail, TV, CDs, DVDs and pocket gizmos that enable them to read mail, call home, write letters and download music and films at the same time, constitute a technology church."[23] These comments indicate that *CSI* is aligned through its audience with the assumption of a high level of competence with virtualization. I suggest that this competence allows members of the "cell-phone generation" to recognize those elements of *CSI: Miami*—such as the abstract cinematography—wherein technological apparatuses like the camera generate opportunities to re-create the self in urban space.[24]

This aspect of the show's reception can be traced in its storylines. In "Murder in a Flash" (3004), a flash mob is summoned to a golf course by e-mails and text messages: the street thus becomes sutured to the screen. While flash mobs are not confined to Miami, it is notable that *CSI: Miami* is the only television show, to my knowledge, to foreground this type of activity. In this way, *CSI: Miami* reflects the increasing virtualization of the city of Miami and also alerts us to new forms of identity—such as flash mobs—that embrace and are even produced through the increasing predominance of virtualization in urban environments.[25] To this extent, the sophistication and intensity of Miami's virtualization, as well as the city's globalization, are reflected and re-worked in the show. *CSI: Miami* offers both a diagnosis of current threats to city living, and a template for how such threats might be countered—even taken advantage of—through new organizations of space and identity.

The notion of flow, which has two meanings in television studies, helps further this line of enquiry into *CSI: Miami*. C. Lee Harrington and Denise D. Bielby note that "First, flow refers to the planned sequence in which segments or strips of TV programming unfold onscreen. . . . Second, flow refers to the movement of television programs and formats through different world markets."[26]

In the first sense of flow, *CSI: Miami* is a pastiche of other texts and media. More particularly, the show often overlays elements of intertextuality in one medium (such as television references) onto the multi-platform intertextuality of a diversity of both new and old media. The televisual and cinematic aspects of the show primarily effect this at the level of form, while the frequent storyline engagements with media such as e-mails, websites, vehicle tracking technology and text messages—not to mention archival television and cinema—replicate intertextuality at the level of content. In "Hard Time" (2003), Caine is stymied in his attempts to convince a parole officer to delay a scheduled hearing. "What we got here," the officer says, "is a failure to communicate." "I love that film too," Caine bats back, concisely implicating his cinema-literate television audience in the intertextuality of *CSI: Miami* (the film, of course, is *Cool Hand Luke*.) In "Game Over" (3018) a motion capture device that portrays humans as virtual wire-frame figures provides evidence related to the murder of an extreme skateboarder. This prompts CSI Calleigh Duquesne to observe, in a nice moment of cross-media, doubled-up intertextuality: "one thing's for sure, it isn't just motion capture. It's a snuff video."

In my reading, intertextuality within and across media in *CSI: Miami* is another index of the link between the show and the virtualization of the city of Miami. This intertextuality draws our attention to the postmodern constitution of identities through a nexus of texts drawn from all points on the spectrums of technology and media.

The second meaning of flow—the international syndication of television products—supplements the engagement in virtualization *within* the text of *CSI: Miami* (in the first meaning of flow), because the show's flow through world markets is also a dissemination of its lessons in urbanism. If *CSI: Mi-*

ami has a pedagogy, that pedagogy concerns both the way in which we live in cities today, and how urbanism might be reconstituted in a world increasingly under the sway of globalization and virtualization. While other shows are also implicated in the international flow of television, *CSI: Miami* suggests a new understanding of *the global viewing context itself* as a space of virtual community that replaces the bonds of traditional urban living. *CSI: Miami* both performs global communication (as one of many sets of media, marketing and screen representations of Miami, it stands out as "the world's most popular TV show")[27] and produces examples of virtualization that provide its viewers, in their local contexts, with both technological and identity-based strategies for planetary interactivity.

IDENTITY UNDER SIEGE

Further identity permutations that suggest elements from Nijman's catalogue of Miami's postmodern urban characteristics emerge if we supplement a formalist perspective on *CSI: Miami* with a more traditional content analysis. One episode touched upon earlier ("Game Over") and another episode, "Identity" (3015), shed light, respectively, on virtual and global identity concerns. They also foreshadow my analysis of the relationship between Horatio Caine's identity and the notions of urban community circulating in *CSI: Miami*.

In "Game Over" Ryan Wolfe partners with Calleigh Duquesne to investigate a murder within an extreme-skateboarding video-games production house. Virtualization and capitalism are here combined. Dave Strong, retired star skateboarder, runs Strong Studios and markets video-simulation games modeled on his own stunts. But it is in fact fellow skateboarder and murder victim Jake Sullivan—employed to impersonate Strong—whose physical prowess is converted into the movements of a wire-frame figure that stands in to represent Strong himself on the video company's motion capture stage. "It's called capitalism," Strong boasts to the CSIs. Virtualization, in other words, allows for a slippage of identities between Sullivan and Strong, which opens up new possibilities for capitalist exploitation. Here, *CSI: Miami* reflects and extends Nijman's observation that "Miami's economy has a decidedly postindustrial profile, one that is barely constrained by the remnants of earlier times."[28] The "rustbelt characteristics" of Los Angeles are largely absent in Miami, and new capitalist formations have the scope to emerge.[29] *CSI: Miami* suggests the nature of some of these formations in future urban locations. "Game Over" prefigures the increased convergence of capitalism and virtualization, and the forms of identity that this convergence might create.

Alongside representations of how virtualization stimulates new identity formations, identity concerns related to globalization are also interrogated in *CSI: Miami*. The aptly named episode "Identity" finds Caine confronted with a case involving Clavo Cruz, a diplomat's son addicted to crime, who relies upon the shelter from prosecution afforded him by the extension of diplomatic immunity to family members. Part of the back story to this episode is Caine's previous apprehension of Clavo's sibling, Ramon: "You're not going to catch me floating around in international waters," Clavo taunts the head of the Crime Lab. Caine gets a lucky break when Clavo spits on Caine's jacket. DNA analysis proves that Clavo is not his father's son, which compromises his diplomatic immunity, thus giving Caine the opportunity to arrest him.

So that Caine can charge him, the man who was led to believe that Clavo was his son re-assigns Clavo's national identity as a citizen of Baracas (as distinct from the rarefied non-identity of international diplomatic immunity). As just another foreign resident in Miami, Clavo is subject to American law. Thus, his connection to Miami is simultaneously made stronger (he becomes liable to arrest in the city) and weaker (his arrest relies on his ties, through citizenship, to a foreign nation). Clavo's fate is significant for the analysis of identity formations and globalization here because it shows how a global scenario—the international conventions governing diplomatic immunity and the flow of migrant populations—can be transformed into a narrative revolving around a transnational urban site within the boundaries of one city: Miami. As in "Game Over," *CSI: Miami* here responds to, and extends, a characteristic of the city of Miami itself: its globalization. Clavo's downfall reveals the flux between national, international, and transnational identity formations at the individual, metropolitan, and exopolitan levels.

Nijman argues that the persistent allegiance of Miami's many immigrants to their "community of origin" results in "a much more flexible existence in two places simultaneously."[30] The episode "Identity" tarries over this notion of "flexible existence," even as it resolves it through the expedient of pulling the diplomatic-immunity crutch out from under Clavo. Thus, Clavo's mode of identity is made much less flexible—indeed it is entirely re-worked—as a result of Caine's investigations. In this manner, *CSI: Miami* actually operates against the manifestations of identity that emerge from globalization. Caine plays the key role on the show in resisting the implication of Nijman's argument regarding Miami's globalized status, which is that the city contains "little in terms of a shared 'American' identity."[31] Caine effectively restabilizes American identity within melting pot Miami (here, by arresting a foreign national).

Lieutenant Caine's attitude towards community does not emerge obviously in *CSI: Miami*. To tease it out, we must examine his relationships with family and the CSI team, which operate as his surrogates for community more generally. Caine's character description in the Cast section on the *CSI: Miami* official website makes explicit how his personal relationships subtend his public activities:

> Raised in 1960s Miami, by age 16 Horatio Caine had experienced a lifetime: Civil Rights marches, Cuban freedom flights, violent race riots and the rise of drug culture. His mother, a single parent in a time that did not favour such a definition of "family," taught Caine that strength resided in your mind, not your hand. Though she was demanding, her love protected him until she stood up to a drug dealer and was killed. At 17, while other teenagers were learning to disco, Caine set out to help the police find her killer. By the time the murderer was sentenced to life, Caine knew he had found his calling: to protect his city.[32]

The death of Caine's mother provides the impetus for his career as a CSI, and in this web-based example of what John Caldwell calls "convergent or 'conglomerating textuality'" we find the narrative origin of a recurring pattern in the television episodes themselves.[33] The prevailing framework for Caine's understanding of his work duties is derived from or informed by his personal life, and this is all the more pronounced given that we almost never see Caine off duty (his work becomes the only outlet for his personal circumstances). Freudian psychoanalytic theory helps to unpack the other salient aspect of Caine's biography mentioned in the character description above.

Caine's representation as both lacking a father figure and fathering Miami (intimated by the phrase "*his* city")[34] suggests the operations of an Oedipus Complex. In fact, we learn in "Collision" (4017) that the Lieutenant's *father* murdered his mother, and that Caine in turn killed that man. At the heart of Freudian theory is the mythical notion of the murder of the father at the hands of his son(s). Because the Complex serves to foreground the symbolic aspect of patriarchy—the "Name of the Father" survives his bodily death—a zone within which the son can exercise paternal authority is opened up.[35] The father's death is not a literal death in the Complex. Rather, the death of the father refers to the son displacing the father—entering the realm of symbolic order—to occupy a position of authority (not least over women) in the social order. However, the son enjoys the father's authority only until the cycle of Oedipus repeats. To this extent, paternal power is always, in theory, vulnerable to subversion. However, as seriality implies the repetition of the same, the serial nature of *CSI: Miami*, which tends to fix character personalities in place, neutralizes this potential for subversion in the Oedipus Complex. On the show, once a patriarch always a patriarch.

Terry Eagleton asserts that the Oedipus Complex is "the structure of relations by which we come to be the men and women that we are. It is the point at which we are produced and constituted as subjects."[36] A Freudian approach is not the only option available for analyzing *CSI: Miami*, and much feminism provides a countervailing analysis to Oedipalism, but Eagleton's comment on the Complex and its enduring significance for identity construction is highly suggestive with regard to Caine. His patriarchal character traits—according to the show's website, derived from his youth—extend beyond the family context as narrowly defined. They shape the organization of Caine's career in terms of his relationships to victims and the CSI team, and his relationship to community in general.

In "Blood Brothers" (2001), Caine's interaction with his sister-in-law, Detective Yelina Salas, underscores his patriarchal intolerance of ambiguity. Caine's brother, Raymond, is believed dead, still Caine is unwilling to have an affair with Yelina, whom he is clearly attracted to. "It is easy to get used to those boundaries," he tells her. Such an effort to preserve clear identity roles is a key characteristic of Freudian patriarchy. Caine resists pursuing any vaguely incestuous involvement with his brother's wife because it would confuse the accepted lines through which the nuclear family is built in Western patriarchy.

Caine's patriarchal character comes through at several levels of the show, including at the level of his understanding of community. An analysis of his relationship to the team he leads shows this. A sequence from "Blood in the Water" (4002) demonstrates both his authority over his team and, by extension, the notion of community that this authority serves to maintain. This episode reveals that Caine's patriarchal relationship with those at work segues into a similarly authoritative yet mildly tolerant understanding of community in Miami. For Caine, Miami community is a cosmopolitan and diverse space that is, however, anchored to the racial identity he owns as a white American.[37]

The relevant sequence comes at the end of the episode. Caine expresses sympathy with crime victim Laura Gannon, who has just witnessed her family life disintegrate; family is "what we all want," Caine agrees. In the following, final scene of the episode, Caine stands on a stairwell looking down on his family—the CSI team—as they go about their daily business in twos or threes. As Kristine Huntley comments, this scene "highlights Horatio's strong feelings for his team and his isolation from them. If the *Miami* team is a family, Horatio is the concerned parent, a position that naturally sets Horatio apart from the rest."[38] What Huntley's analysis neglects to mention, however, is that as a surrogate for Caine's family the CSI team is representative of the Miami community in its mixture of racial and ethnic backgrounds. As Nijman observes, Miami contains "a cosmopolitan class that is of diverse national and ethnic backgrounds, many of them migrants or transients."[39] This sequence in "Blood in the Water" shows that Caine manifests a peculiarly patriarchal tolerance for Miami's multi-nationalism and multiple ethnicities.

To this extent, at least, the three *CSI*s are very similar; the team leader in each case is a white and distinctly unethnic man, while the three CSI teams contain a diversity of racial, ethnic and gender identities. White hegemony presides over a cosmopolitan coalition across the franchise.[40] On *CSI: Miami*, Caine's dislike of ambiguity in personal and family matters is matched on another level by resistance to the variability of cultural identity displayed in Miami's cosmopolitanism. In "10-7" (3024) the pattern of Caine's attitudes toward the globalized community of Miami is revealed explicitly: initial tolerance is replaced by a re-assertion of white hegemony. Horatio invites Colombian-born Yelina and her son, Raymond Junior, to holiday with him in Brazil. However, this is only a ruse to allow her husband (Horatio's brother, now shown to be alive) to leave the city safely with his family. Horatio remains behind in Miami. The family is reunited and *in the same movement* the ethnic difference Yelina represents departs from the community of Miami. Again, the personal aspects of Horatio's life have implications at the level of society in general. Woven through Horatio's attachment to Yelina and his brief marriage to Eric Delko's half-Hispanic sister, Marisol, (see "Shock" [4023] and "Rampage" [4024]) is what might be read as an unconscious impulse opposed to the cosmopolitanism such characters instantiate.

Caine is not an obvious racist; a more nuanced analysis of the issues of identity and community that he raises is required. Recalling Caine's character biography quoted above, what jumps out is his upbringing's imbrication with the history of Miami in the 1960s, a history strongly marked (in the official website's telling) by social and racial disruptions. Commenting on the traumas suffered by Miami a decade or so later in 1980, including the large-scale influx of Cuban refugees and "the worst race riots in American urban history," Jan Nijman suggests that this period "raised anxiety among Anglos to the level of despair. In the eyes of Miami's white establishment, their city was under siege."[41] The official *CSI Miami* website does not spell out the connection between Caine's background and the identity effects that Nijman articulates about Anglo-Miamians, but Caine's patriarchal tendencies and attitude towards community bridge the gap between his character, the fears that Nijman describes, and the history of Miami. At the heart of Caine's character lurks both an anxiety about ethnic and racial diversity and—counteracting this anxiety—a liberal tolerance of difference so long as it is framed (as in the *CSI* trilogy) by the hegemony of white, patriarchal identity. The words of multiculturalism scholar Peter McLaren neatly capture Caine's identity permutation:

Diversity that somehow constitutes itself as a harmonious ensemble of benign cultural spheres is a conservative and liberal model of multiculturalism that . . . deserves to be jettisoned because, when we try to make culture an undisturbed space of harmony and agreement where social relations exist within cultural forms of uninterrupted accord, we ascribe to a form of social amnesia in which we forget that all knowledge is forged in histories that are played out in the field of social antagonisms.[42]

Caine's attitude toward community reveals a weak commitment to Miami's cosmopolitanism because, engineered as it is by his deep investment in patriarchy, this commitment attempts to paper over the powerful differences that both inform his own leadership of the CSI team and contest white superiority.

If Caine's relationship to other characters indicates subtle contestation within *CSI: Miami* over notions of identity and community, another form of tension is manifest in the show's representation of the virtualization and globalization of postmodern urbanism. In the final section of this chapter, I explore the potential of the human body—in alliance with the cinematography and *mise-en-scène* of certain scenes in *CSI: Miami*—to produce a personal and intimate version of urban spatiality that mollifies the extreme spatial effects on identity that virtualization and globalization produce.

THE BODY AND REFIGURED URBAN SPACE

In her analysis of urban identity and spatiality, Celeste Olalquiaga links exopolitanism to a "feeling of being in all places while not really being anywhere."[43] Nijman's description of Miami's urbanism as media-saturated, internationalized in its citizenry, and geographically centrifugal, supports my claim that virtualization and globalization combine on *CSI: Miami* to represent a disorientating spatial habitus for the city's exopolitan inhabitants. Virtualization implicates identity with new media and communications, while globalization destabilizes notions of unified citizenship. Through the combination of these forces, traditional socio-spatial relations are disrupted; in response to this, postmodern identity must be transformed to avoid the "schizophrenic" or "psychasthenic" crisis that Olalquiaga alludes to.

CSI: Miami is as much consumed with bodies as it is with the cinematographic representation of space. Caine's patriarchal method of proofing himself against multicultural diversity may deny rather than draw upon the varied activities of bodies. However, I consider the show's other bodily and spatial preoccupations simultaneously here, in order to show how the spatiality of the body is represented as constituting a powerful antagonist to the destructive spatial impacts of virtualization and globalization in the exopolitan city. To do so, I merge a formalistic approach to television with the feminist tradition of interest in the transformative potential of the body.[44] A recurring theme in *CSI: Miami* is the body that appears dead but is not, which challenges identity at its most fundamental by denying the divide of life and death (see "Hard Time," "The Oath" [2020], and "Whacked"). In "Hard Time," medical examiner Alexx Woods is about to cut open a crime victim to check time of death when Caine intervenes: "Hang on a second, this woman has perspiration on her. Check her." She is alive! Such moments of dramatic impact illustrate the power of the body to transform identity.

This power is mainly released spatially on *CSI: Miami*; the dialectic of the body and space is what interests me here. *CSI: Miami* invites us to reconsider the division between the interior and exterior spaces of the city, as the body inhabits this division. In this way, a new postmodern version of space elides the modernist opposition of private and public space. Throughout the series, the body forms a close alliance with the show's visual apparatus (specifically how interiors are lit and shot) and with its *mise-en-scène*, to bring about a form of interior space that counteracts the combined globalization and virtualization of Miami's exopolitanism. To see how this is accomplished, I detour briefly via the work of Bill Hillier and Gaston Bachelard.

Architectural and Urban Morphology Professor Bill Hillier highlights the fine-grained capacity of space to capture human urban experiences. He argues that "many if not most of the relations between the form of the city and the way it functions seem to pass through space in some sense."[45] Hillier's research unit is the London-based Space Syntax Laboratory; this title captures the insight contained in his work: as a language with its own syntax, spatial awareness can operate as a refined laboratory for urban analysis. Through being sensitive to space, "we can learn to ask questions of the city and get intelligible answers."[46] Hillier's model contains the nuance required to detect the resistance of the body within a virtualized and globalized urbanism that commits violence against identities and bodies of the sort Olalquiaga articulates. By going deeply into the representations of spatiality found in *CSI: Miami*, we can uncover otherwise hidden aspects of the show related to the functioning of Miami's urbanism.

First published in 1958, philosopher Gaston Bachelard's *The Poetics of Space* significantly pre-dates the on-screen spatial experimentation evident in texts like *CSI: Miami*. Nevertheless, it remains intellectually influential for its unsurpassed evocation of the almost imperceptible manifestations of everyday and intimate space. If Hillier activates the idea of space as a language, Bachelard explores the imaginative and personal aspects of this language via vignettes on everything from nests to shells to corners, thus sketching out a rich spatial topography. In combination, Hillier and Bachelard provide a basis for analyzing the intimate and bodily spaces that are represented on *CSI* to lie within exopolitan sites such as Miami. In these spaces, identity treads a middle path between disintegration into new media molecules under the pressures of virtualization, and the confusions of national allegiance brought on by globalization. Such spaces act as sanctuaries for resisting the "feeling of being in all places while not really being anywhere."[47] In this way, new modes of urban identity founded in the body might emerge.

The visual apparatus of *CSI: Miami* gives a special character of spatiality to these bodily sites that populate the city. Furthermore, in underscoring these sites' spatial qualities, the cinematography also insists upon their explicit urbanism through the frequent device of shuttling our view from an aerial panorama of the city into one of Miami's interiors. Phil Hubbard stresses the power of "the mythical 'god's eye' view of cities which informs all manner of maps, plans, models and abstractions of urban space."[48] Contrary to Zygmunt Bauman's comment that globalization radically unsettles our experiences and conceptualizations of the city, *CSI: Miami* gives continuity to the viewer's experience and conceptualization of urbanism, not only in its title, but also through its overhead cinematographic perspectives.

This transition from urban exteriors to interiors on the show often coincides with a sudden cessation of the camera's movement and a signal change in the intensity of the lighting: in the wake of camera speed and bright light, comes sudden stillness and low illumination. The viewer's perceptions are startled for a moment, and then soothed as their eyes become accustomed to the new lighting. This mode of montage, characteristic of *CSI: Miami*, draws us into engagement with the interior spaces of the city, and with all the ways in which (both as viewers and as actual or potential urbanites) we might inhabit these spaces. In the opening credits of the episode "Cop Killer," for example, the camera scans an office block exterior silhouetted against the setting sun, just catching a flare of sunlight in the sky, before the scene shifts to the interior of the morgue. In contrast to the movement and glare of the office-block shot, the morgue shot initially resembles a monochromatic, still-life composition. However, the space soon takes on greater richness and complexity as the camera begins to reveal its various volumes and its palette of filtered colors. In this way, the show's cinematography and lighting effects highlight the unusual spatial qualities of the morgue within the greater urban context.

Staying with this scene, we can consider the content of these sorts of interior spaces on the show. Apart from the camera's explorations of the space of the morgue itself, which are probing without being aggressive, the focus of attention in this scene is on the human body—specifically, the body of a murdered cop. Viewed from all angles, and with its image reproduced in other surfaces of the room, this body in death brings a very personal and intimate character to the space of the morgue. It is almost as if our bodies as viewers are here combining with this representation of a body. To this extent, notions of public and private slip away; the cop's body is open to our gaze (exteriorized to this extent) but this connotes something other than privacy violation or public display. With respect to urban theory, Bauman might call this a "space of flows"[49] in that its "borders are eminently permeable,"[50] while Edward Soja's notion of the city turned "inside-out and outside-in" also comes to mind.[51] This dialectical bodily space suggests a frisson of interiorized-exteriorized urban identity opposed to the identity threats presented by virtualization and globalization.

Besides the dead cop and Caine, Alexx Woods is the other person in this scene. What the Cast section on the *CSI: Miami* official website called Woods's "bedside manner with the dead" is another significant index of how bodies on the show—even, or especially, corpses—contain the transgressive potential to bring alive proximate space.[52] The cop's body, even in the surroundings of the morgue and for a seen-it-all professional like Woods, evokes intimacy, care and gentleness. The interplay here between the body and space resonates with the same spatial vocabulary Bachelard uses regarding intimate spaces: "In that region where being *wants* to be both visible and hidden, the movements of opening and closing are so numerous, so frequently inverted, and so charged with hesitation, that we could conclude on the following formula: man is half-open being."[53] The sexism of the term "man" aside, this last phrase describes the dialectic of space and body (or "being") that the cop's body evokes in the morgue through the effects of cinematography and setting. "Half-open being" is precisely bodily space: space and the body have merged here.[54] The visual apparatus and *mise-en-scène* allied to such interior spaces in *CSI: Miami* therefore help to produce what Bachelard describes as "opening-and-closing," "hesitant" and "inverted" regions.[55] And this interplay of interiority and exteriority, which the spatialized body effects within such interiors of the city, suggests new ways for the urban body to inhabit the intimate architecture of Miami as it is frequently portrayed on *CSI: Miami*.

Certainly the morgue is a privileged site of the body in *CSI: Miami*, not least because the conventions relating to how we engage other bodies in public— what Lyn Lofland terms "civil inattention"—do not apply.[56] But other interiors in the show reveal in their spaces a similar intimacy related to the potentiality of bodies. In "10-7" Caine and Agent David Park meet in a darkened corridor with an angled ceiling-to-floor glass window bordering it. The most significant aspect of the space is not its bare architecture or geometry, but the abstract combination of surfaces and depths it evokes. While obviously an enclosed space, it is also a space that opens up—much as the space of the morgue opens up—into a multiplicity of volumes, reflections and hues, making it hard to know where wall and window separate. While Caine and Park are having a confrontational conversation, the many folds of the space create an embracing and intimate sensation. The space also affects the way in which Caine moves through it. He sidles up to Park by a swaying path, as if the space itself were creating a new identity for him based in his movements (an identity *of* movement inflected by a new twist on *flâneurship* perhaps).

Like the scene in the morgue, this corridor evokes an intimacy of space, related to bodies, that invites description using Bachelard's poetics. The corridor is a space that stands in stark contrast to those other spaces of the city where bodies are virtualized (appearing like distant pixilations on the beach) and/or globalized (like Clavo Cruz, bearing a national identity at odds with the identity assumed in connection with his own body in that he is not, biologically, his father's son). An intimate play of exteriority *within* certain urban interiors emerges. The morgue and this corridor are bolt holes down which the urban body might escape from the identity dissipations of globalization and virtualization. Perhaps the key lesson of *CSI: Miami* is this: that the body, at times, suggests an intimate spatiality—located in "half-open" urban interiors—that provides a node of resistance to the present crisis of exopolitanism brought on by the convergence of globalization and virtualization. As a show with an extremely elastic range of meanings, *CSI: Miami* is simultaneously a fawning advertisement for Miami as a global city and a primer for the most personal and intimate concerns of our bodies.

NOTES

1. Celeste Olalquiaga, *Megalopolis: Contemporary Cultural Sensibilities* (Minneapolis: University of Minnesota Press, 1992), 2.

2. Ackbar Abbas, "Building on Disappearance: Hong Kong Architecture and Colonial Space" in *The Cultural Studies Reader*, ed. Simon During (London and New York: Routledge, 1999), 151.

3. Zygmunt Bauman, "Living (Occasionally Dying) Together in an Urban World" in *Cities, War, and Terrorism: Towards an Urban Geopolitics*, ed. Stephen Graham (Oxford: Blackwell Publishing, 2004), 110.

4. Karen Lury, *Interpreting Television* (London: Hodder Arnold, 2005), 46.

5. The 2000 racial, ethnic and national makeup of Miami is as follows: White persons 66.6 percent; Black or African American persons 22.3 percent; American Indian and Alaska Native persons 0.2 percent; Asian persons 0.7 percent; persons reporting some other race 5.4 percent; persons reporting two or more races 4.7 percent; persons of Hispanic or Latino origin (both white and black) 65.8 percent; foreign born persons 59.5 percent. U.S. Census Bureau, "State & County QuickFacts: Miami (City),

Florida," U.S. Census Bureau, <http://quickfacts.census.gov/qfd/states/12/1245000.html> (1 March 2007).

6. While *CSI: Crime Scene Investigation* also represents a postmodern city—Las Vegas—analysis of this show, and of *CSI: New York*, is impossible here due to space constraints.

7. Jan Nijman, "The Paradigmatic City," *Annals of the Association of American Geographers* 90, no. 1 (2000): 135.

8. Nijman, "The Paradigmatic City," 136.

9. Fredric Jameson, "Postmodernism, or The Cultural Logic of Late Capitalism," *New Left Review* 146 (1984): 53–92.

10. Edward W. Soja, "Inside Exopolis: Scenes from Orange County," in *Variations on a Theme Park: The New American City and the End of Public Space*, ed. Michael Sorkin (New York: Hill and Wang, 1992), 95.

11. Nijman, "The Paradigmatic City," 140 (emphasis added).

12. Nijman, "The Paradigmatic City," 140. Nijman's figures were accurate at the time his article was published in 2000. The 2004 figures have Miami at 58.7 percent foreign born persons and Santa Ana at 55.4 percent foreign born persons. The next highest percentage of foreign born persons is Los Angeles (40.4 percent). U.S. Census Bureau, *2004 American Community Survey*, Table 46. "Nativity and Place of Birth of Resident Population for Cities of 250,000 or More: 2004," U.S. Census Bureau, <http://www.census.gov/compendia/statab/population/> (16 Sept. 2007).

13. John Sinclair, "'The Hollywood of Latin America:' Miami as Regional Center in Television Trade," *Television & New Media* 4, no. 3 (2003): 212.

14. Lury, *Interpreting Television*, 43.

15. Cher Coad, Personal communication with the author, (15 Dec. 2006).

16. Michael Sorkin, "Introduction: Variations on a Theme Park," in *Variations on a Theme Park: The New American City and the End of Public Space*, ed. Michael Sorkin (New York: Hill and Wang,1992), xiii.

17. Jameson, "Postmodernism," 92.

18. Lury, *Interpreting Television*, 43.

19. Adrian Martin, "There's a Million Stories, and a Million Ways to Get There From Here," *Metro Magazine* 142 (2004): 86.

20. Martin, "Million Stories," 84.

21. Martin, "Million Stories," 86.

22. Martin, "Million Stories," 86.

23. Raymond A. Schroth, "The Case of the Beautiful Corpse: A Comparison of Today's TV Crime Dramas with Crime Novels of the Past Shows how our Culture has Changed," *National Catholic Reporter* 40, no. 19 (2004): 16.

24. Schroth, "Beautiful Corpse," 16.

25. Flash mobs are generally considered to have originated in New York City in May 2003. Bill Wasik, "My Crowd, Or, Phase 5: A Report from the Inventor of the Flash Mob," *Harper's Magazine* (March 2006): 56–66.

26. C. Lee Harrington and Denise D. Bielby, "Flow, Home, and Media Pleasures," *Journal of Popular Culture* 38, no. 5 (2005): 834.

27. BBC News, "*CSI* Show 'Most Popular in World,'" BBC, <http://news.bbc. co.uk/2/hi/entertainment/5231334.stm> (7 March 2007).

28. Nijman, "The Paradigmatic City," 138.

29. Nijman, "The Paradigmatic City," 138. "Rustbelt characteristics" references signs of the economic decline of heavy industry, largely in the northeastern US, associated with the move offshore of manufacturing jobs and the rise of new forms of industry.

30. Nijman, "The Paradigmatic City," 141.

31. Nijman, "The Paradigmatic City," 141.

32. CBS, "*CSI: Miami* Official Web-Site," <http://www.cbs.com/primetime/csi_ miami/> (9 Sept. 2005).

33. John T. Caldwell, "Convergence Television: Aggregating Form and Repurposing Content in the Culture of Conglomeration," in *Television after TV: Essays on a Medium in Transition*, ed. Lynn Spigel and Jan Olsson (Durham and London: Duke University Press, 2004), 50.

34. Emphasis added.

35. On the elaboration of the Oedipus Complex in terms of language carried out by Jacques Lacan, Nick Mansfield comments that "Lacan's view of subjectivity repeats the Freudian schema, but with one major variation: the drama of gender and power is displaced from anatomy to language." Nick Mansfield, *Subjectivity: Theories of the Self from Freud to Haraway* (Sydney: Allen & Unwin, 2000), 48.

36. Terry Eagleton, *Literary Theory: An Introduction* (Oxford: Basil Blackwell, 1983), 156.

37. The ethnicity of David Caruso, who plays Horatio Caine, is Italian- and Irish-American. Caruso's father is Italian and his mother is Irish. David Caruso, *NNDB: Tracking the Entire World*, <http://www.nndb.com/people/446/000025371/> (20 Sept. 2007). Caine is presented as effectively white without ethnicity, and from a working-class background.

38. Kristine Huntley, "'Blood in the Water' (Episode 4002)," *CSI Files: CSI: Miami*, <http://www.csifiles.com/reviews/csi/blood_in_the_water.shtml> (1 March, 2006).

39. Nijman, "The Paradigmatic City," 141.

40. Editors Note: with Grissom's departure from *CSI: Crime Scene Investigation* in Season 9 the exact future this hegemony is unclear.

41. Jan Nijman, "Book Review: *City on the Edge: The Transformation of Miami* by Alejandro Portes and Alex Stepick," *Annals of the Association of American Geographers* 84, no. 3 (1994): 526.

42. Shirley R. Steinberg, "Critical Multiculturalism and Democratic Schooling: An Interview with Peter L. McLaren and Joe Kincheloe," in *Multicultural Education, Critical Pedagogy, and the Politics of Difference*, ed. Christine E. Sleeter and Peter L. McLaren (Albany: State University of New York Press, 1995), 141.

43. Olalquiaga, *Megalopolis*, 2.

44. See, for example, Julia Kristeva, *Powers of Horror: An Essay on Abjection* (New York: Columbia University Press, 1982).

45. Bill Hillier, "The Common Language of Space: A Way of Looking at the Social, Economic and Environmental Functioning of Cities on a Common Basis," *Space Syntax Laboratory Web-Site*, <http://www.spacesyntax.org/publications/commonlang.html> (24 Feb. 2006).

46. Hillier, "Common Language of Space."

47. Olalquiaga, *Megalopolis*, 2.

48. Phil Hubbard, *City* (London and New York: Routledge, 2006), 97.

49. Bauman, "Living (Occasionally Dying)," 112.

50. Bauman, "Living (Occasionally Dying)," 113.

51. Soja, "Inside Exopolis," 95.

52. CBS, *CSI: Miami* <http://www.cbs.com/primetime/csi_miami/> (2005). Alexx Woods (played by Khandi Alexander) was replaced by Dr. Tara Price (played by Megalyn Echikunwoke) in Season 7, but is rumoured to be returning to the show in 2009. http://en.wikipedia.org/wiki/CSI_Miami (4 Feb. 2009).

53. Gaston Bachelard, *The Poetics of Space: The Classic Look at How We Experience Intimate Places* (Boston: Beacon Press, 1958), 222.

54. Bachelard, *Poetics of Space*, 222.

55. Bachelard, *Poetics of Space*, 222.

56. Hubbard, *City*, 17.

Chapter Seven

The Crime Scene, the Evidential Fetish, and the Usable Past

William J. Turkel

Nothing in Las Vegas is quite what it seems: no other large city in America has been so explicitly built to complicate and counterfeit its own relationship with the past. Think of the Sphinx and Pyramid of the Luxor, the Statue of Liberty in front of the New York, New York Casino, the Eiffel Tower of Paris, Las Vegas, the statuary and pools of Caesar's Palace. Think of Elton John, John Wayne, and Wayne Newton, together at Madame Tussaud's with Louis Armstrong and Neil Armstrong, George Washington and George W. Bush. The very fact that Las Vegas is fabricated, crafted to deceive, makes it the ideal setting for a television series about crime scene investigators who can determine *what really happened* by closely studying the material evidence of the place itself.

"We scrutinize the crime scene, collect the evidence and recreate what happened without ever having been there," lead CSI Gil Grissom tells the newest member of his team in the pilot episode of *CSI: Crime Scene Investigation*, "Pretty cool, actually." "I just got out of the academy," she replies, "I already know this" (1001). Presumably Grissom's statement was intended, if not for her, then for the viewing audience of October 2000, some of whom may have been unclear about the nature of the CSIs' work. The success of the show and its spin-offs has made it clear what CSIs do, at least on TV. But within a few years of the series' premiere, legal and law enforcement professionals would begin to complain of a "*CSI* effect," whereby jurors are alleged to hold the evidence in real cases to the unrealistic standards of a television show.[1] In actual settings, crime scene investigation is a kind of historical practice, and this limits the uses to which material evidence can be put.[2]

Suppose we rephrase Grissom's statement by changing one word: "we scrutinize the *archive*, collect the evidence and recreate what happened without ever having been there." We now have a succinct description of the historian's craft, rather than the CSI's. Historians, for their part, are quite fond of thinking of themselves as detectives of a sort. An influential methodological essay, "Clues," describes the kinship of microhistory with the activities of Sherlock Holmes. A well-known anthology, *The Historian as Detective*, pairs essays on historians' use of evidence with suggested readings from crime fiction. Stephen Kern's *Cultural History of Causality* is grounded in fictional representations of murder, and so on.[3] Granted, most historians do their work in conditions far removed from the scenes graphically depicted on *CSI*. They are usually surrounded by file boxes rather than brain matter (as in the episode "High and Low" 3010) or arterial spray (as in "Snuff" 3008, "Fur and Loathing" 4006, and "Butterflied" 4012).[4] To handle a papery corpus, they don white cotton gloves rather than latex ones. When we follow CSIs, real and fictional, through the stages of their work we discover that the analogy goes both ways: not only can the archive be thought of as a kind of crime scene but the crime scene as a kind of archive.

SCRUTINIZING THE CRIME SCENE

For both professional CSIs and the ones on TV, the scene of the crime is much more than a location where prior events occurred. Crucially, the scene provides context for interpretation of physical evidence. "Evidence without context is ambiguous at best," Grissom says on one occasion, and on another "evidence without context is not evidence."[5] When Catherine asks him what to make of a scrap of fabric he replies, "Out of context, I don't know" (3023). Through the episodes in a series of crime scenes, we see Grissom using the Socratic method to teach the junior members of his team, not to mention an audience that is still learning the rules of the game. Surrounded by blood and broken glass in an upscale hotel suite Grissom and Nick have the following exchange (1002):

Nick: What do you think, boss?

Grissom: You're CSI three, now. You call it.

Nick: What? You want me to play it blind?

Grissom: You've read the woman's statement. The room is full of evidentiary clues. Talk it out. What does the room say?

Grissom doesn't ask Nick what the clues say. Without context, the clues are mute. It is only the room as a whole that can speak to an interpreter who is prepared to listen. Nick learns: years later we hear him tell Brass that evidence out of context doesn't mean anything (5009).

In the third episode of the first season, "Crate 'N Burial" (1003), a similar exchange occurs between Grissom and Sara as they investigate the house where a kidnapping has occurred. Sara is talking through a scenario when she realizes that Grissom is not paying attention. She asks him if he has found something interesting:

Grissom: Dirt.

Sara: You're . . . so . . . technical. I can hardly keep up, but. . . .

Grissom: Sorry, but out of context, it's just dirt.

Later, outside the house, Sara tells him that she keeps trying to be his star pupil:

Grissom: Sara, that was a seminar. This is real. Pebbles, tiles, the front is all concrete.

Sara: No dirt. Context: there is dirt on the carpeting inside.

Grissom: In an otherwise spotless house.

Sara: You're saying the kidnapper tracked the dirt in.

Grissom: Possible. As of now, that's about all we have, so I guess we follow the dirt.

Sara also learns the lesson of contextualizing evidence at the scene. On another case a year and a half later, Grissom finds her under a bridge at night. When he asks her what she is doing she says, "Contextualizing. A shopping cart in the lab is like a lion in a zoo. I needed to see it in its natural habitat" (2023).

In *CSI* crime scenes can be neatly circumscribed, creating a space in which everything is relevant and outside which almost everything can be ignored. In real life, forensic investigators have much more difficulty determining what is and isn't part of a crime scene. As Larry Ragle, retired Director of Forensic Sciences in Orange County, California notes, "When the crime was in progress there were no out of bounds markers." Often the first officer to arrive has to make an arbitrary decision about what to include in the forensic investigation of the scene, and this "may in fact be made simply because convenient places are available for stringing the standard yellow plastic ribbon, such as street signs, poles, or car radio antennas."[6] The choice of context, in other words, is part of the interpretative process, forcing professional CSIs to confront questions of selectivity, scale and bias. These must be faced by anyone who attempts to reconstruct the past. How do you know which items of evidence make a case and which are irrelevant? How should the story of the crime be framed in time and space? Is it about a person, a relationship, a family, a town? What kind of historical background do you need to understand the crime itself? How do you know you have not subconsciously tailored the context to fit your expectations?

Historians, too, seek context for interpretation, trying to put sources back into their more-or-less original habitats in order to better understand them. These contexts may be political or intellectual or cultural. They may derive from the historian's interests in gender, race, ethnicity, class, religion or sexuality. For ecological or environmental historians, the relevant context is the natural environment. More than most of their colleagues, these historians are likely to study many of the same things that professional and fictional CSIs do, in order to recreate their role in past human affairs: bacteria, algae, fungi, plants, insects, fish, birds, mammals, species boundaries, DNA, disease, soil, agriculture, hunting, the food chain, mining, pollution, fire, climate, among other things.[7] Reading *CSI* from the perspective of environmental history allows us to ask what role material and natural surroundings can play in the reconstruction of past events.

COLLECTING THE EVIDENCE

One of the things made clear to the regular viewer of *CSI* is that clues are everywhere. Sometimes they are caught in the bluish-white beam of a flashlight or made to fluoresce under the alternate light source (ALS), which makes some kinds of latent evidence more visible: technologies of light serve as recurrent emblems for insight on the show. Often these clues are in plain view, seemingly waiting to be photographed, plucked up with tweezers, lifted with tape, swabbed or vacuumed. "There is always a clue," Grissom says in the pilot episode, "I'll find it" (1001). In a later episode in the same season, he tells Nick "People leave us clues. . . . They speak to us in thousands of different ways. It's our job to make sure that we've heard everything they've said. Anything else is reasonable doubt" (1003).

Although clues are ubiquitous on *CSI* and almost always seemingly pertinent to the case at hand, they are not always stable, manifest or easy to interpret. The ephemeral character of some kinds of material evidence is a recurrent problem for the CSIs. "Did you check for fingerprints on the body?" Catherine asks the medical examiner during one case. "Half-life of fingerprints on flesh . . . they're disappearing as we speak" (1013). In other cases, the investigation may be compromised when evidence is blown or washed away during inclement weather.[8] Clues may not always be visible. Looking over Grissom's shoulder into an airplane lavatory, Sara says, "No evidence."

"No patent evidence," Grissom corrects her, "But if there's blood present there may be latent evidence" (1009). Sometimes—à la Sherlock Holmes' "Silver Blaze"—the clue is that the expected evidence is *not* to be found.[9] Investigating a hotel room early one morning, Grissom says to Catherine, "Occasionally I'm struck by the absence of evidence" (1023). In another case, when Warrick and Nick note that there are no signs of struggle in a hallway where they are expecting to see some, Catherine says, "The only clue is no clue" (5018). Once in a while, the clue at first resists interpretation. "Peanuts on the gas pedal?" Nick says to Greg, who says "You're kidding." "Uh-uh," Nick replies. "That's one of those funny clues," Sara says, "Could mean nothing or could mean everything" (1022).

In order for each story arc to fit into the time allotted an episode, the writers make simplifying assumptions that would be untenable in the real world. One of these is that almost every bit of physical evidence that is collected by the CSIs at the crime scene is relevant to the case at hand. When a thread of mercerized cotton is found on a dead runner's body it matches the clothing of a prime suspect (4020), and not, say, the clothing of the victim's girlfriend, mom, training partner, nephew, the guy who brushed past him on the street, or the frat boys who used the machine at the laundromat before him. In the actual world, as in *CSI*, clues are everywhere. Public places are full of the kinds of traces of past human and nonhuman activity that *CSI* plots hinge on: fingerprints, shoeprints, fibers, hairs, blood, urine, semen, epithelial cells, bleaches and deodorizers, cigarette butts, discarded condoms and a nearly infinite number of other things.[10] The catch is that each of these traces could actually be evidence for a nearly infinite number of past events, almost all of which are completely irrelevant to the matter that crime scene investigators are interested in.

Because the fictional crime scenes of *CSI* guarantee that any material evidence found within them will be relevant, Grissom and his team never face the problem of selectivity. Real CSIs and historians, however, have to choose which evidence warrants further study, and even then are usually not able to learn as much as they would like. In the forensic sciences, the key problem is *individualization*. It is often not enough to know that someone made a print with an ulnar loop from their left index finger. That might rule out some suspects, but a large number will remain. In fingerprinting, it is usually essential to determine the *individual* who made a given set of prints. It is often not enough to know that a shoeprint was made by a size 10 running shoe. It has to be matched to an exact shoe, and so forth. A classic definition of the forensic sciences describes the field in exactly these terms: "Criminalistics is the science of individualization." Often, however, the best that actual investigators can do is to *identify* evidence—that is, associate it with a class or group, rather than an individual.[11]

RECREATING WHAT HAPPENED

Unless something goes badly wrong, in the long run the physical evidence on *CSI* tells one story. The CSIs usually do not hit upon the right interpretation at first, especially if they are not working with all the facts, but they eventually get there. "So, what do you think?" Nick asks Warrick as they toss a football back and forth in the break room, "Can two solid theories, each backed by evidence, both be correct?" (1008) Not in the world of *CSI*. As the rookie Holly Gribbs says in the pilot episode, "the key to being a lucid crime scene investigator [is] to reserve judgment until the evidence vindicates or eliminates assumption" (1001). Sometimes the key is to revise judgment. "Hey Grissom," Nick asks, "you know that theory I had?" "Yeah," Grissom replies, to which Nick answers, "I'd like to revise it." Grissom shoots back, "It's a scientist's right to re-examine his theory with each new piece of evidence, Nick" (1018).

Some of the dramatic tension in *CSI* comes from the investigators' struggles to reserve judgment when the physical evidence seems to support a conclusion that they do not like. In these situations the team members often personify the evidence, referring to it as if it could talk to them, lead them around, or play hide-and-seek. "Hey," Warrick says to Catherine as they search a car for clues of a kidnapping, "you don't think I'm feeling this? But we got to follow the evidence even if we don't like where it takes us—it's the job." Later she says to him, "When you want evidence, you can't find it. When you don't want it, it's as big as Dallas" (1003). When Sara reminds Grissom that he often says the CSIs are the "victim's last voice," he replies, "You don't crunch evidence to fit a theory" (1010). It is natural for the investigators to feel empathy for the victims, but that must not interfere with their evaluation of the evidence.

This impartiality becomes most difficult when it seems that one of their own has committed a crime. When a sex worker that Nick slept with is strangled and it seems that he may have done it, the CSIs continue their investigation reluctantly. The medical examiner asks Catherine about the body, "What if I lift his prints from her?" "Then that's what you report. Evidence, Doc," she says shaking her head, "all we've got." Dayshift supervisor Conrad Ecklie, who wouldn't mind seeing his competitor Grissom's team fall apart, tells them, "I'm sorry if you guys don't like where the evidence is pointing. But show me otherwise; tell me where I'm wrong. In the meantime, my hands are tied. I have protocol to follow." None of the *CSI* team disagrees. "Ignore the evidence against [Nick] Stokes and it looks like special favors for CSI," says Ecklie. "Well," the Sheriff replies, "I can't have that" (1013). In the long run, special favors are not needed and the evidence exonerates Nick, underlining the importance of reserving judgment.

In the televisual world of *CSI*, there is only one real past—*what really happened*—and the material evidence found within a tightly constrained crime scene is necessary and sufficient for the fictional CSIs to determine what this past was. Things are rarely so clear for professional CSIs. Although there may be physical evidence at almost all crime scenes, forensic science is used in very few trials.[12] The boundaries of crime scenes are fuzzy; the evidence is often consistent with many interpretations. Actual CSIs have a limited amount of time and money for each investigation and many apparent leads go nowhere. At this point it is useful to introduce the distinction that historians make between *the past*—gone, unchangeable and inaccessible—and *history*, the stories that we tell about the past. For historians and for professional CSIs, stories about the past can only be more-or-less probable, but never certain. Such stories are always biased and often contested; they are always subject to revision. There are no stories about the past that can be told with the objectivity and certainty that characters espouse on *CSI*. This means that physical evidence can never play quite the same role in practice as it does in the show. The fantasies of evidentiary interpretation in *CSI* allow relationships between people to be recast as relationships between people and evidence. Evidence, in other words, is fetishized in *CSI*.

EVIDENCE AS FETISH

In "Slaves of Las Vegas" (2008) a pair of lovers playing in a park at night find the body of a young woman partially buried in a sandbox. Whip and ligature marks on the body, some old, suggest a history of abuse to the CSIs, and yet the woman has not been raped, is otherwise well-groomed and has had expensive plastic surgery. Further clues (traces of liquid latex on the body, the serial number on her breast implant) provide the CSIs with both a name for the victim and a profession: fetish club worker. Later, as we go inside the club, we see a range of props that facilitate the customers' sexual fetishes: whips, paddles, dog-collars, leather masks, cages and faux schoolrooms. The proprietor, Lady Heather, asks Grissom, "Does all this fascinate you?" "Yes," he replies, "I find all deviant behavior fascinating, in that to understand our human nature we have to understand our aberrations."

Grissom is actually inconsistent in his thinking about normal and deviant sexual behavior. Either that, or his repeated encounters with Lady Heather, to whom he is clearly attracted, broadens his perspective (2008, 3015). Two years later, while investigating a death in a community of plushies and furries—people who interact and have sex in animal costumes—Catherine asks Grissom, "whatever happened to normal sex?" "What is normal sex?" he asks. When Catherine asks him in turn if he thinks it is natural "for a grown human only to be intimate with a talking animal," he replies, "Freud said that the only unnatural sexual behavior was to have none at all. And after that, it's just a question of opportunity and preference" (4006).

Although the popular notion of fetishism emphasizes a preference for latex, stiletto heels and ball gags, social theorists distinguish a range of human activities as fetishistic.[13] According to William Pietz, the term fetish "was not proper to any prior discrete society, [but] originated in the colonial spaces of the coast of West Africa during the sixteenth and seventeenth centuries." By the eighteenth century Western students of religion adopted it to refer—with a clear sense of cultural and economic superiority—to cases where people attributed human qualities to non-human entities.[14] In the nineteenth century, the term was appropriated by Marx to describe what he called commodity fetishism. "It is nothing but the definite social relation between men themselves," Marx wrote, "which assumes here, for them, the fantastic form of a relation between things."[15] More prominently in popular imagination, the term was also used by Krafft-Ebing and Freud to refer to cases where sexual attachment is connected to inanimate objects or non-sexual body parts, or where these objects come to stand for (or stand in for) genitalia. Krafft-Ebing gave examples where body odor, braids or items of clothing were associated with sexual satisfaction. More controversially, Freud explained the fetish as an inanimate object that a male child substitutes for the mother's allegedly missing penis in order to mitigate castration anxiety.[16] The anthropologist Roy Ellen has argued that, of all the similarities between religious, economic and psychological uses of the idea of fetishism, the only one that we should reject "is the idea that fetishism is intrinsically aberrant or reflective of a primitive mental condition."[17] Instead, we can see fetishization as a common process whereby inanimate, material things get drawn into social relations between people and take on a life of their own.

In *CSI* the evidence takes on fetishistic qualities. Consider a series of exchanges from the pilot episode. Warrick is interviewing a suspect who says, "I already told you everything." "I understand that," Warrick replies, "But the evidence is telling us something different." Later Grissom says to him, "Forget about the husband, Warrick. Forget about the assumptions. Forget about your promotion. These things will only confuse you. Concentrate on what cannot lie: the evidence." In the same episode, Grissom tells the family of a suspected suicide, "The evidence leads us to believe it was in fact a homicide" (1001). This is not merely a figure of speech; physical or trace evidence is consistently personified in *CSI*. Not only does it speak (truthfully), but it is more reliable than other people's memory (1005), written documentation (1012), or eyewitness testimony (1006, 1009). In fact, in the world of *CSI*, physical evidence almost always trumps testimony. In the series' second episode, Grissom tells a suspect, "We're not detectives. We're crime scene analysts. We're trained to ignore verbal accounts and rely instead on the evidence a scene sets before us." In the third episode, he says, "I tend not to believe people. People lie. The evidence doesn't lie." In the fifth episode, when someone tells Catherine that a suspect had nothing to do with a killing, she says, "The blood evidence is telling us otherwise." In episode after episode, people lie and the CSIs prefer to believe what the physical evidence is telling them.[18] As Sara says to Grissom: "We can bury him under evidence. You're the one who is always saying its better to have one piece of forensic evidence than ten eyewitnesses" (1010).

Bury, indeed. The rhetoric of fetishism in its religious, economic and psychological uses is a normative one. In the colonial context the imagined African fetish was an idol, inferior to the Christians' god. The fact that African people were thought to worship strange things also suggested an economic inferiority, an inability to assess the real value of objects (although this is exactly what happens under capitalism through commodity fetishism).[19] Psychological uses of the term consistently place fetishism in the category of abnormal behavior, thus using it to define normal behavior as "not fetishistic."[20] In *CSI* the accumulated weight of physical evidence also has a normative force. Items of physical evidence—from abrasions and accelerant to Zolpidem and the zygomatic arch—become conflated with abstract concepts like veracity and certainty.[21] In the fictional world of *CSI*, we should only believe in the physical evidence: everything else is deceit. Scientific objectivity is thus portrayed as normal, and anything that is not objective as abnormal.

THE LATENT MADE MANIFEST

Literary scholars argue that a "stable set of rules" was established for crime and mystery writing by the 1920s. On the one hand, the genre was characterized by a conservative outlook "that linked the solution of the crime and the resolution of disorder with the maintenance of social class structures, the protection of property for those who possessed it, and the identification of criminal disorder with social destabilization." On the other, some writing in this genre provided a more radical outlook, through which "crime became a norm rather than a disruption as well as the practice and ethos of the detective, who in the hands of some authors became a champion of ordinary people instead of a defender of the status quo."[22] If we transpose the rules of crime fiction to television, the investigators of *CSI* lie squarely within the conservative tradition. By this I mean that they are presented as

William J. Turkel

upholding the ultimate legitimacy of the criminal justice system at all costs. Rather than break the law, they are willing to follow the evidence even when it seems to incriminate one of their own (1013). Unlike actual CSIs, those on television have powers normally reserved for police, like carrying handguns, interrogating suspects, and ultimately resolving cases.[23] If there is such a thing as the *"CSI* effect," at least some people must perceive the show as a realistic depiction of the power of the forensic scientific method in the prosecution of crime. Even for those who do not see forensic science as a conservative force, the show serves as a text with which the audience can engage in order to imaginatively resolve conflicts in society. By graphically depicting horrors week after week—a family massacred, a mob stomping a sick man to death, a woman murdered in a snuff film, a human body in a meat grinder, a man with a wooden stake in his head, a man buried alive, and so on—*CSI* portrays Las Vegas, and by extension urban America, as a remarkably violent environment.[24] CSI not only poses the problem of social disorder, however, it also offers a solution.

In the world of *CSI*, violence is counterbalanced by the certainty of apprehension and punishment, a certainty based on the ever-multiplying techniques of the forensic sciences. In this, *CSI* draws on a long cultural tradition that envisions a contest between crime and science, running through popular works from *Science Catches the Criminal* (1935) to *Forensics for Dummies* (2004). The former tells us: "to a generation born into a tradition of science-worship, it is scarcely conceivable that men should attempt to solve a mystery of any kind—geologic, criminal or divine—outside the sacred purlieus of the laboratory."[25] The latter puts a comparable claim in more secular terms: "For law enforcement to keep pace with criminal advancements, other techniques had to be developed. Science came to the rescue with methods that depend less on eyewitnesses to identify perpetrators or at least link them to their victims or crime scenes."[26] But death investigation in the US has always been a complicated affair, with a bewildering variety of statewide, district and county medical examiner systems, county and district coroners, and other arrangements.[27] In sharp contrast to the privileged role played by scientific evidence in *CSI*, in professional practice, scientists' claims to certainty are tempered by various qualifications, balanced by a legal system that privileges eyewitness testimony, and opposed by humanists and social scientists who argue that scientific objectivity is at least partially a social construction. The evidence, the reconstructed past, and scientific expertise are almost always highly contested. One exchange in *CSI*—unusual for the show—is more representative of the way that science is actually negotiated in the criminal justice system:[28]

Sheriff Mobley: Captain Brass, do you understand Grissom's insect evidence?

Brass [nods]: To a degree. You know . . . in a general way.

Mobley [to Grissom]: Do you think a jury will understand your 'adjustments'? Or do you think they'll realize your 'conditions' can make the evidence say anything you want it to say?

Grissom: I can make a case to any jury against Scott Shelton for the murder of his wife.

Mobley: Your arresting officer can barely understand it. I read the file. Other than bugs is there anything else? [Grissom shakes his head no]. Get something a jury can understand or move on" (1010).

As a popular textbook on crime scene investigation reminds would-be expert witnesses: "Remember the KISS Principle and keep it simple!"[29]

This uneasy tension between lawyers, scientific experts and trial jurors who are thought incapable of understanding details is the product of a specific historical moment. Up until the second half of the nineteenth century, ordinary people were regularly drawn into death investigations via the mechanism of the coroner's inquest. When a body was discovered, the coroner would summon a jury to view it, listen to the statements of witnesses and determine the cause of death. Over the course of the twentieth century, however, the legal powers of the coroner's inquest were greatly reduced.[30] Scenes of violent death became a place where medical and scientific expertise was negotiated and ordinary citizens were relegated to the roles of bystander, perpetrator, victim or voyeur. Tens of millions of people now tune in weekly to watch *CSI* and its spin-offs, vicariously participating in a mode of historical reconstruction that used to be one of their democratic rights.[31] However, unlike the often irresolvable complexities of evidence that would have confronted them historically at a coroner's inquest, what *CSI* teaches them is that scientific certainty always triumphs over crime, that physical evidence always leads to the truth, that what really happened can be always be figured out. It teaches them that forensic science is limited to a clearly demarcated crime scene, and not linked in any tangible way to the historical, socio-cultural, legal or political contexts within which these crimes occur. If only things were so simple. Beyond the televisual world of orderly verisimilitude portrayed on *CSI* are an infinite number of clues with almost as many possible interpretations, an unending contest for a usable past, and a tangled skein of science and politics, where knowledge is power and vice versa. This is the historian's crime scene.

NOTES

1. For example, see Robin Franzen, "TV's 'CSI' Crime Drama Makes it Look Too Easy," *The Oregonian* (10 Dec 2002). Some legal scholars dispute the putative influence of the *CSI* effect. See Jill Schachner Chanen, "Stay Tuned: With Reality TV Shows, Videotape Evidence and High-Tech Court Presentations, the Medium Has Become the Message in Law," *American Bar Association Journal* 90 (Oct 2004): 44–56. See also Harvey and Derksen's chapter in this volume, "The *CSI Effect:* Science Fiction or Social Fact? An exploratory content analysis of popular press reports."

2. William J. Turkel, "Every Place is an Archive: Environmental History and the Interpretation of Physical Evidence," *Rethinking History* 10, no.2 (2006): 259–76.

3. Carlo Ginzburg, "Clues: Roots of an Evidential Paradigm," in *Clues, Myth, and the Historical Method* (Baltimore: Johns Hopkins, 1989); Robin Winks, ed. *The Historian as Detective: Essays on Evidence* (New York: Harper, 1969); Stephen Kern, *A Cultural History of Causality: Science, Murder Novels and Systems of Thought* (Princeton: Princeton, 2004).

4. The episodes referred to in the text are 3010 (brain matter) and 3008, 4006, and 4012 (arterial spray).

5. These quotes are from episodes 3018 and 4005, respectively.

6. Larry Ragle, *Crime Scene* (New York: Avon, 2002), 62.

7. The episodes in which these occur are: bacteria (1020, 3018), algae (4004, 5005), fungi (3003, 5019), plants (1017, 2007, 3017), insects (1010, 4021, 5016, 5024), fish (3017), birds (2014, 5004), mammals (1022, 3003, 3016, 5002), species boundaries (2015, 2020, 3012), DNA (4017, 5018), epidemic disease (2007), soil (3008), agriculture (2011), hunting (5014), food (3004, 5019), the food chain (2005, 2020), mining (1003, 3016), pollution (5004, 5019), fire (4006), climate (2016, 2021, 4004). For environmental histories that cover some of the same ground, see, for example, Alfred Crosby, *Ecological Imperialism: The Biological Expansion of Europe, 900-1900* (Cambridge, UK: Cambridge, 1993) or Ted Steinberg, *Down to Earth: Nature's Role in American History* (Oxford, UK: Oxford, 2002).

8. Episodes in which this occurs include 1013, 1018, 2013, and 3018.

9. Arthur Conan Doyle, "Silver Blaze," *Strand Magazine* (Dec 1892), Reprinted in *The Memoirs of Sherlock Holmes* (1893). In this story, Holmes draws a Scotland Yard detective's attention to "the curious incident of the dog in the night-time." When the detective replies that the dog did nothing, Holmes says, "That was the curious incident." Later Holmes' reasoning becomes clear. The fact that the dog didn't bark suggests that it must have known the perpetrator of the crime.

10. The episodes in which these occur are: fingerprints (1008, 1014), shoeprints (4010, 5007), fibers (5007, 5016), hairs (4018, 5017), blood (1002, 3008, 5001, 5017), urine (3001, 5001), semen (4021, 5016), epithelial cells (3009, 4017), bleaches and deodorizers (2011, 5017), cigarette butts (4015, 5021), discarded condoms (3021, 3022).

11. The original statement is from Paul L. Kirk, "The Ontogeny of Criminalistics," *Journal of Criminal Law, Criminology, and Police Science* 54 (1963): 235–38; for further discussion see also Harold Tuthill, *Individualization Principles and Proce-*

dures in Criminalistics (Salem, OR: Lightning Powder, 1994); Joe Nickell and John F. Fischer, *Crime Science: Methods of Forensic Detection* (Lexington: University Press of Kentucky, 1999); Ragle, *Crime Scene*; Barry A. J. Fisher, *Techniques of Crime Scene Investigation*, 7th ed. (Boca Raton: CRC Press, 2003).

12. It is difficult to determine how many crime scenes have physical evidence, and estimates range from about 40–90 percent. The number of notifiable offences where forensic science is actually used may be less than 2 percent. (A notifiable offence is one that is serious enough to be recorded by the police.) Mike Redmayne, Expert Evidence and Criminal Justice (Oxford: Oxford, 2001), 17.

13. How do we know which associations are popularly held? I used a digital humanities approach. Search engines like Google provide access to the aggregate behavior of hundreds of millions of people, and thus constitute what John Battelle calls "the database of intentions" (Battelle, *The Search* [New York: Penguin, 2005]). On 20 Aug 2006, the term "fetish" appeared on 46,300,000 web pages, the term "latex" on 87,300,000 web pages and both terms on 10,300,000 pages. Using a metric called the "normalized Google distance" (NGD) we can use information like this to determine the distance between any pair of terms, where a lower number reflects a closer association. The following list shows the distance of each term from the term "fetish," suggesting the degree to which the two terms are popularly associated: latex (0.3856), heels (0.4216), gag (0.4976), choke (0.5499), rubber (0.5534), leather (0.5744), doll (0.5813), dungeon (0.6050), handcuffs (0.6220), smoking (0.6296), balloon (0.6484), cigar (0.7154), fur (0.7879), Freud (0.7922), psychoanalysis (0.7975), Marx (0.8196), Krafft-Ebing (0.9559), commodity (1.006). For NGD, see Rudi Cilibrasi and Paul Vitanyi, "The Google Similarity Distance," IEEE Trans. *Knowledge and Data Engineering* 19, no.3 (2007): 370–383 and William J. Turkel, A Metric for the Popular Imagination (Weblog, 5 Aug 2006) in "Digital History Hacks: Methodology for the Infinite Archive," <http://digitalhistoryhacks.blogspot.com> (1 Sept. 2007).

14. For early attestations see *Oxford English Dictionary*, s.v., "fetish, n." For the history of the term, see William Pietz, "The Problem of the Fetish I," *Res* 9 (1985): 5–17, quote from 5; "The Problem of the Fetish II: The Origin of the Fetish," *Res* 13 (1987): 23–45; "The Problem of the Fetish, IIIa: Bosman's Guinea and the Enlightenment Theory of Fetishism," *Res* 16 (1988): 105–23.

15. Karl Marx, *Capital*, vol. 1 (London: Penguin Classics, 1990), quote from 165.

16. Richard von Krafft-Ebing, *Psychopathia Sexualis*, translated by F. J. Rebman (New York: Pioneer, 1939); Freud, "Fetishism," *The Standard Edition of the Complete Works of Sigmund Freud*, Vol. 21, edited by James Strachey (London: Hogarth Press, 1974), 152–59.

17. Roy Ellen, "Fetishism," *Man*, new ser. 23, no. 2 (1988): 213–35.

18. The episodes referred to in the text are 1002, 1003, and 1005. For more episodes where this happens, see 1007, 1012, 1013, 2006, 3004, 4011.

19. Pietz, "The Problem of the Fetish I."

20. Fetishism is listed as one of the paraphilias in section 302.81 of the *Diagnostic and Statistical Manual of Mental Disorders*, 4th ed. text revision [DSM-IV-TR] (Arlington, VA: American Psychiatric Association, 2000).

21. The "CSI Handbook" at the CBS website for the show lists almost 300 different kinds of physical evidence that have played a role in the series. <http://www.cbs.com/primetime/csi/handbook/index.php?section=evidence>, accessed 27 Aug 2006.

22. Rosemary Herbert, ed. *The Oxford Companion to Crime and Mystery Writing* (New York: Oxford, 1999), s.v., "Conservative vs. Radical Worldview."

23. Ragle, *Crime Scene*, xii.

24. The episodes in which these occur are as follows: massacre (1007), mobs (1009, 3009), snuff film (3008), meat grinder (3011), wooden stake (3016), buried alive (5024). Las Vegas is relatively violent: the FBI Uniform Crime Reports listed about 789 violent crimes per 100,000 people in Las Vegas in 2004 (compared with a national average of about 466 violent crimes per 100,000 people). But Las Vegas is not as bad as Atlanta (1842 violent crimes / 100,000 people in 2004), Detroit (1740), Miami (1677), Tampa (1595), Philadelphia (1408), Dallas (1316), Oakland (1277), Houston (1146), Pittsburgh (1119), Los Angeles (1107), or even Columbus (811). Department of Justice, Federal Bureau of Investigation, *Crime in the United States 2004*, <http://www.fbi.gov/ucr/cius_04/> (27 Aug. 2006).

25. Henry Morton Robinson, *Science Catches the Criminal* (New York: Blue Ribbon, 1935), 14.

26. Douglas P. Lyle, *Forensics for Dummies* (Chichester, West Sussex: John Wiley, 2004), 8.

27. Debra L. Combs, R. Gibson Parrish, and Roy Ing, *Death Investigation in the United States and Canada, 1990* (Atlanta: US Department of Health and Human Services, et al, 1990).

28. For the contested role of scientific experts in real courts, see, for example, Gary Edmund, ed. *Expertise in Regulation and Law* (Aldershot, UK: Ashgate, 2004).

29. Fisher, *Techniques*, 21.

30. "The Coroners and Crime," *Journal of Criminal Law* 3 (1939): 304–19; "The Office of the Coroner versus the Medical Examiner System," *Journal of Criminal Law, Criminology and Police Science* 46 (1955–56): 232–37; D. R. Buchanan and J. K. Mason, "The Coroner's Office Revisited," *Medical Law Review* 3 (1995): 142–60; Ian A. Burney, *Bodies of Evidence: Medicine and the Politics of the English Inquest, 1830–1926* (Baltimore: Johns Hopkins, 2000).

31. The size of the viewing audience for *CSI* is estimated weekly by Nielsen Media Research.

Part III

LATE MODERN SUBJECTS

Chapter Eight

Not the Usual Suspects:
The Obfuscation of Political Economy
and Race in *CSI*

Kevin Denys Bonnycastle

A society is possible in the last analysis because the individuals in it carry
around in their heads some sort of picture of that society.[1]

Now whole sections of society have had to be symbolically expelled in
order to maintain a normative model of a rational society.[2]

THE DISAPPEARED DANGEROUS
UNDERCLASS AS PROBLEMATIC

Prior to this project, I had occasionally viewed *CSI: Crime Scene Investigation*. At first glance, *CSI* reflects mass visual culture's propensity to
dramatize sensational and rare forms of violence, such as predatory killings
and sexual assaults.[3] *CSI* also taps into American culture's support for law-
and-order as seeing justice done, not only by apprehending the guilty, but
exonerating the falsely accused. Toward this end, *CSI* glamorizes a new type
of crime expert—the crime scene investigator (CSI) or criminalist—whose
real and imaginary forensic technologies are coupled to the natural sciences
and Cartesian scientific-deductive rationalities. In contrast, *CSI* links traditional uniformed police to the human sciences and decenters them—for that
reason—as competent crime experts.

Most *CSI* storylines revolve around death—wrongful and accidental. Each
episode of the original series is set in contemporary Las Vegas, an American city rife with conditions that crime drama storylines thrive upon. Death
and despair abound. As of 2003, not only did Las Vegas have one of the
highest crime rates and suicide rates in the United States, but an estimated
8,000 homeless people, among the highest secondary school dropout rates,

burgeoning street gang problems, and entrenched organized crime. A widening economic gap divides the affluent and working or poorer classes in the city. Notwithstanding that Las Vegas' 2003 median household income was nearly $50,000, half of all jobs there are in the low-paying, non-unionized service sector. Every day 25,000 people actively seek work in the city.[4]

Surprisingly, however, in *CSI* storylines, the most economically and politically marginalized segments of society—dubbed *the underclass* by some sociologists—do not figure prominently as either victims or assailants. In particular, the American underclass, denoting the "dangerous" and "largely black and Hispanic population living in concentrated zones of poverty in central cities,"[5] is conspicuously absent. Instead, *CSI* links white, middle-class or bourgeois citizens to predatory killings, as both agents and objects.

These representations stand in stark contrast to the everyday practices and media portrayals of American crime and punishment.[6] According to official crime statistics, in 2005, blacks represented thirteen percent of the U.S. population, twelve years or older, but forty-nine percent of all homicide victims and fifty-four percent of all firearm victims. Overall, African Americans were six times more likely than whites to be homicide victims.[7] Racialized populations are also over-represented among those convicted in violent crime categories. By the beginning of the twenty-first century, black and Hispanic populations constituted over sixty percent of female[8] and seventy percent of male American prison entrants—dubbed the "blackening" of U.S. penal populations.[9]

In actuality, not only is the typical American prisoner young, poor, male, undereducated, underemployed, and racialized, but, according to Barak, "the predatory criminal" in Western mass visual culture is now a euphemism for young black males, who are portrayed as "less human, less rational, and less Eurocentric" than "the rest of us."[10] "Because of the persistent power of racism" writes Angela Davis, "'criminals' and 'evildoers' are in the collective imagination fantasized as people of color."[11] In light of this discussion, the object of my analysis is the virtual absence on *CSI* of the media icon predatory young African American—or phenotypically black male[12]—and other socially and economically disenfranchised underclass populations, as both assailants and victims.

In this chapter, the term "racialized" refers to historically specific discourses about non-white people, which permeate Eurocentric institutions and entrench whiteness as the invisible standard for citizenship. Although much scholarly consensus exists that race has no biological basis, racialized and *racializing* discourses and practices tie phenotypically non-white bodies, communities, and cultures to racial characteristics that authorize unequal and differential access to power and privilege.[13] In turn, "unearned privileges on the basis of whiteness . . . are defended in discourses of denial, innocence, and color-blindness."[14] Historically and today, a key site for the production and dissemination of racializing discourses is the criminal justice system and representations thereof.[15]

At the most general level, my research problematic asks: where is "the dangerous underclass" in *CSI*, and what are some of the effects of this exclusion upon representations of crime, criminality, and crime experts? I begin by setting out my theoretical frameworks and a brief methodological note. Then I sketch the neoliberal economic and political order, and concomitant forms of penality,[16] which effectively co-author *CSI* storylines. I organize my findings within three emergent themes emblematic of new post-welfare forms of punishment: namely, rational choice free-will subjects, responsibilization strategies, and the nation state's retreat from causal crime narratives and experts.

In my discussion, I show how *CSI* dramatizes, stabilizes, and circulates the desired attributes of a historically specific "new good citizen"[17] and, in so doing, rationalizes extant crime policy initiatives. By eliding racialized perpetrators, *CSI* storylines also elide real policing issues afflicting underclass communities, including aggressive, paramilitary police units and corollary inhumane penal systems. These control tactics over-target populations deemed threatening to state-defined social order, including subjects who opt out or are *pushed* out of capitalist labor relationships.[18] These crime control strategies—driven by political and media forces—embody increasingly punitive *neoconservative* motifs and, as such, are irreducible to the rationalizing surveillance technologies and seamless neoliberal logic showcased across my episode sample.[19] I argue that *CSI*, in effect, conjures a two-tiered system of public policing by insinuating an unspoken question: *viz.* if *CSI*'s new arsenal of scientific, dispassionate, and rational surveillance technologies is linked to white, middle class Americans, for whom is the arsenal of military police tactics and weapons intended?

THEORETICAL FRAMEWORKS AND METHODOLOGY

My specific point of departure is Dario Melossi's ideas about the connections between "oscillating" representations of crime and criminality in popular and professional culture, and historical restructurings of political-economic orders. He uses the term "representations" to connote an "elective affinity," rather than a deterministic relationship, between cultural forms (or "aesthetic productions") and economic structures. In short, Melossi argues that the criminal is a malleable but never random social production, whose embodiment reflects the constraints of particular political and economic arrangements.[20] This makes some representations more compelling than others, to some audiences, at particular points in time.

According to Melossi (informed by the work of George Rusche[21]), during times of sustained economic growth and low unemployment—such as the post-war prosperity marking the 1950s and 1960s—the criminal is portrayed with relative sympathy as, for example, a casualty of social inequalities rather than a threat to social order. Under conditions of decreasing economic profitability and high unemployment—which emerged during the mid 1970s in Western democracies—the criminal is reconfigured as "the public enemy" or a "monstrum—a being whose features are inherently different from 'ours' and shocking to the well-behaved."[22]

Melossi's object of study is not *how* representations of the criminal change; however, he includes "fictional accounts"—presumably including media crime drama—as one site of cultural contestation over discursive portrayals of crime and criminality. Certainly, much consensus exists that most of what is known within dominant culture about crime and criminality comes to us through the media.[23] The point taken from Melossi is the affinity between particular representations of criminals and material conditions of existence.

Three other interrelated insights shape my analysis. First is Sherene Razack's suggestion that we consider courtroom trials as providing "moments[s] in public education" that create "national narratives" and "agreed upon public truth about race."[24] Along this vein, Toni Morrison argues that "official stories" developed within and disseminated beyond the courtroom, in effect, impose the dominant culture's will upon its audiences.[25] Third, Wahneema Lubiano's study illuminates how national narratives work, not only by imposition, but by making absent alternative representations and truths.[26] Carrying these insights to popular crime dramas, I propose to read *CSI* as creating official narratives that simultaneously foster and diminish the repertoire of dominant culture stories about crime, criminals, and crime experts.

CHAPTER METHODOLOGY

My data are drawn from viewing twenty consecutive episodes of the original *CSI*, already in syndication, between June and August 2005. I choose here to concentrate on how these episodes treat culpable homicide,[27] which is the most often featured crime category confronting the series' fictional forensic investigators. Using constant comparative analysis,[28] I coded episodes until I reached data saturation.[29] Then, to test the reliability of my themes, I viewed and coded ten more syndicated episodes that aired in December 2005 and January 2006.

I examine the *CSI* effect[30] by asking, first, what explicit and implicit national narratives and public truths about the criminal, the victim, and the crime-expert are enabled and disabled across the *CSI* episodes that I studied. Notwithstanding that there is always room for resistance in the relationship between the viewer and the televisual text,[31] what is it possible to say—in the context of the show— about crime and criminality in American society, and what existing portrayals of motive are not represented or *representable* across these episodes? Second, how do *CSI* storylines reflect, circulate, and reinforce a material reality supportive of these historically specific representations?

A NEOLIBERAL SOCIAL ORDER AND CONCOMITANT POST-WELFARE STRATEGIES OF POWER

Since at least the early 1980s, Western liberal state forms have been shifting from a Keynesian welfare model to a neoliberal model. New neoliberalized logic tries to convince us that a country can no longer provide its citizens with state-based forms of welfare, health, crime control, and social services while remaining competitive in the face of globalized economic production and free trade.[32] Hence, we are witnessing efforts to drastically reduce the individual citizen's claims upon government by dismantling the old welfare state and discursively normalizing new arrangements through public policy and media representations insinuating the requirements and characteristics of the "new good citizen."[33]

The new good neoliberal citizen has eclipsed the old dependent welfare state citizen, who was once relatively shielded from the vicissitudes of capitalism by some state commitment to a Keynesian public policy framework, characterized by a more equitable distribution of wealth through social assistance programs and economic regulation. Now reformed as rational decision-makers who are free to make choices, we are actively "responsibilized"[34] and regulated through discourses about our freedom and duty to manage our own destinies through prudent choices.[35] Within these discursive and material shifts from social to individual responsibility, the lumpen proletariat of over two decades of neoliberal rule and "vampire capitalism"[36] are viewed as architects of their own misfortunes and freely chosen life styles, rather than victims of restructured national economies and vanishing social safety nets. In turn, the state would prefer that these problem populations—embodying the "dark side" and contradictions of neoliberalism—remain invisible and, by extension, unknowable.[37]

Under post-welfarist, post-Keynesian global capitalism, Western systems of penality are undergoing transformations as metaphoric and material as the previous historical shift from sovereign forms of power that targeted the body, to technologies targeting "the soul."[38] In two widely cited papers, Feeley and Simon propose that disciplinary power, which works on and through the penal subject by normalizing and correcting the individual, is no longer the primary vehicle through which contemporary penal power is exercised. Instead, they advance that actuarial tools, which generate mathematical statements about the statistical likelihood of future behaviors within specific sub-populations, are replacing older welfarist quests for causal knowledge of deviance and the deviant. This so-called "New Penology" is making obsolete a multiplicity of old welfare state experts whose authority derives from their claims to understand the individual.[39]

Displacing the old penology is a managerial approach to crime control, the aim of which is not crime's elimination, but its rational management.[40] As a technology developed by the insurance industry, actuarialism no longer requires the clinician's psycho-medical authority for understanding people. Rather than the human sciences, the newest penal experts are trained in advanced statistical theory. As such, rather than talking to actual subjects, experts interact with file data to calculate the qualities of sub-groups to which individuals are thought to belong.[41] Increasingly, actuarial risk expertise lies in the design of new risk and surveillance technologies that remove from the equation any knowledge of the individual, effectively, elevating dehumanization to a virtue. In the age of "responsibilization," then, by claiming to discover the objective factors of risk and deduce effective management strategies, the newest penology can claim the moral ground of doing "responsible science."[42]

I am not suggesting, here, a simple hydraulic shift from older to newer penal regimes. Certainly, residual welfarist effects linger in contemporary post-welfare practices. Moreover, both Garland[43] and O'Malley[44] have identified two contradictory and co-extensive official criminologies within British and American crime control policies. As typologized by Garland, a *criminology of the self*, which normalizes the motivation to commit crimes by presuming a rational, opportunistic offender, much like "us" coexists with a *criminology of the other*, conjuring monstrous, typically racialized "Others" whose seemingly random predatory acts place them beyond the pale of rationality.[45] In common, both criminologies mark the extreme individualizing of crime and remove blame from the structural inadequacies of our political economy. Whereas the former anticipates a potentially reformable neoliberal citizen, the latter imagines the unredeemable anti-citizen and non-citizen targeted for social isolation and permanent exclusion by neoconservative political law-and-order agendas.

FINDINGS: *CSI* AS THE NEW PENOLOGY

Having reviewed the neoliberal framework bracing the newest penal practices, my next section focuses on *CSI* storylines involving culpable homicide in order to isolate *CSI*'s penal DNA. Here I introduce the themes elaborated in the rest of the chapter.

The New Criminal Mind: Making a Rational Choice to Kill

The thirty *CSI* episodes viewed include fifty-one representations of criminal homicides, involving forty-seven perpetrators.[46] Of these, thirty-nine are adults (twenty-nine males and ten females); seven are teenagers (five males and two females); and one is a female child. Throughout these stories, *CSI* instills the criminal—both male and female—with the prerequisites of neoliberal citizenship: rationality, free choice, and self-control. Fostering this characterization, no alcohol-related killings are insinuated among the vocabularies of motive for any culpable killing depicted in these episodes. Without exception in my sample, no perpetrator forms the intent to kill—or actually kills—under the influence of any judgment-impairing substances.[47]

Further embodying the constructed rational choice perpetrator, in forty-eight of the fifty-one killings in these episodes, death is the intended goal, rather than the result of an unintended or reckless effect of force. Across all forty-eight intended deaths, forty-three perpetrators are represented as forming the deliberate and specific intent to kill, animated by the everyday emotions of sane men and women: revenge, sexual jealousy, envy, greed, hatred, resentment, and other motives readily understandable by the average viewer. Only five perpetrators are represented as impulsive or their crimes depicted as spontaneous choices arising in the heat of the moment or triggered by a temporary loss of self-control. No one in these episodes killed for control of the drug trade, during a robbery gone wrong, or in the context of escalating domestic violence.

This dominant representation of killings on the show simultaneously reflects and reverses the "typical [American] criminal homicide."[48] Reflecting the typical homicide, nearly all *CSI* perpetrators act out of "moral emotions" such as the ones listed above. Unlike the typical criminal homicide, however, which stems from "a quickly developing anger" in the context of everyday social relationships, frequently fueled by drugs and alcohol, the majority of the scripted killings on CSI are—to different degrees—pre-meditated, planned, and deliberate, belying even a momentary loss of control over rationality and decision-making.[49]

Finally, although forensic investigators on the show are not predominantly pre-occupied with fathoming the criminal mind, perpetrators are portrayed, variously, as callous, cold, calculating, and cruel—without any emotional effect conveying lack of control. Along this vein, in this episode sample no perpetrator voices culturally circulating scripts for diminishing personal responsibility, such as "I got carried away;" "I didn't know what I was doing;" or "I wasn't myself."[50] Aside from purposive killings, perpetrators are apparently ordinary, lacking any overt mental inadequacies, discrediting attributes, or extensive deviant histories.

Only two storylines depart from these formulaic killings. The first—"Fight Night" (3007)— features two male African American street-gang killings perpetrated against two male African American rival gang members. These killings are represented as impulsive, irrational killings, linked to a Black subculture of violence.[51] The second storyline—"Burked" (2002) —features two young African American males who carry out a contract killing for a white man. Later, in a subplot, the two young men kill each other during an escalating quarrel over stolen property. Other than one white-on-white killing—in "Getting Off" (4016)—precipitated when the assailant discovers his wife in bed with the male victim, these African-American males represent the only perpetrators of heat-of-the-moment or impulsive deliberate killings in the sample. Made manifest across these thirty episodes are—as Garland has proposed—two contradictory and racialized images of the criminal.

De-racializing Criminals and Victims:
"Disappearing the Underclass"

With few exceptions, this sample of CSI episodes lacks explicitly racialized spaces and racialized populations. Across the fifty-one killings represented, only three storylines feature racialized assailants or victims. In "Early Roll-out" (4015) a Hispanic American male boxer rigs his boxing gloves after he decides to kill his African American opponent in the boxing ring. The second and third racialized killings feature the two young African American males hired-to-kill and the intra-racial African American street gang killings, discussed earlier.

Otherwise, these CSI scripts ignore absolutely the key subpopulations of mainstream Western criminologies, namely people at the bottom of political-economic hierarchies, including unemployed working class men, poor racialized welfare-dependent communities, homeless and drug addicted populations, and other people rendered "redundant" by the contemporary global economy.[52] Tellingly, *CSI* portrays the aforementioned African American street-gang leader as a university-educated business entrepreneur. Likewise, the Hispanic American boxer has a professional athletic career and concomitant economic status. In other words, a narrative choice is made across the *CSI* episodes that I viewed to link its meager cast of racialized characters to privilege and power rather than underclass America.[53]

In lieu of widespread cultural images of "the criminal" as Other or "not like the rest of us," the vast majority of these episodes cast a new criminal type that is white, economically stable or bourgeois with no harbingers of deviance from dominant social norms. For instance, in "Grissom Versus the Volcano" (4009), a killer responsible for the bombing deaths of two people is a white, middle class female schoolteacher who helps her young son with his school science projects. She is married to a white man who supports his family through a full time sales job. "Turning of the Screws" (4021) casts a mass killer of six people as a young white man who is an A student on a pending full scholarship to Stanford University, working a summer job in an amusement park. Overall, each white perpetrator is well-groomed, employed or in school, and seemingly imbibes everyday American bourgeois norms centered on traditional nuclear family arrangements, home ownership, post-secondary education, economic independence, full time employment in the legitimate labor market, and non-criminal peers and associates, with only occasional—if any—drift into law breaking.

New Experts and New Technologies: Doing Responsible Science

Across the episodes viewed, the forensic investigators decry a link between understanding the accused subject and solving the crime. For example, in "Grissom Versus the Volcano" (4009), Criminalist Grissom states, "the evidence is only teaching us about the bomb, not the bomber." In "Fur and Loathing" (4006), Criminalist Sidle claims, "I don't try to figure out what people do anymore." Both comments capture and typify one of *CSI*'s core epistemological assumptions. Nested in both statements and peppered throughout *CSI* scripts is the disavowal of ways of knowing mired in understanding human motivation or how the (criminal) mind works. Bearing this out further, the episodes analyzed virtually ignore the most recent policing sciences developed by the FBI, such as personality profiles or geographical profiling, both of which rest on the assumption that human subjects are knowable.[54]

In place of traditional police investigatory practices centered on the interrogation, confession, or interview, the *CSI* subject—as suspect, victim, or witness—is de-centered as the locus of reliable knowledge. Instead, the body is read as the site where the truth about crime can be discovered. For example, in "Homebodies" (4003), Criminalist Grissom does not solicit help from a rape victim until he has exhausted all forensic avenues. Finally, he says to her: "I've done all I can. I need what you saw." In "Cross-Jurisdiction" (2022), rather than asking a young kidnap victim to describe or identify her kidnapper, Criminalist Willow's first statement to her is: "bad people leave behind a part of themselves. I need to look under your fingernails."

Supplanting the human sciences, these forensic investigators use exclusionary technologies, including advanced statistics, DNA profiling, and massive computer-generated population databases, to collect and analyze crime scene evidence. Even though *CSI* forensic experts showcase and meticulously explain these new technologies for their viewers, we are asked, implicitly, on a leap-of-faith, to accept the infallibility of forensic science and the veracity of this new group of police trained and employed scientists.[55]

In contrast to new scientific forensic tools, traditional police investigatory practices are portrayed as inferior governmental technology on *CSI*. Partly for this reason, the show's criminalists are always reiterating their identity as Scientist, *viz.* "he's the cop; I'm the scientist."[56] The actual dividing practice that distinguishes cop and scientist on the show, however, is not technology, but ways of knowing. On *CSI*, cops know, in significant part, by talking and listening to subjects, gut feelings, hunches, intuition, and experientially-based knowledge. For example, in "Last Laugh" (3020), when police Sergeant Brass decides to reopen a case ruled an accidental death, he explains: "I'm chasing something that [CSI] Gil Grissom isn't interested in—a hunch." By contrast, while attending a crime scene in "Bad Words" (4019), Sgt. Brass remarks, "a bomb goes off; people assume it's a hit." Then he asks Grissom, "What do you think?" Grissom replies, "I'm not *thinking*; I'm just looking [for physical evidence]."

As exemplified by Grissom's words, the status of knowledge for these criminalists can only be guaranteed by empiricism or direct observation of the world using scientific positivism. This type of knowledge can be tested and verified by others, allegedly ruling out the knower's subjective biases. Across storylines, examples abound where members of the forensic team dissuade each other from descending into interpretation. "Your notes are great," CSI Willows tells CSI Warrick, in "Homebodies" (4003); "let the case speak for itself." In "Coming of Rage" (4010), CSI Grissom declares, "when you start to get involved with the human element you risk your objectivity" and in "All For Our Country" (4002), "I got ahead of the evidence. It got personal and I don't know why."

This epistemological shift, reflected in the last four quotes, demands and creates a new type of crime expert. On *CSI*, the forensic team's supervisor, Gil Grissom, personifies the ideal-type crime scene investigator and newest penal expert. He is stoic by nature—if not, by training—and purged of all questionable assumptions that might allow his reason to be fogged by emotions. For Grissom, the only true knowledge is discovered through deductive scientific investigations that purportedly eliminate the observer as a layer of data. Grissom mentors his team of criminalists who, in turn, learn to disseminate a new crime solving discourse. For example, in "Cross-Jurisdiction" (2022), Criminalist Willows asserts, "we don't work theories, just evidence," while in "Feeling the Heat" (4005), Criminalist Sidle claims, "if the evidence doesn't support the theory, CSI shouldn't be asking the question." Through statements like these, crime scene investigators on the show ally themselves with doing *responsible* science.

Finally, although the uniformed police play only a secondary role on the show, their inability to solve crime circulates as cultural commonsense or *doxa*. For example, in "Boom" (1013), when Criminalist Grissom clarifies for a bystander that he is a crime scene analyst, not a police officer, the bystander retorts, "yeah, but *we* know who really solves the crime." When featured at all, in the episodes analyzed, regular police officers are portrayed as largely unprofessional, resentful and cynical adjuncts to forensic investigators, trained to do little more than ride in patrol cars and provide lethal force as needed. For example, in "Jackpot" (4007), the local police conspire to sabotage Criminalist Grissom's forensic investigation because it will implicate the town sheriff's brother. In an early scene from that episode, Grissom picks up a beetle, and remarks, "they're perfect. They always do their jobs." Shortly thereafter, we watch him grimace as police officers "compromise the crime scene" through sloppy investigatory techniques. In "All For Our Country" (4002), Sgt. Brass reprimands CSI Grissom because he does not carry his own gun when he serves search warrants on suspects, but assumes instead that the police officers accompanying him are there to provide force if needed.

Although the criminalists work under the direct command of Sgt. Brass, the forensic investigators who are the stars of *CSI* make it clear that their primary allegiance is to science and the scientific method, rather than police politics and public relations. For example, in "All For Our Country" (4002), when Brass tells Grissom, "cops don't take the law into their own hands!" Grissom snaps back incredulously, "in what city?" In this manner, CSIs are portrayed as attached to law enforcement, but above it.

DISCUSSION: "THE *CSI* EFFECT"

Rather than re-cycling racialized crime narratives featuring young, violence-prone African or Hispanic American men, or re-enacting typical homicide scenarios, *CSI* contrives new ones. That *CSI's* representations of criminals, victims, and crime experts do not reflect reality is not the issue here—*CSI* never makes direct ontological claims or appears to aspire to Reality TV status. My concern in this paper is to make manifest the invisible selection and assembly procedures that—over time—have the potential to crystallize into national narratives and agreed upon truths about criminality and new crime control strategies. Although these stories circulate free of the state, through cultural productions, they also do the work of the state. As Brodie points out, neoliberal economic and political restructuring is "unlikely to succeed unless citizens are coerced or more subtly persuaded to act in ways consistent with the logic of the new governing order."[57] The discussion following, then, examines the affinity between *CSI's* representational strategies and discourses, and practices that reflect, stabilize, and legitimate existing neoliberal modes of domination and regulation outside the realm of television.

I begin by considering whether or not my argument imputes too much to an *absence*. Drawing upon Ouellette and Hay's analysis of contemporary *Reality TV* shows, the authors also make links between television and broader economic, political, and cultural trends, noting the "neoliberalizing" effects of television in "disseminating market values to all institutions and social actors" by training viewers to refashion themselves along neoliberal themes of individual responsibility, freedom, and post-welfare forms of good citizenship. Ouellette and Hay draw analogies between *Reality TV* and former welfare state case managers, arguing that the *Reality TV* formula targets "the needy" and attempts to discipline and re-train members of populations who are unable or unwilling to properly care for themselves. The authors emphasize, however, that the *Reality TV* genre "does not hide the truth about changing states of welfare as much as it reconstitutes it."[58]

Continuing along this vein, *CSI* producers' representational choices also contrast starkly with *The Wire*, an American television drama series filmed in Baltimore, which aired from June 2, 2002 to March 9, 2008. Unlike *CSI*, *The Wire's* producer made an executive decision to reflect Baltimore's demographics by casting primarily African American actors. Acclaimed for its realistic portrayals, *The Wire* fractures popular criminology and ideology through humanistic and sympathetic portrayals of criminals and by depicting sociological themes, for example, drawing causal connections among drug prohibition, post-welfare capitalism, poverty, and the war against America's racialized underclass.[59] Whereas the neoliberalizing training at the heart of *Reality TV* shows, and the social commentary undergirding *The Wire,* both work by foregrounding reality and dramatizing contemporary sub-populations viewed as problematic to the new post-welfare social compact, *CSI's* ideological impact is more dependent upon eclipsing the needy and disappearing all dispossessed groups that expose the contradictions at the heart of new governing rationalities. Viewed in light of other TV shows, *CSI*'s narrative omissions appear more glaring, less innocent, and deliberately obfuscatory.

A New Criminal Risk Group: The White, Middle-Class Neoliberal(ized) Criminal

At the most general level, *CSI* dramatizes the individualization of crime, consistent with freedom-of-choice rhetoric and individualism characterizing the political ethos of neoliberalism.[60] With few exceptions, in this sample, each perpetrator is portrayed as a purposive, rational-choice actor whose decision-making embodies a narcissistic form of taking care of the self rather than a cause or symbol of manifold social ills. In this sense, each perpetrator on the show becomes a carrier of neoliberalism.

Viewed over multiple episodes, one of *CSI*'s messages is that the propensity to commit gruesome and calculated killings is ubiquitous across gender and age categories in white, predominantly comfortable or affluent American society. In effect, the cumulative impact of *CSI* scripts *whiten* or de-racialize the rational-choice criminal by making absent, not only media stereotypes of the young predatory African American male, but all racialized population members and the social context in which they act. Moreover, these narrative machinations cloak the reality of who actually is policed and punished in American society. Rather than dramatizing the newest risk groups created by the shifting of federal and state spending from social provision to crime control and the military, *CSI* constantly showcases a white bourgeois criminal. If *CSI* provides moments of public education about the criminal, then what stories are sanctioned and silenced by promoting this new criminal risk group?

First, one effect of *CSI's* choice to exclude African and Hispanic American assailants is that whiteness is articulated to rationality. By implication, rational choice killings seem to animate only white middle-class populations. One tentative reading—born out in the only two storylines involving African-American perpetrators—is that racialized subjects do not commit rational-choice, non-impulsive crimes, but irrational violence. In effect, these narrative choices are racializing strategies that constitute non-white assailants—by commission and omission—outside the white bourgeois norm of rationality, free-will, and self-discipline. In choosing not to represent underclass and racialized Americans among rational-choice subjects, *CSI* strengthens existing cultural and professional crime narratives linking racialized and poor subjects to anti-social, spontaneous, explosive, or random violence, embodying senseless acts of low or no self-control.[61] At a cultural level, such disregard further distances already marginalized segments of society from the rational-choice prerequisites of neoliberal citizenship.

Reiterating, *CSI's* newest risk group of white bourgeois citizens meshes neatly with David Garland's *criminology of the self*. Rather than developing distinctive causal theories of crime, this criminology understands the will to commit crime as a normal feature of modern society.[62] These are the penal subjects imagined by proponents of more rationalized penal strategies, including cognitive retraining programs that endeavor to teach penal subjects how to make correct choices and take responsibility for their own self-management.[63] The return to a facsimile of rehabilitative and reformative objectives in some American and British prisons has been characterized as attempts to "relegitimize" the prison.[64] Certainly, *CSI's* white perpetrators are personified as making purposive choices—bad choices, but intelligible ones nevertheless. As such, this population is potentially manageable and redeemable because members are already tied to disciplinary anchors, including work, school, and family, and share common normative ideals with middle class communities.[65]

By contrast, Garland's *criminology of the other* invoking the animalistic, uncontrollable, unpredictable monstrum "whose features are inherently different from ours"[66] does not figure prominently amongst *CSI's* stock fabrications. As Wacquant notes, the public image of the monster is a *"black"* monstrum personified by "young African-American men from the 'inner city.'"[67] At first glance, *CSI's* choices along color lines could be commended for refusing the "compulsive racialization of criminals."[68] On a deeper level, however, I read the episodes that I viewed as endorsing a "color-blind" approach, a term that Richard Devlin uses to criticize legal analyzes that refuse to acknowledge that race and racism are always factors in policing and punishing crime.[69] Despite its apparent solidarity with color-blindness, then, *CSI's* storylines do not dislodge culturally entrenched fears and representations of the "black monstrum" or criminogenic underclass. Instead, racialized populations—by their omission and selective inclusion—become the excluded and "ungovernable."[70] Severed from criminologies of the everyday self, these groups disappear into "marginalized," "savage spaces" and "anti-communities."[71] Their virtual erasure, in tandem with the erasure of aggressive in-your-face policing, enables viewers to infer that white populations can be more civilly policed at-a-distance by science and surveillance strategies.[72]

CSI's disappeared racialized underclass parallels wider movements within American penology, which has long abandoned earlier penal projects to rehabilitate penal subjects viewed as belonging to "a self-perpetuating and pathological segment of society that is not integratable into the larger whole, even as a reserve labor pool."[73] Bearing this out, African American and Hispanic men are grossly overrepresented in America's sixty brutalizing super-max prisons, dedicated to isolating and confining prisoners in permanent twenty-three hour lock-down.[74] Such penal strategies are more consistent with neo-conservative law-and-order agendas, including repressive "zero-tolerance" policing, chain gangs, indeterminate life sentences, and the return to shaming and stigmatizing the criminal.[75]

In sum, while *CSI*'s portrayal of the new white bourgeois predatory killer shares an affinity with prevailing neoliberal ideals, these subjects are not the inexplicable "monstrum" representation that Melossi associates with an era of rising poverty and unemployment. Instead, the so-called monstrum "who has to be contained through incapacitation or death"[76] is made absent on the show or else is—in two episodes—articulated to young African American males by casting them as more irrational and impulsive and ostensibly less redeemable than their white bourgeois counterparts.

Responsibilization through Disappeared Excuses: A Retreat from Causal Narratives of Crime

I also read *CSI* as "responsibilizing" the criminal,[77] and indirectly, the viewer, through narrative choices that mute political, social, and individual reasons (or excuses) for crime. Foremost, in the episodes analyzed, *CSI*'s consistent choice to whiten the accused and link him or her to constructed middle class normalcy eliminates any vocabulary of choice—vis-à-vis the decision to kill—that implicates existing arrangements of wealth and power in American society. Instead, *CSI* gives life to neoliberal motifs, such as individual responsibility, unconstrained freedom and choice, self-determination, and self-control, by eliminating all culturally circulating narratives for diminishing the culpability of the individual subject of crime.

For example, *CSI*'s narratives personify the extreme individualization and responsibilization of the accused by choosing without exception to sever linkages between alcohol intoxication and culpable homicide. In light of widespread professional and popular discourses that advance a causal nexus between alcohol (ab)use and violent death, this elision needs to be examined. Toward this end, O'Malley's characterization of the "enslaved drug addict" identity as the antithesis of "neoliberal subjectification" is instructive. According to O'Malley, one effect of drug and alcohol addiction discourse is the construction of dependent rather than free citizens. At a discursive level, addicts are simply more difficult to responsibilize.[78] Extended to the *CSI* storylines, alcohol impaired assailants would invite viewers to contemplate violence as at least partially caused by forces beyond the individual's control. Instead of reproducing discourse about alcohol or—to a lesser extent—illegal drugs as a criminogenic risk factor or an excuse, in the episodes considered, *CSI* opts for neoliberal subjectification by instilling killings and killers with sober intelligibility and, by extension, responsibility.

As well, in the episode sample, *CSI*'s virtually exclusive focus on white, middle class perpetrators pulls the rug out from under positivist sociological theories of crime associated with the former welfare state. During the mid-20th century, American sociologists located the sources of crime in individual and social pathology, constructing theories ranging from social ecology, differential association, social disorganization, delinquent subcultures, control and containment, labeling and so on.[79] Despite disagreement over the causes of crime, these mainstream sociological theories associated with the welfare state era shared two constitutive interests. First was a myopic focus on explaining the criminality of individual working-class (or poorer) young males. Second was a belief that crime was only one symptom of systemic social problems—particularly poverty and inequality—that required state-funded social engineering solutions. "Penal-welfare" policies for reducing the frequency of crime during this era included educational programs, social work support, community development, correctional treatment, and welfare spending.[80]

These welfarist theories of crime arose in historically-specific political, economic, and cultural arrangements now eclipsed by neoliberal or post-welfare state discourses, policies, and changing penal ideals. Not only has the state downshifted the problem of crime prevention onto non-state agencies and the individual,[81] these old causal theories of crime cannot be made to fit the material circumstances of *CSI*'s newest risk group. Simply put, the traditional sociological explanations for committing calculated or "cold-blooded" killings were never tailored for normal white bourgeois Americans. Likewise, the decision to incarnate white middle-class predatory killers gives *CSI* license to mute unemployment, poverty, inequality, mental illness, homelessness, racism, street crime, poor single mother families, alienated street cultures and all other manifestations of socially and economically grounded despair once articulated to understandings of and solutions for crime.

Such extreme decontextualization produces at least three effects. First, I believe that, as competent cultural members, we all know how to read social problems as potentially criminogenic. Along this vein, we all know how to link manifestations of socio-cultural malaise to old welfarist causal crime narratives. Whether we read them with sympathy (as reasons) or with disdain (as excuses), we know how to use markers of social inequality and misery to construct culturally salient understandings of those accused of crime.

As backdrop or foreground, sociological particulars enable television crime-drama viewers to construct socially embedded readings of crime and criminality regardless of how the criminal is explicitly portrayed in the televisual narrative. For example, the so-called media icon of an African American predatory male criminal, incarcerated in decrepit Third World public housing, ravaged by the illicit drug trade and cultural isolation, may invoke animalistic imagery. Nevertheless, this provision of social context at least muddies individual responsibilization discourse by insinuating the possibility of a state-driven, *social* justice response. I repeat, there are no culturally salient social reasons for white, middle class citizens to choose to kill—except for drugs and alcohol, mental illness, or loss of self-control through provocation, which is the typical representation for domestic violence. Tellingly, in the *CSI* episodes considered here, all of these reasons are made absent. Certainly one available lesson is that the accused cannot blame society for the crime.

Second and related, since nearly every perpetrator in the storylines examined is white, middle-class, and apparently normal except in relationship to killing, there is no onus on the state in terms of crime prevention. The subtext here—which mirrors extant crime control policies of neoliberal states—is the futility of theories of crime causation and strategies of crime prevention that rely upon traditional forms of policing, judicial sentencing, social engineering and reintegration strategies. The sovereign state cannot prevent crime because crime has no causes; it can only pour resources into the rational management of crime, in this case, crime-solving forensic technologies.[82]

Finally, by almost completely excluding members of the racialized underclass, *CSI's* storylines also disappear the contemporary linkages amongst racism, racialization, social marginality, and criminal justice policy.[83] Instead, *CSI* tends to ignore the state's aggressive physical pursuit and repression of populations constituted as ungovernable through responsibilization strategies. If media representations construct our knowledge about crime, then *CSI* cloaks the reality that criminalization and victimization are basic elements of existence and socialization for African and Hispanic American communities.[84] In pursuing a color-blind approach, *CSI* storylines not only eschew race as a social factor in crime control practices, but lethal victimization. The virtual occlusion of African-American victims of homicides signals that expensive scientific crime-solving technologies are for apprehending perpetrators who kill white people.[85] By dramatizing policing—and more specifically, the policing of white populations, as a rational and dispassionate scientific enterprise, *CSI* also potentially garners the mass support necessary to legitimate modern penal regimes.

Legitimizing and Rationalizing Punitive Sentiments

Continuing along this line, how then can we understand the gap between *CSI's* rational choice model and who is actually policed and punished? What does it ultimately mean that all these bourgeois white Americans are portrayed as killers? Certainly, we could fairly characterize the dominant narratives of the show as "a smokescreen to rationalize intensified crime control and incarceration."[86] Taking up this theme of rationalizing modern punishment, Simon Hallsworth offers a useful analysis for thinking about why *CSI* has de-racialized representations of the criminal for viewers.

For Hallsworth (informed by the work of Norbert Elias), penal regimes are linked inextricably to purely emotive "punitive passions," which—at some level of consciousness—take pleasure in punishment. Following Michel Foucault, Hallsworth describes the spectacle of public forms of punishment in pre-modern societies as unbridling and satisfying "voyeuristic" and "transgressive pleasures" amongst the assembled spectators.[87] As a hallmark of "modern civilization," however, a society's punitive sentiments must be subordinated to intellectually and politically defensible rationalities supportive of the will to punish.[88] In other words, to be perceived as legitimate and civilized, contemporary punishment must be socially constructed as rational, humane, fair, and linked in some manner to civilizing goals versus irrational and purely revengeful inclinations.[89]

By removing race and political economy from representations of policing, then, *CSI* not only depoliticizes policing by fashioning white, rational choice bourgeois criminals who are one hundred percent responsible for their crimes, but sanitizes punishment as a logical and just response undertaken for the greater good of all society. By contrast, marginalized, desperate, racialized "others" as *CSI* targets could evoke sympathy and social conscience, and disturb the sensibilities of many white bourgeois viewers by intimating punishment—and pleasure taken in indulging in punitive sentiments—as irrational and uncivilized.

In sum, *CSI*'s scripted crimes have no causes because they are chosen. Lacking any embeddedness in available knowledges that would allow us to salvage crime causality, *CSI* viewers are left with statements, such as "some people are just born bad" and "biology determines pathology."[90] Accordingly, we need not search for the economic, cultural, patriarchal, racist, or political antecedents of crime and how it is policed and punished. This narrative strategy effectively screens the criminogenic effects of a neoliberal political economy on poor, racialized, and other working-class and underclass communities by normalizing purposive acts of violence and portraying predatory killings as rational choices made by autonomous and free-willed subjects whose punishment can be deemed by *CSI* viewers as legitimate, rational, and civil.

Unmaking People: Crime Scene Investigators and the New Penology

CSI storylines also convey the demise of discipline as the paradigmatic form of power in Western crime control strategies and the advent of new surveillance techniques. Exemplifying the latter, forensic investigators have shifted from practices authorized by the human sciences—as first set out in Foucault's account of the birth of the prison—to new strategies of power coupled to the physical and statistical sciences.[91] Rather than applying science to discern the criminal mind, however, science enables *CSI*'s new crime experts to entirely bypass a thinking subject.

Through the enactment of a cop-scientist divide, *CSI* episodes bring representations of crime control in line with neoliberal trends. First, *CSI* criminalists' apparent disdain for experts and knowledge claims grounded in psychological, psychiatric, or pseudo-scientific policing practices mirrors and amplifies current public and professional frustrations over the failure of traditional criminal justice agencies and actors to regulate and prevent crime.[92] In this manner, *CSI* continues the neoliberal project of dismantling and disqualifying former welfare structures, including the old experts on subjectivity who emerged during the 1960s to administer the welfare state.[93]

Second, the notion that knowledge of the individual—and his or her motivations, desires, and inclinations—is irrelevant to contemporary surveillance technologies resonates generally with the neoliberal retreat from welfarist theories of criminality and crime prevention. Instead, *CSI* idealizes the rational management of crime through science-driven detection technologies.[94] "In the era of racially targeted law-and-order policies,"[95] the overall effect of these representational strategies is to move the problem of crime and its control away from neoconservative politics of over-policing and punishing onto the allegedly neutral terrain of doing responsible science.

In bypassing the criminal's soul, *CSI* personifies—at the level of crime solving—the "return to the body" as the newest focus of penal technologies.[96] For example, rather than compelling knowledge in face to face relationships between crime experts and suspects or witnesses, criminalists on the show most often read crime through measurable bodily signs. Much like the insects that criminalist Grissom relies upon to convey the truth about crime, the show centers the body as an inert object of science—a specimen—that experts need to step outside of to examine.

This scientific-deductive approach to crime solving reflects changing rationalities and managerial tools intended to curb the powers of psychological experts and discourses, in part, by linking scientific administration to perfect justice. For example, mechanical calculations in the form of uniform judicial sentencing tables or actuarial tools for generating individual violence-risk probability scores both appear to excise idiosyncratic, political, or morality-based decision-making.[97] Their common thread is the shift from the individualizing gaze to unmaking the subject by rendering individuals into a collection of observable, quantifiable facts.[98] In so doing, these new practices embrace dehumanization as a goal of our contemporary crime control landscape. Since most of us are relatively unencumbered by scientific and statistical training, we cannot critically interrogate these knowledge claims as readily as (pop) psychological discourse.

New post-welfare epistemological assumptions and practices—already manifest in many judicial and penal initiatives—permeate *CSI*'s scripts. The show, in effect, neoliberalizes the newest crime expert by linking criminalists to doing responsible science. Paralleling the New Penology, *CSI*'s storylines invalidate disciplinary technologies based on knowing the individual—associated with the welfare state—and pursue the management of criminality through new surveillance and detection technologies that not only curtail the powers of older regulation strategies, but mask the punitive turn characteristic of U.S. penality.

CONCLUDING REMARKS: OBFUSCATING THE DANGEROUS UNDERCLASS AND NEOLIBERALIZING THE VIEWER

In this chapter, I locate *CSI*'s scripts within an emergent post-welfarist hegemony about crime and punishment that captures new rationalities, if not actual practices, associated with the shift from a welfare state to neoliberal state. By fashioning a new white, middle class criminal risk group and new crime-fighting experts, while consistently making absent certain ways of making sense of criminality, *CSI*'s narrative machinations can be read, in effect, as a neoliberalizing public education. In particular, *CSI*'s representations of criminals and victims de-racialize American crime, obfuscating the relationships between forms of crime and the economic, social, and cultural injustices that undergird contemporary western political economies. Instead, *CSI* dramatizes neoliberal subjecthood and limitless agency by animating primarily rational-choice white predatory criminals who are rarely disadvantaged or lacking social capital. The effect is that crime can only be read as a choice.

This representation not only depoliticizes crime and legitimates contemporary forms of crime control; it also diverts attention from the dangerous acts actually committed by those in power by misrepresenting the type and extent of culpable killings and social injury perpetuated by white, elite bourgeois citizens. These harms include but are not limited to state-sanctioned civilian and environmental collateral damage from military interventions, planet desecration through green house gases, international human rights violations, species annihilation, occupational health and safety violations, death and disability through marketing drugs with harmful side-effects, conspiracies to inflate the prices of necessary goods, and other global corporate and state crime.[99]

Is it a cosmic fluke that *CSI* does not represent predatory killers or their victims as racialized or the monstrous Other? Notwithstanding that American violent crime rates have been declining, incarceration rates are still increasing. As Angela Davis notes, the military and prisons now represent the American government's pre-eminent social programs.[100] In contrast to *CSI*'s neoliberalized crime narratives, it is primarily poor and racialized people who are victimized by and punished for acts of murder, and who populate American prisons. In casting only white middle-class criminals, "the *CSI* effect" does not democratize violence, but instead constitutes some bodies—particularly, the racialized underclass—as outside normative cultural understandings of criminality, policing, and punishment. Albeit in a clandestine fashion, *CSI* entrenches racism by abandoning racialized perpetrators and victims to irrational and punitive neoconservative crime control strategies.

Traditionally, the so-called dangerous classes have been so viewed because they have the potential to expose contradictions in existing political economic arrangements.[101] Not only in actuality, but in *CSI's* scripts, the racialized underclass—contextualized in inner city American ghettoes—is near impossible to fit into moments of public education about neoliberal subjectification, responsibilization, and dispassionate justice. Hence, this de-racialization of predatory killers disappears the sub-populations that would enable viewers to grasp the state's responsibility for pandemic homicide rates amongst urban "surplus" populations, created by the post-industrial economy and retrenchment of welfarism.[102] As Pratt observes, these are the citizens that the state prefers remain unknowable[103] because they unsettle the neoliberal "myth of a rational society."[104]

In sum, *CSI* has produced a TV crime show that resonates with the cultural and social arrangements of a post-welfare, neoliberal state and provides storylines and new experts supportive of these changes. I am not suggesting that the multiple and shifting groups involved in producing *CSI* actively conspire to create these effects. I am arguing that new representations of crime, criminality and crime experts are never random productions, but draw upon politically and socially bound discourses and practices that our culture makes available to us at a specific point in time. To the extent that *CSI* draws upon ideologies that sustain current power relations, the show also participates in reinforcing those relations and shaping beliefs about the legitimacy of current crime control policies. Accordingly, one of the tasks of critical scholars is to identify and challenge these crime narratives before they become naturalized and culturally ingrained.

NOTES

I gratefully acknowledge Michele Byers and Val Johnson's editorial assistance and thought provoking commentaries.

1. Karl Mannheim, *Ideology and Utopia. Collected Works Volume One* (London: Routledge, 1998), xxv.
2. Richard Osborne, "Crime and the Media: From Mass Studies to Most-Modernism," in *Crime and the Media: The Post Modern Spectacle,* eds. David Kidd-Hewitt and Richard Osborne (London: Pluto Press, 1995), 27.
3. Gregg Barak, "In Between the Waves: Mass Mediated Themes of Crime and Justice," *Social Justice* 21, no. 3 (1994): 135; Osborne, "Crime and Media," 25–48; Richard Tithecotte, *Of Men and Monsters: Jeffrey Dahmer and the Construction of the Serial* Killer (Wisconsin: The University of Wisconsin Press, 1997).
4. *U.S. Census Bureau*, 2003; *Las Vegas Native*<lasvegasnative.us> 2005 (Jan. 2006).
5. Malcolm Feeley and Jonathan Simon, "The New Penology: Notes on the Emerging Strategy of Corrections and its Implications," *Criminology* 30, no. 4 (1992): 467.
6. Carl E. James, "Armed and Dangerous: Racializing Suspect, Suspecting Race," in *Marginality and Condemnation: An Introduction to Critical Criminology,"* eds. Bernard Schissel and Carolyn Brooks (Halifax: Fernwood, 2004), 292–94; Ray Surrette, *Media, Crime, and Criminal Justice: Images and Realities* (Pacific Grove, CA: Brooks/Cole Publishing, 1992).
7. Bureau of Justice Statistics, "Crime and Victims Statistics; Homicide Trends in U.S.," U.S. Department of Justice. 2005 <http://www.ojp.usdoj.gov/bjs/html> (21 Aug. 2007).
8. Julia Sudbury, "Women of Color, Globalization, and the Politics of Incarceration," in *The Criminal Justice System and Women: Offenders, Prisoners, Victims, and Workers*, 3d, eds. Barbara Price and Natalie Sokoloff (New York: McGraw Hill Company, 2004), 221.
9. Loic Wacquant, "Deadly Symbiosis: When Ghetto and Prison Meet and Mesh," *Punishment and Society* 3, no. 1 (2001): 96.
10. Barak, "Between the Waves," 136–37; Wacquant, "Deadly Symbiosis," 114.
11. Angela Davis, *Are Prisons Obsolete?* (Seven Stories Press: New York, 2003), 16.
12. Contemporary American, British, and Canadian crime control practices center on over-policing and over-incarcerating young black males relative to white males. Notwithstanding that the emergence of racialized control practices assumes distinctive genealogies across these nation states, each country constructs race—as signalled by phenotypical non-whiteness—as a causal factor in the development of violence and social disorder. For example, in the U.S., see Waquant, "Deadly Symbiosis." In Canada, see Todd Gordon. *Cops, Crime and Capitalism: The Law-and-Order Agenda in Canada* (Halifax: Fernwood Publishing, 2006). In Britain, see John Solomos and Tim Rackett, "Policing and Urban Unrest: Problem Constitution and Policy Response," in *Out of Order? Policing Black People*, eds. Ellis Cashmere and Eugene

McLaughlin (London: Routledge, 1991), 42–64. Whereas much of *CSI*'s American audience would conflate phenotypical blackness with African American history and culture, UK audiences—and to a lesser extent, Canadian audiences—are more likely to associate phenotypical blackness with Afro-Caribbean populations who emigrated from former British colonies. The commonality is that all three countries impute crime to color. Therefore, in this chapter, the term "black" (with a lower case b) connotes phenotypical color versus a culture or cultures.

13. Erica Lawson and Amanda Hotrum, "Equity for Communities: Integrating Legal Counsel and Critical Race Theory," in *Feminism, Law, Inclusion: Intersectionality in Action* eds. Gayle MacDonald, Rachel L. Osborne, and Charles C. Smith (Toronto: Sumach Press, 2005), 42–43.

14. Frances Henry and Carol Taylor, *Discourses of Domination: Racial Bias in the Canadian English-Language* Press (Toronto: University of Toronto Press, 2002), 11.

15. Elizabeth Comack and Gillian Balfour, *The Power to Criminalize: Violence, Inequality and the Law* (Halifax: Fernwood Press, 2004).

16. I am using David Garland's definition of penality: "the whole of the penal complex, including its sanctions, institutions, discourses, and representations," David Garland, *Punishment and Welfare: A History of Penal Strategies* (Abershot: Gower, 1985), vii and x.

17. Robert Adamoski, Dorothy Chunn, and Robert Menzies, "Rethinking the Citizen in Canadian Social History," in *Contesting Canadian Citizenship*, eds. Robert Adamoski, Dorothy Chunn and Robert Menzies (Peterborough, Ontario: Broadview Press, 2002), 12–41; Alan Hunt, "Moral Regulation and Making-up the New Person: Putting Gramsci to Work," *Theoretical Criminology* 1, no. 3 (1997): 277–78. Barak, "Between the Waves," 137; Surette, *Media, Crime and Criminal Justice*.

18. Mark Neocleous, *The Fabrication of Social Order: A Cultural Theory of Police Power* (Pluto Press: London, 2000).

19. Simon Hallsworth, "Rethinking the Punitive Turn," *Punishment and Society* 2, no 2 (2004): 145.

20. Dario Melossi, "Changing Representations of the Criminal," *British Journal of Criminology* 40, no. 2 (Spring 2000): 296, 300, 297, 311.

21. Very simply, a Ruschian analysis focuses on the links between changes in labor market conditions and changing penal forms. George Rusche and Otto Kirchheimer, *Punishment and Social Structure*. (New York: Russell and Russell, 1968).

22. Melossi, "Changing Representations," 297.

23. Melossi, "Changing Representations," 311.

24. Sherene Razack, "R. D. S. v. Her Majesty the Queen: A Case about Home," in *Feminism, Law, Inclusion: Intersectionality in Action*, eds. Gayle MacDonald, Rachel L. Osborne, and Charles C. Smith (Toronto: Sumach Press, 2005), 202.

25. Toni Morrison, "The Official Story: Dead Men Golfing," in *Birth of a Nation'hood*, eds. Toni Morrison and Claudia Brodsky (New York: Pantheon Books, 1997), xxviii.

26. Wahneema Lubiano, "Black Ladies, Welfare Queens, and State Minstrels: Ideological War by Narrative Means," in *Race-ing Justice, En-gendering Power:*

Essays on Anita Hill, Clarence Thomas, and the Construction of Social Reality, ed, Toni Morrison (New York: Pantheon Books, 1992), 323–63.

27. Homicides can be divided into culpable and non-culpable. Whereas non-culpable homicides are forms of accidental killings, culpable homicides are killings where the offender commits an unlawful act that he or she knows, or ought to have known, is likely to cause death. I use the terms 'culpable killings' and 'criminal homicide' interchangeably. Technically, however, 'criminal,' 'homicide' and, to some extent, 'culpable' are legal designations that do not apply until a suspect has been found criminally responsible beyond a reasonable doubt by a judge and jury, pursuant to criminal charges.

28. Constant comparative analysis is where the researcher analyzes her or his data after each interview or, in this case, after viewing single *CSI* episodes. Subsequent episodes are viewed with an eye toward testing the reliability of emergent themes. See Anselm Strauss and Juliet Corbin, *Basics of Qualitative Research: Grounded Theory Procedures and Techniques* (Newbury Park: Sage, 1990).

29. Data saturation refers to the point in data collection where additional data apparently contribute no new information. See Anselm Strauss and Juliet Corbin, *Basics of Qualitative Research: Grounded Theory Procedures and Techniques* (Newbury Park: Sage, 1990).

30. I have appropriated the term "*CSI* effect" to open up alternative ways of thinking about the effects of *CSI* upon viewers, which are less apparent than the conventional meaning of this term, which refers more narrowly to the unrealistic forensic expectations of jurors in criminal cases.

31. Michele Byers, in an editorial comment.

32. Pat O'Malley, "Risk Societies and the Government of Crime," in *Dangerous Offenders: Punishment and Social Order*, eds. Mark Brown and John Pratt (London and New York: Routledge, 2000), 189–207; John Pratt, "The Return of the Wheelbarrow Men; Or, The Arrival of Postmodern Penality," *British Journal of Criminology* 40, no. 1 (Winter 2000): 133–57; Thom Workman, *Social Torment: Globalization in Atlantic Canada*, (Halifax: Fernwood Press, 2003).

33. Janine Brodie, "Canadian Women, Changing State Forms, and Public Policy," in *Women and Canadian Public Policy*, ed. Janine Brodie (Toronto: Harcourt, Brace and Company, 1996); David Garland, *The Culture of Control: Crime and Social Order in Contemporary Society,* (Chicago: University of Chicago Press, 2001); Marlee Kline, "Blue Meanies in Alberta: Tory Tactics and the Privitization of Child Welfare," in *Challenging the Public/Private Divide: Feminism, Law, and Pubic Policy*, ed. Susan B. Boyd (Toronto: University of Toronto Press, 1997), 330–59; Pat O'Malley, "Risk, Power, and Crime Prevention," *Economy and Society* 21 (1996): 252–75.

34. As defined by David Garland, "the responsibilization strategy involves a number of new techniques and methods whereby the state seeks to bring about action on the part of 'private' agencies and individuals—either by 'stimulating new forms of behaviors' or by 'stopping established habits'" David Garland, "The Limits of the Sovereign State: Strategies of Crime Control in Contemporary Society," *The British Journal of Criminology* 36, no. 4 (1996): 452.

35. O'Malley, "Risk and Crime Prevention;" Nikolas Rose, "Governing 'Advanced' Liberal Democracies," in *Foucault and Political Reason*, ed, Andrew Barry, Thomas Osbourne, and Nikolas Rose (Chicago: University of Chicago Press, 1996), 37–64; Lealle Ruhl, "Liberal Governance and Prenatal Care: Risk and Regulation in Pregnancy," *Economy and Society* 28, no. 1 (1999): 95–117.

36. Dorothy Chunn, "Feminism, Law and 'the Family'": Assessing the Reform Legacy," in *Locating Race/Class/Gender* Connections ed. Elizabeth Comack (Halifax: Fernwood, 1999), 256.

37. John Pratt, "Governmentality, Neoliberalism and Dangerousness," in *Governable Places: Readings on Governmentality and Crime Control*, ed. Russell Smandych (Aldershot Brookfield VT: Ashgate, 1999), 133–57; Steven Spitzer, "Toward a Marxian Theory of Deviance," *Social Problems* 22, no. 5 (1975): 638–59.

38. Michel Foucault, *Discipline and Punish: The Birth of the Prison* (London: Peregrine Books, 1979); Carolyn Strange, "The Undercurrent of Penal Culture: Punishment of the Body in Mid-Twentieth Century Canada," *Law and History Review* 19, No. 2 (Summer 2001): 1–39.

39. Feeley and Simon, "New Penology;" Foucault, *Discipline and Punish*; David Garland, "Governmentality and the Problem of Crime: Foucault, Criminology, and Sociology," *Theoretical Criminology* 1, no. 2 (1997): 173–214; Rose, "Governing Democracies," 37–64; Nikolas Rose, "Government and Control," *British Journal of Criminology* 40, no. 2 (Spring 2000): 321–39.

40. Feeley and Simon, "New Penology"; Garland, "Limits of Sovereign State," 452.

41. Robert Castel, "From Dangerousness to Risk," in *The Foucault Effect: Studies in Governmentality* eds. G. Burchell, C. Gordon, and P. Miller (Chicago: University of Chicago Press, 1991), 281–96; Mark Brown, "Calculations of Risk in Contemporary Penal Practice," in *Dangerous Offenders: Punishment and Social Order*, ed. Mark Brown and John Pratt (Routlege: London and New York, 2000), 93–104.

42. Kevin Bonnycastle, "Sex Offenders in *Con*text: Creating Choices in the Age of Risk" (PhD Diss., Simon Fraser University, 2004); Mona Lynch, "Rehabilitation a Rhetoric: The Ideal of Reformation in Contemporary Parole Discourse and Practices," *Punishment and Society* 2, no. 1 (2001): 40–65; Vernon Quinsey, Grant Harris, Marnie Rice, and Catherine Cormier (eds.), *Violent Offender: Appraising and Managing Risk* (Washington, DC: American Psychological Association, 1998).

43. Garland, "Limits of Sovereign State."

44. Pat O'Malley, "Volatile and Contradictory Punishment," *Theoretical Criminology* 3 (1999): 175–96.

45. Garland, "Limits of Sovereign State."

46. The episodes in my sample were as follows: Season 1, 1013 "Boom," 1018 "$35K O.B.O"; Season 2, 2001 "Burked," 2005 "Scuba Doobie-Doo," 2011 "Organ Grinder," 201 "You've Got Male," 2020 "Cats in the Cradle," 2022 "Cross Jurisdictions"; Season 3 3007 "Fight Night," 3008 "Snuff," 3011 "Recipe for Murder," 3012 "Got Murder?" 3014 "One Hit Wonder," 3019 "A Night at the Movies," 3020 "Last Laugh"; Season 4, 4002 "All for Our Country," 4003 "Homebodies," 4004 "Feeling the Heat," 4005 "Fur and Loathing," 4006 "Jackpot," 4009 "Grissom Versus the

Volcano," 4010 "Coming of Rage," 3011 "Eleven Angry Jurors," 4013 "Suckers," 4015 "Early Rollout," 4019 "Getting Off," 4019 "Bad Words," 4021 "Turning The Screws," 4022 "No More Bets," 4023 "Bloodlines."

47. One of the editors points out that at least two individual episodes outside my sample exist in which illegal drug use—albeit not alcohol—leads to murder (for example, "Friends and Lovers," 1005).

48. Jack Katz, *Seductions of Crime: Moral and Sensual Attractions in Doing Evil* (New York: Basic Books, 1988). To arrive at his conclusions, Katz re-analyzed all previously published material on American homicides, produced through ethnographic life histories, police records, biographies and autobiographies, and participant observation. He concentrated on what was said and done, and the context in which killings arose, rather than trying to delve into the perpetrators' minds (326). Ultimately, Katz does not recognize that these moral emotions are also gendered, racialized, and class-based, hence shaped by material conditions that buffer some persons and not others from their effects. In a more recent discussion, Bierne and Messerschmidt confirm Katz's characterization of murder as predominantly arising in unplanned everyday interactions. Piers Bierne and James W. Messerschmidt, *Criminology* 4d (Los Angeles: Roxbury Publishing Company, 2006), 125.

49. Katz, *Seductions*, 18.

50. Katz, *Seductions*, 25; Bonnycastle, "Sex Offenders."

51. Feeley and Simon, "New Penology," 192–93; Malcolm Feeley and Jonathan Simon, "Actuarial Justice: The Emerging New Criminal Law," in *The Futures of Criminology* ed. David Nelkan (Thousand Oakes: Sage, 1994), 174–201; James, "Armed and Dangerous," 289–308.

52. Zygmunt Bauman, *Life in Fragments: Essays in Post-Modern Morality*, (Oxford: Blackwell, 1995), 74.

53. No African-American women are cast as victims or perpetrators of culpable homicide; however one African American woman is featured as the victim of an accidental shooting and a second African American woman is featured as a suicide victim. Neither character is linked to the racialized underclass. The first woman—in "Coming of Rage" (4079)—is portrayed as residing in an affluent, middle class neighbor and the second woman—in "Grissom Versus the Volcano" (4078) enjoys a pampered lifestyle as the wife of an acclaimed African American jazz musician. That being said, exceptions exist outside my sample. For example, according to one of the book's editors, "No Humans Involved" (5010) features an African-American woman who is a sex worker, welfare cheat, and killer of a young African American boy.

54. Kim Rossmo, *Geographical Profiling* (Boca Raton, Florida: CRC Press, 2000). Tithecotte, *Men and Monsters.*

55. Significant evidence exists that some of these technologies are very unreliable. For example see David Lyon "Technology vs. 'Terrorism': Circuits of City Surveillance Since September 11,' in S. Graham (ed.) *Cities, War, and Terrorism* (Malden, MA: Blackwell, 2004).

56. $35K O.B.O.

57. Brodie, "Canadian Women," 21.

58. Ouellette, Laurie and James Hay, *Better Living Through Reality TV: Television and Post-Welfare Citizenship* (Blackwell Publishing, 2008), 35, 40.

59. *The Wire* <www.hbo.com/thewire> (11 Oct. 2008).

60. Comack and Balfour, *Power to Criminalize*; Rebecca Johnson, "If Choice is the Answer, What is the Question? Spelunking in Symes v. Canada," in *Law as a Gendering* Practice eds. Dorothy Chunn and Dany Lacombe (Toronto: Oxford University Press, 2000), 199–221.

61. R. J. Herrnstein, "Criminogenic Traits," in *Crime* eds. James Q. Wilson and Joan Petersilia (San Francisco: ICS Press, 1995), 58–62; Michael Gottfredson and Travis Hirschi, *A General Theory of Crime* (Stanford: Stanford University Press, 1990).

62. Garland, "Governmentality," 451, 461.

63. Bonnycastle, "Sex Offenders"; Kathryn Fox, "Changing Violent Minds: Discursive Correction and Resistance in the Cognitive Treatment of Violent Offenders in Prison," *Social Problems* 46, no. 1 (1999): 88–103.

64. Pratt, "Governmentality," 134; Richard Sparks, "Can Prison Be Legitimate? Penal Politics, Privitization and the Timeliness of an Old Idea," *British Journal of Criminology* 34 (1994): 14–28.

65. Feeley and Simon, "New Penology," 468; Lynch, "Rehabilitation as Rhetoric," 41.

66. Melossi, "Changing Representations," 311.

67. Wacquant, "Deadly Symbiosis," 118.

68. Wacquant, "Deadly Symbiosis," 104.

69. Richard Devlin, "We Can't Go On Together With Suspicious Minds: Judicial Bias and Racialized Perspective in R. vs. R. D. S.," *Dalhousie Law Review* 18, no. 2, (1995), 44-11-46; Razack, "*R. D. S.*," 200–219.

70. Pratt, "Governmentality," 134.

71. Rose, "Government and Control," 331.

72. Gordon, "*Cops and Capitalism.*"

73. Wilson, cited in Feeley and Simon, "New Penology," 92.

74. Davis, "*Are Prisons Obsolete?*"

75. Gordon, "*Cops and Capitalism*," Pratt, "Wheelbarrow Men," Wacquant, "Deadly Symbiosis."

76. Melossi, "Changing Representations," 311.

77. O'Malley, "Risk and Crime Prevention," 252–75; Garland, "Governmentality," 452.

78. Pat O'Malley, "Governing Through the Democratic Minimization of Harms," in *Institutionalizing Restorative Justice*, eds. Ivo Aertsen, Tom Daems, and Luc Roberts (London: Willan Publishing, 2006), 225.

79. Bierne and Messerschmidt, *Criminology.*

80. Garland, *Culture of Control*, 62–72.

81. O'Malley, "Risk and Restorative Justice," Pratt, "Governmentality;" Garland, *Culture of Control.*

82. Garland, "Limits of Sovereign State," 448; Garland, *Culture of Control*; Lynch, "Rehabilitation as Rhetoric," 40–65.

83. Katherine Beckett and Bruce Western, "Governing Social Marginality," *Punishment and* Society 3, no. 1 (2001): 43–59; Wacquant, "Deadly Symbiosis."

84. Wacquant, "Deadly Symbiosis."

85. Judith Butler, "Endangered/Endangering: Schematic Racism and White Paranoia," in *Reading Rodney King, Reading Urban Uprising* ed. R. Gooding-Williams (London: Routledge, 1993).

86. Val Marie Johnson in her editorial comment.

87. Simon Hallsworth, "Punitive Passions, Civilisation, and Punishment," <http://psep.free.ngo.pl/a-eg/04shkara.html> (Sept. 1 2006): 2–3.

88. Norbert Elias, *The History of Manners* (Oxford: Basil Blackwell, 1978).

89. By the same token, Hallsworth argues that expressive, decivilizing punishment can be justified and indulged in where a targeted population can be discursively dehumanized and distinguished as a threat to existing social order. *CSI* producers have aligned themselves with civilizing punishment. Hallsworth, "Punitive Passions," 6.

90. Snuff.

91. Foucault, *Discipline and Punish*; Feeley and Simon, "New Penology."

92. Garland, "Limits of Sovereign State," 447.

93. Pratt, "Governmentality,"151.

94. Feeley and Simon, "New Penology," 455; Lynch, "Rehabilitation as Rhetoric," 41.

95. Wacquant, "Deadly Symbiosis," 118.

96. Pratt, "Wheelbarrow Men."

97. Feeley and Simon, "Actuarial Justice;" Pratt, "Governmentality;" "Wheelbarrow Men."

98. Castel, "Dangerousness to Risk," 282, 288; Bonnycastle, "Sex Offenders," 182.

99. See Susan C. Boyd, Dorothy E. Chunn, and Robert Menzies, eds, *Toxic Criminology* (Fernwood: Halifax, 2002); Laureen Snider, "Relocating Law: Making Corporate Crime Disappear," in *Locating Law: Race/Class/Gender Connections* ed, Elizabeth Comack (Halifax: Fernwood Press, 2003), 185.

100. Davis, *"Are Prisons Obsolete?"*

101. Spitzer, "Marxian Theory," 638–59.

102. Wacquant, "Deadly Symbiosis," 105.

103. Pratt, "Governmentality," 149.

104. Osborne, "Crime and Media," 27.

Chapter Nine

Troping Mr. Johnson: Reading Phallic Mastery and Anxiety on Season One of *CSI: Crime Scene Investigation*

Mythili Rajiva

"If you want to learn about forensics, master everything else first."[1]

—Gil Grissom, *CSI* Investigator

The following discussion uses a feminist psychoanalytic framework to analyze how American cultural narratives of racialization, gender, class, age, and sexuality are represented in the pilot season of *CSI: Crime Scene Investigation*. Popular culture is an arena filled with contradiction and contestation, where a society's conscious and unconscious impulses, anxieties and desires are played out through representation.[2] Therefore, although *CSI*'s central storylines do not, in general, deal explicitly with racialized relations of power, I argue that the historical legacy of slavery underpinning contemporary race relations in the US informs the content of many mainstream television shows such as *CSI*.

I use two main concepts to build my analysis: the psychoanalytic concept of the Phallus and the literary concept of the trope. The Phallus,[3] as the symbol of patriarchy, also includes (but is not exhaustive of) several hierarchical relations in contemporary western societies: the privileged status of men over women; of racialized white men over both racialized white women, and racialized men and women of color; economically privileged men and women over working class men and women; and heterosexual men over gay men and women. According to Craib, "It is the symbol of the penis, the phallus, that is important. The penis is usually a rather flabby piece of flesh; its symbol, the phallus, is a powerful tool that can appear anywhere and everywhere." Phallic mastery signifies white, supremacist, capitalist patriarchy,[4] but even for those who occupy a master status (primarily white, elite, heterosexual men), this mastery is never finally and irrevocably attained; it is always contested, which produces the anxieties represented and performed in popular culture. On the other hand, according to White, tropes cement existing relations of power in both dominant and marginalized discourses.[5] For example, discourses used to justify European colonial expansion frequently employed the "animalization" trope to frame colonized populations as animals (or at best barbarians), existing in an uncivilized state in comparison to their white, western, European conquerors. Tropes, then, are part of the symbolic means through which material inequalities are created and sustained in particular societies at particular historical junctures. Shohat and Stam argue that tropes are not historically and culturally fixed, and can also function as moments of contestation, interpretation and subversion.[6]

On *CSI*'s pilot season, we can read phallic mastery and anxiety through at least three sets of tropes used in various storylines and character arcs. First, there is a trope of lost innocence (primarily portrayed through the fleeting character of Holly Gribbs' life and death in the first two episodes), which underpins the absence of young, white, middle class, heterosexual femininity in the show's main characters. This trope is constructed and maintained through a trope of danger, represented by violent black masculinity (the gangster who takes Holly's life) and aided and abetted by weak black masculinity (Warrick, the *CSI* investigator whose actions, unintentionally, are partially responsible for her death). Secondly, the series' five main characters function as tropes of mastery (Grissom and Nick) and anxiety over threatening Otherness (Catherine, Sara and Warrick). Finally, given its infrequent presence except through minor characters, black femininity is troped as a dummy presence, a form of tokenism that re-asserts the series' dominant racialized, gendered, aged and classed norms.

I conclude with a reflexive counter-reading of the show that recognizes the "multiple, shifting, and highly subjective" nature of viewer interpretations.[7] Diverse viewers' interpretations of storylines and characters will necessarily diverge from my particular readings; the latter are also susceptible to their own moments of contradiction and ambivalence. This underscores Fiske's point that television is not a do-it-yourself meaning kit, but it is also not a box of ready-made meanings available for passive consumption.[8] Television consumers consume television texts in an ambiguous and ambivalent fashion, which reflects how practices, meanings and representations are sites of struggle across and within difference.[9]

LITTLE GIRL LOST: HOLLY GRIBBS AS
A TROPE OF INNOCENCE

In this section, I examine how *CSI*'s first season represents young, white, middle class girlhood and womanhood through its *absence*, or its lack of representation in central characters whom audiences could identify as symbols of normative femininity within mainstream American televisual traditions.[10] In popular US culture, idealized representations of normative femininity generally take the form of white, blonde, youthful, middle-class femininity. According to both hooks and Podlesney, America's obsession with blondness suggests unconscious national worries over questions of racial purity: "within white supremacist culture, a female must be white to occupy the space of sacred femininity and she must also be blond. . . . blond. . . . embodies the white supremacist aesthetics that inform the popular imagination of our culture."[11] If blondeness represents "racial unambiguity"[12] within the American imagination, then its absence and/or narrow representation on a crime show such as *CSI* may reflect an attempt to maintain metaphorical racial boundaries between white innocence and the implicitly racialized danger of crime.

I focus on a central storyline that launched *CSI*'s pilot season: the murder of rookie Holly Gribbs. In the violent, morally bankrupt world of crime, innocence (troped as young, blonde, white and female) is quickly and brutally snuffed out. In the pilot episode, Gribbs, a young, blonde, female rookie, has just joined the *CSI* team after graduating from the academy.[13] Gribbs spends the episode struggling to find her professional footing: she is yelled at by her older male boss; throws up at the sight of a dead body; gets held up at gunpoint; and is described by co-workers as "cute," and "the new girl." The pilot ends with her courageously entering an empty house (the scene of a break-in), only to encounter the perpetrator, who shoots her. Gribbs ends up in a coma and by the start of the next episode, she is dead. For the rest of season one there is no explicit recovery of the subject position represented by Holly Gribbs; yet her life and death represent a central foreshadowing of how race, gender, class, sexuality and age intersect on *CSI* to produce certain images of racialized white femininity that are compatible/acceptable with/in this televisual world of crime and criminal investigation. This compatibility is organized through a particular set of subject positions: if the subject is a brunette, an older (thirty or forty something) blonde, a sexually aggressive or non-heterosexual blonde, or a non-middle class blonde, there is a space for her in the narrative content of the show, as part of the *CSI* team, as a secondary character, or as a criminal.[14] If, on the other hand, the subject is a blonde, identifiable as either a girl or a young woman, and represents respectable, middle-class, white femininity (that is neither sexually aggressive nor resistant to heterosexual norms), then her main role in the pilot season is as the quintessential crime victim, whose passive innocence symbolizes what must be protected or avenged by the show's heroes.[15] Gribbs' speedy exit suggests that, as an active subject, there is no place for her or what she represents in the world of crime scene investigation. She is the constitutive but passive outside through which racialized Otherness is produced. Thus, she becomes a symbol of what must be protected by active white masculinity, as represented through the team under Grissom's leadership.

But protected from what, specifically? Here, we must ask whether on *CSI*, the absence of (white, feminine, young) innocence is bound up with another conspicuous absence: that of dangerous black masculinity. Interestingly, crime on *CSI*'s first season is not explicitly racialized; despite the stereotypes of racialized crime ubiquitous in mainstream American cultural discourses, *CSI*'s pilot season depicts an almost raceless world where most of its heroes, heroines, perpetrators and victims are white.[16] Does the show's consistent idealizing of the supposedly neutral, always unfailing objectivity of science mean that race and racism cannot even be acknowledged as part of the world of crime or its detection?[17] How does race then return sub-textually at specific moments? One instance is Gribbs' murder. Warrick, the potentially "good" black cop, is asked to "babysit" Gribbs during a crime scene investigation but, instead, abandons his responsibility to go off and gamble. When Gribbs attempts to navigate the crime scene alone, the "bad" black man (in the convenient scapegoat role of gangster villain, here returning to the scene of his crime) shoots her. If we read this as a pivotal moment in the series' genesis, then the suggestion is that white, blonde, female innocence is brutally murdered by dangerous, amoral, black masculinity (the gangster who shoots Holly) working in tandem with weak or inept black masculinity (Warrick). Black masculinity in its specific manifestation as a violent threat to white female innocence then disappears entirely for the rest of the season, yet its phantom presence haunts the show's landscape: the gangster's "mere existence" as a trope of danger justifies the need for law and order in the *CSI* world.[18] Blackness as a threat to whiteness has been contained, but its traces remain. Gribbs' tragic death (and Warrick's subsequent rehabilitation over the season), are implicit reminders of the racialized nature of violent crime.

This sub-text underlying *CSI*'s otherwise seemingly raceless narrative can be read specifically through the fear of miscegenation that haunts contemporary American popular culture. Like women of all hues, the undeniable presence of racialized Others in the public sphere undermines the supremacy of white, imperial, heterosexist masculinity, and contributes to continuing sexual anxieties around relations between black men and white women.[19] On *CSI,* this anxiety plays out by having Holly murdered as a result of actions taken by two black men. In their brevity and stereotyped framing, neither encounter between Gribbs and these two men offers the potential for complex or intimate involvement between white womanhood and black masculinity. According to Pellegrini, among others, we can never admit that a white woman might actively desire and willingly "'submit' to a black man."[20] Racialized phallic anxiety must be resolved by denying the subject positions that make this desire possible. First, idealized femininity must be excluded from the public sphere; second, black masculinity must be either controlled or destroyed to eliminate the threat of interracial desire. In *CSI*'s pilot episode, this is accomplished first through the abandonment of a young, innocent, blonde woman by a seemingly indifferent black investigator, and her subsequent murder at the hands of a black gangster.

READING GRISSOM, CATHERINE, SARA, AND WARRICK AS TROPES OF PHALLIC MASTERY AND ANXIETY

In this section, I move from looking at absence on *CSI* to examining how race, gender, class and sexuality are made actively *present* on the show. My contention is that in the first season, the series' five main characters are interesting, not so much as specific personalities, but rather as tropes of phallic mastery (Grissom and Nick) and anxiety (Catherine, Sara and Warrick). The anxiety over threatening Otherness is contained by making it knowable. By drawing on stock cultural understandings of difference to construct the latter three characters, Otherness becomes a recognizable object that can be controlled and redeemed by phallic mastery.

Catherine Willows

Catherine represents a form of white femininity that is both not young and ambiguously classed. Catherine is a well-dressed, well-educated professional woman, but she is also a single mother with a deadbeat ex-husband; a former exotic dancer and a recovering cocaine addict, she has a past that many viewers might read as less than respectable.[21] Details of Catherine's less than respectable and vaguely working-class background are actually revealed in later seasons, when we find out that her mother was a showgirl and her biological father a shady casino owner about whose wealth she feels ambivalent, but of which she still selectively takes advantage. The character performs an active and slightly threatening kind of sexuality not commonly associated with young, respectable, middle class femininity. Catherine is red-haired (or strawberry blonde); she often appears wearing tight, revealing clothing; and she responds to masculine allusions about her past with lighthearted and mildly flirtatious banter:

Greg: So you used to work at the French Palace. . . . My friends and I used to go there. . . . Maybe I saw you perform.

Catherine: Oh I doubt it. . . . You would've remembered. ("Who Are You?" 1006)

Greg: Did you ever wear one of these [a headdress] while you were dancing?

Catherine: I wore nothing but skin.

Greg: Ooh. ("Table Stakes" 1015)

What complicates a surface reading of Catherine as mature, unselfconscious and sexually liberated is her ambiguous class identity. As work building on Foucault has taught us, sexual regulation in the context of modern capitalist society has entailed classifying groups through social categories of race, gender and class.[22] While respectable, bourgeois Victorian womanhood was predominantly constructed as asexual, working-class sexuality (for both genders) was narrated as active and unrestrained. Until fairly recently, there was no mainstream subject position available to white, middle class women as active sexual subjects (versus objects of white masculine desire). If this discourse still haunts dominant representations of white, middle-class, respectable womanhood in North American culture, is Catherine's active and potentially threatening sexuality on *CSI* explicable and even acceptable only by reading her through an ambiguous—i.e. not obviously bourgeois—class identity?

Sara Sidle

In the first season of *CSI*, Sara functions as a trope of undesirable femininity. For example, the first season character profile describes her as "sharp," "no nonsense" and having a "brash manner."[23] Sara's difficulties on the show can be seen as an understandable product of feminist struggles for gender equality. However, her lack of sensuality, a personal life, or human connection also suggests phallic anxiety about gender equality and can be read as an implicit warning for young female viewers about embracing professional success in the masculine world of work. Introduced in "Cool Change" (1002) as an investigator of Holly Gribbs' attack, Sara subsequently replaces Holly (who has died). Sara is a brunette, evoking an American post-war cultural understanding of brunettes as smarter (but less attractive) than blondes.[24] Unlike Holly, Sara is not young, delicate, fragile or easily intimidated. Middle class, in her late twenties when she joins the team, Sara has no personal or romantic life, but instead devotes all her time to her investigations, is emotionally shut down and only expresses real feeling during cases of violence against women:[25]

Grissom: Sara, do you have any diversions? . . . you max out on overtime every month. You go home and listen to your police scanner. You read forensic textbooks . . . you need something outside of law enforcement. Catherine has her kid, you know?[26]

She is described in the current official CBS website profile as a brilliant but socially backward young woman, who finally managed to date at Harvard University.[27] In later seasons, she continues to struggle with emotional connection. In seasons four to six, she starts to fall apart (developing a drinking problem). According to the CBS profile, "like any tragic figure worth her salt, Sara has a single flaw: people. She can solve any problem except the problem of other people and how she's supposed to relate to them."[28]

Warrick Brown

As the only major African-American character on *CSI*'s first season, Warrick functions primarily as a foil for both white femininity and white masculinity. His subordinate relationality illustrates Herman Gray's argument about frames of containment that confirm dominant white notions of what blackness is and, thus, reproduce racialized discourses circulating in American society.[29] *CSI's* pilot season repeatedly provides evidence that Warrick is a liability to the *CSI* team. This persistent undermining of the show's only major African American character suggests, as mentioned earlier, a kind of haunted narrative of American race relations, part of which includes white, liberal guilt about slavery and its legacies. According to Meek, "any claim to self-identity will always be punctuated by specters . . . who unsettle us with their ghostly (non) presence."[30] In this context, white American identity is indelibly tied to the legacy of slavery. In its first season, *CSI* handles this specter by positioning black masculinity as naturally inferior in two ways, first as dangerous (the gangster) and second, as weak or incompetent. In the latter scenario, represented by Warrick's character, white responsibility for (and privilege grounded in) the history of black-white relations is assuaged by the comforting thought that there has been a survival of the fittest quality to white supremacy. The transformation of white guilt into complacency is thus effected through the positioning of Warrick as the trope of the racial Other in desperate need of the White civilizing mission.

Warrick, in the pilot episode, is presented as a good but deeply flawed man, in danger of being swallowed up by his gambling addiction.[31] He must choose between, on the one hand, his habit and a coercive relationship with a corrupt white judge who explicitly stands in for the slave master by asserting to Warrick, "I own you,"[32] and, on the other, Grissom, as the benevolent paternal voice of white rational masculinity. Again, a narrative of white liberal guilt that can only be resolved by what psychoanalytic theory would call a splitting haunts this storyline. Phallic mastery's destructive side must be acknowledged because of the undeniable history of slave relations. However, the American cultural psyche, caught up in its myths of freedom, democracy and benevolent intervention in other nations' problems, has to compensate for this national ghost by reminding itself of its good guys: the founding fathers who supposedly believed in equality for all, Abraham Lincoln the great emancipator of slaves, civil rights champions such as John F. Kennedy and Bobby Kennedy, and, of course, the scientists who brought the world reason and enlightenment. On *CSI,* the corrupt judge becomes the repository for all that was/is oppressive about white masculinity, while the show's lead, Grissom, represents democracy, rationality and support for civil liberties. And even here, there is a profound denial to be read between the lines of the *CSI* world: although the corrupt white judge is, on the surface, a caricature of the slave master, after a third viewing of the episode (with sub-titles on), it was fascinating to discover that the judge's name is "Cohen." Phallic anxiety, thus, further displaces the specter of "bad" whiteness onto the ambiguously racialized figure of a Jewish man.[33]

Warrick's troubles set him up as the embodied space across which crude stereotypes of good and bad white masculinity do battle. Again, this power struggle over who controls black bodies is also about protecting white womanhood.[34] As I discussed earlier, the resolution of the Holly Gribbs story arc (which launches the pilot episode and the series itself) allows Warrick's presence to be dealt with in a way that addresses phallic anxiety around white women and black men. For example, after the *CSI* team has caught the black man accused of Holly's murder, the camera pans over the faces of the five main characters, all of whom are white, except for Warrick. My reading of this camera shot is that it suggests an imperial gaze, shared by both the white characters and Warrick. Faced with the choice between racial solidarity (between Warrick and the black male accused)[35] or justice (read here as white and masculine), Warrick has made his choice. The episode ends with Warrick telling Grissom "I won't let you down again," and cuts to the scene of the black accused being taken away in a police car. The wrapping up of these storylines, both literally and metaphorically, suggests that if confronted with the temptation of young, white, respectable femininity (represented by Holly Gribbs), black masculinity has only two options: to perform the dangerous or incapable Other and be punished for it (in this case, along with his white female partner), or to be the castrated black man who will protect white womanhood without ever desiring her. And while Warrick's bi-racial status allows him to be cast as the "good" black man (whiter and therefore potentially more redeemable than the black gangster), in *CSI*'s first season he is still repeatedly constructed as the Other, thus rendering him an unsuitable partner for white femininity.

Finally, without wanting to overstate of the significance of Warrick's involvement in Gribbs' death and his role as racialized scapegoat in the show's foundational narrative, it is worth noting how Warrick's character ultimately exits the series. In the season eight finale, Warrick is arrested for allegedly murdering someone and is taunted by the arresting officer about his involvement eight years before in the death of Holly Gribbs.[36] Thus, once again, viewers are reminded of the failed beginnings of Warrick's *CSI* career, which involved the death of a young, innocent, white woman. And while Sara Sidle also leaves the show in an earlier season, Warrick's departure is interesting precisely because, as the show's only African-American lead character, he dies violently at the hands of a crooked white cop.

Nick Stokes

While Catherine, Sara and Warrick can be read as various tropes of anxiety-producing Otherness on *CSI*, Nick, the handsome and perpetually smiling investigator, appears to be Grissom's successor to the project of phallic mastery as white, western, privileged, rational masculinity. He is described in the official first season character profile as "equal parts, charm and chops . . . self-assured and focused . . . [with] a revolving-door reputation with women."[37] In direct contrast to Warrick, Nick rarely has to be reprimanded or lectured by his boss. Even his one weakness is heroic. In "Boom" (1012), Nick is the white knight to a beautiful prostitute with whom he has a brief but necessarily doomed affair. The prostitute first appears in the pilot episode as someone who drugs and robs her clients.[38] Right away, there is a certain flirtation between her and Nick; he figures out what she is doing, but lets her off, warning her that next time he will arrest her. In "Boom," after he rescues her from an abusive pimp/lover, they end up having sex. She is murdered the same day by the pimp/lover and Nick is a potential suspect until he solves the case. His superiors chastise him for his lapse in judgment (both in sleeping with this woman as well as getting involved in her personal conflicts), which has not only put him at risk, but potentially even contributed to her murder. But this is still a far cry from Warrick, whose mistakes put the entire team in danger, and whose gambling addiction has no undertones of virtue. In contrast, Nick's sexual and emotional weakness in terms of this woman can be read as evidence of both a chivalrous nature and sexual prowess.

It is important to read Nick's performance of phallic mastery relationally, that is, through his interactions with the series' other two central male characters. Regular episodes of playful masculine ribbing and an avid interest in betting (on football or who will clear the most cases) punctuate Nick's interactions with Warrick, indicating to the audience that Nick, despite his sensitive, metrosexual traits, is actually very heteronormative.[39] Nick's interactions with Grissom have a father-son undertone: several characters on the show, but most often Grissom, refer to Nick affectionately as "Nicky." Furthermore, in "Friends and Lovers" (1005), Catherine responds to Nick (who is quoting from the gospel of Grissom), "hey Nick, Grissom's not always right. Do yourself a favor and think for yourself."

Nick's performance of hegemonic white, bourgeois, heterosexual masculinity is highlighted in "Pledging Mr. Johnson" (1004), when an allegedly accidental death during a fraternity hazing requires further investigation. The episode is significant, both in terms of setting Nick up as a trope of hegemonic masculinity as well as understanding the broader narrative of phallic mastery that underpins the show's pilot season. In this episode, "Johnson" refers both to the pledge who is murdered (James Johnson), and to a phallic hazing ritual involved in the case, which required that each pledge get his penis (in slang terms, johnson), signed by a member of sorority row. During the episode, two important facts are revealed: 1) Grissom promotes Nick to a CSI level 3 investigator over Warrick because of the latter's screw-up regarding Gribbs' murder and 2) we find out that Nick was a frat boy in college. The latter point is crucial because when it appears that one of the frat boys has murdered the pledge over a woman, Nick does not deny the legitimacy of fraternities but, instead, draws on an ideal form that symbolizes all that is noble about white, male solidarity:

> Nick: Hey Matt, you know why I joined a fraternity? Because I wanted to belong to something—the brotherhood. That's what it was all about for me . . . you come clean, you might be able to save the brotherhood, but if you don't, everything you're trying to protect, you'll destroy.[40]

The episode's resolution suggests that fraternities can be worthy brotherhoods (rather than simply spaces of corrupt privilege); furthermore, it is Nick as an embodiment of the trope of white, privileged masculinity (like Grissom), who represents the benevolent possibilities of phallic mastery.

Gil Grissom

If Nick is successor to the project of phallic mastery, then Grissom, as leading man, is the reigning patriarch, performing a fantasy of benevolent white masculine domination over unruly Others. *CSI* is Grissom's kingdom: he is in charge of his team; he makes executive decisions; the actor who plays him leads in the opening credits (and is a *CSI* executive producer). Grissom's character, described as "old school," performs a trope of western scientific rationality; he is the quintessential Cartesian man, as illustrated by his encounters with the other main characters.[41] Throughout the first season, viewers are given clues as to what Grissom holds most dear: the scientific ideals of objectivity, truth and reason in the pursuit of justice.

In terms of his interactions with his team, Grissom's encounters with Warrick play into the fantasy of the kindly (white) father watching over his imperial family; he advises, warns, supports and encourages Warrick, using the language of paternalistic condescension ("I'm proud of you" and "I can only help you out so much. After that, it's up to you").[42] The colonial discourse of the "white man's burden" haunts the two men's relationship to one another: in a later season, when the team has come together to grieve Warrick's death and clear his name, they find a videotape of Warrick speaking to an unknown interviewer about his love and respect for Grissom, the one man who has never failed him, and to whom he owes everything.[43] As such, despite being called "For Warrick," the episode might better have been called "For Grissom," given that it is essentially a paean to Grissom, highlighting his noble failure in trying to redeem what, ultimately, could not be redeemed (the inferior racialized Other).

Similarly, in his gendered interactions with Catherine and Sara, Grissom embodies both moral righteousness and paternal benevolence. In "Pledging Mr. Johnson" (1004), Catherine compromises the integrity of a case by telling the victim's husband, against Grissom's wishes, of his late wife's affair. Catherine's feminine reasoning, meant to represent women's supposedly emotional, subjective and relational logic, proves faulty when the husband incorrectly assumes that his wife's lover is also her murderer (and murders the lover). Catherine is horrified and ashamed at the consequences of her poor decision, and the story arc's unhappy conclusion reasserts phallic authority. Grissom's interactions with Sara also reassert the emotional/feminine—rational/masculine divide. He regularly chastises Sara for being too emotionally cut off and married to her work. However, in "Too Tough to Die" (1016), where Sara is clearly upset about the crime, Grissom cautions her about letting her emotions get the better of her. This fits with Grissom's own approach to personal life: that it is secondary, even superfluous, to the pursuit of science and justice. An example of this can be found in his clumsy attempts, on several occasions, to woo another scientist.[44] Although he manages to arrange a dinner date with this woman, the date ends before it has even really begun, with Grissom being called back to work by his team and, in effect, back to the public sphere where his real passion lies. This conclusion works to reassert the traditional divide between masculinity as synonymous with the public world of work, and femininity as naturally suited to the private sphere of emotional connection and family.[45]

Finally, Grissom's phallic mastery is demonstrated by the seemingly innocuous fact that, in the first season, Catherine, Sara, Warrick and even Nick are referred to almost exclusively by their first names, but Grissom is almost always called by his last name.[46] Naming is central to the question of power relations and who has the authority to name and un-name others. During slavery, and even after it in the American South, black men were called by their first names, and were often called "boy" regardless of their age, as a clear discursive strategy of diminishment. The moniker and, thus, subject position "man" (and the family name linked with it) was reserved for white masters and, after slavery and before civil rights, for white men. Similarly, before second wave feminism, it was common and even expected for men to refer to women as girls, regardless of their age or status. These naming practices are about the power of knowing and ultimately owning the subjectivity (and objectivity) of the Self and the Other. The distinction between the familiar first name use for Catherine, Sara, Warrick and Nick, and the unambiguously masculine and proper last name use for Grissom draws a small but significant difference between the *CSI* team and their natural superior: the older, white, middle class, heterosexual man of science, embodied by Gil Grissom.

TOO TOUGH TO DIE, TOO DUMB TO SPEAK: THE SHADOW PRESENCE OF BLACK FEMININITY

In this section, I examine how black femininity occupies a space between *absence* and *presence*, or what I see as a "shadow presence," on *CSI*'s first season.[47] While a black female medical examiner has a small recurring role,[48] and there are a handful of episodes where there are very minor black female characters,[49] there are only two episodes with storylines that center on black female characters: "Crate and Burial" (1003), where a young black man accidentally kills a little black girl in a hit-and-run accident, and "Too Tough to Die" (1016), where the perpetrator (also a young black man), shoots and puts a young black woman into a coma.

These storylines ambiguously locate black femininity along a continuum of silence and voice in relation to the show's major and minor characters. In some ways, this location parallels the show's exclusion of idealized white femininity and dangerous black masculinity (represented, respectively, by Holly Gribbs and the gangster who kills her). However, Gribbs is an active, speaking subject until she dies in the pilot episode, thereby becoming a central device through which the show's moral narrative is secured. Dangerous black masculinity is also active briefly, as a type of racialized villain (i.e. perpetrator of crimes against whiteness), and then disappears entirely from the first season. As I mentioned earlier, on *CSI* this absence can be read, sub-textually, as the unnamed, and un-nameable ghost of failed "race relations" in America. In contrast to both these conspicuous absences, black femininity is simultaneously absent and present. Rather than functioning as an active presence that is then erased in order to present the dangers of crime to (white, gendered, aged) innocence, or as a spectral presence haunting the show's whitened landscape, black femininity is somewhat arbitrarily inserted at certain points in the season, in order to further certain storylines along. For example, it is absent generally over the course of the season and in episodes such as "Crate and Burial" (1003), where the little girl functions as an off-stage victim: we see only one very quick, somewhat blurred flashback of the accident and another quick shot of the body being examined; however, unlike many of the other victims on the show, we never hear her speak in flashbacks or find out anything about her, even her name. Black femininity is vocally and substantially present in the show's first season only through the sporadic appearance of the medical examiner, who speaks in a few brief sentences here and there, the Jane Doe in the coma who is voiceless, and the Gangster's mother who speaks only to defend the indefensible.

My reading, therefore, of *CSI*'s first season is that black femininity is performed through what I call the Dummy trope, a gesture to neoliberal tolerance that allows for the minimal presence of the unthreatening, but still unwelcome, Other. The following are four definitions of the word Dummy found in the Macmillan dictionary: "1) figure of the human body used to represent or serve as a real person: department store dummy, a ventriloquist's dummy 2) imitation object made to resemble the real thing, as a false drawer 3) one unable to speak; mute 4) one seeming to act independently or for his own interests but really serving another."[50] These four definitions, while not exhaustive, resonate with respect to representations of black femininity on *CSI*'s first season. Starting with definition one, the medical examiner does speak but as a token representation of black femininity; like the department store dummy, she imitates real personhood. She is rarely on screen for longer than a few minutes, and we know absolutely nothing about her, except that she is the examiner who delivers (without much emotion) neutral scientific facts about death.

Moving to definition two, the hit and run victim in "Crate and Burial" (1003) is an imitative object to the extent that she implies violent death (the grist for the *CSI* mill), but unlike the vast majority of the cases explored on the series, her death is accidental, the result of reckless driving, rather than human malice. She is, figuratively speaking, a false drawer in the pursuit of justice, a victim without a real victimizer. In *CSI*'s first season, the only black victims (either male or female) have died either as the result of accidental death or black on black violence.[51] White on black violence is never presented. In this set of narratives, black victimization is never the fault of white criminals for reasons of gain, pathology or racism. Given the history of white racist violence perpetrated against blacks in the US, the lack of even one case with a black victim and a white perpetrator on *CSI*'s first season seems, once again, to conveniently deny the reality of American race relations. This is particularly noteworthy since the pilot episode of the series *begins* with a black man murdering an innocent white person, through the implied negligence of another black man. In this phallic fantasy, *white* racialization and racism are never motivations: white men are sometimes heroic (Grissom and Nick), when ambiguously white (as in the case of Judge Cohen), they are corrupt but not violent or they are criminals who appear to be completely indifferent to race (the numerous white criminals who appear throughout the season and whose victims are other whites, male and female).

Definitions one and three are particularly mobilized in "Too Tough to Die" (1016), where a comatose victim—aptly introduced as a Jane Doe, and revealed later in the episode to be Pamela Adler—never speaks but is spoken about, to, and for, by Sara Sidle. Ironically, Sara finds a chain with Saint Catherine on it among the comatose woman's things and says to the latter about Saint Catherine: "she was tough, outspoken." But while Sara sees a likeness between Saint Catherine and the victim, given the victim's actual silence, it is Sara's pain and anger at violence against women that is rendered most emotionally present to the audience. While it might be argued that the investigators often speak on behalf of (dead) victims on *CSI*, white victims are extremely common on the show. Within the *CSI* landscape, whiteness functions as a norm and is, therefore, allowed a broad range of subject positions (from victim to villain to witness to investigator). Furthermore, a significant majority of episodes in the first season (at least nineteen) contain flashbacks, where white victims are seen speaking and interacting with other characters. In contrast, in the first season, black characters in general and black women specifically rarely appear. When they do, they are generally silent, and are portrayed either as very minor characters or as victims.

This racialized displacement is common in popular cultural representations; according to Berlant and Freeman, it is "the historic burden black women in cinema have borne to represent embodiment, desire and the dignity of suffering on behalf of white women. . . . the black woman signifies, but will not, does not, or cannot speak for herself."[52] Again, while this inability to speak on one's own behalf is, to some extent, true of many of *CSI*'s victims, two things set this Jane Doe apart from the rest: first, there is no other episode in the first season that is centered on a victim that is neither dead nor really alive; and second, no other episode has a *CSI* investigator hold lengthy conversations with this silent victim who has no voice to answer back. It is precisely this *absent* presence that suggests the imitative or "dummy" quality of black femininity as presented on *CSI*. It is, perhaps, only a coincidence that there is an actual plastic dummy in the same episode, used by Catherine and Warrick to deduce the logistics of a crime scene on a separate case, and described by Catherine as "lifelike . . . doesn't talk . . . and self-healing."[53] If we juxtapose these two images, it is not entirely clear which is the real dummy: the white blow-up doll or the black woman in a coma, spoken for by her white, female ventriloquist.

Finally, moving on to definition four, the main speaking positions allotted to black femininity on *CSI* actually reinforce the phallic mastery that underpins the show's universe. First, the medical examiner speaks as the voice of science, the civilized Other whose presence has a mirroring effect: she reflects back to Grissom (with whom she has the most contact) the superiority of western scientific rationality. Second, in "Too Tough to Die (1016), Shaunda, the shooter's mother, speaks, but seemingly without remorse. In *CSI*'s cultural script, where discovering and punishing criminals is the *raison d'être*, the mother attempts to defend her violent son. She is, thus, configured as speaking against justice, and her words are effectively de-legitimized. One can also read an even deeper hostility in this scenario, with black maternity being troped as the mother of black violence that affects both blacks and whites. Given that the gangster's father is noticeably absent in this story arc, is an allusion being made to all those single black welfare mothers raising sons? In such a narrative, black mothers are held at least partially responsible for producing the violent "boyz in the hood" who have turned America's allegedly peaceful (white) cities into deadly war zones.

WRITING AGAINST YOUR OWN TEXT: CONCLUDING THOUGHTS ON THE AMBIVALENT SELVES OF TELEVISION WRITERS AND VIEWERS

The discussion so far has explored how, on *CSI*'s pilot season, story and character arcs can be read as representations of larger social concerns around the question of difference. Employing a feminist psychoanalytic framework, I examined how gender, race, class, age and sexuality are performed on the show through certain tropes; these tropes can be read as texts of phallic mastery and anxiety emanating from the project of white, privileged, heterosexual masculinity, as those performing it attempt to navigate a world characterized by resistance to hegemonic forms of economic, political and cultural power. I began by arguing that, in the pilot episode, the young, blonde cop's murder represents a trope of lost innocence in the dangerous world of *CSI*. In this gendered fantasy of phallic mastery, the ostensibly neutral narrative of benevolent and objective science is accompanied by a racialized sub-text or, following Derrida, a ghost narrative that tropes the "real" threat to young, white girlhood and womanhood as black masculinity (in both its dangerous and inadequate manifestations). I then examined how the show's main characters operate as tropes of both mastery (Grissom and Nick) and threatening difference (Catherine, Sara and Warrick). I concluded with a discussion of the absence/ presence of black femininity on the show through the dummy trope. I looked at the few episodes where black femininity has a presence and argued that given the particular subject positions allotted to black femininity, this inclusion of black femininity is little more than lip service to an abstract concept of racial equality/visibility in a neo-liberal landscape.

Having made a case for the above arguments, I want to conclude by deconstructing my own interpretations. My intention here is to point out that authors, performers and audiences always create space for resistance and subversion in cultural texts. How a particular show gets written and read is often what is at stake in the debates around popular culture and the so-called effects of popular culture on larger society. As Julie D'Acci points out, "the hegemonic status of any discourse is, by its very nature, always open to change, negotiation, and displacement."[54] Therefore, I want to re-visit some of the mastery/anxiety narratives that I have outlined with an eye towards identifying slippages or moments of contradiction. While I offer this counter-hegemonic reading, I am not necessarily arguing that it takes the place of, or radically interrupts, the relations of power underlying the show's founding myth. Rather than undermining my prior claims, I simply want to open up the possibility for alternative viewer interpretations of what is at stake in these representations, to drive home the point that television audiences are not the mindless dupes of Adorno and Horkheimer's famous culture industry. Instead, as Haralovich and Rabinovitz argue, viewers are also "resistant readers," who appropriate, remake and reinterpret mainstream productions in ways that demonstrate cultural agency rather than simply consumerist practices.[55]

To begin with the mourning for Holly Gribbs that opens the series, we might read this, not just as a trope of lost innocence, but also as a critique of an infantilized form of womanhood.[56] After all, both Catherine and Sara (who replaces Gribbs) are strong, competent and highly intelligent career women, who do not have to be protected or saved from modern urban dangers. Moreover, Catherine's sexuality, while ambiguously classed, also represents the active sexuality of women over forty, something that, until recently, has been largely absent from mainstream cultural depictions of female sexuality. Catherine's highly embodied sexual performance is a pleasurable and even powerful aspect of her self; it is neither a way to get ahead, nor is it a source of shame. We might read Catherine as both an object of male desire and an actively desiring subject. The show's writers are, thus, offering a radical re-visioning of female sexuality, which allows female viewers to relate to im-ages of feminine desirability outside the realm of anorexic, eternally young female bodies. This representation also affords male viewers the opportunity to recognize and embrace their own desire for adult women, rather than the barely pubescent girl-women that the mainstream fashion and entertainment industries consistently tout as epitomizing female beauty.

Warrick's character might also be read in a subversive fashion. For ex-ample, the pilot episode where Warrick is first introduced does not shy away from addressing race, even if it is through a superficial, almost playful discus-sion. The following exchanges are set up to allow Warrick the space to speak about race and racial inequality, in ways that, at the very least, interrupt his subordinate status throughout the first season:

Warrick (to Nick on the subject of who will be promoted): I'm like Tiger, man. I'm heavily favored.[57]

Warrick (to Catherine about his suspicions regarding a white male crime victim): That's why I took this job, I can always tell when Whitey is talking out his ass.[58]

Finally, there is the trope of phallic mastery itself, as performed by Gil Grissom. In the pilot season of *CSI: Crime Scene Investigation* Grissom is consistently depicted as a noble, heroic man of science who is dedicated to making the world a better place, but there are repeated suggestions that his public life is not an adequate substitute for a private or emotional life. Gris-som has no personal stuff, no attachments, no family or close friends and, thus, no real emotional life. There is a very minor character that appears throughout the season as a potential romantic interest for Grissom: a brilliant, blonde, older female scientist. She is Grissom's equal in terms of intelligence and independence, as well as socially (through her race, class and age sta-tus). Her sporadic appearance, when she shows up to help him with a case and then disappears, might be read as a kind of wish fulfillment, a desire for emotional intimacy with the gendered Other. It might, perhaps, even indicate a subconscious desire for equality with that Other. Of course, in season one, Grissom, when forced to choose between private, individual love and his team's needs, chooses the latter. So is this a clear triumph of phallic mastery? It may be. But it is worth noting, as this book goes to press, that *CSI*'s ninth season finds Grissom making the startling decision to retire from forensics and leave *CSI*.[59] Leaving *CSI* brings a resolution to Grissom's struggle with his personal/professional demons, albeit in a somewhat clichéd fashion: the last scene of the departure episode finds Grissom wandering through the proverbial forest where he meets and embraces Sara Sidle, with whom he has had a complicated professional and romantic relationship in past seasons.[60]

While this "fairytale" ending is somewhat problematic, in that it appears to redeem Sidle's troubled character primarily through the role of the feminine, nurturing Other, Grissom's departure does usher in a new era for *CSI* through the addition of Dr. Ray Langston, played by African-American actor Laurence Fishburne. Interestingly, this dual departure/addition returns us to the scene of the imperial drama between Grissom and Warrick Brown, wherein Langston represents a strange composite of the two. Like Grissom, Langston is a Ph.D., and a mature man; yet as someone with little "field" experience, he takes up what Grissom himself describes as an entry-level position, thus, replacing Warrick in the racial hierarchy of the show (a clue to this replacement can even be found in one of the episode's final scenes, which has Grissom staring fondly at Warrick's picture).[61] Langston also shares a disturbing similarity to Warrick in his potential for violence, and his guilt over past professional mistakes of a tragic nature.[62] Still, it is Grissom who seeks Langston out for help with a case and then suggests that he join *CSI*. While the show's imperial subtext has hardly been challenged by this move, it should be pointed out that Fishburne, already a full-fledged movie star, gets top billing in the new credits.

Finally, it is Catherine Willows who takes over as the new head of *CSI*, a shift that is significant, given the gender dynamics that inform the show's foundational narrative. Perhaps, then, the final completion of Grissom's storyline can be read as a kind of wish fulfillment on the part of the show's writers: the demand for a sincere effort by the white masculine imperial masters to work not only *with* but *for* their subordinated Others, in order to clean up a society whose ills (poverty, racism, gendered violence) these masters are largely responsible for creating.

NOTES

1. Character Profile for Gil Grissom, "*CSI: Crime Scene Investigation*," Official CBS Website, http://www.cbs.com/primetime/csi/.

2. Allan J. Gedalof et al., *Cultural Subjects: A Popular Culture Reader*, (Toronto: Thomson Nelson, 2005), 15.

3. Ian Craib, *Psychoanalysis and Social Theory: The Limits of Sociology* (Amherst: The University of Massachusetts Press, 1989), 124–25.

4. bell hooks, *Outlaw Culture: Resisting Representations* (New York and London: Routledge, 1994), 116.

5. Cited in Ella Shohat and Robert Stam, *Unthinking Eurocentrism: Multiculturalism and the Media* (London: Routledge, 1994), 137.

6. For instance, the above trope of animalization has been openly challenged by formerly subjugated communities, who argue that western civilizing projects of slavery, apartheid and indigenous genocides are actually indictments of European barbarism.

7. Herman Gray, *Watching Race: Television and the Struggle for Blackness* (Minneapolis: University of Minnesota Press, 1994), 4–10.

8. John Fiske. "Moments of Television: Neither the Text nor the Audience," in *Remote Control: Television, Audiences and Cultural Power*, ed. Ellen Seiter et al (London and New York: Routledge, 1989), 56–78.

9. Herman Gray, *Watching Race: Television and the Struggle for Blackness* (Minneapolis: University of Minnesota Press, 1994), 4–10.

10. Julie D'Acci. "Gender, Representation and Television," in *Television Studies*, ed. Toby Miller (London: BFI Publishing, 2002), 91–93.

11. Bell hooks, *Outlaw Culture: Resisting Representations* (New York and London: Routledge, 1994), 19.

12. Teresa Podlesney. "Blondes," in *The Hysterical Male: New Feminist Theory*, ed. Arthur Kroker and Marilouise Kroker (Montreal: New World Perspectives, 1991), 80.

13. "Pilot" (1001).

14. In "Friends and Lovers" (1005), the young blonde murder suspect's clothing exposes most of her cleavage, sending a visual cue that this is not innocent femininity; she is also a lesbian who, with her lover, committed the murder in order to avoid exposure and ruin.

15. In "To Halve and to Hold" (1014), the young blonde murder suspect is trying to protect the real murderer, her jealous fiancé. In "Who are you?" (1006), the ex-lover's brunette wife kills the young blonde murder victim out of jealousy. In "35k O.B.O" (1018), the blonde accident victim turns out to be the lover of a husband who has hired someone to kill his wife.

16. See Bonnycastle in this volume for further discussion of this and related issues.

17. Take, for example, the comment that Grissom makes to Warrick early on in the season: "the minute you started thinking about yourself instead of the case, you lost him. There is no room for subjectivity in this department. We handle each case objectively without presupposition, regardless of race, color, creed or bubblegum flavor. Okay?"

18. In a similar fashion to what Engle describes about 9/11: "Producing their own Hauntology, the dead towers operate as an absent presence whose mere existence *as such* explains the US invasions of Afghanistan and Iraq, as well as the nation's domestic policies of surveillance and deportation." Karen J. Engle "Putting Mourning to Work: Making Sense of 9/11," *Theory, Culture and Society*, vol. 24, no. 1 (2007): 61–88.

19. Ironically, this nebulous fear contrasts sharply with the historical realities of slavery and post-slavery America, where it was actually black women who were most vulnerable to forced sexual relations with white men. The cultural denial of this vulnerability has been accompanied by fears about white women's violation by black

men, anxiety that can be read, psychoanalytically, as a classic displacement strategy. According to Gaines, "Here is a sexual scenario to rival the Oedipal myth; the black woman sexually violated by the white man, but the fact of her rape repressed and displaced onto the virginal white woman, and thus used symbolically as the justification for the actual castration of the black man." Jane Gaines. "White Privilege and Looking Relations," in *Feminism and Film*, ed. E. Ann Kaplan (Oxford: Oxford University Press, 2000), 349. Also see bell hooks, *Black Looks: Race and Representation* (Boston: South End Press, 1992).

20. Ann Pellegrini, *Performance Anxieties: Staging Psychoanalysis, Staging Race* (New York: Routledge, 1997), 139. Also see "Ida B. Wells-Barnett Exposes the Myth of the Black Rapist, 1892" in *Major Problems in the History of American Sexuality*, ed. Kathy Peiss (Boston: Houghton Mifflin, 2002), 155–58.

21. Here is Catherine as described by cast members (*CSI: Crime Scene Investigation*, DVD, Season One, Cast Interviews):

Marg Helgenberger (Catherine): Catherine Willows did come from the world of exotic dancing, I like to refer to it as, instead of stripping. It sounds classier . . . and is now a very well-respected criminalist in the city of Las Vegas . . . that fascinated me when I first read the script and I thought "wow, that's quite a path that she's taken, from where she came and where she ends up."

William Peterson (Grissom): Catherine Willows is more from the streets, she's an ex stripper.

22. Gary Kinsman. "Constructing Sexual Problems: 'These Things may lead to the Tragedy of our Species,'" in *Power and Resistance: Critical Thinking about Canadian Social Issues*, ed. Les Samuelson and Wayne Antony (Halifax: Fernwood Publishing, 2003), 85–120.

23. *CSI: Crime Scene Investigation*, DVD, Season One, Character profile.

24. Teresa Podlesney. "Blondes," in *The Hysterical Male: New Feminist Theory*, ed. Arthur Kroker and Marilouise Kroker (Montreal: New World Perspectives, 1991), 87.

25. In the first season viewers are not told why she is particularly affected by violence against women.

26. "Too Tough to Die" (1016).

27. Character Profile for Sara Sidle, "*CSI: Crime Scene Investigation*," Official CBS Website, http://www.cbs.com/primetime/csi/.

28. Character Profile for Sara Sidle, "*CSI: Crime Scene Investigation*," Official CBS Website, http://www.cbs.com/primetime/csi/.

29. Herman Gray, *Watching Race: Television and the Struggle for Blackness* (Minneapolis: University of Minnesota Press, 1994), 8.

30. Allan Meek. "Mourning, Media and the 'Virtual Space of Spectrality,'" *Space and Culture*, vol. 3, no. 5, 2000, 104.

31. "Pilot" (1001).

32. Warrick becomes tied to Judge Cohen when he places a bet for him in return for a blank warrant that the CSI team does not have the evidence to legally procure. I do not have the space to address here the criminological complexities around how Warrick's racialized weakness for gambling is complicated by this linked quest to

enact a strong law and order approach (that is often employed by all the characters on the show). Thanks to Val Johnson for highlighting this.

33. This construction points to the arbitrary and historically specific nature of racial categories: although conventionally understood to be a marker of power and status, whiteness is neither stable nor is it a unitary identity. It is, instead, a struggle for belonging among groups variously categorized as not white, not quite white, not white enough and sometimes, but not always, white.

34. The feminization/emasculation of black men, both physically and representationally, was and is a primary tactic of white supremacist thought. Thus, the disabling of Warrick as a potential threat to phallic mastery occurs, not only through the above storyline, but on varying levels. It is, perhaps, more than coincidental that Warrick's light skin and hair and blue eyes construct him as bi-racial and sexually desirable within a dominant white aesthetic; yet, in the first season, his only interactions with white women are work related. The contradiction between his whitened aesthetic appeal and the lack of actual sexual interaction suggests that his racial liminality may also be a gendered liminality: as the castrated black man who lacks any real sexual identity, Warrick, in the first season, may be standing in for both black masculinity and passive white femininity.

35. According to Pellegrini, the refusal to recognize specificity "is one of the better known mechanisms of subjugation." Ann Pellegrini, *Performance Anxieties: Staging Psychoanalysis, Staging Race* (New York: Routledge, 1997), 8. Black masculinity is homogenized throughout the first season, subtly reminding the viewer that Warrick is part of a larger "race problem" in the US. For example, in the pilot, a young black man (assisting Grissom in the lab) finds evidence to support Warrick's claim and says to Grissom with great pride "the brother was right, wasn't he!" In the same episode, Warrick goes to Judge Cohen's house at night and is mistaken by police as a criminal: "Sorry, Judge, we got a call from a neighbor about a black man at your house and responded." At the end of the episode, we are introduced to the black gangster who murders Holly Gribbs. In "Cool Change" (1002), Catherine sets up Holly's murderer on the phone by pretending to be interested sexually in him; but her language is blatantly mocking "gansgta talk" (she mentions "a little bling bling" and tells him "invite me over to your crib, baby"). In "Crate and Burial" (1003), Warrick's investigation of a young black man's hit and run killing of a little black girl leads him to the young man's car. When the car is started, the sound system starts blaring hip hop music: Warrick starts moving his head to the music and says to Catherine "this is good stuff." Viewers are reminded of Warrick's similarity to this young man (who is also guilty of a crime).

36. Season Eight "For Gedda" (8017).

37. (*CSI: Crime Scene Investigation*, DVD, Season One, Character profile).

38. "Pilot"(1001).

39. For example, in "Boom" (1013), where Nick is initially suspected of murdering a prostitute, he gets unusually emotional (in contrast to the stoic masculinity of the other lead male characters) when he is cleared of all charges and hugs Catherine gratefully, almost crying. In "Who Are You?" (1006), while he is being held at gunpoint by a murderer, he is actually shown crying.

40. "Pledging Mr. Johnson" (1004).
41. William Peterson, the actor who plays Grissom describes him in the following way: "My character is an academic, he's been through a Master's and a Ph.D." (*CSI: Crime Scene Investigation*, DVD, Season One, Cast Interviews).
42. "Cool Change" (1002).
43. "For Warrick" (9001).
44. "Who are you?" (1006); "Face Lift" (1017); "To Halve and to Hold" (1014).
45. Again, this divide can be seen in Grissom's chastising of Sara for her lack of emotional connection (see page 5) as well as Catherine's guilt in the first season, over loving her job so much that it pulls her away from her mothering responsibilities.
46. There is some gender distinction here; for example, Warrick is very occasionally addressed as Brown by some of the senior men. Interestingly, most of the minor characters referred to by their last names are all older, white men in positions of authority: Brass the former *CSI* head, now in charge of homicide; Ecklie, a *CSI* head and rival of Grissom's; and O'Reilly, the chief of police.
47. I have borrowed this phrase from Nancy Lesko. *Act Your Age! A Cultural Construction of Adolescence* (New York and London: Routledge Falmer, 2001).
48. Dr. Jemma Williams, played by the actress Judith Scott.
49. In "Blood Drops"(1007), there is a tiny role for a black female psychiatrist who speaks a few words; in "Friends and Lovers"(1005), again there is a tiny role for a black, female lawyer who doesn't speak; in "Fahrenheit 932" (1012), two black female characters have a small speaking role: the dead victim of the accused killer, his wife (seen in flashbacks), and his current girlfriend.
50. *Macmillan Contemporary Dictionary* (New York and London: Macmillan and Collier Publishers, 1979), 315.
51. For instance, in "Fahrenheit 932" (1012), a black man accidentally kills his wife and child in a fire. In "Too Tough to Die" (1016), Grissom draws on implicit racist imagery, through his animalizing of gangsters: "gang shooters mark their kills by tossing down their hats, some sort of anthropological quirk of territoriality, like cats spraying on a bush."
52. Cited in Ann Pellegrini, *Performance Anxieties: Staging Psychoanalysis, Staging Race* (New York: Routledge, 1997), 55.
53. "Too Tough to Die" (1016).
54. Julie D'Acci. "Cultural Studies, Television Studies and the Crisis in the Humanities," in *Television after TV: Essays on a Medium in Transition*, ed. Lynn Spigel and Jan Olsson (Durham and London: Duke University Press, 2004), 435.
55. Mary Beth Haralovich and Lauren Rabinovitz. Introduction to *Television, History, and American Culture*. Ed. Mary Beth Haralovich and Lauren Rabinovitz (Durham and London: Duke University Press, 1999), 5.
56. "Pilot" (1001) and "Cool Change" (1002).
57. "Pilot" (1001).
58. "Pilot" (1001).
59. "19 Down" (9009).
60. "One to Go" (9010).
61. "One to Go" (9010).

62. "On the characterization of Langston, CBS previously explained, "His focus on understanding criminal behavior, how and why people commit acts of violence—tendencies he disturbingly sees in himself.'. . . Langston was once a doctor, working in a hospital. A co-worker murdered 27 patients and all the evidence showed up before him, but he never put the evidence together." <http://en.wikipedia.org/wiki/Crime_Scene_Investigation> (Feb. 10 2009).

Chapter Ten

Forensic Music: Channeling the Dead on Post-9/11 Television

Lawrence Kramer

The subject of this chapter is the communications medium as spirit medium: television, literally far-seeing, as séance. The analytic medium, correspondingly, is a network of apparitions, the flitting imagery and disembodied music broadcast via the title sequences of three American crime melodramas that became very popular in the years following 2001: *CSI: Crime Scene Investigation*, *CSI: Miami*, and *Cold Case*. They are all shows devoted to the dead, whose demands upon the living became a source of debate and anxiety in the United States in the aftermath of the event that gapes in my network's reticulations: the black hole designated simply 9/11.[1]

The trauma so named is incapable of being represented by so slight and utilitarian a thing as a TV title sequence. That is part of my point: the trauma is not so represented; what *is* represented is a narrative genre. But this genre, the TV police procedural as forensic investigation, dwells on trauma with particular intensity. For some years after 9/ll, serial television drama became preoccupied with visualizing an endless parade of grotesque and disfiguring deaths. The resulting images were shocking at first in their apparent realism; although they gradually devolved into something like a baroque convention, this predictable change has not so much altered their meaning as normalized it. In the immediate post 9/11 period, these graphic representations of trauma at the core of criminal melodrama acted as if they were byproducts of more a primary trauma their narrative genre was incapable of representing directly. One wound covered another like scar tissue; the fictional narratives spun from insulted bodies covered, in every sense of the term, an unspoken historical event inflecting and punctuating them.

We should not underestimate the poetic economy, the dreamlike condensation, with which title sequences could draw these threads together. Like the frame of a painting, the title sequence confers identity on a work in relation to which the sequence stands simultaneously on both the outside and the inside.[2] The title sequence both represents the genre it introduces and possesses a genre of its own. It is more than just a portal; it is the shibboleth that lets you through the portal. The title sequence condenses the general plot of a film or a television series into a narrative image and conveys that image in enhanced form by conjoining it with music.

We need to dwell for a moment on that last sentence, each element of which requires glossing. "Narrative image" is Stephen Heath's term for the emblem, usually involving both words and images (the newspaper ad, the film poster, the DVD cover), by which a film is traditionally marketed. Meant to be easily recognized and remembered, the narrative image forms a synoptic portrayal that both identifies the genre of a film and promises a surplus of the pleasure and excitement proper to that genre.[3] Audiences often give a film cultural currency beyond its commodity value by adopting or even inventing such images. Famous lines, even lines that were never spoken—"Come up and see me sometime," "Play it again, Sam," or, to switch to television, "Beam me up, Scotty"—together with the appropriate poses, gestures, and intonations, become parts of a common vocabulary subject to endless reapplication.

The concept of narrative image is relevant here because it can be broadened to refer to any compressed or synoptic form of narrative, for example a title sequence. In other words, the concept may cover any compressed representation through which an extended narrative can be grasped as an immediate whole—grasped in the double sense of perceived and interpreted. Narrative images are not just mnemonic and synoptic; they're hermeneutic.

The concept of narrative image translates especially well to series television, in which the plot to be grasped belongs not just to the individual episode, but to the series as a whole. The episodes are concretizations of a general series plot that cannot be represented directly. This general plot is an ideal type, of which each realization, each episode, is a variant. The general plot is a kind of narrative essence. The job of the title sequence is to convey it. To that end the sequence requires the combination of music with a succession of visual forms that compose the narrative image. The visuals specify content; the music gives that content a narrative shape independent of any particular story. The visuals furnish the unassembled materials of a narrative; the music embodies the impetus that drives the general series plot.

The result of this combination of visuals and music is a form of interpellation shaped by the needs of the serial medium. Television series are designed to be rerun, the more often the better. The audience is invited to watch and listen in order to revisit a fictional world, with certain favorite characters, regardless of what happens on any particular episode or along any multi-episode narrative thread. The music of the title sequence is a kind of acoustic insignia, like a logo on a T-shirt. Unlike the background music that accompanies the narrative specific to each episode, the title music is supposed to be listened to, not just absorbed. But because it is repeated with every episode, this music does not have the status of an independent musical event, in contrast, for example, to the title music for a movie (sequels aside). The title music to a television series is ritualistic; it both induces a disposition in the audience to follow the general plot and inducts the audience into the corresponding fictional world.

The three series under the lens here are *CSI: Crime Scene Investigation*, set in Las Vegas; a spinoff, *CSI: Miami*; and *Cold Case*, set in Philadelphia. The first two are forensic rhapsodies, Holmesian or Cornwellian romances of trace evidence, blood spatter, hair, fiber, and DNA. The third is forensic in a more deliberative sense, a study of belated justice achieved by rewriting the past, reimagining more than reconstructing the track of the crime. These series epitomize the post 9/11 trend toward forensic romance in crime narratives—they were chosen because the two *CSI*s establish the model for television drama and *Cold Case* provides its complement—but they have lots of company.

There are also another *CSI* spinoff, *CSI: New York*, which I mention briefly, and *Without a Trace*, also set in New York. A more recent entry, *Bones*, is set in the other target city of the 9/11 attacks, Washington, DC. I can give only a trace of *Without a Trace*. Suffice it to say that this is the post-9/11 fantasy series par excellence. It portrays a New York in which the key fact of life is that people abruptly go missing—they vaporize on screen in the prelude to each episode—only to be found, more often alive than dead, by a special team of dedicated FBI agents, one of whom (a woman this time) is named Sam Spade. The series is darker and more complex than this summary suggests. There is a continual tension between the traumatizing details of the show's narratives and the fantasy of recovery that most of the narratives support. This is also true of *Cold Case*, but not of either *CSI* or *CSI: Miami*, both of which insist on facing up to inexplicable actions and irrevocable consequences. As for *Bones*, it is a hybrid that testifies to the normalizing and conventionalizing effect I spoke of earlier. The show's deaths are probably the most bizarre on offer (though they are sometimes rivaled by those on *CSI: New York*) but its narratives embrace elements of both situation- and sex comedy, which mingle unapologetically with forensic detail. Hence the series title, which refers both to human remains and to the nickname conferred on the brilliant but clueless forensic heroine by her partner. With *Bones*, trauma is no longer traumatic. Another popular series, *Criminal Minds*, involving FBI profilers, is, so to speak, the un-*Bones*; it maintains the somber tone of the original *CSI: Crime Scene Investigation* even more consistently than the founding original itself.

Most of these series depend on the idea of speaking for the dead, and more than that of speaking *with* them, achieving an intimacy with them despite their apparent muteness. This is certainly true of the three series to be analyzed here, each of which has a protagonist whose uncanny sensitivity is mediumistic—one to material traces, one to guilty personalities, and one to hidden suffering. Each of these series depicts a relentless criminal investigation that channels the departed by discerning and preserving their identities, telling the true story of their lives by discovering the truth of their deaths.

This address to the dead replicates the memorial practices that quickly arose in the wake of 9/11: the *New York Times* printing the names and faces of all the victims, the dignitaries at the anniversary of the attacks reading the list of names aloud. These efforts represent attempts to reverse the traditional petrifaction of the name carved on memorial stone; the reading, the imagery, reanimates the names, if only for the space of a single breath or glance. The aim is to prevent the trauma of the day from receding into a spiritless death toll, a mere number. Disagreement over how to inscribe the names of the victims on the memorial at Ground Zero in New York City perhaps reflected this difficulty, famously solved in another context by Maya Lin's use of polished black granite to reflect the images of visitors to the Vietnam Veterans' Memorial Wall in Washington, D.C. One might also mention in this connection the musical memorial to the victims of 9/ll commissioned by the New York Philharmonic, John Adams's *On the Transmigration of Souls*. The composition is a threnody, a formal musical lament. It incorporates the reading of the names of the dead and reanimates the victims by absorbing their names into the current of the music that mourns them. The threnody becomes a processional of vanished spirits.

The connection of public mourning after 9/11 to *CSI* and other television crime series, let alone to the series' title sequences, is obviously indirect. The cultural network that entwines these things together does so precisely by indirection; it proliferates by lines and zones of suggestion, allusion, resemblance, association, connotation. Its boundaries are fluid, its chronology nonlinear. It is more like one of the rhizomes described by Deleuze and Guattari, crisscrossed by multiple "lines of flight," than like a clearly delineated moment or locale.[4] What I refer to as "9/ll" rippled back through Oklahoma City and Columbine and forward through Baghdad. The television series caught in such ripples also contribute to them; after *CSI*, the bodies of the dead assumed a social entitlement and especially a visibility that they rarely (if ever) had before. The most potent "*CSI* effect" may finally prove to have been less the fantasy of combining an all-powerful rationality with empathy and decency than the establishment of the fictional dead as interlocutors of the living.

This loop of cultural influence operates even as these three series, true to their type, waver in their profile from week to week and change in response to ratings sweeps and other vicissitudes of production. (Not to mention cast changes: as of this writing, *CSI: Crime Scene Investigation* has killed off a major character, Warrick Brown, and the departure of William Peterson's Gil Grissom from the show is imminent.) The odd ontology of series television seems to be that things are so until they are not. The need to vary and sometimes jettison the series' formulas, the tendency of long-running series to become self-referential and at times self-parodistic, and the changing cultural climate that forms a continuous background to series television, all tend to limit whatever interpretive claims the series may provoke. General remarks of the kind one would be more comfortable making about a film or a book have to be referred to samples or trends or clusters rather than to totalities. What this means about the *CSI* series in particular is that the techniques of representation I discuss below have become less central and less consistent as the series have aged. They have to some extent become artifacts of an impulse no longer sustainable at its original strength. But that is the most one can expect. Interpreting culture along its lines of flight might be said to be an art of approximation, something between a shadow play and a simulation, except that there is no way to stabilize the distinction between the interpretation and its object. The object does not become perceptible until the interpretation has begun, which, however, compresses the energies of cultural becoming into an object.[5]

CSI: Crime Scene Investigation and *CSI: Miami* depend on intimacy with the bodies of the dead, *Cold Case* on intimacy with their histories. Let's take the bodies first. The space of the *CSI* narratives is oriented around bodies displayed (or splayed out) fully and often: at the crime scene, a site legibly marked by the fate inflicted there; on the autopsy table, the arena of physical manipulation, mechanical penetration, and the examination of wounds; and in camera-eye close-ups of the body inside and out, nearly always accompanied by amplified noise overlaying or replacing the musical underscore. This acoustic form of display is especially important and forms a trademark in all three *CSI* series. The moment of visualization is also a moment of *audialization*; the offended body protests to the ear as it distorts to the eye. In many cases, the noise comes from the crime itself. When we see what must (or might) have happened, we also hear how it sounded, as if the criminalist's perceptions were sharp enough to detect acoustic as well as visual trace evidence, in defiance of the apparent truth that vanished sound leaves no trace.

This visual-acoustic intimacy is progressive on *CSI*. The closer one gets to the truth of the body, the closer one gets to the truth of the crime. The better one can account for the mechanics of bodies, whether of organisms, nonliving matter, or machines—the investigations make little distinction—the better one can say what really happened. That the truth lodges in matter, not in mind, is part of the point. The forensic narrative is an analysis in the strictest sense: as the body is broken down the story of the crime is built up. There is a tacit progression from material truth to the truth of events, and no going the other way; whatever the evidence says is the truth. People fool each other and themselves; physical evidence never lies. So powerful is the fantasy underlying this principle—that our technology and rationality, confronting the truth of bodies, will save us—that some argue it has spilled over into real life and begun to shape public expectation, much to the dismay of real forensic experts. "It's not like *CSI*" is said to have become a familiar mantra in law enforcement.

But the fantasy says it *should* be like *CSI*, and in character as well as action. The shows' forensic discovery process finds a narrative parallel in the investigators' intimacy with the corpses entrusted to them. No one is ever supposed to shrink from a victim's body, no matter how horrific the wounds. Lapses may occur, but the primary protagonists of *CSI* and *CSI: Miami*, Gil Grissom and Horatio Caine, never falter. *CSI: Miami*'s medical examiner has (or had, until the character left the show) a habit of holding conversations with the bodies she examines, complete with caresses and endearments. The original *CSI* often brings Grissom and his ME together at the autopsy table for long colloquies across the exposed corpse of the victim, the silent interlocutor or interpellator who has brought them together. All the CSIs—the term designates the characters as well as the shows—keep vigilant faith with the dead, the story of whose lives is in their hands. They observe a meticulous decorum both at the crime scene and in the morgue, with a detachment that paradoxically humanizes their duty to handle human remains by defining what they do as a form of recognition.

The title sequences for *CSI: Crime Scene Investigation* and *CSI: Miami* give these intimacies both a general form and a specific feeling. The *CSI: Crime Scene Investigation* sequence keeps its visuals fairly rudimentary, with an obvious emphasis on forensic evidence and technique. The primary work of constructing the narrative image is done by the music, an extract from "Who Are You," a song by Pete Townshend of The Who (*CSI: Miami* and *CSI: New York* also use Townshend songs.) The *CSI* sequence uses only the song's refrain, and only a part of that: "Who are you? Who, who? Who, who? I really wanna know." As these fragmentary lyrics suggest, and as the music's phrase structure confirms, the titles to *CSI* embody the troubled but unyielding will to memory. The drive for an answer to the seemingly simple question "Who are you?" is the show's version of the memorial promise never to lose the identity of a single victim. That promise potentially extends to the viewer—each viewer—who, hearing the song, may also feel addressed by its reiterated "you."

Although the criminalists generally "know" who the victim is in the literal sense of knowing a name, the identity they really want to know is the truth of the life that the name names. Knowing the victim in that deeper sense enables them to find the perpetrator, whose name they do not know and to whom the question "Who are you?" equally applies. But it applies only through the medium of the victim's identity, the full truth of which culminates in the plural *you* that binds the victim to the killer. The melodic line of "Who Are You" moves from wistfulness to urgency, as if to progress from sympathetic advocacy for the victim to relentless pursuit of the perpetrator. It would be hard to find a better expression of the general plot of *CSI*, which turns precisely on the technique of transforming sympathetic advocacy into relentless pursuit. The multiplicity of possible *you*'s in "Who Are You" articulates the underlying logic of that transformation.

The music consists of an introductory riff plus three phrases, A A B. The first two phrases are nearly identical, but the one small difference between them is crucial; it breaks the symmetry of the pair and turns the first A into an antecedent phrase and the second into a consequent. In both phrases the backup voices sing the first half of the refrain while leaving gaps in the text—"Who are you. . . . Who, who? . . . Who, who?"—to register the persistence of unsolved mystery. The vocal line of the first A pointedly ends too soon, as if thwarted; it leaves its questions hanging over the vocal silence. When the second A reaches this point, however, it fills the silence with a strident solo outburst of "I really wanna know." Instead of answering the question "Who are you," the outburst heightens the desire for an answer and makes that desire personal: there is someone speaking, an "I," and he really wants to know. Where the antecedent intimates, the consequent insists.

The questioning in both these A phrases is lyrical at first, almost yearning, with a sweetly prolonged vocalic sound for the initial "Who." But the sweetness curdles into irony with the owl-like echoes of "who, who," sung falsetto. Perhaps "Who are you" is a foolish question, or a question without a good answer. The consequent phrase, the second A, ends by abruptly sweeping this ambivalence aside in favor of raw urgency—but only to introduce another and more pointed ambivalence. The guttural melodic cadence on "I really wanna know" suggests frustration and determination, anger and desire, in equal measure. So, too, does the B segment into which the cadence overlaps: a crescendo focused on four gapped repetitions of a single word, the "you" of the refrain's insistent questioning. The fourth "you" is set a little apart from the others. The crescendo peaks on it but also begins to fade as the syllabic setting of the first three *you*'s (one syllable to one note) expands into a brief melisma (one syllable to more than one note). The voice uncoils to snag its quarry in a final cadence, spider to fly, but all it finds there is the token of a still unknown other.

These phrase structures in the titles synopsize the general plot of *CSI*: dedicated curiosity seeks the identity of the victim and therefore of the murderer, but the curiosity is never fully satisfied even when its success is greatest. Crimes can be analyzed, evil cannot. Thus in the *CSI: Crime Scene Investigation* episode "Got Murder?" (3012) a teenage girl with "Electra" feelings (the pseudo-Freudian allusion is explicit) kills her mother in a fit of jealous rage. The teen's feelings for her father also reveal themselves when she suffers from a hysterical pregnancy accompanied by real lactation. The father, suspected by the investigators of the sexual abuse of his daughter as well as of the murder, is innocent of both in a literal sense. But he is guilty for not having intervened in his daughter's fantasy, which he allows because, as his facial expressions and body language all but shout out, he unconsciously shares it.

This Freudian reading symbolically proceeds through the mother's eye: that is, through her eyeball, found at the start of the episode in a tree, where a raven has stashed it. "Got Murder?" answers the question "Who are you?" for the victim by showing both what she could see and to what she was blind, and then makes visible the objects of her blindness. Her symbolically restored vision or insight extends (via the CSIs) to enlighten the father, who must see his own complicity by revoking his denial of what was right before his eyes. Only the daughter remains blind, as in blind hatred or rage.

At the start of the episode Grissom quotes Poe to underline the allusion conveyed through the raven, anticipating the psychopathology of father and daughter. Poe's "The Raven" is also about obsessive love for an unattainable object. Typically for the series, the pivotal clue to the daughter's crime and the father's complicity is a material trace, not a psychodynamic symptom. The clue is a breast-milk stain, the true sign of the daughter's false pregnancy, the literal substance of the unattainable. The milk continues the train of allusions started with "Quoth the Raven, 'Nevermore'" and the misbegotten Electra complex. (Such ironic allusiveness is characteristic of the series, which makes a point of its sophisticated postmodernity, also symbolized by its Las Vegas setting.) "Got Murder?" is a Freudian play on the dairy industry ad slogan "Got Milk?" The title catches both the spirit and the form—one word displacing another—of Oedipal ambivalence, a crime consisting of not being able to give the right answer to the question "Who are you?"

In relation to narratives like this the hoarsely shouted fourfold "you" that ends the music in the *CSI: Crime Scene Investigation* title sequence is partly defensive, a wall of sound thrown up against the mystery of iniquity. Whoever you are, the musical cry seeks to arrest you like a jabbing finger. But to what end? It remains unclear whether the song's explosive "you" is angry, defiant, accusatory, elective, or mocking. Likewise unclear is the point at which the identity of "you" passes from the victim to the perpetrator, thus fulfilling the show's forensic principle that to know the first is to discover the second. All this indeterminacy is compounded further by the viewer's potential awareness of the legend surrounding the full lyrics to the original song, in which a drunk or disorderly narrator confronts (with the question "Who the fuck are you?") a kindly but intrusive policeman alleged to be a stand-in for God.

Or does the policeman stand in for someone else? Once the events of 2001 caught up with *CSI*, another "you" lurked behind the usual suspects. After 9/11, many Americans became either inspired or appalled by the search for retribution against unknown killers. To post-9/11 ears, The Who's "Who Are You" might be addressed to threatening figures cloaked in the malignancy that seemed to envelop the event: figures of roving death, of violence out of the blue sky. The Who themselves seemed to endorse this message when they gave a performance of "Who Are You?" right after 9/11 at The Concert for New York City (October 20, 2001), on a stage framed by both the Stars and Stripes and the Union Jack.[6] At one level, the title music as used on *CSI* had come, in the wake of 9/11, to suggest a deep unease about the pursuit of justice for the dead. The progression from curiosity, to the fierceness of forensic desire ("I really wanna know"), to urgent interpellation ("You, you, you. . . You!") took on an apocalyptic tinge. At its climax in the B phrase, the song as heard in the title sequence expresses both a hunger for justice and a deep need for reassurance that justice can be done.

CSI: Crime Scene Investigation is at times blunt about the possibility that the truth is inadequate to the demands of justice. Even so, Grissom and company insist on pursuing both. They take what comes. By contrast, *CSI: Miami* bluntly insists that the truth will out and justice with it; as Horatio Caine is fond of saying, "We never close." Like its counterpart for the original *CSI*, the phrase stricture of the title music for *CSI: Miami*, Townshend's "Won't Get Fooled Again," synopsizes the general plot of the series. As with the original *CSI*, the *CSI: Miami* titles use only a fragment of the song's refrain: "We don't get fooled again, don't get fooled again, no, no." Here, however, there is no closed or balanced form, no A A B, but just a repetition of the key phrase (minus its pronoun) and the pugnacious, "No, no." We do not even hear these lyrics until the titles are nearly over. This deferral corresponds to the rhythm of the series' general plot, in which tension slowly builds to a *gotcha!* moment at the end of each episode. At that point a CSI confronts the skeptical perpetrator with irrefutable evidence of guilt: proof positive that, whatever it takes, we don't get fooled again.

The vocals in the *CSI: Miami* titles do not emerge, they erupt. Where the original *CSI* disciplines its drive for answers, *CSI: Miami* puts its musical and narrative discipline at the disposal of sheer drive. The extract from "Won't

Get Fooled Again" begins with a war whoop and never looks back. Its music is loud and aggressive to the point of belligerence, the equivalent of tough policing in sound; it echoes the suppressed undertones of righteous indignation in Caine's soft, self-interrupting, but foreboding voice. The lyric's "no, no" forms the intimidating inverse of the original *CSI*'s bemused "who, who." The visuals in the *CSI: Miami* sequence concur by suggesting a force of elucidation that nothing can resist. Establishing shots feature aerial views of the city and coastline with emphasis on sunlight and waterways. Mathematical formulae morph on screen into the actors' names. Translucent vertical panels, similar to the glass panels of the interrogation room, slide across the screen in a continual movement from obscurity to clarity, albeit momentary clarity. In contrast, the title sequence of the original *CSI* offers nocturnal shots of Las Vegas, leaving the dark corners of the heart in place amid glitter and corruption. In *CSI: Miami* everything comes to light; in *CSI*, even the light deceives.

The syntax of the key phrase in the *CSI: Miami* title sequence also conveys the impression of an indomitable, quasi-vindictive justice. In the original song, "We don't get fooled again" is a dependent clause referring to an uncertain future. The speaker is both attacking a failed revolution and attacking himself for the hope he placed in it. Unable to give up the hope, he thinks of trying prayer: "I'll get down on my knees and pray / We don't get fooled again." The resolutely secular *CSI: Miami*, with its *CSI* credo of faith in the substance of things seen, will have none of that. Its title sequence makes "We don't get fooled again" an independent clause in the narrative present, the perennial time of storytelling. What the statement says in the show's titles is what happens *in the story*: it tells us that in the kind of story we're about to watch, we don't get fooled again, or, as the song phrases it, we *don't* get fooled a-*gain*. No, no.

All of this raises an obvious question. If we don't get fooled *again*, who fooled us the first time? The answer corresponds to nothing shown directly in the plots of particular episodes. Although the show has offered narrative threads involving long-running secrets (a mole in the lab, the whereabouts of Caine's supposedly dead brother), Caine and his team typically have no need to second-guess themselves. And who has fooled "us" in the recent past? First and foremost, given that *CSI: Miami*'s first season started in 2002, the answer is the 9/11 hijackers. The connection comes up indirectly in "MIA/ NYC Nonstop" (0213), the episode through which *CSI: Miami* introduces the second spinoff, *CSI: New York*. Not only has Mack Taylor, the protagonist of the latter show, lost his wife in the destruction of the twin towers, but the transitional plot between the two series also tracks its villain from a Miami crime scene to Manhattan on the basis of trace evidence from Ground Zero. In post-9/11 America, this is the ultimate form of trace. Immediately recogniz-able to the forensic eye, it is literally a part of the nationwide impact of the event, a microscopic souvenir of catastrophe.

There's another obvious question we need to ask. Why do the *CSI* series use the strident, violent, anti-establishment rock music of The Who—songs of the 1970s still trailing the antinomian spirit of the 1960s—to embody the spirit of twenty-first century law enforcement? Why shift the speaker of "Who Are You?" from the policed to the police? Why take the words of "Won't Get Fooled Again" out of the mouth of a failed revolutionary and make them speak for the Law? The questions are no less pointed because The Who that performed "Don't Get Fooled Again" and "Who Are You?" at that post-9/11 concert might not have a problem with this appropriation of their earlier selves. The redeployment of the songs is neither more nor less appropriative because The Who do it, too.

One straightforward answer, a good old-fashioned Hobbesian one, is that the title sequences show the state reclaiming its monopoly on violence, a monopoly that is legitimated by the subsequent narratives of detection on both *CSI* shows. The music may be angry, but its anger has become both dis-ciplined and disciplinary and is therefore justified. The anger that was once directed against the law by rebellious rock music—always a shade dubiously, given its commodity value in the very society it attacked—has now become the anger of the law itself. *CSI* converts the violence of the music from a protest against injustice to an instrument of justice. The critique of society as criminal morphs into the defense of society against criminals.

But why? To what end? Joined with visuals that emphasize forensic proce-dures and equipment, the music of The Who in the *CSI* title sequences associ-ates the search for justice with two apparently contradictory impulses that are at bottom the same: a devotion to technocratic rationality as an instrument of truth, and a deep, irrational rage spurring the desire to reverse, and more, to revenge, the unjust meting out of violent death. Each impulse is unswerving, each unquestioned, each uncompromising. Working together, they create a powerful new mythology in which state power feeds on the very forces of anarchy—from criminality to aggressivity to dissidence—that the state seeks to hold in subjection. This is the mythology of police who do The Who. Both the title sequences and the general plots of *CSI: Crime Scene Investigation* and *CSI: Miami* suggest that the social institutions of retributive violence are impossible to distinguish from the personal defense mechanisms of those who administer them. Music that shouts and bangs is the anthem of both.

This fusion shows itself particularly in the two shows' protagonists, both of whom are emotionally maimed. Gil Grissom is sexually repressed and emotionally withdrawn (even—as of this writing, and except in the immediate aftermath of Warrick's death—with Sarah Sidle, a protégé with whom he was "revealed" to be romantically involved after a good many seasons). Fully at home only in the lab, Grissom sees the world as a crime scene writ large. He is more comfortable with bodies than with persons except when he confronts a killer with the serenely logical chain of deductions that establishes guilt. He is kind, fair, even-tempered, and famously fond of insects, but these virtues only serve to uphold an impenetrable reserve that Grissom maintains even from himself.

Horatio Caine seems doomed to private despair, a point on which *CSI: Miami* is almost sadistically insistent. In earlier seasons he is guiltily in love with his brother's widow, from whom he tries to conceal both his own feelings and his brother's infidelity. Caine trammels his private life in deception while upholding utter probity in public. After discovering that his brother is still alive and reuniting husband and wife (in effect renouncing his feelings for Yelena, his sister-in-law, as if in obedience to the incest taboo, which remains in force even when the brother eventually does die[7]), Caine marries the terminally-ill sister of one of his team only to have his wife promptly killed off in a gang hit in "One of Our Own," season four's finale (4025). Like Grissom's self-denials, Caine's deprivations form part of the allegorical conception of his character. Caine—the name has its irony, given that the biblical Cain kills his brother Abel because God appears to favor the latter—is a man who sublimates his anguish into the coldly vindictive pursuit of impersonal justice. And for this he is a heroic figure, just as Grissom is. The two are heroes for the post-9/11 age; both inwardly and outwardly, they reconstruct justice from the debris of trauma.

Cold Case communicates with the dead by reconstructing traumatized memories rather than traumatized bodies, a form of restitution that also constitutes an indirect response to 9/11 and an echo of the memorial practices associated with it. The show works with texts, interviews, and competing narratives, not with material detritus, but like the two *CSI* shows examined here, it issues the reassurance that nothing is too small to notice, that nothing will be permanently forgotten. The storage medium for the cold case files symbolizes this principle; it constitutes a monument, not just a database. The files fill a room, set on library stacks in white cardboard boxes inscribed with the victims' names. The result is a mute archive of injustice, a block of material rather than digital data that resists manipulation and decipherment. The material relics are calcified ghosts. The secrets they conceal can be reanimated only by acts of empathy and insight; technological wizardry will not help.

The show's title sequence is a collage in three distinct parts: a wail of ritual mourning in a woman's voice, vaguely Eastern and redolent of the choral laments of a Greek tragedy; the elaboration of a short theme that gives narrative continuity to the visuals, which flash to and fro among the show's main characters, Philadelphia landmarks, and the white case boxes; and an abrupt cadence, decisive but obviously tacked on, a *deus ex machina* to the tragic plot. The ambivalence of the cadence announces the essential ambivalence at the heart of the show. Justice is done for the victims, each story is recovered, tribute is paid, but only after a lapse of years or even generations of misery. The show's general plot insists that the truth is redemptive, but its episodes often dwell more forcefully on suffering, loss, and the weight of guilty se-crets. The emphasis falls about equally on the outraged innocence of the dead and the burdens of the living who are called on to do them justice. The survivors owe the lost a symbolic debt that the law insists they pay, but that it may be impossible to pay in full.

This dilemma of justice in hindsight demands an investigator wounded enough to grasp it instinctively. Like Grissom and Caine, Lilly Rush, the protagonist of *Cold Case*, is solitary and withdrawn, haunted, as Caine is, by an old trauma that must remain her secret. The trauma itself carries a whiff of soap opera—her sister apparently seduced the love of Rush's life—but its lingering impact seems to owe more to its quasi-incestuous entanglements than to simple betrayal. Rush's personal life is almost nonexistent. Until season three's finale, "Joseph," in which she begins a liaison with a former suspect, Rush is unable to support a romantic relationship with a man; she has cats instead. (She goes back to the cats early in the following season after the short-lived romance fizzles.) She is a kind of widow for her work, and in that respect she may recall the 9/11 widow, the new memorial persona that developed after the twin towers fell. The wail that starts the *Cold Case* title sequence is, musically speaking, a widow's wail, a mourning wail. It does not come from Rush herself—as stoical as any of her male colleagues, she would never utter her pain aloud—but the wail symbolically evokes her sympathy, even her identification, with the victims of cold murder cases and especially with those whom the victims have left behind.

As with the *CSIs*, one or two episodes of *Cold Case* make allegorical al-lusions to the nation's disarray, but with an eye on the consequences of 9/11 rather than on the event itself. In "Red Glare," the victim is hounded by the McCarthy-era FBI and killed on the eve of deciding whether to name names to Congress. The motive for murder turns out to be jealousy over a woman whose name is at risk of being reported, but most of the dramatic emphasis falls on the excesses committed by the government in the name of national se-curity. The analogy with homeland security in the neo-McCarthyite age of the *U.S.A. Patriot Act* (2001) is painfully clear. In "Mind Hunters," the killer is a police wannabe who works in the Cold Case detectives' own records office. Impersonating a patrolman, he kidnaps women who have fought off earlier attackers, strips them, releases them in the woods, and hunts them down. In the wake of the prisoner abuse scandal in Iraq, the practice of extraordinary rendition, and revelations of torture at Guantanamo Bay, the depiction of sexual humiliation and death at the hands of a quasi-military figure is, to say the least, politically resonant. And in this episode, although his identity is discovered and he even confesses under interrogation, the killer gets away for lack of hard evidence. He literally walks free, animating the cliché, strolling contentedly across the squad room in slow motion as music (Phil Collins' "Long Long Way to Go") swells in the background. The irony is cutting: the law has a long way to go before it can do anything about the killer who sees in himself only the image of the law.

In the second season finale, "The Woods," Rush confronts this psychopathic nemesis again and shoots him dead. But the shooting borders on vigilante justice, compounding the earlier irony by suggesting that the killer's view of the law as intrinsically violent may contain an element of truth. The implication is especially dark because *Cold Case* normally treats its lead characters as softer, more workaday versions of the gifted but driven Grissom and Caine. Rush and her colleagues are just ordinary people who sacrifice their personal well being in the interests of justice.

Like its counterpart in the two *CSI* shows, the title music of *Cold Case* traces the narrative of the series' general plot. Overall, the wail introduces the wrong that the final cadence sets right. The middle section grounds this outcome in a phrase structure that anticipates it, thus connecting the general plot to a primary musical rhythm. Excerpted from "Nara," a track by the eclectic band E. S. Posthumus, the middle section reiterates a simple phrase, two measures of antecedent and two of consequent. The melody moves in even quarter notes in three-quarter time. Measures one to three state rising two-note motives after the downbeat; measure four adds a melody note on the downbeat and reverses direction, creating a single slurred phrase that voices the melodic cadence of the phrase. The result discloses something unapparent in the first three measures, a hidden truth: the rising motives are fragments of a familiar musical figure, a turn, but a turn that remains unachieved until the fourth measure articulates it. The internal drama of the phrase is an allegory for the detectives' work: it fills the gaps in the story and closes the case.

The repetition of this phrasal allegory in the title sequence does to the visuals that accompany it what the *Cold Case* detectives do to the past; it makes a whole of scattered traces. Yet the result in the music has a slight flaw, like the belatedness of the justice achieved by the end of each episode. The melodic cadence ends weakly, off the beat, as if to acknowledge the residue of damage that no amount of justice can undo after the fact. From here the melody line continues without a break to start over again in the following measure, simultaneously completing and restarting the turn on the downbeat. This circle turns without closure through five rotations, necessitating the cadential cutoff after the fifth turn. The cadence is an imposition; it installs resignation in the place where resolution is lacking. This much, says the cadence, you can have—nothing more.

As convention dictates, the title music does not occur within the show's narratives, where music serves more as texture than as utterance. The title music stands to the narrative of any given episode as a moral does to a fable; it interprets the story from outside. This restriction keeps the musical articulation of the series' general plot intact and leaves the individual episodes free to find music appropriate to their particular stories. The *CSI* shows observe the same principles.

But there is more. *CSI* in all its versions adds a third narrative dimension, the forensic present. As the investigators reconstruct them one by one, the elements of the crime appear as flashbacks. Most of these recreations are accurate; some are hypothetical and subject to later correction. Either way, the flashbacks distinguish themselves from the narrative present both visually and acoustically: by the use of different film stock to create changes in texture and coloration; with abrupt changes in visual scale or rhythm; by presentation as "ghost" images superimposed on the narrative stream; and with collisions or overlaps between musical underscore and noise. It is as if the traumatic past constituted a parallel narrative universe, to be reclaimed in fragments as the result of forensic work in the present.

Some of these flashbacks focus on narrative action, some on matter and motion, some on bodily surfaces and interiors. The most significant involve extreme close-ups or microscopic visualization, bringing the viewer into intimate contact with the material world or, more exactly, with the world regarded as purely material. Objects and substances clash or splash or invade intimate bodily spaces; magnification and slow or jagged motion render them visually monstrous; their destructive impact registers acoustically as noise, as by a sonogram. At every level, the forensic present fills a distorted visual-acoustic space that punctures the space of the story in order to be recuperated into it by the *CSI* teams. The teams treat these narrative ruptures much as they do bodily wounds: they understand them and then they close them. Each return to the narrative present restores both the standard forms of narrative visualization and the hierarchy of music over ambient noise as an accompaniment to action. In the typical episode, musicalized narrative is especially prominent during scenes showing the painstaking work of evidence collection or lab testing. The noise track kicks in when investigation blossoms into insight. Of course the two types of scene may mix or overlap; their vocabulary is both visually and acoustically versatile.

Similarly, *Cold Case* creates a musical frame that regularly makes inroads into the story. Each episode concludes in music-video style, with a song as underscore to shots of the captured perpetrator being led away amid ghostly images of the victims to whom justice is being rendered. These spectral epiphanies suggest—fantasize—that the music can reanimate the dead just enough to win recognition from them that their case has been closed at last, the symbolic debt to them discharged. In one memorable instance, from "Sleepover," the victim is a girl last seen happily riding her bike down a leafy suburban street. The closing image is the same but viewed through Rush's eyes, with the added ambiguity that the second girl may not be the victim at all, but one of the innumerable girls who might on any day be riding her bike through suburban America. Both Rush and the viewers see the present through the eyes of the past.

In these closing segments the music assumes the role of a narrative voiceover. This is a common enough device but in *Cold Case* it is asked to assume particular gravity. The show makes extensive use of period-appropriate music to frame its episodes, thus linking the viewer acoustically to the era of the crime. There is a fan site that keeps track of these usages.[8] Each episode culminates in the closing video by musically transposing the past into the present and absorbing the finished narrative into the music. The song of an earlier day becomes the conjoined celebration and lament that emerges when the case is finally solved. Suppressed emotions find catharsis in a sentimentality licensed by the music's historical distance. In this symbolic fusion of underscore with diegesis, the concluding song becomes several things at once: a rendering-articulate of the opening wail, a means of reclaiming the past, and an illocutionary act that symbolically renders the justice that the law could not give before. This restitution is especially important because, in contrast to those of most crime melodramas, the victims in this series are tragic protagonists, rarely complicit in their deaths but often sacrificed to intolerance—malignant snobbery in "Sleepover," red-baiting in "Red Glare."

Cold Case also has its own version of *CSI*'s forensic present, which I will call the time print—a narrative version of computerized age regression. Here the identity of a present-day character suddenly vanishes and the character briefly appears as he or she did in the period when the crime took place. The reversal is equally sudden and the sequence almost always the same: backward-forward, tock-tick. Because a violent contingency separates the two, the present self disfigures the past self in ways that the past self could never anticipate. The time print reveals that the present self has crusted like a shell around the past self; the past self forms the kernel of an unresolved trauma as long as the crime remains unsolved. The traumatic disfigurement sometimes reflects suffering, sometimes guilt, and sometimes both. This disruption in the structure of identity is also a disruption in the musicalization of the narrative. The time prints have no musical signature; they just occur to a low-pitched, hollow *whoosh*. Only during the closing video is there a union of music and time print, a harmonization of past and present, of crime and punishment, that is marked by the use of slow motion when the handcuffed perpetrator is led away.

But where, then, are we led by *Cold Case*? Where are we led by *CSI: Crime Scene Investigation* and *CSI: Miami*? What shall we make of the shows' musical devices that construct memory as they shape forensic narrative? And how do we distinguish between memory as a narrative function and memory as a historical burden?

The burden is tied up with the concept of trauma, which is fundamentally troubled in relation to the concept of history. Theorists of the topic now widely regard trauma as a hole in history. A trauma is an overwhelming shock that both persists long beyond its occurrence and thwarts all attempts to represent it—attempts that it also persistently elicits. The persistence feeds on the thwarting. To vary Cathy Caruth's formulation, a trauma is an event in the past that has not yet taken place because no symbolic means can suffice to place it.[9] But for whom is this true?

The locus of its truth is necessarily the subject whose consistency trauma disrupts. Traumatic damage is radically individual. Even amid general disaster trauma is acutely, disastrously intimate. Originally applied to bodies by nineteenth-century medicine, the concept of trauma evolved during the twentieth century to encompass minds as well. In the process it may well have become one of the fundamental concepts of mind: trauma exposes the condition of the human subject when all the social, symbolic, and linguistic resources of subjectivity have catastrophically failed. In a strict literal sense, therefore, events such as 9/11 can be traumatic only for those who lived through them. Strictly speaking, societies can be disrupted, even devastated, even destroyed, but they cannot be traumatized. Collective trauma is a metaphor for the failure of social structures and institutions to assimilate a disaster—be it 9/11, Hurricane Katrina, or worse.

But collective trauma is not a *mere* metaphor. The metaphor is inescapable, and its presence is signaled, indeed imposed, precisely by a crisis of symbolization. The general effect of a collective trauma is the proliferation of efforts to incorporate it within the symbolic order. These efforts do not primarily seek to represent the trauma directly, but, on the contrary, to patch the hole in history with a fabric of indirect references, allusions, and metaphorical substitutions. The traumatic event is placed in history by displacing it in discourse. To be sure, direct representations are not at all lacking; they are just insufficient. Just a few years after the event the footage of the twin towers on 9/11 became iconic, the dramatizations for movies and television began, and a genre of 9/ll fiction emerged. But just as one of the most durable representations of the Vietnam War has proven to be Francis Ford Coppola's *Apocalypse Now*, a mythological film that fuses the war with the plot of Joseph Conrad's *Heart of Darkness*, the most potent representations of 9/ll may well have come in the form of novels like Ian McEwen's *Saturday*, which is concerned precisely with the memories and fantasies induced by the event rather than with the representation of the event itself. Collective trauma cannot be dammed up by direct representation; it has to be worked out through its ripple effects.

Enter *CSI*. Earlier I noted that the connection between 9/11 and television's forensic melodramas is indirect. It more or less has to be. The *CSI* series were never meant to remind audiences of the trauma of that day, and all the less so as time passes, but they do tacitly enact a fantasy-structure that ameliorates the event's emotional and social residues.[10] Or not a structure: a patchwork. Time and again, these series address matters that, unspeakable in an everyday sense, become surrogates for the unspeakable in a larger sense. But the series refuse to be traumatized. Through their fantasy patchwork they in turn make the unspeakable articulate. Forensic expertise cannot rationalize malice, but it can track down those whom malice drives; the silence of the dead cannot be broken, but the criminalist knows the ventriloquizing art of making their bodies speak; the past cannot be undone, but it can be rewritten as a meaningful narrative.

These reversals, however, are not meant to negate the unspeakable but, on the contrary, to preserve it. The media since 9/ll have become so inured to graphic violence, terrorism, victimization, and mass death that the representation of these things, real or fictional, has largely lost its former power to appall. Television, movie, and computer screens ameliorate trauma all too well by becoming machines for its reproduction; they miniaturize it. (Perhaps it is no accident that a continuing plot thread in season 7 of *CSI: Crime Scene Investigation* involved a reign of terror by "the Miniature Killer," a figure who foretold his crimes by constructing detailed dollhouse-like replicas of the intended crime scenes—and who took aim at Grissom through Sarah.[11]) Led by *CSI*, television's forensic melodramas have tried to recover the value of traumatic shock by constructing narratives that reanimate trauma on a small scale and demand that trauma be met and discharged by narrative itself. The violence that prevails on these series is not absolved from the media's trade in trauma. But the series balance their complicity by allowing their fictions of individual trauma to merge indirectly, by intimation, with the metaphors of collective trauma. In the process, these little traumas symbolically reconnect the big one to the nexus of justice, commemoration, and rationality from which the big one seems to have broken loose. Trauma becomes unspeakable again so that we can reassume the burden of speaking about it. This symbolic brinksmanship finds its most immediate voice in the music by which the series frame and accompany their narratives. The forensic present erupts in grating noise on *CSI: Crime Scene* Investigation and *CSI: Miami* but the narrative present restores the musical underscore; the period music on *Cold Case* takes control of the image stream when a cold case is resolved. On all three series the insignia music of the title sequences raises this rhythm to the necessary level of symbolization. Part allegory, part catharsis, the preamble makes the story viable. Phrases unite across gaps to form a whole; music hostile to the social order becomes that order's new anthem; a scream erupts but a cadence quells it. The music gives the fantasy-patchwork a consistency resonant with the practices of post-9/11 memory while absolving the audience of the need to name the connection. Perhaps it even absolves them, for a moment, of the need to remember. The fantasy can remember for them; 9/11 has become part of their unconscious. They—we—live within its echo.

NOTES

A shorter version of this paper was delivered at the conference "Over the Waves: Music in Broadcasting," organized at McMaster University in March 2005, by Christina Baade, James Deaville, and Sandy Thorburn.

1. Although I did not know it while writing, the metaphors that thread this paragraph transmit a historical relationship between spiritualism and early television, in view of which my argument might be characterized as premised on the uncanny return of that relationship, on an uncanny return of the uncanny. See Stefan Andriopoulos, "Psychic Television," *Critical Inquiry* 31 (2005): 618–37.

2. On framing, see Jacques Derrida, "The Parergon," in his *The Truth in Painting*, trans. Geoff Bennington and Ian McCloud (Chicago: University of Chicago Press, 1987), 39–118, esp. 55–67; for more on music and the fantasy structure of title sequences, see my *Musical Meaning: Toward a Critical History* (Berkeley: University of California Press, 2001), 188–92.

3. Stephen Heath, *Questions of Cinema* (Bloomington, IN: Indiana University Press, 1983), 133.

4. Gilles Deleuze and Felix Guattari, *A Thousand Plateaus: Capitalism and Schizophrenia* (1980), trans. with a foreword by Brian Massumi (Minneapolis: University of Minnesota Press, 1987), 3–4, 88–89, 121–22.

5. The original *CSI* is an exemplary case in point: a success when it started in 2000, the series has become a phenomenon in the years since, with ubiquitous reruns in multiple venues as well as the spinoffs. Its narrative devices have been widely imitated. The only comparable franchise is *Law and Order*, which in the present context is notable for its musical emptiness. Far more than its title music, some version of

which introduces all three of its current series, its acoustic signature is the famous *doink-doink* sound, suggestive at once of the knock of the police on the door (law) and the rap of a judge's gavel (order). The sound has become as much a cultural icon as the four-note motto of the old *Dragnet* series, but without actually bothering to become music.

6. My thanks for this information to Susan Fast, who pointed it out to me during the "Over the Waves" conference.

7. The narrative arc begins with episode 0324, "10-7," and concludes with episode 0501, "Rio."

8. Music Guide, "Cold Case—Source #1," <http://coldcase.net/index. php?categoryid=125> (22 Oct. 2008).

9. Cathy Caruth, *Unclaimed Experience: Trauma, Narrative, and History* (Baltimore: Johns Hopkins University Press, 1996), 17–18.

10. For an account of this amelioration across the television medium in the immediate aftermath of 9/ll, see Lynn Spigel, "Entertainment Wars: Television Culture After 9/ll," *American Quarterly* 56 (2004): 235–70. Spigel remarks on the quick return to business as usual despite the industry's instant claim that 9/11 had changed things forever. In effect the industry escaped the shadow of the event by returning to escapism. My argument in the present paper includes the suggestion that forensic melodramas offer a more durable and resonant form of amelioration made possible by their indirect means of representation. Among other things, they restore to narrative an epistemic power threatened, indeed shattered (as Spigel observes), by television news coverage of 9/ll and other catastrophes.

11. The narrative arc framed the season, starting with episode 0701, "Built to Kill, Part One," and ending with episode 0724, "Living Doll," with subsequent resolution in episode 0801, "Dead Doll." Incidentally, "his" victims should be "hers": the Miniature Killer turns out to be a woman.

Appendix A

Primary Character List

CSI: CRIME SCENE INVESTIGATION

Riley Adam (Lauren Lee Smith)
Capt. Jim Brass (Paul Guilfoyle)
Warrick Brown (Gary Dourdan)
Dt. Sofia Curtis (Louise Lombard)
Gill Grissom (William Peterson)
David Hodges (Wallace Langham)
Dr. Raymond Langston (Laurence Fishburne)
Dr. Al Robbins (Robert David Hall)
Greg Sanders (Eric Szmanda)
Sara Sidle (Jorja Fox)
Nick Stokes (George Eads)
Catherine Willows (Marg Halgenberger)

CSI: MIAMI

Natalia Boa Vista (Eva La Rue)
Lt. Horatio Caine (David Caruso)
Eric "Delko" Delektorsky (Adam Rodriguez)
Megan Donner (Kim Delaney)
Calleigh Duquesne (Emily Proctor)
Dr. Tara Price (Megalyn Echikunwoke)
Det. Yelina Salas (Sofia Milos)
Tim "Speed" Speedle (Rory Cochrane)
Det. Frank Tripp (Rex Linn)

Ryan Wolfe (Jonathan Togo)
Chief M.E. Alexx Woods (Khandi Alexander)

CSI: NY

Det. Stella Bonasera (Melina Kanakaredes)
Aiden Burn (Vanessa Ferlito)
Det. Donald "Don" Flack, Jr. (Eddie Cahill)
Dr. Sid Hammerback (Robert Joy)
Dr. Sheldon Hawkes (Hill Harper)
Danny Messer (Carmine Giovinzzo)
Lindsay Munroe (Anna Belknap)
Adam Ross (A.J. Buckley)
Det. Mack "Mac" Taylor (Gary Sinise)

Appendix B

Episode Guide

CSI: CRIME SCENE INVESTIGATION

Epi.#	Air Date	Title	Writer	Director
1001	6-Oct-2000	Pilot	A.E. Zuiker	Danny Cannon
1002	13-Oct-2000	Cool Change	A. E. Zuiker	Michael Walkins
1003	20-Oct-2000	Crate 'n Burial	A. Donahue	Danny Cannon
1004	27-Oct-2000	Pledging Mr. Johnson	Josh Berman	Richard J. Lewis
1005	3-Nov-2000	Friends and Lovers	A. Lipsitz	L. Antonio
1006	10-Nov-2000	Who Are You?	C. Mendelson/ J. Berman	Danny Cannon
1007	17-Nov-2000	Blood Drops	T. McCarthy/ A. Donahue	Kenneth Fink
1008	24-Nov-2000	Anonymous	E. Talbert/ A. Zuiker	Danny Cannon
1009	8-Dec-2000	Unfriendly Skies	A. Lipsitz/A. Zuiker	Michael Shapiro
1010	22-Dec-2000	Sex, Lies and Larvae	J. Berman/A. Donahue	Thomas J. Wright
1011	12-Jan-2001	I-15 Murders	C. Mendelson	Oz Scott
1012	1-Feb-2001	Fahrenheit 93	Jacqueline Zambrano	Danny Cannon
1013	8-Feb-2001	Boom	A. Donahue/ J. Berman / J. Medelsohn	Kenneth Fink
1014	15-Feb-2001	To Halve and to Hold	Andrew Lipsitz	Lou Antonio
1015	22-Feb-2001	Table Stakes	E. Devine/C. Mendelsohn/ A. E. Zuiker	Danny Cannon
1016	1-Mar-2001	Too Tough to Die	Elizabeth Devine	Richard J. Lewis
1017	8-Mar-2001	Face Lift	Josh Berman	Lou Antonio
1018	29-Mar-2001	$35K O.B.O.	E. Talbert	R. Wagner
1019	12-April-2001	Gentle, Gentle	A. Donahue	Danny Cannon
1020	19-April-2001	Sounds of Silence	A. Lipsitz/J. Berman	Peter Markle
1021	26-April-2001	Justice is Served	Jerry Stahl	Thomas J. Wright
1022	10-May-2001	Evaluation Day	A. E. Zuiker	Kenneth Fink
1023	17-May-2001	Strip Strangler	Ann Donahue	Danny Cannon

2001	27-Sept-2001	Burked	C. Mendelson/A. Zuiker	Danny Cannon
2002	4-Oct-2001	Chaos Theory	E. Talbert/J. Berman	Ken Fink
2003	11-Oct-2001	Overload	J. Berman	Richard J. Lewis
2004	18-Oct-2001	Bully for You	Ann Donahue	Thomas J. Wright
2005	25-Oct-2001	Scuba Doobie-Doo	A. Lipsitz, E/Devine	J. Levy
2006	1-Nov-2001	Alter Boys	Ann Donahue	Danny Cannon
2007	8-Nov-2001	Caged	E. Devine/C. Mendelsohn	Richard J. Lewis
2008	15-Nov-2001	Slaves of Las Vegas	Jerry Stahl	Peter Markle
2011	13-Dec-2001	Organ Grinder	A. Donahue/E. Devine	A. Lidd
2012	20-Dec-2001	You've Got Male	M. Dube/C. Miller	C. Correll
2013	17-Jan-2002	Identity Crisis	A. Donahue/A.E. Zuiker	Keneth Fink
2014	31-Jan-2002	The Finger	D. Cannon/C. Mendelsohn	Richard J. Lewis
2015	7-Feb-2002	Burden of Proof	Ann Donahue	Kenneth Fink
2016	28-Feb-2002	Primum Non Nocere	Andrew Lipsitz	Danny Cannon
2017	7-Mar-2002	Felonius Monk	Jerry Stahl	Kenneth Fink
2020	25-April-2002	Cats in the Cradle	K. Dobkin	R. J. Lewis
2021	2-May-2002	Anatomy of a Lye	A. Lipsitz/J. Berman	Kenneth Fink
2022	9-May-2002	Cross Jurisdiction	A. Zuiker/A. Donahue	D. Cannon
2023	16-May-2002	The Hunger Artist	Jerry Stahl	Richard J. Lewish
3001	26-Sept-2002	Revenge is Best Served Cold	C. Mendelsohn/A.E. Zuiker	Danny Cannon
3003	10-Oct-2002	Let the Seller Beware	A. Lipstiz/A.E. Zuiker	Richard J. Lewis
3004	17-Oct-2002	A Little Murder	N. Shankar/A. Donahue	Tucker Gates
3005	31-Oct-2002	Abra Cadaver	D. Cannon/A.E. Zuiker	Danny Cannon
3007	14-Nov-2002	Fight Night	A. Lipsitz/N. Shankar	R. J. Lewis.
3008	21-Nov-2002	Snuff	A. Donahue/B. Harris	K. Fink
3009	5-Dec-2002	Blood Lust	J. Berman/C. Mendelsohn	Charlie Correll
3010	12-Dec-2002	High and Low	E. Talbert/N. Shankar	Richard J. Lewis
3011	9-Jan-2003	Recipe for Murder	A. Zuiker, A. Donahue	R.J. Lewis/ J.M. Tobin
3012	16-Jan-2003	Got Murder?	S. Goldfinger	K. Fink
3014	6-Feb-2003	One Hit Wonder	C. Miller	F. E. Alcala
3015	13-Feb-2003	Lady Heather's Box	J.Berman et. al.	Richard A. Lewis
3016	20-Feb-2003	Lucky Strike	E. Talbert/A.E. Zuiker	Kenneth Fink
3017	13-Mar-2003	Crash & Burn	Josh Berman	Richard J. Lewis
3018	3-April-2003	Precious Metal	N. Shankar/A. Lipsitz	Deran Sarafian
3019	10-April-2003	A Night at the Movies	A. Zuiker/D. Cannon	M. E. Beesley
3020	24-April-2003	Last Laugh	A. Zuiker/B. Harris	R. J. Lewis
3021	1-May-2003	Forever	Sarah Goldfinger	David Grossman
3022	8-May-2003	Play With Fire	N. Shankar/A. Lipsitz	Kenneth Fink
3023	15-May-2003	Inside the Box	A. Zuiker/C. Mendelsohn	Danny Cannon
4001	25-Sept-2003	Assume Nothing	A.E. Zuiker/D. Cannon	Richard J. Lewis
4002	2-Oct-2003	All for Our Country	R. Catalani/A. Lipsitz/ C. Mendelsohn	R. J. Lewis
4003	9-Oct-2003	Homebodies	S. Goldfinger/N. Shankar	K. Fink
4004	23-Oct-2003	Feeling the Heat	E. Talbert/A. Zuiker	K. Fink
4005	30-Oct-2003	Fur and Loathing	J. Stahl/C. Mendelsohn/ N. Shankar	R. J. Lewis
4006	6-Nov-2003	Jackpot	J. Berman/C. Mendelsohn/A. Zuiker	D. Cannon
4009	11-Dec-2003	Grissom v. the Volcano	J. Berman/C. Mendelsohn/A. Zuiker	R. J. Lewis

4010	18-Dec-2003	Coming of Rage	S. Goldfinger/R. Catalani	N. McCormick
4011	8-Jan-2004	Eleven Angry Jurors	J. Berman/A. Lipsitz	M. E. Beasley
4012	15-Jan-2004	Butterflied	David Rambo	Richard J. Lewis
4013	5-Feb-2004	Suckers	J. Berman/D. Cannon	D. Cannon
4015	19-Feb-2004	Early Rollout	E. Devine/C. Mendelsohn	D. Clark
4016	26-Feb-2004	Getting Off	J. Stahl/A. Zuiker	D. Clark
4017	11-Mar-2004	XX	E. A. Vare	Deran Sarafian
4018	1-April-2004	Bad to the Bone	Eli Talbert	David Grossman
4019	15-April-2004	Bad Words	S. Goldfinger/J. Berman/ R. Catalani/C. Mendelsohn	R. Bailey
4020	29-April-2004	Dead Ringer	Elizabeth Devine	Kenneth Fink
4021	6-May-2004	Turning The Screws	J. Berman/R. Catalani/ C. Mendelsohn	D. Sarafian
4022	13-May-2004	No More Bets	D. Abraham/A. Lipsitz/ J. McCreary/ C. Mendelsohn/N. Shankar	R. J. Lewis
4023	20-May-2004	Bloodlines	N. Shenkar/C. Mendelson S. Goldfinger/E. Talbert	Kenneth Fink
5001	23-Sept-2004	Viva Las Vegas	D. Cannon/C. Mendelsohn	Danny Cannon
5002	7-Oct-2004	Down the Drain	Naren Shankar	Kenneth Fink
5004	21-Oct-2004	Crow's Feet	Josh Berman	Richard J. Lewis
5005	28-Oct-2004	Swap Meet	D. Rambo et. al.	Danny Cannon
5007	11-Nov-2004	Formalities	N. Shankar/D. L. Abrahams	Bill Eagles
5009	25-Nov-2004	Mea Culpa	C. Mendelsohn/J. Berman	David Grossman
5011	6-Jan-2005	Who Shot Sherlock	R. Catalani/D. Rambo	Kenneth Fink
5014	10-Feb-2005	Unbearable	C. Mendelsohn/J. Berman	Kenneth Fink
5016	24-Feb-2005	Big Middle	N. Shankar/J. McCreary	Bill Eagles
5017	10-Mar-2005	Compulsion	J. Berman/R. Catalani	Kenneth Fink
5018	31-Mar-2005	Spark of Life	A. MacDonald	Kenneth Fink
5019	14-April-2005	4X	S. Goldfinger et. al.	Terrence O-Hara
5021	28-April-2005	Committed	S. Goldfinger/U. Narsu	Richard J. Lewis
5024	19-May-2005	Grave Danger	Q. Tarantino et al.	Quentin Tarantino
6001	22-Sept-2005	Bodies in Motion	C. Mendelsohn/N. Shankar	R. J. Lewish
6019	6-April-2006	Spellbound	Jacqueline Hoyt	Jeffrey G. Hunt
7001	21-Sept-2006	Built to Kill, Part One	S. Goldfinger et. al.	Kenneth Fink
7024	17-May-2007	Living Doll	N. Shankar et. al.	Kenneth Fink
8001	27-Sept-2007	Dead Doll	N. Shankar et. al.	Kenneth Fink
8017	15-May-2008	For Gedda	D.Abraham/R. Catalani/ Kenneth Fink	Kenneth Fink
9001	9-Oct-2005	For Warrick	A. MacDonald/R.J. Lewis/ C. Mendelsohn	R.J. Lewis
9009	11-Dec-2008	19 Down	N. Shankar/C. Mendelsohn	K. Fink
9010	15-Jan-2009	One to Go	N.Shankar/C. Mendelsohn	A. Smight

CSI: MIAMI

Epi.#	Air Date	Title	Writer	Director
1021	28-April-2003	Spring Break	Steven Maeda	Deran Sarafian
1023	12-May-2003	Freaks and Tweaks	E. Devine/T. Haynes	Deran Sarafian

2001	22-Sept-2003	Blood Brothers	Ann Donahue	Danny Cannon
2003	6-Oct-2003	Hard Time	Elizabeth Devine	Deran Sarafian
2020	19-April-2004	The Oath	I. Modrovich et. al.	Duane Clark
2023	17-May-2004	MIA/NYC—Nonstop	A. E. Zuiker et. al.	Danny Cannon
3004	11-Oct-2004	Murder in a Flash	A. McGrail/S. Nayar	Fred Keller
3013	17-Jan-2005	Cop Killer	S. Maeda/K. Houghton	Jonathan Glassnen
3015	14-Feb-2005	Identity	A. Donahue/I. Modrovich	Gloria Muzio
3018	21-March-2005	Game Over	M. Ostrowski/C. Miller	Jonathan Glassner
3023	16-May-2005	Whacked	A. Donahue/E. Devine	Scott Lautanen
3024	23-May-2005	10-7	M. Ostrowski et. al.	Joe Chappelle
4002	26-Sept-2005	Blood in the Water	S. Nayar/D. Widenmann	Duane Clark
4017	6-March-2005	Collision	Dean Widenmann	Sam Hill
4023	8-May-2006	Shock	C. Miller/B. Davidson	Karen Gaviola
4024	15-May-2006	Rampage	I. Modrovich/M. Dube	Scott Lautanen
4015	22-May-2006	One of Our Own	E. Devine et. al.	Matt Earl Besley
5001	18-Sept-2006	Rio	Sunil Nayar	Joe Chapelle

CSI: NEW YORK

Epi.#	Air Date	Title	Writer	Director
1012	12-Jan-2005	Recycling	T. A. Lea/Z. Reiter	Alex Zarkrzewski
1017	2-Mar-2005	The Fall	A. McGrail/H. Haynes	Norberto Barba
1022	11-May-2005	The Closer	Pam Veasy	Emilio Estevez
2002	5-Oct-2005	Grand Murder at Central Station	Zachary Reiter	Scott Lautanen

Appendix C

Dataset of Press Sources on *CSI* and the *CSI* Effect, 2002–2005

Compiled by Elizabeth Harvey and Linda Derksen and listed by year of publication

2002

1. Jeffrey Kluger. "How Science Solves Crimes." *Time* (Saturday Oct. 12 2002).
2. Robin Franzen. "'CSI Effect' on Potential Jurors Has Some Prosecutors Worried." *Al Menconi Ministries.* Entertainment News Section for December 19, 2002. <http://www.almenconi.com/news/dec02/121902.html> (May 10, 2005).

2003

3. Bill Brioux. "Chalk It Up to Experience: How The Experts Make Television's Hottest Show Seem So Realistic." *Canoe—Jam!* (2003). <http://ja.canoe.ca/Television/television_Shows/C/CSI/2003/01/28/pf-734856.html> (Aug. 5, 2005).
4. Mark Sappenfield. "From Lindbergh to Laci, a Growing Forensics Fancy." *The Christian Science Monitor* (2003), <http://www.csmonitor.com/2003/0424/p01s01-ussc.htm> (July 5, 2005).
5. Rob Owen. "Science is the Star on 'CSI: Miami.'" *Pittsburgh Post Gazette,* interactive edition. <http://www.postgazette.com/printer.asp> (July 5, 2005).

6. Kevin Finneran. "Prime Time Science." *Editor's Journal* (Fall 2003):23
7. Carlene Hempel. "Television's Whodunit Effect." *The Boston Globe Magazine* (2003) <http://www.bafo.org.uk/television1.htm> (May 28, 2005).
8. Dan Vergano. "'CSI' Episode Wasn't What the Doctors Ordered." *USA Today,* February 25, 2003 edition, Life Section: 12d.
9. Kirk Monroe. "New Poll Shows Dramatic Rise in Americans' DNA I.Q." *EurekAlert* (2003). <kirk@kmcpr.com> (June 7, 2005).
10. Cyril H. Wecht. "Science Fiction: Television Programs Fail to Show Busy Overworked Forensic Labs." *Patriot News,* May 4, 2003. D03.
11. Associated Press. "CSI: Real World. Debunking Some of the CSI Bunk." *UnknownNews* (2003), <http://www.unknownnews.net/030909csi.html> (May 28, 2005).

2004

12. Dave Scheiber. "Crossing the Line: Reality Becomes Fiction When a Real-Life Detective, Who Makes His Home In St. Petersburg, Embarks on a New Career Advising the CBS Drama, CSI: Miami." *St. Petersburg Times Online* (2004), <http://www.sptimes.com/2004/01/01/news_pf/Floridian/Crossing_the_line.shtml> (July 17, 2005).
13. Dan Skantar. "Prime-Time Crime Television Exposed." *Firearms ID.com,* (2004), <http://www.firearmsid.com/Feature%20Articles/crimetelevision/crimetelevision.htm> (June 8, 2005).
14. Richard Willing. "'CSI Effect' Has Juries Wanting More Evidence." *USA Today* (2004). <http://www.usatoday.com/news/nation/2004-08-05-csi-effect_x.htm> (May 10, 2005).
15. Sydney Morning Herald. "The Real CSI." *The Sydney Morning Herald* (2004). <http://radar.smh.com.au/archives/2004/09/the_real_csi.html> (July 17, 2005).
16. Patrick S. Pemberton. "Crime Dramas Have Yet to Solve Problem of Realistic Depiction." *The San Diego Union Tribune* (2004), <http://www.signonsandiego.com/uniontrib/20040913/news_mz1c13crimet.html> (April 6, 2005).
17. Valerie Kalfrin. "'CSI: Tampa' Not as Glamorous as Television Version, But Very Effective." *TBO.com,* (2004), <http://multimedia.tbo.com/multimedia/popup/MGBKJ1C415E.html> (June 20, 2005).
18. James Poniewozik, Jeanne McDowell, Desa Philadelphia, and Kate Novack. "Crimetime Lineup: How the Slick Show Changed Televi-

sion—in Part By Dragging it Back Into the Past." *Time,* Vol. 164, Issue 19, 11/8/2004.

19. Amy Lennard Goehner, Lina Lofaro, and Kate Novack. 2004. "Ripple Effect. Where *CSI* Meets Real Law and Order." *Time.* Vol. 164, Issue 19, 11/8/2004.

20. Lyric Wallwork Winik. "The Real CSI." *Parade* (2004). <http://archive .parade.com/2004/1121/1121_intelligence.html> (June 8, 2005).

21. Kirk Makin. "The Reliance on Science as a Cure For Injustice." *Injusticebusters,* First reported in the Globe and Mail, Nov. 22, 2004. <http:// www.injusticebusters.com/04/CSI_Effect.shtml> (May 10, 2005).

22. Jane Ann Morrison. "'CSI Effect' May Have Led Binion Jurors to Demand Harder Evidence." *Las Vegas Review-Journal* (2004). <http:// reviewjournal.com/lvrj_home/2004/Dec-02-Thu-2004/news/25387405 .html> (June 20, 2005).

23. Emilie Lounsberry. "Lawyers' New Credo: Keep It Entertaining." *The Philadelphia Inquirer,* Sunday, December 26, 2004. http://www .philly.com/mld/philly/news/breaking_news/10497840.htm (May 28, 2005).

2005

24. Ross MacDowell. "The Real CSI." *Australian Institute of Criminology,* (2005). <http://www.aic.gov.au/services/careers/csi.html> (June 20, 2005).

25. Johnnie L.Roberts. "'CSI' to News: Drop Dead." *Newsweek.* Vol.145, Issue 4:8.

26. John L. Smith. "Evidence Lab Labors in Real World of Biker Gangs, Not 'CSI' Fantasy." *ReviewJournal.com* (2005). <http://www.review-journal.com/lvrj_home/2005/Feb-02-Wed-2005/news/25783233.html> (June 20, 2005).

27. Vince Gonzales. "The CSI Effect." *CBS News* Video (2005). <http://www .cbsnews.com/stories/2005/02/10/eveningnews/main673060.shtml>

28. Alan Boyle. "Crime Sleuths Cope With 'CSI' Effect." *MSNBC.com* (2005). <http://www.msnbc.msn.com/id/7003715/print/1/displaymode/ 1098/> (June 8, 2005).

29. Bruce Lieberman. "Forensics: Fact Vs Fiction. Television Shows Make Crime Solving Look Easy But In Real Life It's Not So Simple." *The San Diego Union-Tribune* (2005). <http://www.signonsandiego.com/ uniontrib/20050221/news_1n21forensic.html> (May 28, 2005).

30. Jeff Loew. "'CSI' Effect or Just Flimsy Evidence?" *Scryptic Studios* (2005) <http://www.scrypticstudios.com/index.php/news/354> (June 7, 2005).

31. Hattie Kauffman. "The CSI Effect." *CBS News* (2005). <http://www.cbsnews.com/stories/2005/03/21/earlyshow/printable681949.shtml> (July 17, 2005).

32. Josh Gildea. "America Falls For the 'CSI Effect.'" *The Daily Cardinal* (2005). <http://www.truthinjustice.org/CSI-effect.htm> (May 27, 2005).

33. Stephanie Peters. "Forensic Science Arrests Television Viewers Attention." *Northeastern News-The Inside* (2005). <http://www.nunews.com/media/paper600/news/2005/03/30/TheInside/Forensic.Science.Arrests.Television.Viewers.Attention-906596.shtml> (June 6, 2005).

34. Regis Behe. "CSI: Pittsburgh." *Pittsburgh Tribune-Review* (2005). <http://pittsburghlive.com/x/tribune-review/entertainment/books/s_319427.html> (June 2, 2005).

35. Maryanne Kocis MacLeod. "Television Shows Don't Reflect Reality of Using DNA to Solve Crimes." *The Macomb Daily, Online Edition* (2005). <http://www.macombdaily.com/stories/040605/loc_forensic001.shtml> (June 7, 2005).

36. Brian Handwerk. "DNA Freed Death-Row Inmates, Brings Others To Justice." *National Geographic News* (2005). <http://news.nationalgeographic.com/news/2005/04/0408_050408_television_dnadeath.html> (April 13, 2005).

37. Ted Landphair. "Television Crime Shows Make Forensic Studies a Hot Career." *NewsVOA.com* (2005). <http://www.voanews.com/english/AmericanLife/2005-04-08-voa34.cfm> (June 7, 2005).

38. Maggie Newhouse. "Real Life CSI." *Pittsburgh Tribune-Review* (2005). <http://pittsburghlive.com/x/tribune-review/trib/pittsburgh/s_323238.html> (August 5, 2005).

39. Alex Massie. "'CSI Effect' Evident in US Courtrooms-(Possible Reason Jury Acquitted Robert Blake.)" *The Scotsman.com*, (2005). <http://www.freerepublic.com/focus/f-news/1390431/posts> (June 12, 2005).

40. Mike Smythe. "The CSI Effect." *KFVS12 Viewpoint With Mike Smythe* (2005). <http://www.kfvs12.com/global/story.asp?s=3244320.htm> (June 6, 2005).

41. Kit R. Roane. "The CSI Effect." *U.S. News & World Report.* Vol. 138, Issue 15:48–53.

42. Steve Mirsky. "Crime Scene Investigation: Television Supersleuths Affect Real Courts, Campuses and Criminals." *ScientificAmerican*

.com (2005). <http://www.sciam.com/articleID=0008FDFF-100E-1264-8F9683414B7F.htm> (June 7, 2005).

43. GatorSports.com. "CSI: Accidental Education. Criminals Can Pick Up Tips On How To Thwart Efforts By Law Enforcement." *Gainesvillesun .com* (2005). <http://gatorsports.com/apps/pbcs.dll/article?AID=/20050426/LOCAL/50425072/1078.htm> (June 7, 2005).

44. Katharhynn Heidelberg. "CBI a Far Cry From 'CSI.'" *Montrose Daily Press* (2005). <http://www.montrosepress.com/articles/2005/08/02/local_news/2.prt> (August 2, 2005).

45. Paige Newman. 2005. "Secrets of 'CSI' Success: Great Characters, Tawdry Topic Help Make Drama Television's Top Show." MSNBC (2005). <http://www.msnbc.msn.com/id/7434546/print/1/displaymode/1098/> (August 5, 2005).

46. Kate Coscarelli. 2005. "The 'CSI' Effect: Television's False Reality Fools Jurors." *The Star-Ledger*, (2005). <http://www.newhousenews .com/archive/coscarelli050205.html> (July 17, 2005).

47. CBS Denver. "CSI Has 'Major Effect' On Real Life Juries." *CBS4 Denver* (2005). <http://news4colorado.com/crimeaccidentreport/local_story_125123936.html> (April 6, 2005).

48. Jeffrey Toobin. "Toobin: 'CSI' Makes Jurors More Demanding." *CNN .com.*, (2005). <http://cnnstudentnews.cnn.com/2005/LAW/05/05/otsc .toobin> (June 6, 2005).

49. Paul Rincon. "CSI Shows Give 'Unrealistic View.'" *BBC News* (2005). <http://news.bbc.co.uk/go/pr/fr/-/1/hi/sci/tech/4284335.stm> (May 10, 2005).

50. Cole, Simon and Rachel Dioso. "The Law and the Lab: Do Television Shows Really Affect How Juries Vote? Let's Look at the Evidence." *The Wall Street Journal* (2005). <http://www.truthinjustice.org/law-lab .htm> (May 23, 2005).

51. Jennifer Parker. "CSI Effect and Corpus Christi." *Corpus-Beat Magazine* (2005). <http://www.corpusbeat.com/ViewPost .ASPX?PostObjectID=1878> (June 21, 2005).

52. CNN.com. "The Real CSI: Investigators' Jobs Less Glamorous, More Personal." *CNN.com* (2005) <http://cnnstudentnews.cnn.com/2005/LAW/05/05/murder.overview> (August 5, 2005).

53. Jamie Stockwell. "Defense, Prosecution Play to New 'CSI' Savvy. Juries Increasingly Are Expecting Television-Style Forensics." *MSNBC.com* (2005). <http://msnbc.com/id/7902971/> (May 23, 2005). Previously in the *Washington Post.*

54. Patrick Mattimore. "Television's Effect on the Courtroom." *San Francisco Examiner* (2005). <http://www.sfexaminer.com/articles/2005/05/24/opinion/20050524_op03_jurors.prt> (June 20, 2005).
55. Meggan Clark. "'CSI' Effect Causing Crime Lab Backlog." *New Haven Register.com* (2005). <www.nhregister.com/site/1281&dept_id=517515> (June 20, 2005).
56. Flynn McRoberts, Steve Mills, and Maurice Possley. 2005. "The 'CSI Effect': Fact or Fiction?" *The Chicago Tribune* (2005). <http://www.journalstar.com/articles/2005/06/10/top_story/extras/doc42a> (July 17, 2005).
57. Sheryl Marsh. "Real-Life Forensic Work Not What You See On Television." *Taphophilia.com* (2005). <http://taphophilia.com/modules.php?name=News&file=print&sid=2632>
58. Ed Treleven. "'The CSI Effect' On Real Juries." *Wisconsin State Journal* (2005). <http://www.madison.com/wsj/home/local/index.php?ntid=44090&ntpid=3> (June 21, 2005).
59. John Sharp. "Beeney Case Shocks Police. East Peoria Police Chief Says Television Crime Shows Are Affecting Real-Life trials." *PJStar.com* (2005). <http://www.pjstar.com/stories/062505/TRI_B6Q4JRJU.061.shtml> (July 17, 2005).
60. Zofia Smardz. "The Jury's Out. How 12 Reasonable People Got Hung Up on Reasonable Doubt." *The Washington Post* (2005). <http://www.washingtonpost.com/wp-dyn/content/article/2005/06/25/AR2005062500078_print.html> (July 17, 2005).
61. Clarence Walker. "CSI (T.V. Crime Dramas) Affects the American Criminal Justice System." *American Mafia.com*, (2005). <http://www.americanmafia.com/Feature_Articles_301.html> (June 21, 2005).
62. Katie McDevitte. 2005. "'CSI Effect' Turns Jurors Into Instant Experts." *Arizona East Valley Tribune* (2005). <http://www.eastelevisionalleytribune.com/index.php?sty=43932> (July 17, 2005).
63. Mark Billingham. 2005. "Tarantino is Perfect For This Kinky Crime Show." *The Telegraph.co.uk* (2005). <http://www.telegraph.co.uk/arts/main.jhtml?xml=/arts/2005/07/12/bvtaratin09.xml> (July 17, 2005).
64. Tom Dworetzky. "Final Reckoning." *Popular Mechanics* (2005),Vol. 182, Issue 7:56-9.
65. Susan Ormiston. "The Current Part 2: The CSI Effect." CBC Radio program broadcast on April 5, 2005. Can be found at: <http://www.cbc.ca/thecurrent/2005/200504/20050405.html> (July 17, 2005).
66. Dawn Stevens. "CSI Effect in Madison." *Channel 3000* (2005), streaming video report. <http://www.channel3000.com/technology/4250198/detail.html>

67. Ted Landphair. 2005. "Ted Landphair Report." Video/audio. At *NEWSVOA.com* (2005). <http://www.voanews.com/english/American-Life/2005-04-08-voa34.cfm> (June 7, 2005).
68. Marsha Kazarosian. "Hollywood: Fact or Fiction in Court?" *The Power of Attorney Show on The Legal Talk Network* (2005). Audio broadcast. <http://www.legaltalknetwork.com/modules.php?name=News&file=article&sid=20>
69. Barbara Pierce. "The CSI Effect" CBS News video. Feb. 10, 2005. <http://www.cbsnews.com/stories/2005/02/10/eveningnews/main673060.shtml>
70. Nancy Beardsley. "Forensic Scientists: America's New Pop Culture Heroes." *Coast to Coast* report in streaming video for NewsVOA.com (2004). <http://www.voanews.com/english/AmericanLife/2004-10-20-voa80.cfm> (July, 2005).

Bibliography

Ackbar, Abbas. "Building on Disappearance: Hong Kong Architecture and Colonial Space." Pp. 146–68 in *The Cultural Studies Reader*, edited by Simon During. London and New York: Routledge, 1999.

Adamoski, Robert, Dorothy Chunn, and Robert Menzies. "Rethinking the Citizen in Canadian Social History." Pp. 12–41 in *Contesting Canadian Citizenship*, edited by Robert Adamoski, Dorothy Chunn and Robert Menzies. Peterborough, Ontario: Broadview Press, 2002.

Adler, Leo. "Commentary: Convicted by Juries, Exonerated by Science." *The Voice of the Criminal Defence Bar*, 1996.

Allen M., ed. *Reading CSI: Crime TV Under the Microscope*. London: IB Tauris, 2007.

"Andrea Yates" <http://en.wikipedia.org/wiki/Andrea_Yates> (2 Feb. 2009).

Andrews, Carol. *Egyptian Mummies*, 2nd ed. London: British Museum, 1998.

Andriopoulos, Stefan. "Psychic Television." *Critical Inquiry* 31 (2005): 618–37.

Bachelard, Gaston. *The Poetics of Space: The Classic Look at How We Experience Intimate Places*. Boston: Beacon Press, 1958.

Ballard, J. G. "In Cold Blood." *Guardian*. (June 25 2005): Review sec.19.

Bandes, Susan, and Jack Beermann. "Lawyering Up." *The Green Bag* (Autumn 1998).

Bandura, Albert. "Social Cognitive Theory of Mass Communication." Pp. 121–53 in *Media Effects: Advances in Theory and Research*, edited by J. Bryant and D. Zillman. New Jersey: Earlbaum, 1994.

Barak, Gregg. "In Between the Waves: Mass Mediated Themes of Crime and Justice." *Social Justice* 21, no. 3 (1994): 133–47.

———. "Mediatizing law and order: Applying Cottle's architecture of communicative frames to the social construction of crime and justice." *Crime, Media, Culture* 4, no.3 (2007): 101–9.

Barry, Andrew, Thomas Osborne, and Nikolas Rose, eds. *Foucault and Political Reason: Liberalism, Neo-Liberalism and Rationalities of Government*. Chicago: University of Chicago Press, 1996.

Bauman, Zygmunt . *Life in Fragments: Essays in Post-Modern Morality*. Oxford: Blackwell, 1995.

———. "Living (Occasionally Dying) Together in an Urban World." Pp. 110–19 in *Cities, War, and Terrorism: Towards an Urban Geopolitics*, edited by Stephen Graham. Oxford: Blackwell Publishing, 2004.

Beck, Ulrich. *Risk Society: Toward a New Modernity*. Translated by M. Ritter. London: Sage, 1992.

Beckett, Katherine, and Bruce Wester. "Governing Social Marginality." *Punishment and Society* 3, no. 1 (2001): 43–59.

"The Best of Television: The Inaugural Flow Critics' Poll" (Posted by Jason Mittell, September 22nd, 2006) <http://flowTV.org/?p=8> (30 Jan. 2009).

Beyer, J. C., Y.F. Enos and M. Stajic, "Drug identification through analysis of maggots." *Journal of Forensic Science* 25 (1980): 411–12.

Bierne, Piers and James W. Messerschmidt. *Criminology* 4. Los Angeles: Roxbury Publishing Company, 2006.

Biressi, Anita and Heather Nunn. *Reality TV: Realism and Revelation*. London: Wallflower, 2005.

Black, Joel. *The Reality Effect: Film Culture and the Graphic Imperative*. New York and London: Routledge, 2002.

Bonnycastle, Kevin. "Sex Offenders in Context: Creating Choices in the Age of Risk." PhD Diss., Simon Fraser University, 2004.

Born, Georgina. "Against Negation, for a politics of cultural production: Adorno, aesthetics, the social." *Screen* 34, no. 3 (1993): 223–42.

Bowers, Vivien. *Crime Science: How Investigators Use Science to Track Down the Bad Guys*. Toronto: Owl, 1997.

Boyd, Susan C., Dorothy E. Chunn, and Robert Menzies, eds., *Toxic Criminology*. Fernwood: Halifax, 2002.

Brennan, Lisa. "Pitching the Gen X Jury." *The National Law Journal*. June 6 2004. <http://www.judicialaccountability.org/trialsusingtechnology.htm> (17 Jan. 2009).

Brioux, Bill. "Chalk It Up to Experience: How the Experts Make Television's Hottest Show Seem So Realistic." *Canoe-Jam!* (2003). <http://jam.canoe.ca/Television/TV_Shows/C/CSI/2003/01/28/734856.html> (16 Jan. 2009).

Brodie, Janine. "Canadian Women, Changing State Forms, and Public Policy." Pp. 1–28 in *Women and Canadian Public Policy*, edited by Janine Brodie. Toronto: Harcourt, Brace and Company, 1996.

Brottman, Mikita. "The Fascination of the Abomination." Pp. 171–188 in *Film and Television After 9/11,* edited by W.W. Dixon. Carbondale IL: Southern Illinois University Press, 2004.

Brovard, James. *Attention Deficit Democracy*. New York: Palgrave Macmillan, 2005.

Brown, Mark. "Calculations of Risk in Contemporary Penal Practice." Pp. 93–104 in *Dangerous Offenders: Punishment and Social Order*, edited by Mark Brown and John Pratt. Routlege: London and New York, 2000.

Brown, Sheila. *Crime and Law in Media Culture*. Buckingham and Philadelphia: Open University Press, 2003.

Brown, Wendy. "Neo-liberalism and the End of Liberal Democracy." *Theory & Event* 7, no.1 (2003): 1–19.

———. "American Nightmare: Neoliberalism, Neoconservatism, and De-Democratization." *Political Theory* 34, n.6 (2006): 690–714.

Brunsdon, Charlotte. "Structure of Anxiety: Recent British Television Crime Fiction." *Screen* 30, no.3 (1998): 223–43.

Buchanan, D. R., and J. K. Mason. "The Coroner's Office Revisited." *Medical Law Review* 3 (1995): 142–60.

Burchell, Graham, Colin Gordon, and Peter Miller, eds. *The Foucault Effect: Studies in Governmentality*. Chicago: University of Chicago Press, 1991.

Bureau of Justice Statistics. "Crime and Victims Statistics; Homicide Trends in US." US Department of Justice. 2005. <http://www.ojp.usdoj.gov/bjs/cvict.htm> (16 Jan. 2009).

Burney, Ian A. *Bodies of Evidence: Medicine and the Politics of the English Inquest, 1830–1926*. Baltimore: Johns Hopkins, 2000.

Butler, Judith. "Endangered/Endangering: Schematic Racism and White Paranoia." Pp. 15–22 in *Reading Rodney King, Reading Urban Uprising*, edited by R. Gooding-Williams. London: Routledge, 1993.

Byers, Michele, and David Lavery, eds. *"Dear Angela:" Remembering My So-Called Life*. Lanham: Lexington, 2007.

Caldwell, John T. "Convergence Television: Aggregating Form and Repurposing Content in the Culture of Conglomeration." Pp. 41–74 in *Television After TV: Essays on a Medium in Transition*, edited by Lynn Spigel and Jan Olsson. Durham, NC: Duke University Press, 2004.

Carroll, Noël. *Theorizing the Moving Image*. Cambridge: Cambridge University Press, 1996.

Caruth, Cathy. *Unclaimed Experience: Trauma, Narrative, and History*. Baltimore: Johns Hopkins University Press, 1996.

Castel, Robert. "From Dangerousness to Risk." Pp. 281–96 in *The Foucault Effect*.

Cather, H. "The *CSI* Effect: Fake TV and its Impact on Jurors In Criminal Cases." *The Prosecutor* 38, no.2 (March–April 2004): 9–15.

Caughie, John. "Adorno's reproach: repetition, difference and television genre." *Screen* 32 no. 2 (1991): 127–51.

Cavender, G. "Media and Crime Policy: A Reconsideration of David Garland's The Culture of Control." *Punishment & Society* 6, no.3 (2004): 335–48.

Cavender, G. and S. Deutsch. "*CSI* and moral authority: The police and science." *Crime Media Culture* 3, no.1 (2007): 67–81.

Chaffee, S. H. and A. R. Tims. "Interpersonal Factors in Adolescent Television Use." *Journal of Social Issues* 32, no. 4 (1976): 98–115.

Chambliss, Bill, Aaron Doyle and Jimmie Reeves. "Panel Discussion on 'Deviance.'" *Velvet Light Trap* 53 (Spring 2004): 4–9.

Chanen, Jill Schachner. "Stay Tuned: With Reality TV Shows, Videotape Evidence and High-Tech Court Presentations, the Medium Has Become the Message in Law." *American Bar Association Journal* 90 (Oct 2004): 44–56.

Chunn, Dorothy. "Feminism, Law and 'the Family'': Assessing the Reform Legacy." Pp. 236–59 in *Locating Law: Race/Class/Gender Connections* ed. Elizabeth Comack. Halifax: Fernwood, 1999.

Chunn, Dorothy and Robert Menzies. "'So what does all of this have to do with Criminology?': Surviving the Restructuring of the Discipline in the Twenty-First Century." *Canadian Journal of Criminology and Criminal Justice* (September 2006): 663–76.

Chunn, Dorothy and Shelley Gavigan. "From Welfare Fraud to Welfare as Fraud: The Criminalization of Poverty." Pp. 217–35 in *Criminalizing Women*, edited by Comack and Balfour. Halifax, NS: Fernwood Publishing, 2006.

Cilibrasi, Rudi and Paul Vitanyi. "The Google Similarity Distance." IEEE Trans. *Knowledge and Data Engineering* 19, no.3 (2007): 370–83.

Clarke, Mike. *Teaching Popular Television*. London: Heinemann Educational in association with BFI, 1987.

CNN/USA Today-Gallup. "Simpson verdict opinion poll" October 3, 1995, <http://www.cnn.com/US/OJ/daily/9510/10-04/poll/index.html> (2 Feb. 2009).

Cole, David. *No Equal Justice*. New York: New Press, 2000.

Cole, Simon and Rachel Dioso. "The Law and The Lab: Do Television Shows Really Affect How Juries Vote? Let's Look At the Evidence." *The Wall Street Journal.* 2005. <http://www.truthinjustice.org/law-lab.htm> (17 Jan. 2009).

Comack, Elizabeth, and Gillian Balfour. *The Power to Criminalize: Violence, Inequality and the Law*. Halifax: Fernwood Press, 2004.

Combs, Debra L., R. Gibson Parrish, and Roy Ing. *Death Investigation in the United States and Canada, 1990*. Atlanta: US Department of Health and Human Services, et al, 1990.

"The Coroners and Crime." *Journal of Criminal Law* 3 (1939): 304–19.

Craib, Ian. *Psychoanalysis and Social Theory: The Limits of Sociology*. Amherst: The University of Massachusetts Press, 1989.

Crane, Jonathan Lake. *Terror and Everyday Life: Singular Moments in the History of the Horror Film*. Thousand Oaks, CA: Sage, 1994.

"Crime Shows Dominate Ratings." <http://www.cnn.com/2005/SHOWBIZ/television/08/03/nielsens.ap/>

Crosby, Alfred. *Ecological Imperialism: The Biological Expansion of Europe, 900–1900*. Cambridge, UK: Cambridge, 1993.

"CSI: Crime Scene Investigation" <http://en.wikipedia.org/wiki/CSI:_Crime_Scene_Investigation#U.S._television_ratings; www.nielsen.com> (30 Jan. 2009).

"CSI Effect." *Double-Tongued Dictionary* 2005. http://www.doubletongued.org/index.php/citations/csi_effect_1/ (17 Jan. 2009).

"CSI Effect." *Do You Speak American: Track That Word at PBS.org*. 2003. <http://www.pbs.org/speak/words/trackthatword/ttw/?i=513> (17 Jan. 2009).

"The CSI Effect: Forensic Science in the Public Imagination." Symposium, in *Worldwide Public Understanding of Science*, American Academy for the Advancement of Science 2005 Annual Meeting (Audio-Visual Education Network, 2005): AS5187.

"CSI: Maricopa County. The *CSI* Effect and its Real-Life Impact on Justice. A Study by the Maricopa County Attorney's Office." June 30, 2005. <www.maricopacountyattorney.org/Press/PDF/CSIReport.pdf> (21 Sept. 2007).

"CSI show 'most popular in world,'" (31 July 2006) <http://news.bbc.co.uk/1/hi/entertainment/5231334.stm> (30 January 2009).

D'Acci, Julie. "Gender, Representation and Television." In *Television Studies*, edited by Toby Miller. London: BFI Publishing, 2002, 373–88.

———. "Cultural Studies, Television Studies and the Crisis in the Humanities," in *Television after TV: Essays on a Medium in Transition*, ed. Lynn Spigel and Jan Olsson (Durham and London: Duke University Press, 2004), 418–46.

Davis, Angela. *Are Prisons Obsolete?* Seven Stories Press: New York, 2003.

"Defense Lawyers Hinge Cases on 'CSI' Savvy." *The Washington Post* (May 22, 2005): A1.

Deleuze, Gilles, and Felix Guattari, *A Thousand Plateaus: Capitalism and Schizophrenia* (1980), trans. with a foreword by Brian Massumi. Minneapolis: University of Minnesota Press, 1987.

Derksen, Linda. "Towards a Sociology of Measurement: The Meaning of Measurement Error in the Case of DNA Profiling." *Social Studies of Science* 30 (2000): 803–45.

———. "Agency and Structure in the History of DNA Profiling: The Stabilization and Standardization of a New Technology." Ph.D. Dissertation, Science Studies Program and Department of Sociology, University of California, San Diego, 2003.

Derrida, Jacques. "The Parergon." Pp. 39–118, in his *The Truth in Painting*, trans. Geoff Bennington and Ian McCloud. Chicago: University of Chicago Press, 1987.

———. *Spectres of Marx*. New York: Routledge, 1994.

Devlin, Richard. "We Can't Go On Together With Suspicious Minds: Judicial Bias and Racialized Perspective in R. vs. R. D. S." *Dalhousie Law Review* 18, no. 2 (1995): 408–46.

Dillon, Mick, and Jeremy Valentine. "Introduction: Culture and Governance." *Cultural Values: The Journal for Cultural Research* 6 (2002): 5–9.

Douglas, Mary. *Purity and Danger: An Analysis of the Concepts of Pollution and Taboo*. London: Routledge & Kegan Paul, 1969.

Doyle, Arthur Conan. "Silver Blaze." *Strand Magazine* 4 (December 1892), 645–60.

Dubber, Mark. *Victims in the War on Crime: The Use and Abuse of Victims' Rights*. New York: New York University Press, 2002.

Duncker, Patricia. Letter. *Guardian* (July 2 2005): Review sec., 8.

Eagleton, Terry. *Literary Theory: An Introduction*. Oxford: Basil Blackwell, 1983.

Edmund, Gary, ed. *Expertise in Regulation and Law*.Aldershot, UK: Ashgate, 2004.

Elias, Norbert. *The History of Manners*. Oxford: Basil Blackwell, 1978.

Engle, Karen J. "Putting Mourning to Work: Making Sense of 9/11." *Theory, Culture and Society* 24, no. 1 (2007): 61–88.

Ericson, Richard, and Aaron Doyle. *Uncertain Business: Risk, Insurance and the Limits of Knowledge*. Toronto: University of Toronto Press, 2004.

Ericson, Richard, and Kevin Haggerty. *Policing the Risk Society*. Toronto: University of Toronto Press, 1997.

Eschholz, Sarah, Brenda S. Blackwell, Marc Gertz, and Ted Chiricos. "Race and Attitudes Toward the Police: Assessing the Effects of Watching 'Reality' Police Programs." *Journal of Criminal Justice 30 (2002)*: 327–41.

Feeley, Malcolm, and Jonathan Simon. "The New Penology: Notes on the Emerging Strategy of Corrections and its Implications." *Criminology* 30, no. 4 (1992): 449–74.

——. "Actuarial Justice: The Emerging New Criminal Law." Pp. 174–201 in *The Futures of Criminology*, edited by David Nelkan. Thousand Oakes: Sage, 1994.

Ferrell, J., and C. R. Sanders. "Toward a Cultural Criminology." Pp. 297–326 in *Cultural Criminology*, edited by J. Ferrell and C. Sanders. Boston: Northeastern University Press, 1995.

Feuer, Jane. "The MTM Style." Pp. 32–60 in *MTM 'Quality Television'*, edited by Jane Feuer, Paul Kerr, and Tish Vahimagi London: BFI Books 1984.

"Final 2007–8 Season To Date Broadcast Shows By Viewers" (Posted 25 September 2008 by Bill Gorman) <http://tvbythenumbers.com/category/nielsen-network-tv-ratings-season-to-date/nielsen-tv-ratings-top-broadcast-shows-season-to-date> (30 Jan. 2009).

Fisher, Barry A. J. *Techniques of Crime Scene Investigation*, 7th ed. Boca Raton: CRC Press, 2003.

Fiske, John. "Moments of Television: Neither the Text nor the Audience." Pp. 56–78 in *Remote Control: Television, Audiences and Cultural Power*, edited by Ellen Seiter et. al. London and New York: Routledge, 1989.

Flynn, John L. "The Office of the Coroner versus the Medical Examiner System." *Journal of Criminal Law, Criminology and Police Science* 46, no. 2 (1956): 232–238.

Foley, Elizabeth, and Adrienne LeFevre. "Understanding Generation X." *Trial* (June 2000): 58–62.

Forman, Murray. "Freaks, Aliens, and the Social Other: Representations of Student Stratification in U.S. Television's First Post-Columbine Season." *Velvet Light Trap* 53 (Spring 2004): 66–82.

Foucault, Michel. *Discipline and Punish: The Birth of the Prison*. London: Peregrine Books, 1979.

Fox, Kathryn. "Changing Violent Minds: Discursive Correction and Resistance in the Cognitive Treatment of Violent Offenders in Prison." *Social Problems* 46, no. 1 (1999): 88–103.

Franzen, Robin. "TV's 'CSI' Crime Drama Makes it Look Too Easy." *The Oregonian* (10 Dec 2002).

——. "'CSI Effect' on Potential Jurors Has Some Prosecutors Worried." *Almenconi News*. December 19 2002. <http://www.almenconi.com/news/dec02/121902.html>

Freud, Sigmund. "Fetishism." Pp. 152–59. *The Standard Edition of the Complete Works of Sigmund Freud*, Vol. 21, edited by James Strachey. London: Hogarth Press, 1974.

Gaines, Jane. "White Privilege and Looking Relations." Pp.336–55 in *Feminism and Film*, edited by E. Ann Kaplan. Oxford: Oxford University Press, 2000.

The Gallup Poll. Public Opinion 2005. Lanham, MD: Rowman & Littlefield, 2007.

Garland, David. *Punishment and Welfare: A History of Penal Strategies.* Abershot: Gower, 1985.

———. "The Limits of the Sovereign State: Strategies of Crime Control in Contemporary Society." *The British Journal of Criminology* 36, no. 4 (1996): 445–71.

———. "Governmentality and the Problem of Crime: Foucault, Criminology, and Sociology." *Theoretical Criminology* 1, no. 2 (1997): 173–214.

———. *The Culture of Control: Crime and Social Order in Contemporary Society.* Chicago: University of Chicago Press, 2001.

Gedalof, Allan J. et al. *Cultural Subjects: A Popular Culture Reader.* Toronto: Thomson Nelson, 2005.

Gerbner, George, Larry Gross, Michael Morgan, and Nancy Signorelli. "A Curious Journey Into the Scary World of Paul Hirsch." *Communication Research* 8 (1981): 39–72.

Gever, M. "The spectacle of crime, digitized." *European Journal of Cultural Studies* 8, no.4 (Nov. 2005): 445–63.

Gibbs, Jewelle Taylor. *Race and Justice: Rodney King and O. J. Simpson in a House Divided.* New York: Josey Bass, 1996.

Ginzburg, Carlo. "Clues: Roots of an Evidential Paradigm." Pp. 96–125 in *Clues, Myth, and the Historical Method.* Baltimore: Johns Hopkins, 1989.

Goehner, Amy Lennard, Lina Lofaro, and Kate Novack. "Where CSI Meets Real Law and Order." *Time* 164, no. 19 (8 November 2004).

Goff, Madison Lee. "Problems in estimation of postmortem interval resulting from wrapping of the corpse: A case study from Hawaii." *Journal of Agricultural Entomology* 9, no. 4 (1992): 237–43.

Goff, Madison Lee, and Wayne D. Lord. "Entomotoxicology. A new area for forensic investigation." *American Journal of Forensic Medicine and Pathology* 15, no. 1 (1994): 51–57.

Gordon, Todd. *Cops, Crime and Capitalism: The Law-and-Order Agenda in Canada.* Halifax: Fernwood Publishing, 2006.

Gottfredson, Michael, and Travis Hirschi, *A General Theory of Crime.* Stanford: Stanford University Press, 1990.

"Governor Ryan's Capital Punishment Moratorium and the Executioner's Confession: Views from the Governor's Mansion to Death Row." *St. John's Law Review* 75 (Summer 2001): 401–18.

Gray, Herman. *Watching Race: Television and the Struggle for Blackness.* Minneapolis: University of Minnesota Press, 1994.

Guider, Elizabeth. "'CSI' on Euro most-wanted list," *Variety* (Oct. 12, 2005).

Gunther, M. "You Have the Right to Remain Silent." *TV Guide* (18 December 1971): 8.

Hallett, Michael. *'COPS' and 'CSI': Reality Television?* 15 Oct. 2005. <www.unf.edu/coas/ccj/Faculty/Hallett/COPS%20and%20CSI%20Reality%20Television.doc> (17 Jan. 2009).

Hallsworth, Simon. "Rethinking the Punitive Turn." *Punishment and Society* 2, no 2 (2000): 145–60.

——. "Punitive Passions, Civilisation, and Punishment." *PSEP* <http://psep.free .ngo.pl/a-eg/04shkara.html> (17 Jan. 2009).

Hansen, Mark. "The Uncertain Science of Evidence," *ABAJournal.Com* 2005. <http://www.abanet.org/journal/redesign/07fcle.html> (17 July 2005).

Haralovich, Mary Beth, and Lauren Rabinovitz. "Introduction." Pp.1–16 in *Television, History, and American Culture: Feminist Critical Essays*, edited by Mary Beth Haralovich and Lauren Rabinovitz. Durham and London: Duke University Press, 1999.

Harcourt, Bernard. "The Shaping of Chance: Actuarial Models and Criminal Profiling at the Turn of the Twenty-First Century." *University of Chicago Law Review* 70, no.105 (2003): 105–28.

Harrington, C. Lee, and Denise D. Bielby. "Flow, Home, and Media Pleasures." *Journal of Popular Culture* 38, no. 5 (2005): 834–54.

Harrington, E. Burton. "Nation, identity and the fascination with forensic science in Sherlock Holmes and *CSI.*" *International Journal of Cultural Studies* 10, no.3 (Sept. 2007): 365–82.

Harris Poll on Major Institutions (2004–2008) <http://www.pollingreport.com/ institut.htm> (2 Feb. 2009).

Harvey, David. *A Brief History of Neoliberalism.* New York: Oxford University Press, 2005.

Hayes, Brian. "Wisconsin's Lethargic Response to the 'CSI Effect.'" *Wisconsin Interest* (Fall 2005): 7–13.

Heath, Stephen. *Questions of Cinema.* Bloomington, IN: Indiana University Press, 1983.

Heintz-Knowles, Katharine E. "Images of Youth: A Content Analysis of Adolescents in Prime Time Entertainment Programming." 2000. <http://www.frameworksinstitute.org/products/youth.pdf>

Henry, Frances, and Carol Taylor. *Discourses of Domination: Racial Bias in the Canadian English-Language Press.* Toronto: University of Toronto Press, 2002.

Herbert, Rosemary, ed. *The Oxford Companion to Crime and Mystery Writing.* New York: Oxford, 1999.

Herczog, Mary. *Frommer's Portable Las Vegas for Non-Gamblers*, 2nd ed. New York: Wiley, 2005.

Hermer, Joe, and Janet Mosher, eds. *Disorderly People: Law and the Politics of Exclusion in Ontario.* Halifax: Fernwood Publishing, 2002.

Herrnstein, R. J. "Criminogenic Traits." Pp. 58–62 in *Crime*, edited by James Q. Wilson and Joan Petersilia. San Francisco: ICS Press, 1995.

Hillier, Bill. "The Common Language of Space: A Way of Looking at the Social, Economic and Environmental Functioning of Cities on a Common Basis." *Space Syntax Laboratory Web-Site.* 2006. <http://www.spacesyntax.org/publications/ commonlang.html> (24 Feb. 2006).

Holt, Jennifer. "Vertical Vision: Deregulation, Industrial Economy and Prime-Time Design." Pp. 11–31 in *Quality Popular Television*, edited by Mark Jancovich and James Lyons. London: Bfi Publishing, 2003.

hooks, bell. *Black Looks: Race and Representation*. Boston: South End Press, 1992.
——. *Outlaw Culture: Resisting Representations*. New York and London: Routledge, 1994.
Houck, Max M. "CSI: Reality." *Scientific American* 295 (2006): 85–89.
Hubbard, Phil. *City*. London and New York: Routledge, 2006.
Hunt, Alan. "Moral Regulation and Making-up the New Person: Putting Gramsci to Work." *Theoretical Criminology* 1, no. 3 (1997): 275–301.
Hurd, Geoff. "The Television Presentation of the Police." In *Popular Television and Film: A Reader*, edited by Tony Bennett et al. London: BFI/Open University, 1981.
"Ida B. Wells-Barnett Exposes the Myth of the Black Rapist, 1892." Pp. 155–58 in *Major Problems in the History of American Sexuality*, edited by Kathy Peiss. Boston: Houghton Mifflin, 2002.
The Innocence Project, <http://www.innocenceproject.org/> (2 Feb. 2009).
Introna, Francesco, Carlo Pietro Campobassa and Madison Lee, Goff. "Entomotoxicology." *Forensic Science International* 120 (2001): 42–47.
Jacobs, Jason. *Body Trauma TV: The New Hospital Dramas*. London: BFI, 2003.
James, Carl E. "Armed and Dangerous: Racializing Suspects, Suspecting Race." Pp.210–17 in *Marginality and Condemnation: An Introduction to Critical Criminology*, edited by Bernard Schissel and Carolyn Brooks. Halifax: Fernwood, 2004.
Jameson, Fredric. "Postmodernism, or The Cultural Logic of Late Capitalism." *New Left Review* 146 (1984): 53–92.
Jasanoff, Sheila. "The Eye of Everyman: Witnessing DNA in the Simpson Trial." *Social Studies of Science* 28, nos. 5–6 (October–December 1998): 713–40.
Jenkins, Henry. "Why Fiske Still Matters." FLOW. June 10, 2005. <http://flowTV.org/?p=585>
Johnson, Rebecca. "If Choice is the Answer, What is the Question? Spelunking in Symes v. Canada." Pp. 199–221 in *Law as a Gendering Practice*, edited by Dorothy Chunn and Dany Lacombe. Toronto: Oxford University Press, 2000.
Katz, Jack. *Seductions of Crime: Moral and Sensual Attractions in Doing Evil*. New York: Basic Books, 1988.
Kazarosian, Marsha. "Hollywood: Fact or Fiction in Court?" *Power of Attorney* Radio Show. <http://www.legaltalknetwork.com/modules.php?name=News&file=article&sid=20>
Kern, Stephen. *A Cultural History of Causality: Science, Murder Novels and Systems of Thought*. Princeton: Princeton, 2004.
Kerr, Paul. "Drama at MTM: Lou Grant and Hill Street Blues." Pp.132–65 in *MTM 'Quality Television.'*
King, Stephen. *Danse Macabre*. London: Warner, 1993.
Kinsman, Gary. "Constructing Sexual Problems: 'These Things may lead to the Tragedy of our Species.'" Pp. 85–120 in *Power and Resistance: Critical Thinking about Canadian Social Issues*, edited by Les Samuelson and Wayne Antony. Halifax: Fernwood Publishing, 2003.
Kirk, Paul L. "The Ontogeny of Criminalistics." *Journal of Criminal Law, Criminology, and Police Science* 54 (1963): 235–38.

Kline, Marlee. "Blue Meanies in Alberta: Tory Tactics and the Privitization of Child Welfare." Pp. 330–359 in *Challenging the Public/Private Divide: Feminism, Law, and Pubic Policy*, edited by Susan B. Boyd. Toronto: University of Toronto Press, 1997.

Kluger, Jeffrey. "How Science Solves Crimes." *Time*. 12 October 2002. <http://www .time.com/time/magazine/article/0,9171,1003480,00.html>

Krafft-Ebing, Richard von. *Psychopathia Sexualis*, translated by F. J. Rebman. New York: Pioneer, 1939.

Kramer, L. *Musical Meaning: Toward a Critical History*. Berkeley: University of California Press, 2001.

Kristeva, Julia. *Powers of Horror: An Essay on Abjection*, trans. Leon S. Roudiez. 1980. New York: Columbia University Press, 1982.

Lacks, R. Diehl. "The 'Real' CSI: Designing and Teaching a Violent Crime Scene Class in an Undergraduate Setting." *Journal of Criminal Justice Education* 18, no.2 (July 2007): 311–21.

Lane, Philip J. "The Existential Condition of Television Crime Drama." *Journal of Popular Culture* 34, no. 4 (2001): 137–51.

Laskowski, Gregory E. "The CSI Effect: Good or Bad For Forensic Science." 2005. <http://www.clpex.com/Articles/TheDetail/100-199/TheDetail187.htm.> (20 June 2005).

LaTempa, Susan. "The Women of CSI." *Written By*. 2002. <http://www.wga.org/ WrittenBy/1002/csi.html>

Lawson, Erica, and Amanda Hotrum. "Equity for Communities: Integrating Legal Counsel and Critical Race Theory." Pp. 41–49 in *Feminism, Law, Inclusion: Intersectionality in Action*, edited by Gayle MacDonald, Rachel L. Osborne, and Charles C. Smith. Toronto: Sumach Press, 2005.

Lawson, Mark. "Art in the Aftermath." *Guardian*. July 16, 2005. <http://www.guardian .co.uk/film/2005/jul/16/media.television>

Leca, Ange-Pierre. *The Cult of the Immortal: Mummies and the Ancient Egyptian Way of Death*, trans. Louise Asmal. London: Souvenir, 1980.

Lee, Joseph, and A. G. Page. "Use and Admissibility of 'High Tech' Evidence." *California Litigation* 11, no. 3 Spring/Summer 1998. <http://74.125.47.132/search?q= cache:kjDuIENTAjoJ:www.calbar.ca.gov/calbar/pdfs/sections/litigation/v11n3_ callit_feature.pdf+Use+and+Admissibility+of+'High+Tech'+Evidence+california +litigation&hl=en&ct=clnk&cd=2&gl=ca&client=firefox-a>

Lemke, Thomas. "'The birth of bio-politics': Michel Foucault's lecture at the Collège de France on neo-liberal governmentality." *Economy and Society* 30, no.2 (2001): 190–207.

Lesko, Nancy. *Act Your Age! A Cultural Construction of Adolescence*. New York and London: Routledge Falmer, 2001.

Lewis, Tyson. "The Surveillance Economy of Post-Columbine School." *The Review of Education, Pedagogy, and Cultural Studies* 25 (2003): 335–55.

Lieberman, Bruce. "Forensics: Fact or Fiction. TV Shows Make Crime Solving Look Easy But In Real Life It's Not So Simple." *The San Diego Tribune*. 2005. <http:// www.signonsandiego.com/uniontrib/20050221/news_1n21forensic.html>

Lord, Wayne D., et al. "Isolation, amplification, and sequencing of human mitochondrial DNA obtained from human crab louse, *Pthirus pubis* (L.), blood meals." *Journal of Forensic Science* 43, no. 5 (1998): 1097–1100.

Lubiano, Wahneema. "Black Ladies, Welfare Queens, and State Minstrels: Ideological War by Narrative Means." Pp. 323–63 in *Race-ing Justice, En-gendering Power: Essays on Anita Hill, Clarence Thomas, and the Construction of Social Reality*, edited by Toni Morrison. New York: Pantheon Books, 1992.

Lury, Karen. *Interpreting Television*. London: Hodder Arnold, 2005.

Lyle, Douglas P. *Forensics for Dummies*. Chichester, West Sussex: John Wiley, 2004.

Lynch, Michael. "God's Signature: DNA Profiling, the New Gold Standard in Forensic Science." *Endeavour* 27, no. 2 (June 2003): 93–97.

Lynch, Mona. "Rehabilitation a Rhetoric: The Ideal of Reformation in Contemporary Parole Discourse and Practices." *Punishment and Society* 2, no. 1 (2001): 40–65.

Lyon, David. "Technology vs. 'Terrorism': Circuits of City Surveillance Since September 11." Pp. 297–311 in *Cities, War, and Terrorism*, edited by S. Graham. Malden, MA: Blackwell, 2004.

Mannheim, Karl. *Ideology and Utopia. Collected Works Volume One*. London: Routledge, 1998.

Manning, Peter K. "Media Loops." Pp. 25–39 in *Popular Culture, Crime and Justice*, edited by Frankie Bailey, Y. and Donna C. Hale. Belmont, CA: West/Wadsworth, 1998.

Mansfield, Nick. *Subjectivity: Theories of the Self from Freud to Haraway*. Sydney: Allen & Unwin, 2000.

Mares, Marie-Louise. "The Role of Source Confusion in Television's Cultivation of Social Reality Judgments." *Human Communication Research* 2 (23 December 1996): 278–97.

Martin, Adrian. "There's a Million Stories, and a Million Ways to Get There From Here." *Metro Magazine* 142 (2004).

Marx, Karl. *Capital*, vol. 1. London: Penguin Classics, 1990.

Massie, A., "CSI effect' evident in US courtrooms" *Scotsman*. 2005. <news .scotsman.com/archive.cfm?id=436302005.>

McKnight, Brian E. *The Washing Away of Wrongs: Forensic Medicine in Thirteenth Century China by Sung T'zu*. Ann Arbor: Center for Chinese Studies, Univ. Mich., 1981.

McNeely, Connie L. "Perceptions of the Criminal Justice System: Television." *Journal of Criminal Justice and Popular Culture* 3, no. 1 (1995): 1–20.

Meek, Allan. "Mourning, Media and the 'Virtual Space of Spectrality." *Space and Culture* 3, no. 5 (2000).

Melossi, Dario. "Changing Representations of the Criminal." *British Journal of Criminology* 40, no. 2 (Spring 2000): 296–320.

Merck, Mandy. "American Gothic: Undermining the Uncanny." Pp. 61–72 in *Reading "Six Feet Under": TV to Die for*, edited by Kim Akass and Janet McCabe. London: I.B. Tauris, 2005.

Meyer, David S., and William Hoynes, "Shannon's Deal: Competing Images of the Legal System in Primetime Television." *Journal of Popular Culture* 27 (Spring 1994): 31–41.

Meyrowitz, Joshua. "Television and Interpersonal Behavior: Codes of Perception and Response." Pp. 253–72 in *INTER/MEDIA. Interpersonal Communication in a Media World*, edited by Gary Gumpert and Robert Cathcart. New York: Oxford University Press, 1979.

Mittel, Jason. *Genre and Television*. London: Routledge, 2004.

Morrison, Toni. "The Official Story: Dead Man Golfing." Pp.vii–xxviii in *Birth of a Nation'hood: Gaze, Script and Spectacle in the O.J. Simpson Case*, edited by Toni Morrison and Claudia Brodsky. New York: Pantheon Books, 1997.

National Center for Victims of Crime. *America Speaks Out: Citizens' Attitudes About Victims' Rights and Violence, Executive Summary*. Arlington, VA: National Center for Victims, 1991.

Neale, Steve. *Genre and Hollywood*. London: Routledge, 2000.

———. "Studying Genre" and "Genre and Television." In *The Television Genre Book*, edited by Glen Creeber. London: BFI Books, 2001.

Neocleous, Mark. *The Fabrication of Social Order: A Cultural Theory of Police Power*. Pluto Press: London, 2000.

Neuman, Lawrence W. *Basics of Social Research: Qualitative and Quantitative Approaches*. New York: Pearson Education Inc., 2004.

Nevada's Forensic Science Center, "Crime Lab Fundraising Project" <http://www.hendersoncrimelab.com/media_coverage.html> (30 Jan. 2009).

Nickell, Joe, and John F. Fischer. *Crime Science: Methods of Forensic Detection*. Lexington: University Press of Kentucky, 1999.

Nijman, Jan. Review of *City on the Edge: The Transformation of Miami* by Alejandro Portes and Alex Stepick. *Annals of the Association of American Geographers* 84, no. 3 (1994): 526–28.

———. "The Paradigmatic City." *Annals of the Association of American Geographers* 90, no. 1 (2000): 135–45.

O'Brien, Susie, and Imre Szeman. *Popular Culture: A User's Guide*. Scarborough, Ontario: Nelson, 2004.

Olalquiaga, Celeste. *Megalopolis: Contemporary Cultural Sensibilities*. Minneapolis: University of Minnesota Press, 1992.

O'Malley, Pat. "Volatile and Contradictory Punishment." *Theoretical Criminology* 3 (1999): 175–96.

———. "Risk Societies and the Government of Crime." Pp. 189–207 in *Dangerous Offenders: Punishment and Social Order*, edited by Mark Brown and John Pratt. London and New York: Routledge, 2000.

———. "Governing Through the Democratic Minimization of Harms." Pp. 216–36 in *Institutionalizing Restorative Justice*, edited by Ivo Aertsen, Tom Daems, and Luc Roberts. London: Willan Publishing, 2006.

Ormiston, Susan. "The Current Part 2: The CSI Effect." *The Current*. 2005. <http://www.cbc.ca/thecurrent/2005/200504/20050405.html>

Osborne, Richard. "Crime and the Media: From Mass Studies to Post-modernism." Pp.25–48 in *Crime and the Media: The Postmodern Spectacle,* edited by David Kidd-Hewitt and Richard Osborne. London: Pluto Press, 1995.

Ostrom, Brian J., and Roger A. Hanson. *Efficiency, Timeliness, and Quality: A New Perspective From Nine State Criminal Trial Courts.* Rockville, MD: National Institute of Justice, 2000.

Ouellette, Laurie and James Hay. *Better Living Through Reality TV: Television and Post-Welfare Citizenship.* Blackwell Publishing, 2008.

Palmer, Gareth. *Discipline And Liberty: Television and Governance.* Manchester: Manchester University Press, 2003.

Parks, Lisa. "Brave New Buffy: Rethinking TV Violence." Pp. 118–33 in *Quality Popular Television,* edited by Mark Jancovich and James Lyons. London: BFI, 2003.

Patton, Michael. *Qualitative Research and Evaluation Methods.* Thousand Oaks, California: Sage Publications, 2002.

Peesker, Saira. "New '*CSI*' game lets viewers in on the mystery," CTV News.ca. Dec. 11 2006. <http://www.ctv.ca/servlet/ArticleNews/story/CTVNews/20061205/CSI_interview_061205/20061211/> (17 Aug. 2007).

Pellegrini, Ann. *Performance Anxieties: Staging Psychoanalysis, Staging Race.* New York: Routledge, 1997.

Peña, Yesilernis L., Christopher Federico, and Jim Sidanius. *Race and Support for the Criminal Justice System: A Matter of Asymmetry.* Working Paper 181. New York: Russell Sage Foundation, 2006.

Pietz, William. "The Problem of the Fetish I." *Res* 9 (1985): 5–17.

———. "The Problem of the Fetish II: The Origin of the Fetish." *Res* 13 (1987): 23–45.

———. "The Problem of the Fetish, IIIa: Bosman's Guinea and the Enlightenment Theory of Fetishism." *Res* 16 (1988): 105–23.

Podlas, Kimberlianne. "Should We Blame Judge Judy? The Messages Television Courtrooms Send Viewers." *Judicature* 86, no. 1 (July–August 2002): 38–43.

———. "'The CSI Effect:' Exposing the Media Myth." *Fordham Intellectual Property, Media and Entertainment Law Journal* 16 (2006): 429–65.

Podlesney, Teresa. "Blondes." In *The Hysterical Male: New Feminist Theory,* edited by Arthur Kroker and Marilouise Kroker. Montreal: New World Perspectives, 1991.

Poniewozik, James, Jeanne McDowell, Desa Philadelphia, and Kate Novack. "Crimetime Lineup: How the Slick Show Changed Television—In Part By Dragging It Back Into the Past." *Time* 164, no.19. 11 August 2004. <http://www.time.com/time/magazine/0,9263,7601041108,00.html>

Pratt, Anna, and Mariana Valverde. "From Deserving Victims to 'Masters of Confusion': Redefining Refugees in the 1990s." *Canadian Journal of Sociology* 27, no.2 (2002): 135–62.

Pratt, John. "Governmentality, Neoliberalism and Dangerousness." Pp. 133–57 in *Governable Places: Readings on Governmentality and Crime Control,* edited by Russell Smandych. Aldershot Brookfield VT: Ashgate, 1999.

——. "The Return of the Wheelbarrow Men; Or, The Arrival of Postmodern Penality." *British Journal of Criminology* 40, no. 1 (Winter 2000): 133–57.

Quinsey, Vernon, Grant Harris, Marnie Rice, and Catherine Cormier, eds. *Violent Offender: Appraising and Managing Risk.* Washington, DC: American Psychological Association, 1998.

Rafter, Nicole. *Shots in the Mirror: Crime Films and Society*, 2nd ed. New York: Oxford University Press, 2006.

——. "Crime, film and criminology: Recent sex-crime movies." *Theoretical Criminology* 11, no.3 (2007): 403–20.

Ragle, Larry. *Crime Scene.* New York: Avon, 2002.

Ramsland, Katherine. "IQ, EQ, and SQ: Grissom Thinks and Caine Feels, but Taylor Enlightens." In *Investigating CSI: An Unauthorized Look Inside the Crime Labs of Las Vegas, Miami and New York*, edited by Donn Cortez. Dallas: BenBella Books, 2006.

Rapping, Elayne. *Law and Justice As Seen On Television.* New York: New York University Press, 2003.

Razack, Sherene. "R. D. S. v. Her Majesty the Queen: A Case about Home." Pp. 282–94 in *Feminism, Law, Inclusion: Intersectionality in Action*, edited by Gayle MacDonald, Rachel L. Osborne, and Charles C. Smith. Toronto: Sumach Press, 2005.

Redmayne, Mike. *Expert Evidence and Criminal Justice.* Oxford: Oxford, 2001.

Reeves, Jimmie, Marc Rodgers, and Michael Epstein. "Rewriting Popularity: The Cult *Files*." Pp. 22–35 in *"Deny All Knowledge," Reading the X-Files*, edited by David Lavery, Angela Hague, and Marla Cartwright. New York: Syracuse University Press, 1996.

Reiner, Robert. "Media Made Criminality." Pp. 376–416 in *The Oxford Handbook of Criminology*, edited by M. Maguire, R. Morgan & R. Reiner. Oxford: Oxford University Press, 2002.

Richardson, Ruth. *Death, Dissection and the Destitute*, 2nd ed. London: Phoenix, 2001.

Robben, Janine. "The 'CSI' Effect: Popular culture and the justice system." *Oregon State Bar Bulletin.* 2005. <http://www.osbar.org/publications/bulletin/05oct/csi.html> (30 Jan. 2009).

Robbers, Monica L. P. "The Media and Public Perceptions of Criminal Justice Policy Issues: An Analysis of Bowling For Columbine and Gun Control." *Journal of Criminal Justice and Popular Culture* 12, no. 2 (2005): 77–95.

Robinson, Henry Morton. *Science Catches the Criminal.* New York: Blue Ribbon, 1935.

Robinson, Paul H. "Should the Victims' Rights Movement Have Influence Over Criminal Law Formulation and Adjudication?" *McGeorge Law Review* 33 (2003): 749–88.

Rogers, Everett M. , Arvind Singhal, and Avinash Thombre. "Indian Audience Interpretations of Health Related Content in The Bold and the Beautiful." *Gazette: The International Journal for Communication Studies* 66, no. 5 (2004): 437–58.

Rose, Nikolas. "Governing 'Advanced' Liberal Democracies." Pp. 37–64 in *Foucault and Political Reason.*

———. "The death of the social? Refiguring the territory of government." *Economy and Society* 25, no.3 (1996): 327–56.

———. "Government and Control." *British Journal of Criminology* 40, no. 2 (Spring 2000): 321–39.

Rose, Nikolas, and Peter Miller. "Political Power beyond the State: Problematics of Government." *British Journal of Sociology* 43, no.2 (June 1992): 173–205.

Rossmo, Kim. *Geographical Profiling*. Boca Raton, Florida: CRC Press, 2000.

Roy, Ellen. "Fetishism." *Man*, new ser. 23, no. 2 (1988): 213–35.

Ruhl, Lealle. "Liberal Governance and Prenatal Care: Risk and Regulation in Pregnancy." *Economy and Society* 28, no. 1 (1999): 95–117.

Rusche, George, and Otto Kirchheimer. *Punishment and Social Structure*. New York: Russell and Russell, 1968.

Sadler, D. W., et al. "Drug accumulation and elimination in *Calliphora vicina* larvae." *Forensic Science International* 71, no. 3 (1995): 191–97.

Saferstein, Richard. *Criminalistics. An Introduction to Forensic Science*. 9th ed. Upper Saddle River, N.J.: Prentice Hall. 2007.

Sappenfield, Mark. "From Lindbergh to Laci, a Growing Forensics Fallacy." *The Christian Science Monitor* (24 April 2003) <http://www.csmonitor.com/2003/0424/p01s01-ussc.htm>

Scheiber, Dave. "Crossing the Line: Reality Becomes Fiction When a Real-Life Detective, Who Makes His Home in St. Petersburg, Embarks on a New Career Advising The CBS Drama, CSI: Miami." *St. Petersburg Times Online* (1 January 2004) <http://www.sptimes.com/2004/01/01/news_pf/Floridian/Crossing_the_line.shtml>

Schroth, Raymond A. "The Case of the Beautiful Corpse: A Comparison of Today's Television Crime Dramas With Crime Novels of the Past Shows How Our Culture Has Changed." *National Catholic Reporter* 40, no. 19. 12 March 2004. <http://natcath.org/NCR_Online/archives2/2004a/031204/031204m.htm>

Sherman, Lawrence W. "Trust and Confidence in Criminal Justice." *National Institute for Justice Journal* 248 (2002): 22–31.

Sherwin, Richard K. *When the Law Goes Pop: The Vanishing Line Between Law and Popular Culture*. Chicago: University of Chicago Press, 2000.

Shohat, Ella, and Robert Stam. *Unthinking Eurocentrism: Multiculturalism and the Media*. London: Routledge, 1994.

Simon, Jonathan. *Governing through Crime: How the War on Crime Transformed American Democracy and Created a Culture of Fear*. New York: Oxford University Press, 2007.

Sinclair, John. "'The Hollywood of Latin America:' Miami as Regional Center in Television Trade." *Television & New Media* 4, no. 3 (2003): 211–29.

Smardz, Sophia. "The Jury's Out." WashingtonPost.Com. 25 June 2004. <http://www.washingtonpost.com/wpdyn/content/article/2005/06/25/AR2005062500078_p.htm>

Snider, Laureen. "Relocating Law: Making Corporate Crime Disappear." In *Locating Law: Race/Class/Gender Connections*, edited by Elizabeth Comack. Halifax: Fernwood Press, 2003.

Soja, Edward W. "Inside Exopolis: Scenes from Orange County." In *Variations on a Theme Park: The New American City and the End of Public Space*, edited by Michael Sorkin. New York: Hill and Wang, 1992.

Solomos, John, and Tim Rackett. "Policing and Urban Unrest: Problem Constitution and Policy Response." Pp. 42–64 in *Out of Order? Policing Black People*, edited by Ellis Cashmere and Eugene McLaughlin. London: Routledge, 1991.

Sorkin, Michael. "Introduction: Variations on a Theme Park." Pp. 407–10 in *Variations on a Theme Park: The New American City and the End of Public Space*, edited by Michael Sorkin. New York: Hill and Wang,1992.

Sparks, Richard. *Television and the Drama of Crime: Moral Tales and the Place of Crime in Public Life*. Buckingham: Open University Press, 1992.

———. "Can Prison Be Legitimate? Penal Politics, Privitization and the Timeliness of an Old Idea." *British Journal of Criminology* 34 (1994): 14–28.

Spigel, Lynn. "Entertainment Wars: Television Culture After 9/11." *American Quarterly* 56 (2004): 235–70.

Spitzer, Steven. "Towards a Marxian Theory of Deviance." *Social Problems* 22, no. 5 (1975): 638–59.

Steinberg, Shirley R. "Critical Multiculturalism and Democratic Schooling: An Interview with Peter L. McLaren and Joe Kincheloe." Pp. 129–54 in *Multicultural Education, Critical Pedagogy, and the Politics of Difference*, ed. Christine E. Sleeter and Peter L. McLaren. Albany: State University of New York Press, 1995.

Steinberg, Ted. *Down to Earth: Nature's Role in American History*. Oxford, UK: Oxford, 2002.

Stockwell. "Defense, Prosecution Play to New "CSI" Savvy: Juries expecting TV-style Forensics." *Washington Post* (2005): A01.

Strange, Carolyn. "The Undercurrent of Penal Culture: Punishment of the Body in Mid-Twentieth Century Canada." *Law and History Review* 19, No. 2 (Summer 2001): 1–39.

Strauss, Anselm, and Juliet Corbin. *Basics of Qualitative Research: Grounded Theory Procedures and Techniques*. Newbury Park: Sage, 1990.

Sudbury, Julia. "Women of Color, Globalization, and the Politics of Incarceration." Pp. 219–34 in *The Criminal Justice System and Women: Offenders, Prisoners, Victims, and Workers*, 3d, edited by Barbara Price and Natalie Sokoloff. New York: McGraw Hill Company, 2004.

Surette, Ray. *Media, Crime, and Criminal Justice: Images and Realities*. Pacific Grove, CA: Brooks/Cole Publishing, 1992.

———. "Some Unpopular Thoughts About Popular Culture." Pp. xiv–xxiv in *Popular Culture, Crime and Justice*, edited by Frankie Y. Bailey and Donna C. Hale. Belmont, CA: West/Wadsworth, 1998.

Taylor, John. *Body Horror: Photojournalism, Catastrophe and War*. Manchester: Manchester University Press, 1998.

Tithecotte, Richard. *Of Men and Monsters: Jeffrey Dahmer and the Construction of the Serial Killer*. Wisconsin: The University of Wisconsin Press, 1997.

Toobin,Jeffrey."TheCSIEffect."*TheNewYorker*.May7,2007.<http://www.newyorker.com/reporting/2007/05/07/070507fa_fact_toobin>

Turkel, William J. "Every Place is an Archive: Environmental History and the Interpretation of Physical Evidence." *Rethinking History* 10, no.2 (2006): 259–76.

——. A Metric for the Popular Imagination (Weblog, 5 Aug 2006) in "Digital History Hacks: Methodology for the Infinite Archive." <http://digitalhistoryhacks
.blogspot.com> (1 Sept. 2007).

Turow, Scott. "Still Guilty After All These Years." *New York Times.* April 8 2007.
<http://www.nytimes.com/2007/04/08/opinion/08turow.html>

Tuthill, Harold. *Individualization Principles and Procedures in Criminalistics.* Salem, OR: Lightning Powder, 1994.

Tyldesley, Joyce. *The Mummy: Unwrap the Ancient Secrets of the Mummies' Tombs.*
London: Carlton, 1999.

Tyler, T. "Viewing CSI and the Threshold of Guilt: Managing Truth and Justice in
Reality and Fiction." *Yale Law Journal* 115, no.5 (March 2006): 1050–85.

"Ultra Concentrated Media" <http://www.mediachannel.org/ownership/chart.shtml>
(30 Jan. 2009).

U.S. Census Bureau. *2004 American Community Survey.* Table 46. "Nativity and Place
of Birth of Resident Population for Cities of 250,000 or More: 2004." U.S. Census
Bureau, <http://www.census.gov/compendia/statab/population/> (16 Sept. 2007).

——. "State & County QuickFacts: Miami (City), Florida." U.S. Census Bureau.
<http://quickfacts.census.gov/qfd/states/12/1245000.html> (1 March 2007).

U.S. Department of Justice. *New Directions from the Field: Victims' Rights and Services for the 21st Century.* Washington, DC: Office for Victims of Crime. 1998.
<http://www.ojp.usdoj.gov/ovc/new/directions/> (2 Feb. 2009).

Valverde, Mariana. *Law & Order: Images, Meanings, Myths.* New Brunswick, NJ:
Rutgers University Press, 2006.

Van den Bulck, Jan, and Heidi Vandebosch. "When the Viewer Goes to Prison:
Learning Fact From Fiction. A Qualitative Cultivation Study." *Poetics* 31 (2003):
103–16.

Wacquant, Loic. "Deadly Symbiosis: When Ghetto and Prison Meet and Mesh."
Punishment and Society 3, no. 1 (2001): 95–133.

Walker, Clarence. "CSI (Television Crime Dramas) Affects the American Criminal
Justice System." *American Mafia.Com.* 2005. <http://www.americanmafia.com/
Feature_Articles_301.html>

Wasik, Bill. "My Crowd, Or, Phase 5: A Report from the Inventor of the Flash Mob."
Harper's Magazine (March 2006): 56–66.

Webb, James P. Jr. et al. "The chigger species *Eutrombicula belkini* Gould (Acari :
Trombiculidae) as a forensic tool in a homicide investigation in Ventura County,
California." *Bulletin of the Society of Vector Ecology* 8 (1983): 141–46.

Weisberg, Robert. "Introduction." *Stanford Law and Policy Review* 15 (2004): 323–28.

Wells, Jeffrey D., and Felix A. Sperling. "DNA-based identification of forensically
important Chrysomyinae (Diptera: Calliphoridae)." *Forensic Science International*
120 (2001): 110–15.

Willing, Richard. "'CSI Effect' Has Juries Wanting More Evidence." *USA Today.* 8
May 2004. <http://www.usatoday.com/news/nation/2004-08-05-csi-effect_x.htm>

Wilson, Z., S. Hubbard, S., and D.J. Pounder. "Drug analysis in fly larvae." *American Journal of Forensic Medicine and Pathology* 14, no. 2 (1993): 118–20.

Winks, Robin, ed. *The Historian as Detective: Essays on Evidence.* New York: Harper, 1969.

Workman, Thom. *Social Torment: Globalization in Atlantic Canada.* Halifax: Fernwood Press, 2003.

Index

9/11, xv11, xxii–xxiv, xxx, xxxvn32, xxxvin34, xxxvin36, 85–86, 89n24, 195n18, 202, 239–40, 203–4, 209–211, 220n10; September 11, 2001, xvi, xxii, xxx

"10-7" (*Miami* 3024), 123, 127, 220n7

"19 Down" (*CSI* 9009), 198n61

"$35K O.B.O." (*CSI* 1018), 101, 173n46, 174n56, 196n15

24, xiii, xxiii, xxv, 112

ABC, xvi, 103

"A Night at the Movies" (*CSI* 3019), 173n46

abjection, 93–110, 130n44

"Abra Cadaver" (*CSI* 3005), 98, 141

absence, xxiii, 9, 49, 137, 150, 160, 178–81, 188–89, 192; absent, xx, xxix–xxx, 119, 150, 152, 161, 163, 165, 168, 189–92, 195

actuarialism, xxi–xxii, xxxvn31, 54, 174n51, 176n96

aesthetic(s), xxviii, 79, 81, 88n3, 93, 103, 117, 151, 179, 197n34

African, 141

African American, 93, 128n5, 150, 156–57, 159–63, 165, 170n12, 175n53, 183, 185, 194

agency, xx, 28n113, 69, 168, 192

alcohol, 42, 102, 155–56, 163, 165, 173

Alexander, Khandi, 131n52

"All for Our Country" (*CSI* 4002), 158–59, 173n46

Alternate Light Source, 34–36, 136

American (also North American), xvi–xviii, xxvii, 3, 5–6, 12, 18, 21–22, 41, 61, 63–70, 82, 107–8, 114, 120, 122–23, 149–69, 174n48, 177–83, 186, 188, 190, 201, 210

The Anatomy Act, 94–95

"Anatomy of a Lye" (*CSI* 2021), 98

"Anonymous" (*CSI* 1008), 34, 36, 97

Apocalypse Now, 218

architecture, xxxi, 101, 116, 127

archive, 133–34, 212

Arrested Development, xiii

assailant, 41, 150, 157, 162, 163

"Assume Nothing" (*CSI* 4001), 103

attorney, xx, 7, 10, 12–14, 16–17, 20, 24n24, 25n56, 25n64, 27n91, 30, 67–68, 74n28

audience, xiv, xvii, xxii–xxx, 7–8, 19, 54, 65–66, 69–87, 89n28, 93, 97, 107, 109, 117–18, 134–35, 142, 146n31, 152, 170n12, 179, 185, 190, 192, 202–3, 218–19

autopsy, 48–49, 51, 69–70, 79, 93, 96, 100, 205–6

Editors and Contributors

Gail Anderson received her PhD (1992) and MPM (1986) from Simon Fraser University, in entomology, and her BSc (Hon.) (1983) from Manchester University. Dr. Anderson is associate professor in forensic entomology in the School of Criminology at Simon Fraser University, associate director of the School of Criminology, and a forensic consultant to the RCMP and City Police across Canada (and other countries). She has testified as an expert witness in court many times, and is developing a database of forensic insects across Canada. Her work has been featured in television programs including "Journeys—Grave Testimony," "Forbidden Places—Silent Witness" and "The Nature of Things—Postmortem." She was a recipient of Canada's "Top 40 under 40" award in 1999, and was recently listed in *Time* magazine as one of the top five innovators in the world this century in the field of criminal justice. Dr. Anderson was presented with the Derome Award in 2001.

Kevin Denys Bonnycastle is assistant professor at Saint Mary's University. Her PhD in Criminology was from Simon Fraser University (2004). She has published "Rape Uncodified: Reconsidering Bill C-49 Amendments to Canadian Sexual Assault Laws" in *Law as a Gendering Practice*, Chunn and Lacombe, eds. (2001), and "The Future of Research on Woman Battering," in *Unsettling Truths: Battered Women, Policy, Politics, and Contemporary Research in Canada*, Bonnycastle and Rigakos, eds. (1999). Bonnycastle has also collaborated in prisoner-driven research on Hepatitis C, HIV and TB and Prisoner Practices, a Safe Prison Tattoo Project proposal, and Prospective Needle-Exchange Programs for men in Federal Canadian Penitentiaries (2002–2004).

Michele Byers is associate professor at Saint Mary's University in Halifax, Nova Scotia. She has published extensively in the areas of television, gender, youth cultures, and identity, most recently in *Atlantis, Canadian Ethnic Studies, Shofar, Culture, Theory & Critique, The Essential Cult TV Reader, You Should See Yourself: Jewish Identity in Postmodern American Culture,* and *Programming Reality: Perspectives on English-Canadian Television.* Michele is the editor of *Growing Up Degrassi: Television, Identity and Youth Cultures* and co-editor (with David Lavery) of *"Dear Angela": Remembering My So-Called Life.* She and David have also just finished compiling a new edited collection, tentatively entitled *On the Verge of Tears: Why the Movies, Television, Music, Art, and Literature Make Us Cry.* Her most recent work involves the study of television and ethnicity.

Linda Derksen is currently chair of the Department of Sociology at Vancouver Island University, where one of her deepest interests is in mentoring undergraduates in student-led research projects. Her own recent research interests and publications are in the fields of DNA profiling, knowledge utilization in nursing, hierarchical linear modeling, and co-citation analyses of the growth of the knowledge utilization field between 1945 and 2004. Her teaching focuses on classical and contemporary social theory, science and technology studies, and research methods.

Nichola Dobson is an independent scholar based in Edinburgh. She completed her PhD in animation genre at Queen Margaret University, Edinburgh, where she lectured in media studies, media language and cultural studies. She was researcher on a joint project between Glasgow Caledonian University and Universitat Rovira i Virgili Tarragona, Catalonia on national identity in TV soaps, and also lectured there on Discourse and Ideology. Her research interests are divided between animation, television studies, and genre, demonstrated by the range of publications in journals, book chapters, and conference papers. A member of the Society for Animation Studies since 2001, she is the founding editor of their journal *Animation Studies.* She has recently finished her first single authored book *Historical Dictionary of Animation and Cartoons,* and is currently continuing her research on TV animation and genre, and genre in the UK series *Life on Mars.*

Basil Glynn received his PhD for the thesis, "It's a Wrap: A Developmental Study of the Mummy in Film from Its Origins to the Fifties" from the University of Nottingham. He lectures in film and media in the Department of Film, Media and Communication, Liverpool Hope University, United Kingdom. He is currently working on articles on American sci-fi, Asian television, and British and American horror.

Elizabeth Harvey has an MA in integrated studies from Athabasca University with a specialization in adult education, and a BA with distinction in anthropology and sociology from Vancouver Island University (formerly Malaspina University-College). She is currently completing a post-graduate certificate in counseling, and hopes to begin work on her doctoral degree in fall 2009 with an emphasis on post-secondary educational systems, particularly Universal Design for Learning. Besides the *CSI* effect, her research interests include the impact of the accommodations-based approach in post-secondary education on adults with disabilities, and the impact of ancient Scythian biological weapons. She is published in *Developmental Disabilities Bulletin*, and has several other articles under review. Harvey is employed as a professional tutor and advocate for adults with learning disabilities and other cognitive issues.

Kurt Hohenstein is associate professor of history at Winona State University in Minnesota. He received his JD from the University of Nebraska and his PhD from Virginia. He is the author of *Coining Corruption: The Making of the American Campaign Finance System* published by Northern Illinois University Press in 2007. He is currently working on a political novel about a runaway constitutional convention.

Val Marie Johnson is an Associate Professor at Saint Mary's University in Halifax, Nova Scotia. She wrote her doctoral dissertation on moral citizenship and governance in New York City, 1890–1920 (New School for Social Research 2003), and is revising this for publication as a book in 2009–2010. Johnson has published articles on the New York City history of how the regulation and performance of gender and sexuality intersected with the production of citizenship and identity, urban communities and politics, and policing and law in *The Journal of Urban History*, *The Journal of Women's History*, the *Journal of American Ethnic History*, and the *Journal of the History of Sexuality*. She has just completed a co-edited volume (with Diane Crocker) on the criminalization of poverty, and her most recent research is a socio-political analysis of Canadian youth justice law reform and changes in liberalism from 1960 to 1982.

Jeongmee Kim is senior lecturer in film and television studies, Department of Interdisciplinary Studies, Manchester Metropolitan University, United Kingdom. Kim's PhD was on contemporary British cinema. She has published an article on the export of Korean cultural products and is currently editing a book on Asian television drama.

Lawrence Kramer is professor of English and music at Fordham University and editor of the journal *19th-Century Music*. He is the author of nine books on the interrelations of music, society, and culture, some of which (notably *Musical Meaning: Toward a Critical History* and *Why Classical Music Still Matters*) take up questions of media. He is also contributing co-editor, with Richard Leppert and Danniel Goldmark, of the collection *Beyond the Soundtrack: Representing Music in Cinema.*

Mythili Rajiva is assistant professor in the Department of Sociology and Criminology at Saint Mary's University (Halifax, Nova Scotia). Her areas of expertise are youth culture, feminist theory/method, and race/postcolonial theory. She has a recent article on race, adolescence, and girlhood in the *Canadian Review of Sociology and Anthropology* (2006). Her current research explores the issue of bullying among non-adults; she is co-editing a volume for Canadian Scholars' Press that explores the intersections of race, gender, class, age, and sexuality in the 1997 murder of Reena Virk, a fourteen-year-old Canadian girl of South Asian ancestry, who was the victim of a violent "swarming" by her peers that involved torture and culminated in her death at the hands of a teenage boy and girl.

William J. Turkel is assistant professor of history at the University of Western Ontario, where he teaches courses on digital history and the history of science, technology, and environment. His research focuses on the ways that people reconstruct the past from its material traces, and the possibility of building historical interpretations into physical devices and environments. He is the author of *The Archive of Place: Unearthing the Pasts of the Chilcotin Plateau* and co-editor of *Method and Meaning in Canadian Environmental History.*

Sherah VanLaerhoven received her PhD (2001) from the University of Arkansas, in entomology, and her MPM (1997) and BSc (1995) from Simon Fraser University. VanLaerhoven is chair of forensic science in the Centre for Inter-Faculty Programs and associate professor in the Department of Biology at University of Windsor. She is a consultant and expert witness for police, medical examiners/coroners, and lawyers in Canada and internationally, including the high profile cases *Regina v. Truscott* and *Regina v. Baltovitch.* Her research in insect behavioral ecology focuses on interactions between insects and variability in communities, as applied to insect evidence and beneficial insects. Her work has been featured numerous times in different media including Discovery Channel, *Discovery Magazine, Globe & Mail,* NPR, and CBC Radio. She was awarded Canada's "Top 40 under 40" award (2006) and nominated as one of the IBC "Foremost Scientists of the World" 2008 (awaiting results).

Patrick West is senior lecturer in professional and creative writing in the School of Communication and Creative Arts, Deakin University, Melbourne, Australia. Patrick's PhD from the University of Melbourne was a psychoanalytic and feminist analysis of Julia Kristeva. He is a widely published essayist, literary journalist, and short-story writer with research and creative interests across the fields of screen studies, literary studies, and screenwriting. Patrick's academic work has been published in journals such as *Critical Studies in Television: Scholarly Studies in Small Screen Fictions, Antipodes: A North American Journal of Australian Literature*, and *JNZL: Journal of New Zealand Literature*. His prize-winning short stories have been published twice in the annual collection *The Best Australian Stories* (2006 and 2008) and in journals like *Southerly* and *Idiom 23*. Patrick's literary journalism and reviews appear frequently in national and international venues. In 2007 he edited, with Jeannette Delamoir, the Adapt issue of *M/C Journal*, which may be accessed at http://journal.media-culture.org.au/0705/.